D1617478

THE EDUCATION OF A CANADIAN

H. Gordon Skilling with the Order of the White Lion, 1993

THE EDUCATION OF A CANADIAN

My Life as a Scholar and Activist

H. GORDON SKILLING

PUBLISHED FOR CARLETON UNIVERSITY

BY MCGILL-QUEEN'S UNIVERSITY PRESS
MONTREAL & KINGSTON • LONDON • ITHACA

ISBN 0-88629-357-X

Printed and bound in Canada

Publication of this book was made possible with the help of grants from the Centre for East European Studies, the Office of the Vice President, Research and International Relations, and the Office of the Provost, University of Toronto; the International Academic Relations Division, Department of Foreign Affairs and International Trade; the Simons Foundation; and the Bata Foundation.

McGill-Queen's University Press acknowledges the financial support of the Government of Canada through the Book Publishing Industry Development Program (BPIDP) for our publishing activities. It also acknowledges the support of the Canada Council for the Arts for its publishing program.

Canadian Cataloguing in Publication Data

Skilling, H. Gordon (Harold Gordon), 1912-
The education of a Canadian : my life as a scholar and activist

Includes bibliographical references and index.
ISBN 0-88629-357-X

1. Skilling, H. Gordon (Harold Gordon), 1912-
2. Czechoslovakia—Politics and government—1945-1992.
3. Communism—History—20th century. *4*. Scholars—Canada—Biography. *5*. Political activists—Biography. *6*. College teachers—Canada—Biography. I. Title.

JC253.S53A3 2000   320'.092   C99-901573-7

Jacket: Jane Francis Design
Interior: Lynn's Desktop Publishing

To Sally Bright

who married me in Prague,
shared my life for more than 50 years,
and watched with me the destruction of a country,
    long hoped with me for its people's liberation,
    and shared with them and me the joy of its rebirth

and to our sons, David Bright and Peter Conard,
who also came to know and love
that distant land and its people

BY THE SAME AUTHOR

Canadian Representation Abroad (1945).

Communism, National and International (1964).

The Governments of Communist East Europe (1966).

Editor, *The Czech Renascence of the Nineteenth Century: Essays in Honour of Otakar Odložilík* (1970). With Peter Brock.

Interest Groups in Soviet Politics (1971). With Franklyn Griffiths.

Czechoslovakia's Interrupted Revolution (1976).

Charter 77 and Human Rights in Czechoslovakia (1981).

Samizdat and an Independent Society in Central and Eastern Europe (1989).

Editor, *Czechoslovakia, 1918-1988: Seventy Years from Independence* (1991).

Civic Freedom in Central Europe: Voices from Czechoslovakia (1991). With Paul Wilson.

T.G. Masaryk, 1882-1914: Against the Current (1994). Czech edition: *T.G. Masaryk, Proti proudu, 1882-1914* (1995).

CONTENTS

IV
SOWING THE SEEDS OF FREEDOM

ILLUSTRATIONS

FOREWORD

Dear Friends

I am delighted that readers throughout the entire world can now read the memoirs of H. Gordon Skilling, my friend, the well-known chronicler of August 1968 and expert in Czech history. Professor Skilling is widely recognized for his many books dealing with Czech and Czechoslovakian history. I met him a number of times before November 1989 and like to remember our long conversations concerning the failures of the communist system in Czechoslovakia and our collaboration in promoting rights through Chapter 77.

I greatly appreciate Professor Skilling's life-long work which, for the most part, has been dedicated to Czechoslovakia, the country for which he has always had a profound feeling. I am certain that this publication will help readers throughout the world to gain a deeper knowledge of our nation and its poignant history.

Václav Havel

PREFACE

AS PEOPLE REACH, AND PASS, the proverbial three score years and ten, they inevitably look back more often on their past life and become curious about half-forgotten episodes and events, and the actions and beliefs these evoked at the time. They may be tempted to record such events and thoughts for descendants and friends, or even for a wider public. Only after overcoming doubts and inhibitions did I embark on writing a memoir devoted to the two central themes of my life: world communism and its manifestations in central and eastern Europe, and Czechoslovakia, a small country unfamiliar to most Canadians. By an unexpected twist of history — the seizure of power by the Communists in Czechoslovakia in 1948 — these two themes became interwoven and remained so until the peaceful overthrow of Communism in 1989. Together they formed a major current through much of my adult life.

This book is in the first place an exploration and explanation of one Canadian's thinking about communism in central and eastern Europe. Why was I so fascinated by a worldwide movement alien to most Canadians, and why was I destined to devote a lifetime to attempting to understand it? As a young man I experienced the Depression and witnessed the birth of Canadian socialism; as a result I became a convinced socialist. In England, faced with the threats of fascism and impending war, I, like so many students, moved steadily to the Left and became enamoured of communism. My belief was strengthened by the failure of the West to stand up to Japanese, Italian, and German aggression, especially the Western sellout of Czechoslovakia at Munich, and the enormous Soviet contribution to victory in World War II. I was not alone in succumbing to illusions about communism, but I took longer than many to awaken to its realities. During the 1950s, in the United States, I tried to preserve some degree of political detachment and objectivity and thus became increasingly out of step with the prevailing American anti-Communist mood. I grew more and more aware of the imperfections and evil feaures of the various communist systems, and became actively engaged in the struggle for human rights in the communist world.

As for Czechoslovakia, why did a Canadian-born scholar, of Scottish and English descent, develop a deep and abiding interest in this faraway country, of which the Western world knew so little? My sympathy was kindled during my time at Oxford in the late 1930s. Unlike its neighbours, this country had maintained a democratic system and it was also the linchpin in the system of security designed to block the expansion of Nazi Germany. These distinctive features led me to enter on research on Czech history for a doctorate at the School of Slavonic and East European Studies in London. By sheer chance, while I was doing research in Prague on my chosen subject, I was thrown into the vortex of world affairs as an eye-witness of events that led directly to war.

My initial interest in Czechoslovakia and its people developed into a lifelong study of the history and politics of what became a kind of second homeland. When Communism came to "my country" by violent means, what remained of my sympathy for the Soviet Union and for communism was shaken to the core, while my sympathy with Czechoslovakia deepened. When the Prague Spring was crushed in 1968, I became increasingly concerned with repression in the country, and turned my attention to the investigation, and support, of the Charter 77 movement as an expression of independent thought and action, and as a rebirth of deeper national traditions. I was happy when the long fusion of Czechoslovakia and Communism came to an abrupt and surprising end in 1989 but saddened by the breakup, a few years later, of the country I had known so well.

This volume represents a conscientious attempt to trace the evolution of my thinking about communism and about Czechoslovakia over 70 years. As I review this record, I am more than ever impressed by how little I was prepared at each stage for the events that followed, and how often I had to adapt to new and unexpected situations and demands. Although my development may in retrospect appear to be a natural and logical course, with each step planned beforehand, in fact it was often the product of chance and surprise. One cannot predict or forecast the future, or even the course of one's own life; it is a constant process of education as new happenings and experiences illuminate earlier events and suggest novel interpretations of them.

For the appearance of this memoir I owe much to many people who gave aid and encouragement in the course of its development. First, I am indebted to Julius Molinaro, my fellow Harbordite, and his wife Matie, who became my literary agent, for reading the manuscript chapter by chapter and persuading me that it was worth publishing. Kay Riddell Rouillard gave me the same kind of moral support and carefully edited the original. I am grateful also to many others who read individual chapters and made comments and criticisms, and to Joan Robinson, who patiently listened to my worries during the many years of writing and revision, made critical comments, and sustained my spirits. I am indebted to John Flood of Carleton University Press, for his initial support, Carter Elwood and Jamie Glazov for their generous praise as readers for the Press, and Jennie Strickland, its production editor, for her unflagging interest and enthusiasm.

The manuscript went through several revisions, five by my own hand, but was greatly improved by others who edited and worked on successive versions: my son, Peter Skilling, Rebecca Spagnolo, computer expert, Lilit Žekulin for Czech references, the typesetter, Lynn Julian, Jennie Strickland for the final polishing, and Jean Wheeler for the index. I owe a debt to Garron Wells and Harold Averill of the University of Toronto archives, for classifying my papers; Maria Gabánková, for the splendid portrait used on the cover; Jane Francis and her husband David Skilling, for the beautiful cover design.

For financial support I would like to thank, warmly, Robert Johnson, director of the Centre for Russian and East European Studies (CREES), for raising and contributing funds, the vice president (research and international relations), provost, and chair, political science, of the University of Toronto, for their genereous contributions, and Tomáš Bat'a and Jennifer Allen Simons, of the Simons Foundation, for their additional assistance.

The book opens with the dramatic events of the destruction of Czechoslovakia that Sally and I witnessed in the years 1938 and 1939 and then continues with the story of my life from 1912.

I

DEATH OF A COUNTRY

IT WAS AT A MOMENT OF HIGH CRISIS, in May 1938, that the Czechoslovak Broadcasting Corporation offered, and I accepted, a job broadcasting on radio, in English. My new wife, Sally, and I left London to return to Prague.[1] We had married in the glorious central European capital the previous autumn while I was doing research there for my doctoral studies at the University of London. Somewhat ironically, my thesis topic was the Czech-German national conflict in late-nineteenth century Czech history. During a stopover in Paris we spent much of our time in cafés and parks reading the newspapers about the Czechoslovak crisis. For a time it seemed as though we might not be able to continue to Prague. We proceeded, however, stopping off at Cheb (Eger), which had been the scene of the shooting of two Germans by a Czech policeman only a few days before. Their funeral turned into a great political demonstration by the Nazis, and their shooting was depicted as an illustration of Czech oppression. Hitler sent two wreaths, which were laid by German officers. In fact Eger seemed as though it were already part of Nazi Germany. In the streets people were giving the Nazi salute and the greeting "Heil Hitler." Pictures of Henlein (local Nazi leader) and Hitler were everywhere. But there was a strong movement of resistance among the Czech minority and the few anti-fascist Germans. We attended meetings of German and Czechoslovak Social Democrats and another of all anti-Nazi elements. We also met with a number of the local leaders, who expressed their determination, one and all, Czech and German, to fight to the bitter end against Nazi intervention. We admired their courage in the face of rising Nazi terror and the danger of war and German occupation.

In Prague, with the help of two friends, Lisa and Zdeněk Rudinger, we found a small apartment — really only a single room, with shared kitchen and bath, in a modern building on Fochová třída (named after the French general Marshal Foch, renamed during the Nazi occupation after the German Marshal Schwerin, and again under the Communists after Marshal Stalin: the Avenue of the Three Marshals, as a Czech wag later called it). Our flat was located close to the main railway station and across the street from Radiožurnál, the broadcasting station where I was to work.

My duties, shared with an English colleague, Oswald Bamborough, were to translate and record an English-language radio news bulletin for broadcast to England and North America. The items were prepared by Czech editors, but I tried to liven them up in English. The work, some three to four hours every evening, was at first not too demanding and left time for me to do the occasional translation — for instance, a speech by Prime Minister Hodža — and to read widely in the Czech and Slovak and the world press. I also prepared a special broadcast on the Czech-German question, but it was thought to be too historical to be used. During the daytime I was able to carry on my research.

In early June we witnessed a great parade celebrating the 60th anniversary of the founding of the Czechoslovak Social Democratic party. Later that month Prague was inundated with 30,000 children for the Slet, the gymnastic performance organized by the nationalist association Sokol (Falcon), founded in the 1860s. There were a number of performances in the Strahov stadium by different age groups. In absolute unison, 25,000 men and women did gymnastic exercises to music, their movements and costumes creating colourful and ever-changing patterns. On other evenings there were historical pageants representing the need to defend the country against aggressors. The stadium was usually packed with some 200,000 persons and seats were at a premium. It was a great manifestation of strength and unity in the face of imminent danger.

In mid-August Sally went with Lisa Rudinger to the Sudeten regions, where they visited Jáchymov, the site of dangerous radium mines, and several neighbouring villages where people plied the ancient crafts of lace- and violin-making at home. They were both welcomed into homes and took part in a march in support of the republic. It was a moving display of the solidarity of members of the Czech National Socialist, Social Democratic, and Communist parties and of Czechs and Germans. Later, Sally and I started out for a holiday in the mountains in the German districts of northwestern Bohemia, near Liberec. Alas, I fell ill with jaundice, and it rained day and night for six days. We remained cooped up in our hostel the whole time.

Meanwhile, secret political negotiations between the government and representatives of the Henlein party were breaking down. If Henlein's demands had been accepted, Czechoslovak independence would have been gravely undermined. If they were rejected, everything would depend on whether Hitler was ready to act, and on whether London and Paris would warn him against doing so. If France honoured its obligations to Czechoslovakia and persuaded Britain to join in, the situation would be saved, probably without war. If Paris gave way to London, Czechoslovakia would be lost, and peace as well.

In August Lord Runciman arrived to study the situation for the British government. This visit provoked a German campaign of propaganda, with distorted and falsified reports on the oppression of Germans. There were concentrations of German troops along the borders. I watched a great procession of railway workers below our windows — the so-called Blue Army. Thousands of labourers in blue uniforms from all over the republic, together with peasants in bright costumes, carried banners proclaiming "We Shall Defend Our Boundaries" and "For the Defence of Democracy and World Peace." As German pressure continued, I wrote on 28 August that Hitler would surely strike now or later and would be prevented from doing so only if Britain threw its full weight behind resistance to aggression. The war had, in effect, been going on for seven years in other parts of the world, such as China and Spain, and its spread could be prevented only if London acted. Even Ottawa had a responsibility, since this was a worldwide offensive and could be met only by worldwide resistance.

A week later everyone was cheered by massive demonstrations and the formation of a new government in Prague pledged to defend the country. Suddenly, without warning, general mobilization was declared. In her letter home on 8 September, Sally described the unforgettable scenes in the streets. The women accompanied the men who had been called up, carrying their bags to the stations. Truckloads of men shouted "Long live the Czechoslovak Republic! Long live the army!" At last the long uncertainty was over, and they could go into battle for the defence of their country. That night a total blackout of the city began. We had black paper thumbtacked to our windows, and dark blue or black cellophane over all lights. We needed a flashlight but none was to be purchased, as everyone had had the same idea. We had already been issued gas masks. At the end of the month, because of the threat of war and of bomb attacks on the railways, we moved to the Rudingers' apartment in the Old Town. Zdeněk had been called up, and Lisa was alone with her two children. There was a possibility that the Czechoslovak broadcasting service might be evacuated somewhere

to the east, in which case Sally could stay with Lisa. Although we recognized the danger of war, we decided to stay on and do what we could
to help.

As the crisis intensified, my radio work increased, and research
came to a full stop. I was working about twelve hours every day. I was
also invited to prepare several special commentaries, some for the U.S.
National Broadcasting Corporation (NBC). My parents at home tried
desperately to track down my broadcasts and were finally able to hear
my voice a couple of times. We had to help a host of radio broadcast-
ers who descended on Prague to cover the crisis from hour to hour —
the first major occasion of international radio broadcasting. In one
case, on the eve of Munich, we discreetly arranged for a famous but
inebriated American to read his script into a dead microphone.

In early September a fiery speech by Hitler set sparks to the in-
cendiary atmosphere that had been created by Henlein's followers.
Throughout the German districts there were attacks on government
offices, on the police, and on the homes and stores of democratic
Germans and Czechs; these were led by Henlein storm-troopers and
endorsed by the Sudeten German party. Henlein left the republic and,
in an inflammatory broadcast over German wireless, openly demanded
the secession of German-speaking areas to Germany. The government
crushed what amounted to a rebellion by firm police action and
declared martial law in 16 townships. It was a tense time, Sally wrote
home, and war was possible. Yet, in the midst of this crisis, life went on
and, contrary to Germany's lying reports, an admirable order and discipline were maintained. Hitler, however, did not move his troops,
probably because he feared that he would have Britain, France, and the
Soviet Union ranged against him. We were confident that he would
not challenge the whole world and that in the event of war the Soviet
Union would be on the side of Czechoslovakia.

Chamberlain had decided to fly to Germany, and we feared that
the British and the French had agreed on the cession of Czechoslovak
territory to avert war. This would mean giving up the fortifications
along the mountainous frontiers and would leave the republic exposed
and helpless before the German onslaught. At the end of September
we still hoped against hope that Britain and France would refuse to
accept German demands. In a letter of the 21st, a week before the
Munich conference, we wrote: "What we had feared has come true.
France and Britain have betrayed Czechoslovakia, leaving her isolated
and alone in the face of an assault by Germany." It was not known

whether the Soviet Union, which was bound to help Czechoslovakia only if France did so, would support the Czechs and Slovaks if they were abandoned by the West.

In Prague the workers in all factories and stores went on strike and, in huge, orderly columns, converged on the square in front of the university and the Parliament. There they listened to political and military leaders who called on the new government to reject the pressure from abroad. It was inspiring to watch this massive demonstration of the will to resist. Britain was never so hated and despised, we wrote, but many were still hoping that the British people would repudiate the sell-out and force Chamberlain to resign. Some Czechs, including my boss at Radiožurnál, manifested their disgust with France by throwing their French medals into the Vltava.

THE CONSEQUENCES OF MUNICH

The Munich settlement did not come as a surprise, and it had the expected disastrous consequences. I wrote in a letter of 23 October to friends in England that Czechoslovakia, now completely isolated diplomatically, was subject to the full force of pressure from Berlin and had to give in to all demands. President Beneš was forced to resign but managed to get out of the country before a trial was staged. Newspapers and journals were severely censored, and a purge of the civil service began. The slogan of the day was "National Unity," and anyone who attacked the government was regarded as a traitor. The Communist party was dissolved, and its publications were banned. The Social Democrats left the Second International and united with the Czech National Socialist party in a left-wing bloc. The main parties of the right and centre, including the Agrarians, formed an all-national bloc.

The cession of territory to Germany and the granting of autonomy to Slovakia changed the balance of power in the state in favour of Slovakia, and the new central government in Prague was made up almost exclusively of Czech Agrarians and Slovak Clericals. The right-wing parties seized the opportunity to denigrate everyone and everything connected with the Masaryk-Beneš tradition — one year after everyone, over the bier of Masaryk, had pledged that "we shall remain faithful." Their newspapers sought to discredit the foreign policy of Edvard Beneš and to justify yielding to Germany's every demand; they also launched a wave of chauvinist propaganda directed against Jews and democratic Germans. Some of the progressive elements sold out and advocated "selfish nationalism" and "loyalty to Berlin." Other progressives still defended internationalism and democracy. The autonomy granted to Slovakia gave complete control of that province to the Clerical Hlinka party. The Slovak prime minister, Dr Tiso, opened cabinet meetings with prayers to God and publicly stated that the main enemy was Jewish Bolshevism. The first act of the government was to dissolve the Communist party.

After Munich our broadcasts became more and more distorted by self-censorship and official restrictions, so that the work lost all purpose. I resigned at the end of October and worked henceforth only once a week to relieve my English colleague. This left me free to resume full-time research on my thesis, although it was not easy given the atmosphere of impending war. The Parliamentary Library was shut down for lack of heating fuel, and I had to study in the Klementinum and at home. I worked very hard, and Sally had to persuade me to take short breaks once in a while. I began writing the first chapter in early January 1939 and finished it, over 100 pages long, by the end of February.

By this time Sally and I had moved to the plebeian district of Žižkov. We lived in a room with two large beds and their bulky bolsters, which left hardly any free space. Sally had the use of the kitchen where our landlady, Mrs Kadrnožková, who was a widow, ran a corset-making establishment. Sally took up her study of German with a friend, Heinz Frank, a German-speaking communist from the Sudeten region. I turned to studying the Czech language, taking regular conversation with Gustav Bareš (formerly Breitenfeld), a Czech communist journalist who had lost his job (later, under Communist rule, he became a top party leader). Once more Sally and I began to live a more normal life, going to concerts and seeing our friends. One evening we went the rounds of Prague taverns with Heinz Frank. We made frequent excursions into the countryside, including a visit to the villa where Mozart had lived during his stays in Prague.

Another day we went out to Brandýs nad Labem and talked with my friend Zdeněk Prokop about his military service on the frontier. He told us of one group of soldiers who refused to withdraw when the land was being occupied by German troops. They shut themselves up in a fortress and blew it up when they ran out of food. At an evening with our good friends the Rudingers, Zdeněk, also back from military service, told us of the terrible shock of the surrender on the minds of soldiers who were ready to fight. The Rudingers told us of their fears for the future. Zdeněk, general manager of a glass cartel, was Jewish and spoke perfect Czech and German; Lisa was the daughter of a Hungarian aristocrat. They spoke German at home with their two children. They were both ardent Communists and faced the prospect of exile. Under the new regime, life for democratically minded and Communist Germans — and for Jews — would be grim.

On 15 October I wrote to my thesis supervisor in London, Professor R.W. Seton-Watson: "I can guess your feelings. To one so intimately connected with the fortunes of Czechoslovakia from the beginning, the trend of events must have been, to put it mildly, profoundly discouraging. I, too, have come to admire this state, not only for what it had accomplished within its borders, but also for what it could have been expected to do in the maintenance of European peace. The useless sacrifice of one of the most loyal European states and the last democracy of Central Europe is in my mind a political crime, and not the first or the last of its kind." I was later glad to hear that Seton-Watson had formed a committee in Britain to assist the refugees.

In a letter home on 26 October, Sally wrote of the follies of this so-called peace and placed the blame squarely on Chamberlain and his clique. Ever since 1931 Britain had consistently given way to the aggressors — in Manchuria, Ethiopia, Spain, Austria, and now Czechoslovakia. In doing so, they had two aims, she thought: first, to undermine the democratic France of the Popular Front and to force on it a government pliable to Britain's wishes; and second, to isolate the Soviet Union, which for years had striven for peace and aided democracy all over the world. In a letter to an English friend on 29 October I referred to those who had been laughed at when they described Czechoslovakia as a possible second Spain but who were now shown to have been foresighted. There was no reason to expect any more resistance to German expansion in central Europe than to Japan in China or to German and Italian intervention in Spain. Only the extreme left in Britain sensed the wind's true direction and warned of the danger. If Prague, with Soviet support, had resisted Germany, the opposition forces in the West might have been successful in their efforts to press the British and French governments into helping Czechoslovakia. Yet if Czechoslovakia had resisted, with Soviet help, Britain and France would probably have joined Germany in a war against the "Bolshevist front."

One month later, on 19 November, I wrote that the situation in Czechoslovakia was almost unrecognizable compared to the days before

September. Then, Czechoslovakia was in the forefront of the peace movement and the League of Nations, and stood in the way of German advance into the whole of Central Europe. Now, powerless, she was dominated by Germany and forced to give way to every demand by Hitler. Then Czechoslovakia was, in many ways, a model democracy politically, with a high degree of national tolerance. Now it was a land where the undemocratic and chauvinist elements had seized the upper hand; people were turning against everything foreign and toward things "national" and Czech, even to anti-semitism. In early December a relatively unknown judge, Emil Hácha, had become president, and a new conservative government was formed. In Slovakia there was a completely fascist regime, which was a willing instrument for Hitler.

The outlook was by now gloomy indeed. Munich had simply postponed war for the time being but also made it more likely, perhaps even inevitable. "With nothing standing in his way, Hitler will plan his next aggression, either in the East, or in the West against France or Britain. Hitler will always have new demands, and finally resistance will have to be made to his desires for world expansion," I wrote on 2 November. If there had been resistance a year earlier, or even in September, war might have been avoided. After Munich a firm hand would still be necessary, finally, but Hitler was now so strong that he would willingly risk war. We should see within the year, I wrote home, whether my father's confidence that Munich brought permanent peace was justified.

The main question confronting our Czech friends was the plight of the refugees, not only those from the German Reich and from Austria, who had been given refuge in Czechoslovakia, but the even larger number — some 40,000 — from the Sudeten German areas ceded to Germany. An asylum had to be found abroad for the half-million Czech and German Jews involved as well as thousands of German and Austrian political refugees who faced great danger if they remained in the Protectorate and certain death if they returned home. Four months of almost fruitless efforts abroad on their behalf had created a feeling of hopelessness concerning their future. The refugees were living in camps scattered through the country — about 60 in all, housing some 140,000 persons. These camps were supported by the Czech National Fund, the Lord Mayor of London's Fund, and Czech local municipalities.

On Christmas Day 1938 we visited one of the camps in a Workers Club House in Beroun, a large town near Prague. There lived 180 people; 60 Czechs and 120 Germans. All had been active in the struggle against the Henlein movement in the Sudeten region and feared that, on Hitler's demand, they would be sent back to face their fate. They had built up a remarkable camp life, with an elected leadership, a regular general meeting, a so-called Wall Newspaper, a kitchen, a dining-room, a tailor, and shoe-repair shops. We attended a gala concert in the evening, which included a play that dramatized the plight of the refugees and demonstrated their unshakable belief that the fall of Hitler would mean a quick return home.

We were greatly concerned with the future of these victims of the Munich settlement. I had written on 26 October to the Canadian High Commissioner in London, Lester Pearson, urging that Canada provide a home for these victims of political and racial persecution and consider admitting some of them to form a self-supporting communal colony somewhere in the Canadian countryside. Many were political leaders, tried and tested in their devotion to democracy, others were skilled workers. "It was a unique opportunity for Canada to demonstrate her humanism and at the same time to gain new citizens of inestimable worth." This letter may have contributed to the eventual decision by the Canadian government to admit some 50,000 refugees and settle them on land in northern Alberta. Sally took on some very practical work in an office run by the Friends Service Committee, which conducted a program of relief for the refugees.

Meanwhile winter came, bringing heavy snow at the end of the year and skaters to the frozen Vltava. Large Christmas trees all over town served as centres for the collection of food and clothing for poor children. We celebrated Christmas eve with a friend, Leopold Grünwald, former editor of *Rote Fahne*, the Communist German-language newspaper, for whom Sally had been translating news bulletins into English. Still quite young, he had been among the founding members of both the Austrian and the Czechoslovak Communist parties in the 1920s. Both he and his wife faced an uncertain future and probable exile. Although both were Jewish, they served us the traditional Catholic Christmas supper of carp, potato salad, and fruit compote.

On New Year's Day we visited several small churches, all filled with worshippers, with the usual beggars at the doors. In one church there was a great cross, "the Cross of the Republic," with two round shields. Both showed maps of the republic: one, in black, had a crown of thorns superimposed; the other, in white, a laurel wreath and a red cross. Above the cross was the inscription, "Protect the Republic."

WITNESSES OF DISASTER

On 25 February 1939 we honoured St Matthew's Day — traditional-
ly regarded in Czechoslovakia as the end of winter and a harbinger of
spring. We joined the pilgrimage, an annual event since 1598, to the
tiny church of St Matthew, which overlooked the Šárka valley and was
packed with worshippers. We sent home a postcard showing the
church and bearing the inscription: "At St Matthews, when the sun
smiles on the pilgrimage, there are as many pretty maidens as when
poppy seeds are sown." Nearby was a fair, with sideshows for shooting
or gymnastics, and stands selling hotdogs (horké párky), which hung in
great festoons, and honeyed marzipan biscuits, often in the shape of
hearts. In this gay atmosphere it was hard to recall the fate that had
befallen the country.

The Britain was showing a complete lack of interest in the fate of what
remained of the republic and had reneged on its promise of economic
assistance. Germany was stepping up pressure on Czechoslovakia,
which could no longer be considered an independent country. The
threat of Slovak separation was so serious that Prague cracked down on
the separatist movement and appointed a new government in Slovakia.
In several articles for the *Canadian Forum,* dated July 1938 and March
and April 1939, I concluded that a German occupation was one of
several likely possibilities.

The crisis began one Tuesday evening, 14 March, when Slovakia
declared itself independent. Loudspeakers throughout the town called
at intervals for order and discipline. Great numbers of policemen lined
the main streets. A troop of fifty mounted police rode up and down Na
příkopě where the Deutsches Haus and German student quarters were
located. Nazi students paraded through the main streets in uniform,
chanting "Ein Volk, ein Reich, ein Führer." In the face of similar
provocative actions throughout Bohemia and Moravia, the Czechs
preserved admirable discipline and only minor disorders occurred. As
we prepared for bed that night the wireless announced that President
Hácha was on his way to Berlin and German troops had occupied some
border towns. At seven-thirty in the morning, on 15 March, we were
awakened by our landlady, who told us tearfully that German troops
had been marching from the border since six o'clock and people were
out buying up goods. By ten we were on Wenceslas Square, where we
saw the first advance German motorcyclist arrive, in a severe March
snowstorm. A few Germans ran up to shake his hand, but thousands of

Czechs looked on grimly and refused to give him directions. Soon the motorized divisions, including tanks with machine-guns at the ready, poured into the city centre. They were driving on the right side of the road (in a city with left-hand traffic) and were sometimes blocked by trucks and taxis moving in the opposite direction. At certain points the crowds formed a solid human barrier, booing, hissing, and shaking their fists into the very muzzles of the machine-guns. The police had to clear a way for the invaders. At other points the people were silent and gazed with hatred or contempt at the passing vehicles. Others continued on their way to work or business. In the very heart of the city, at the foot of Wenceslas Square, we were part of a crowd that began to sing the national anthem, heads bared in the driving snow — a stirring moment.

Throughout the day the German troops poured in, occupying barracks vacated by the Czechoslovak soldiers. The Chief of the German General Staff set up its headquarters at the Hotel Alcron. The airport, radio studios, police stations, and postal and telegraph offices were all placed under police control. And then came the culminating indignity, which sent a cold shudder down the spine of every Czech — the entry of Hitler, together with the German foreign minister, Von Ribbentrop, General Keitel, and Himmler, the head of the SS, into the Prague Castle, where the swastika was raised for all to see. In the morning we climbed up to the Castle heights and witnessed a crowd of five thousand Germans, chanting over and over: "Lieber Führer, sei so net, zeig dein Gesicht am Fenster brett" (Dear Führer, be so kind; show your face at the windowsill). He did at last appear and could be seen behind a curtain. We were sickened by the irony and the falsity of this Nazi demonstration, high above a city with a population of almost eight hundred thousand Czechs and fewer than 50,000 Germans.

The work of "totalitarianizing" a democratic country began at once. With Himmler came hundreds of his secret police, who began arresting former high officials and hunting down the "politicals," not only those who had fled from Germany after 1933, or from Austria in March 1938, or the Sudeten districts in September 1938, but also now their Czech comrades. Days and nights of psychological terror began for the politically endangered, who slept in friends' homes and wandered the streets in the daytime. House searches began, at first by lenient Czech policemen, who warned suspects to burn everything incriminating. Meetings of all kinds were forbidden — the press was incorporated into the Nazi press service — and there was a curfew at eight o'clock every night. The civil administrator of Bohemia was

Konrad Henlein, the Sudeten German leader. The Czech General, Gajda, who had been dismissed from the General Staff in the 1920s for betraying military secrets, and led an abortive fascist putsch in the 1930s, was made the leader of the Czech National Committee, an instrument of German rule.

At his midnight meeting in Berlin President Hácha capitulated when Hitler threatened him with the destruction of Prague by bombing, because he knew there was no help forthcoming from the British or French governments. To interpret Hácha's act of delivering the Czech nation into the hands of the German chancellor as a voluntary expression of a desire to live under the rule of Hitler is to insult a brave and steadfast people, whose hearts were boiling under their calm exteriors. At the statue of St Wenceslas, the patron saint and king of Bohemia, and at the resting place of the Czech Unknown Soldier, crowds of people, bare headed and weeping, gathered and left thousands of little bouquets. Flowers were also placed at the Jan Hus monument and the statue of Woodrow Wilson. The old Czechoslovak flag was raised throughout the city, and the swastika was seldom seen. Such was the enthusiasm of Prague for their liberation by the Führer!

The newspapers at home in Canada carried headlines about a "Toronto boy" who had disappeared after the German invasion. A few days after the event I received a call from the British embassy asking if I was safe; my brother Andy had asked the government in Ottawa to inquire after us. Friends urged us to leave as soon as possible, but with our British and American passports we felt relatively safe. We hated the prospect of staying on but were reluctant to give up when my studies were so close to completion. During the days of crisis I had stopped work on my thesis, and I now found it hard to get back to it. But there seemed no alternative to pushing on as fast as possible. Using a new typewriter, with Czech diacritics, we buckled down to the task of typing several more chapters.

Sally redoubled her work at the Friends Committee. When a big transport of women and children received permission to pass through Germany, Tessa Rowntree, the head of the office, accompanied them and left Sally in charge of the office. Sally dispensed money to the refugees to keep them alive while they waited for arrangements to cross the narrow frontier into Poland. This they did by paying high fees to often-unreliable smugglers who were to guide them through the mountains to the border. The "politicals" were hidden by railway workers in the coal carriages of trains or led by miners through disused mine shafts under the frontier.

My friend Grünwald was living in hiding and had lost contact with the Soviet embassy, which had promised him a visa. I kept in touch with him through a prearranged contact with a shoemaker. On one occasion I made a nighttime visit, on his behalf, to the Soviet consulate general. It was terrifying, standing outside the high wall in full view of a police guard, to ring the bell at a spotlit gate. Later I had a conspiratorial meeting with a Soviet representative in Rieger Park, by the statue of the Czech political leader F.L. Rieger, where he identified himself by a prearranged signal, whistling to his dog. Grünwald in the end escaped across the border into Poland, picked up his visa in Warsaw, and spent the war years in the USSR.

In April 1939 when spring came, Prague began to look beautiful again. We got out for some good walks, once in the steep and rocky valley of Šárka, another time on the slopes of Petřín Hill, where one could see the blossoms in the huge monastery gardens. We also joined the tens of thousands of Praguers who made excursions on Sundays by train or by bus to the woods on the Labe river or to the Sázava river. Once we went with Professor Otakar Odložilík, who told us of his plans to go to the United States for the summer. When he found a Canadian penny he was delighted with this good omen! The rivers were filled with bathers and canoeists, and the steamers took excursionists up the river. We made an overnight trip to the industrial city of "red" Kladno, a bastion of communist strength, and stayed with a family of workers. In the morning the children rushed in expecting to see "Red Indians" from Canada!

By the time of our departure from Prague in the early summer of 1939 I had completed five chapters of my thesis in final draft and sent them back to England. We began putting our passports in order, getting the necessary documents from the police and the Nazi occupation authorities, and packing our suitcases. Since we were "more or less in rags" by this time, we took the opportunity of getting some clothes made cheaply — in my case, by a little tailor across the street, and in Sally's, by one of the girls who worked in our landlady's corset establishment. Finally, all was in order, and we bade a sad farewell to the city that we had come to love and to Czech friends who had to remain in occupied Prague. We spent our final evening with the Rudingers, whose son and daughter were already in England and who expected themselves to reach that refuge before we did. We left on July 8, stopping for a final visit at the historic city of Tábor, centre of the Hussite movement in the fifteenth century.

NOTE

1.   I base parts of this chapter on my letters to family and friends during this period. University of Toronto Archives (UTA): Gordon Skilling Papers, boxes 8 and 9.

I
GETTING MY BEARINGS

2

GROWING UP ON COLLEGE STREET

MY MOTHER, ALICE STEVENSON, was born in the village of Stanwell Moor, near Staines, Middlesex. The daughter of a gardener on a large estate near the village, she lived with her parents in Park Lodge, the coach-house at the manor, and served as a children's helper and as maid or cook. She was 19 years old in 1893, when she married my father, William, who was 21. A shoemaker, he peddled around Stanwell and other villages on a bicycle, picking up shoes to be repaired. His father, a Scot from Leith, was also a cobbler, as were his four brothers and two of his brothers-in-law. Like her husband, Alice was almost entirely without education, having left school at age 12. Moving first to Ashford and then to Brighton, they had four children: my three brothers, William John (born 1894), Edward Donald (1898), and Andrew Douglas (1903), and one daughter, Alice Evelyn, who died shortly after her birth in 1901. I entered the world in 1912, their only child to be born in Canada, and was given names as Scottish as those of my brothers.

I do not know the reasons for my parents' emigration to Canada in 1907 — perhaps worsening economic conditions or simply my father's search for adventure and a new life. Certainly the decision to migrate to a new country at the age of 35 with his wife and three sons (then 10, 13 and 15 years old), was a bold one, an act which entailed uprooting their lives from traditions, friends, and family to embark on a risky and challenging new course. One can only imagine the "joys" of the voyage to Canada in the steerage of a small steamship. My mother remembered it as a nightmare of constant seasickness, and the huge rats which scuttled around the cabin — the "pussy cats," as my brother Andy called them — terrified her. They spent two or three years adapting to the new and strange life in Montreal. Once or twice in the summer Dad went "harvesting" in the West, but he was not attracted to the hard life of a farmer. For reasons unknown, he and his family pushed

The shoe-repair shop on College Street: Andy, Mother, Don, and Father, in 1912

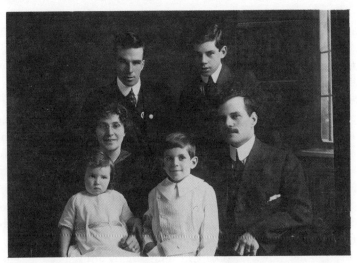

Our family, July 1917: me at centre, Bill and Andy in back, Mother and Father with Bill's daughter Margaret

on to Toronto, living for a brief period on Ontario Street, in the heart of the city, among other newly arrived immigrants. They then moved west to the major thoroughfare of College Street, where they lived at number 633, near Grace Street, in a flat above my Dad's shoe store. I was born there on February 28, 1912.

Dad always seemed chained to his shop, which was open daily from eight o'clock in the morning until eight at night, and on Saturday until almost midnight. Hour by hour, in the flat above the store, we could hear the pounding of the hammer and the whirring of the machines. It was a good business, and my father was not hard-up. He was able to purchase his store and later bought, rented and sold half a dozen houses and stores, then built a large store on the Danforth. In early 1926, during the real estate boom, he went down to Florida alone and bought a lot in Coral Gables. In my eyes he seemed to be a slave to work and money-making, but he was an industrious and ambitious man who achieved much from humble beginnings.

My father had no hobbies and took no interest in sports. He enjoyed reading biography, and sometimes went to downtown theatres on passes given in return for his placing a poster in his shop window. He did not drink (except some port wine on special occasions) but was a constant smoker of foul-smelling cigars. We had family parties at home or on weekend outings to the suburb of Long Branch, where Dad built a little cottage. He loved to travel, and in 1924 purchased a used Ford Sedan for $427, making possible car trips to Muskoka and Niagara Falls, into the States and to Quebec. After the armistice in 1918, *wanderlust* led my father further afield, first to Ottawa in 1919, where he was an "instructor in rehabilitation," teaching the art of shoe-repair to returning veterans. Soon afterward he spent a year or so in Brooklyn where he worked in a shoe-repair shop in Flatbush. From there my parents made their first trip home to England. Dad continued in business until the mid-1930s, then retired to a small cottage in the suburb of West Hill. They later moved back into the city, resettling in the east end. In 1953 they celebrated the 60th anniversary of their marriage.

My mother was a devoted wife and parent, bearing sole responsibility for bringing up the children and looking after our home. Her life was one of hard and unremitting work on frugal means, and she was expected to follow my father's will in all matters. She was a woman of sensitivity and intelligence, affectionate to her family and generous and kind to all. Although she had only elementary schooling, she appreciated the value of education and was a constant support to me in my studies from childhood on. She and my father were regular church-goers; we walked every week in our Sunday best to a neighbouring Presbyterian church, later belonging to the United Church of Canada. In the east end, when life was a little easier at home, she was active in churchwomen's groups. The loss of my brother Don, in the war, was a source of lasting grief to her. Each year, on Armistice Day, I went with her to the ceremony of remembrance at City Hall, where she placed a wreath on the cenotaph in his memory. In the mid-1930s, after visiting me in Europe, she gave frequent talks on her impressions of the battlefields of France and of the meetings of the League of Nations

My brother Don, before leaving for the war, 1917

Assembly that we attended in Geneva. She became active in peace work in the League of Nations Society and revealed latent talents that were never fully developed due to lack of education and opportunity.

In 1916 two of my brothers enlisted for war service. The older, Bill, was seriously wounded but survived. Don died of wounds on his first day in action at the front. My brother, Andy, was closest to me since he lived at home while I was a lad. He became a successful photographer and was active in the Kiwanis Club. I was greatly saddened by his early death in 1958, after several heart attacks, at 55 years of age, only one year before my permanent return to Toronto.

Two of my earliest memories related to the two great tragedies, World War I and the world Depression, that symbolized the times in which I grew up. I vividly recall the day, in May 1917, when my father came up the staircase from the store below, bearing the telegram with the news that my brother, "Pte. Edward Donald Skilling," had "died of wounds — gunshot wound in left thigh." As my mother wept at the head of the stairs, I crept into the kitchen to cry against the wall. Some 12 years later I remember just as acutely the day my brother Bill, in the same hallway, jokingly announced to my mother that he had joined General Cox's army, that is, the army of unemployed, having lost his job as carpenter.

My own "war effort," at age five or six, was to wear a little military uniform, replete with Scottish tam, and to return the salute of a friendly officer who regularly led his company down College Street beneath our front room window. Finally, on Armistice Day, I remember the singing and cheering, the bonfires on College Street, and after the war the snapshots taken by my parents during their trip to Europe in 1919, of ruined Ypres and Vimy Ridge, and of Don's grave in Aubigny, France.

During my year or two at Grace Street Public School, just around the corner from my father's store, I remember being intensely shy and hiding behind my mother when I was introduced to someone. There were about four hundred boys and girls of Jewish or Italian origin at my school. Most of them left school at age 14, for lack of the means to continue. The teachers were almost all women, and the few men were away on war service. When we moved to Ottawa in 1919, I received farewell letters, written on a Jewish holiday, from my teacher, Alice Brabazon, and those few classmates who were present that day.

I can fill in bits of our time in Ottawa and Brooklyn, and later in Montreal, from a skimpy diary. From Ottawa I have a recollection, no doubt preserved by my mother's frequent recounting, of a librarian's joking comment that I had read all the books in the local public library. I often read to my mother at home. For Brooklyn, my diary records frequent movies, occasional churchgoing, and sightseeing with Andy in New York City and even further afield. I remember nothing of my life in Brooklyn except the anxieties connected with frequent bed-wetting. In Montreal I stayed with my Aunt Lill, my mother's sister, during my parents' trip to England and France, and the summer months were passed in games and reading, outings with my grown-up cousins, Ted, Flo, and Grace, and with Ted's man friend.

Back in Toronto again, we lived in the east end in a small house on Monarch Park Avenue, then above the store that Dad had built at 2217 Danforth Avenue. I attended Wilkinson Public School, more modern than Grace Street; it served a largely middle-class and fairly well-to-do population, mainly British in origin. The teachers were again almost all women, including Mildred Sloan, with whom I was apparently a great favorite. In walking to and from school I passed through the playground, and I remember an encounter with a bully from whose attack I was rescued by a fellow student. About this time I tried my hand at writing a short story entitled "Adventures in the Rockies," a romantic tale of trappers who struck it rich by finding gold. A letter of rejection from an editor of the *Boys Tely*, a section of Toronto's *Evening Telegram*, described the story as "wonderful for a boy of your age" (I was then 11). Someday, he thought, I might be writing stories for the press. "Do not be discouraged by a few failures at the start."

Our move back to College Street in 1924 was a return to the scenes of my early childhood and to the district which would be "home" for me during my public and high school days and through my first year in university. Clinton Street Public School had a high proportion of foreign born students. Boys and girls were segregated into separate classes. I was in room 10, for the best students, and had one of the few male teachers, Andrew Wilkie, who was a pianist and formed an orchestra and choir. I played for the school baseball team, took part in a play, and was a member of the cadet corps. Later, in 1928, when a Clinton Old Boys' Reunion was organized during a trip by steamboat to Port Dalhousie, I was elected president.

As a boy aged 12 to 16 I was generally good at school, though there were occasions when I got my hands strapped. Much of my time was spent doing homework and reading, and visiting the library. I kept long lists of words and their meanings, as well as brief reviews of books I had read. Homework essays dealt with such exotic subjects as the Renaissance, the Reformation and the Industrial Revolution. I was obsessed with crossword puzzles and even tried to construct some for the *Evening Telegram,* but they were not accepted. Having begun piano lessons on "the Danforth," I went on to study with Fair Cockburn at the Toronto Conservatory of Music. I took the examinations year by year, always with honours or first class honours, and eventually obtained the degree of ATCM (Associate of the Toronto Conservatory of Music). I also gave piano lessons, teaching four students every Saturday morning and earning 75 cents an hour.

I was closely associated with the church, first at Clinton Street Methodist, then at West Presbyterian on College Street, and first took communion in October 1925. I attended Sunday School regularly, later teaching a class for several years. Our teacher, John Burgar, a businessman, spent little time on the Bible and read to us instead from *Les Misérables.* He openly discussed the sexual problems of growing boys. He also ran the West Church Club, of which I was secretary. We met weekly for games in the gym, devotional services, talks, book reports, and debates; in one I remember opposing the abolition of cadet-training in schools. The club followed the program of the Tuxis Trail Rangers, and I zealously sought to win badges for specific achievements. The club sponsored occasional picnics, paper chases or banquets, including one for fathers and sons, and (more unusually), one for mothers and sons. For these gatherings I often attempted humorous speeches on subjects such as "If I were my father's father" and "Raising a large family." In 1928 and 1929 I myself ran a junior boys' club at the church.

"Minding the store" in the evenings was one of my responsibilities, especially when both my parents were out. Between customers, I read and did homework amid the smell of leather, ink and polish. Most bothersome was the need to rush downstairs during mealtimes, whenever the bell rang, to serve customers. I learned to do some of the minor work: sanding, inking and polishing, sharpening skates and even heeling shoes. There were also numerous odd jobs such as cleaning the store windows, shovelling snow, sometimes helping to scrape and paper or paint the walls, not only at number 633, but at other of my Dad's properties. I often did errands on my bike, collecting the rents from Dad's tenants. I received a small allowance and had a bank account of my own, which reached the grand sum of $40 by the end of 1924. I even made a loan of $20 to my father when he acquired his first car and did not have enough in the bank to cover it — a debt he soon repaid.

I have vague memories of playing with toy soldiers in the postage stamp-size garden behind the store, and of swimming at Sunnyside; of football and baseball games in the summers, and in winter, playing hockey, skating to music, and sleighing in the ravines. I was an ardent fan of the Toronto Maple Leafs although I rarely went to games at the Lakeshore stadium. I played the hand-wound "Victrola" and listened, often in vain, to a crystal set radio. In the evenings there were sometimes card games at home, as well as cribbage and crokonole. We made frequent visits to the local movie-house, at first to see silent thrillers, which were accompanied by a pianist, and later the "talkies." The great stars of the day were Charlie Chaplin, Rudolf Valentino, Harold Lloyd, and Douglas Fairbanks. A special treat was to attend a play at a downtown theatre with one of my parents. We had frequent social gatherings of friends and relatives. The big occasions were Christmas and New Year's, with these parties lasting past three a.m. After a huge dinner, we played parlour games and cards, and sang at the piano, with me at the keyboard and my cousin, Ern, playing his trumpet.

I was growing up in the thoroughly urban environment of a rapidly developing city whose population reached over a half million in the 1920s. Toronto retained a predominantly British character well into the 1930s, but its ethnic profile was actually changing rapidly as a result of immigration. Our own district became more and more cosmopolitan as European immigrants, including many Jews, moved in. Almost all our neighbours and fellow shopkeepers were Jewish. I do not remember any anti-semitism on the part of my father, but I deplored his habit of referring to Italians or Ukrainians as "foreigners," even though they might have been born in Canada. I was horrified by the taunt, "Ye killee Christ," chanted by some of the neighbourhood children, as they held up three fingers at the bearded "rag and bones" man in his horse-drawn cart. My diary recorded some mildly negative comments on the overwhelmingly Jewish composition of my classes, both at Clinton and Harbord, I had many Jewish friends and classmates, and I used to go to Holy Blossom Synagogue occasionally to hear the eloquent sermons of Rabbi Eisendrath.

In 1925 we drove to Washington DC, New York, and Montreal in our Model-T Ford, covering about 2500 miles, never at more than 25 miles per hour, over rough and dusty roads, with frequent stops for repairs and many detours. Another trip in 1926 took us to Detroit and Chicago, where my brother Andy was working. In Detroit we visited the enormous Ford assembly-line factory and I took my first flight by airplane at the Dearborn Airport. In Chicago the bloody slaughter of sheep and steers at the Swift Packing Company sickened us.

In the summer of 1926 I first experienced the beauty of the lake country to the north of the city. We spent a wonderful week at the cottage of our friends and neighbours the Martins (Mr. Martin ran a grocery store near us), swimming, canoeing, berrying, fishing, chopping wood, and playing golf in an open field. The following summer I spent two weeks across Lake Muskoka at Pine Crest, a boys' camp run by the YMCA. I lived in a tent with other boys and eagerly imbibed Indian lore around the campfire in the evenings. There I learned to swim and canoe properly. In the summer of 1928 I had quite a different experience as a counsellor at the Bolton Summer Camp, not far from Orangeville, which was run by the Neighbourhood Workers Association. There I had my first contact with underprivileged children from the city's poorest districts.

In 1930 I took an unforgettable canoe trip in the wilds of Lake Temagami with Mr Burgar, my Sunday school teacher. He was an experienced outdoorsman, and introduced me to life in the wilderness: the joys of setting up camp, cooking over a campfire, sleeping in a tent or in the open air, and the arduous hours of paddling, sometimes bucking high winds and waves in difficult lake crossings, and portaging our canoe and supplies for several hundred yards. In our ten days we met only one other canoe and felt like early explorers or *coureurs de bois*.

In September 1926 I got my first job, as an office boy at the *Star Weekly*, but it only lasted one week. There I delivered messages and performed menial tasks like clearing the wastebaskets, but I got to hobnob with the "famous," such as writer Gregory Clark (a Harbord graduate). In the summer of 1927 I had several jobs, first at the Nu Tec Sign Co. on Queen Street, where I did my first piecework. In one week I earned over $20, and was glad to give $5 to my mother. Later I worked briefly in the ladies' hat department of Simpson's department store.

In 1929 I got a summer job as a bellboy at the Royal Muskoka, a luxury hotel on Lake Rosseau, where for eight weeks I combined business with pleasure. Carrying baggage and catering to the needs and whims of the well-to-do, I earned a total of $250, which I used to cover the expenses of my final year at high school. The staff, many of them students like me, shared some of the privileges of paying guests; in our off-duty hours we could swim, canoe, golf, and dance in the ballroom. We lived, however, in bug-infested wooden tenements. My glimpse into the life of the leisure class at the Royal Muskoka offered a sharp contrast to my memories of the poverty of the kids at Bolton Camp. The following year, just before entering college, I was again employed at the Royal, but because of the Depression, my job lasted only two weeks. I spent most of the summer at home on the Danforth, walking down to Lake Ontario to swim and sunbathe, and hitch-hiked with my brother Andy to Montreal and Ottawa.

These were my years of growing up. I began to be interested in girls and sex, at least in my thoughts. I had my first crush in the summer of 1925, on Violet Dodds. After a Sunday school picnic at Queenston we enjoyed the ferry trip home together on the open deck. In the summer of 1927 I fell for Lorraine Sanderson, formerly of Clinton, who served with me on the executive of the Old Boys' Reunion. That autumn I acquired my first suit of clothes with "longers" (long pants) and my first man's hat — a fawn fedora. I began to go steady in the later years of high school with Harriet Mills, the daughter of a high school classics teacher (whose approval I won by my good work in Latin and Greek). Harriet and I went to school dances together and sometime went into nearby High Park for a little necking and kissing.

On 2 September 1925, I registered at Harbord Collegiate Institute, just south of Bloor Street West, near Bathurst. By this time well over half, perhaps even 90 percent, of my fellow-students were Jewish. "The Old School," to which I wrote a dedication in the *Harbord Review* in my final year, was "an ancient red-brick place" with "a massive incongruous tower" and strange "Oriental turrets," and with "time-worn classrooms, ill-lit corridors ... and a bare old-fashioned Assembly Hall." This "dark, poorly ventilated building," was replaced by a more modern building the year after my departure. Old Harbord had a good library and a gymnasium, but no cafeteria or swimming pool. Whatever its physical defect I wrote, it still "stood loftily in our hearts."

The school was headed by Lt.-Col. E.W. Hagarty, a veteran of the Great War whose own son was killed in 1916. He had been a teacher of Latin and Greek since Harbord opened in 1892, and principal for more than 20 years. He was very patriotic and a strong advocate of military training in schools. Widely considered to be a "martinet" in disciplinary and academic matters, he tended to run the school like an army, but he also possessed a profound dedication to scholarship. He ran a staff of excellent teachers, for whom I had great respect at the time and fond memories years later. Year after year the scholarly record of the school remained outstanding and its students garnered many scholarships. It had many distinguished graduates over the years and Harbordites developed an extraordinary loyalty to the old school.

I ranked high in academic work and was usually first in my class. However, I was somewhat bored by the slowness of classroom work and it was not unusual for me to be sent out to the hallway for whispering or passing notes. Homework took up an average of one to two hours daily, and as much as five in my final year. Practising the piano took another hour or two each day. I was busy with extracurricular activities, eventually becoming president of the Lit (Literary Society), associate editor of the *Harbord Review,* and battalion commander of the cadet corps. I played defense on the junior basketball team; Harbord won the city high school championship in 1928-29. This qualified me for the coveted badges, Harbord H and V. The undoubted climax of my teen years was graduating with12 firsts in 12 subjects, with an average of 89 percent. This brought university scholarships in general proficiency, Greek, and Latin, and a gold medal in mathematics. I was also lucky enough to win a special Gundy-Doran scholarship in Canadian history, valued at $1,200. These awards secured financial support for my studies and meant that I could pay my mother for room and board.

When I re-read my school essays and other writings now, they seem empty of original ideas and and full of clichés and prejudices. I exalted "great men," such as Nelson and Lincoln, celebrated patriotism, both British and Canadian, and had effusive praise for Loyalists, the Royal Canadian Mounted Police, the monarchy, and Canada as a nation. In an essay for the Simpson's Essay Contest, I waxed eloquent on the romance and achievement of that company: I won sixth prize ($10). I was equally romantic in an essay submitted to a contest of the Canadian Progress Club (1927); here I wrote enthusiastically of Canada's progress during 60 years of confederation and the country's "glorious future." I believed, naively, that "the two races," English and French, would always work harmoniously together, united by the ties of common interest and allegiance to the empire. In an oratorical contest on the subject, "Canada Among the Nations," I spoke of Canada as a country on its way to equality status within the empire and "an enormous future." I said Canada should take a stand for world peace and international good will; its relationship with the United States offered testimony that "all disputes between nations can be settled by reason, not force." I won a gold medal for this effusion. My Gundy-Doran essay on the settlement of Ontario before confederation was a more solid piece, based on research and reading some 70 sources. I ended by expressing pride in the heritage of our ancestors, both the United Empire Loyalists and the later immigrants from Europe, who together "ushered the new-born Ontario into the world, not with bloodshed and plunder, but with the ring of the woodsman's axe as he felled the trees to build his forest home."

My school essays make almost no mention of the glaring social problems of the time and the two great tragedies of my boyhood and youth — the Great War and the Depression — appear to have had a negligible impact on my thinking. I seemed to have little or no social conscience, and took no interest in politics, national or provincial, or in international affairs. I uttered platitudes on the undefended Canadian-American border but did not so much as mention the League of Nations. Yet my seeming disinterest in events abroad and unawareness of the mounting international crisis in Europe and Asia, and the growing threats of Fascism and Communism, may have been typical of my age and class. I expressed no sympathy for the new currents of organized labour and socialism in Europe, and served blithely as an officer in the cadet corps. Appearing in uniform at the Armistice Day ceremony at the war memorial, which commemorated the 75 Harbordites killed in World War I, seemed a proud honour.

One school essay, entitled "Poverty: Its Causes and Its Remedies," and written after the stock market crash of October 1929, was an exception to my general lack of concern with society and its problems. Still, it barely differed from my other efforts in its smug and self-satisfied conclusions. The causes of poverty were carelessness in handling money, the pursuit of pleasure, the worship of our neighbours, and the desire to emulate them. "To rise out of poverty" was by no means easy, I conceded. Success required "patience, industry, perseverance and courage." Another essay on "success" effusively praised Henry Ford, who "disposed of his millions in charitable ways," and "was able to create a low cost of living, a comfortable home-life, and good wages for his employees." In my valedictory address, given in the fall of 1930 after my graduation, there was not a single reference to the Depression and the tragedy of unemployment or to the gathering clouds of war. I spoke in clichés of the virtues of the "successful man," and quoted Bruce Barton: "He had an aim. He studied. He worked."

Perhaps it is too much to expect that a youth of 17 or 18 would have begun to sense the ills of the society in which he was growing up and to seek solutions to some of its problems. My own life had been a serene one, largely without personal tragedy apart from the death of one brother and the imprisonment of another for harassment of his children. There were no serious conflicts within my family (at least none that I was aware of), nor did I experience difficulties in growing to maturity. I was successful academically and socially, and was well enough endowed financially to pursue the studies I loved. I could therefore proceed to university with my optimistic assumptions of a good life ahead completely intact. In an essay written during my first term at college I actually agreed with William Osler, who, in a speech at Yale University, declared that students should "stop worrying about the future and the past," the "unborn tomorrows" and the "dead yesterdays," and concentrate on "the year's tasks." Our university years, I wrote, would be "the period in which we established the mental, social and moral basis for a straight, unfaltering journey through life."

It only took a year or two of higher education to challenge these illusions and to bring me into touch with the realities of the contemporary world. Many, many years later, speaking at the Harbord reunion dinner in 1985, I observed that our studies at Harbord did not prepare us for the unexpected and unpredictable life ahead: the effects of the Depression, the Second World War, the Holocaust, nuclear weapons, or the Cold War. Harbord was but a beginning in the life-long process of education, but it had been "a good place to start, a place of good teachers, high standards, rich opportunities in music, literature and sports, a place of good friendship and happy associations, of racial harmony."

3

BECOMING A SOCIALIST: TORONTO

IT WAS A FOREGONE CONCLUSION that I would study at the University of Toronto since I had won scholarships for that institution and I could live at home and avoid the expense of residence. My choice of non-denominational and cosmopolitan University College, instead of Victoria College, which was affiliated with the United Church, was probably influenced by my declining religious faith and my upbringing in the most ethnically mixed part of Toronto. My selection of political science and economics was more surprising, because my scholarships had been for the most part in classics; perhaps a factor was my meeting Irene Biss, a charming young lecturer in economics, at the registration desk.

The University of Toronto, under its scholarly president Sir Robert Falconer, was pre-eminent among Canadian institutions of higher learning. University College (UC) had great strength in the traditional courses of classics, modern languages, and philosophy and was headed by the urbane and liberal-minded principal Malcolm Wallace. The department of political economy had established a high standard of scholarship and bore a decidedly British stamp, which was only gradually modified by the Canadian influence of Harold Innis and other, younger professors. Its classical "political economy" approach was being newly counterbalanced by modern socialist and Canadian tendencies of thought.

Work in the honours course, political science and economics, was rigorous and demanding; it involved compulsory lecture courses, sometimes in large classes and, less often, small tutorial groups. Most important was the writing of essays, a constant exercise that counted for nothing in one's ultimate standing but disciplined one to devote enormous time and effort to a given topic. The curriculum was highly structured with only limited freedom to choose among subjects, and the whole course demanded a high degree of specialization, mainly in economics. The thrust of the program was British and Canadian although it tended to be more European in its historical and theoretical aspects. There was not a single course on Canadian government. There was a benign neglect of foreign countries such as Soviet Russia, China, African states or even the United States.

I was lucky to study under a galaxy of stimulating scholars. The more senior academics included Vincent Bladen, a fervent believer in Adam Smith, who touched on Marx only at the end of his course; Harold Innis, dean of Canadian economic historians, whose lectures (quite dull and uninspiring) were based on his massive pioneering studies of Canadian staple production; and Alex Brady, a specialist on the governments of the dominions, who lectured on political thought from Plato to the present. Among more recently appointed lecturers were Wynne Plumptre, who was fresh from studying at the feet of John Maynard Keynes at Cambridge (he was an ardent advocate of a central bank for Canada); Joe Parkinson, a specialist in international trade and finance; and Harry Cassidy, an expert in social problems and social insurance. Many of these newer recruits were moderate socialists and participated in the founding of the Cooperative Commonwealth Federation (CCF). More radical was Lorne T. Morgan, an economic historian whose eloquent and witty lectures on European economic development (including Russia and the Soviet Union) attracted several hundred students. A lecturer from Holland, the eccentric Otto Berlenbach van der Sprenkel, gave me my first insights into Marxism through his interpretation of political theory. I studied British and colonial and some modern Canadian and American history under leading scholars such as George Brown and George Glazebrook. Outside the classroom I was influenced by the radical historian, Frank Underhill, a leading figure in the CCF.

I devoted much of my time to study, and especially to the essays. Well trained in the art of writing exams in high school, I was able to achieve first class standing in all years and, in all but the final year, stood first in my class. I also won the Southam and Mackenzie scholarships in political science. At the same time I was very active in campus politics, including the University College Literary and Athletic Society (the Lit, as we called it). In my senior year I conducted a hard-fought campaign for the presidency, using posters and leaflets, and won by a vote of 314 to 158 over my conservative opponent, Dick Bell, with whom I often locked horns in debate. Our honorary president was the extraordinarily young-looking and witty Wynne Plumptre. On

February 22, 1934, when the Lit celebrated its 80th anniversary with a great banquet in the Hart House dining hall, the university's chancellor, Sir William Mulock, proposed a toast to the Lit. In my reply I paid tribute to it as a central current in the stream of college days that constituted our initiation into real life. At other commemorative occasions in the great hall, such as the retirement of Sir Robert Falconer or Dean De Lury, I had to preside or speak. The first meeting of the Lit under my presidency passed a motion eliminating all bribery (peanuts, cigarettes, and blotters), as well as campaign advertising in future elections. The Lit also adopted, after a competition, a new college cheer or "yell," which gave prominence to UC as "the home of knowledge," citing its motto "*Parum claris, lucem dare* [To give light where it is needed]." As president of the Lit I became a member, and later an elected vice-president, of the Students' Administrative Council (SAC) and represented it at the annual meeting of the National Federation of Canadian University Students (NFCUS). The Lit found many lighter outlets in such galas as the Arts Ball and the UC Follies, and the highly polemical and often witty debates in its Parliamentary Club. As "governor general" in the autumn of 1933 and again in January 1934, I read, on behalf of the government, a markedly socialistic Throne Speech declaring support for the League of Nations. On other worthy occasions I condemned the English accent, the restoration of knighthoods in Canada, and even Santa Claus — as an exemplar of crass commercialism.

My life at the University of Toronto was one of perpetual motion. Living at home, I had to walk daily to the campus, trudging along College Street during my first year, and later taking the streetcar from our home on the Danforth. I spent many hours attending lectures in the then rather dilapidated but pleasant halls and classrooms of UC, and in the junior common room, where the Lit had its meetings. I was proud to see my name inscribed in gold on the wall with other members of the Lit executives, dating back to 1852. There was so much to do in the splendid neo-gothic Hart House, where annually elected student committees planned and organized activities involving art, athletics, music, and debating. I was elected to the debates committee and was thus able to take lunch or dinner at the high table. There I enjoyed a personal association with the warden, J.B. Bickersteth, an Englishman who was a graduate of Oxford and a war veteran. A confirmed bachelor, Bicky resided in the House and seemed to embody its spirit of collegiality and all-roundedness. I was also a news editor, and later associate editor, of the *Varsity*.

Our evenings were sometimes spent in informal discussion circles which gathered, by invitation, at Wynne Plumptre's house in Rosedale. The Historical Club met at the homes of other professors or Toronto business magnates such as Sir Joseph Flavelle and J.S. McLean. Somewhat contradictory to my emerging socialist beliefs was my pledge to a fraternity (Psi Upsilon) — costly and elitist as these clubs were — and I played an active part in its affairs. I found time to play basketball and swim in the Hart House pool. In the early university years I regularly trekked down to the Conservatory of Music for music lessons and the occasional recital. During this hectic life I found welcome relaxation with my girlfriend, Eileen Woodhouse, a quiet, attractive young woman from Niagara Falls. She was not active in student affairs and had little interest in politics, but we enjoyed many happy hours together, going to the college balls and to dances at her sorority or my fraternity.

My other close friends included Sydney Hermant, son of the owner of a large optical firm. On the first day of registration he clipped my freshman tie at the entrance to University College and enlisted me in debating activities. Sydney liked to bring together Jews and gentiles at parties at his father's big home on Heath Street. After graduation he married Madge Shaw and took over his father's firm. He remained passionately devoted to the university and dedicated spare time for the rest of his life to work on its governing bodies. Another good friend was Marvin Gelber, also Jewish and the son of a businessman. A serious, scholarly person, he was strongly anti-Nazi and once tried to get me to boycott a concert by Walter Gieseking. He remained a bachelor all his life, succeeded to his father's business, and became a patron of the arts, an MP, and an active participant in international affairs, including serving as a delegate to the United Nations. Other friends were Arnold Smith, active in debating and the Lit, a fellow socialist, who in later life became a diplomat and secretary general of the Commonwealth, and George Ignatieff, the scion of a distinguished Russian family, who also rose high in the diplomatic service. I made other friends through debating and student politics: Dick Bell, who became a lawyer and a leading Conservative; and Sam Hughes, later a justice of the Ontario Supreme Court. I also relished my friendship with Saul Rae, song and dance star in the UC Follies, a socialist who later became a prominent diplomat, and Max Patrick, a witty debater, who later taught school in England and in Canada.

The campus was seething with politics, as was reported in the student newspaper, the *Varsity*; there were active Conservative and

The Hart House Debates Committee, 1934. Back row: H.G. Skilling, H.J. Fair, Prof. E.W. McInnis, R.A. Bell, A.R. Tilley.
Front row: R.J. Miller, S.K. Hermant, Prof. G.W. Brown, J.B. Bickersteth (Warden), and J.S. Woods

Liberal associations as well as the new CCF Club. Frequent public meetings aired the dangers of war, the evil of rearmament, and the value of the League of Nations, in speeches by local lecturers or famous visitors such as Sir Norman Angell, Fenner Brockway, Professor Alfred Zimmern, and Anna Louise Strong. Some speeches were hostile, others favourable, to German and Italian fascism, and anti-semitism was both openly justified and condemned. The Soviet Union received more favourable treatment, and the new communist society was more often praised than denounced. In Hart House debates a motion deploring the existence of the Soviet Union was roundly defeated. There were frequent speeches in favour of socialism from leaders of Christian movements and by J.S. Woodsworth and Agnes McPhail, leaders of the CCF and the United Farmers of Ontario. Once, in early 1934, the *Varsity* deplored the fact that most students entertained socialistic sympathies and were bombarded with these ideas by professors inside and outside the classroom. There were public proposals to abolish the Canadian Officers' Training Corps on campus. On the other hand, voices were raised against excluding women from Hart House, the ban on their participation in debates, and even for the idea of coeducational residences. It was openly deplored that women were not welcomed as members by the various political clubs, although the CCF Club opened its doors to them.

My studies were leading to profound changes in my way of thinking. To start with, I had moved away from my earlier religious faith. In an essay that sought to answer the question "What We Believe," I wrote that I could not accept the notion of a personal God or the divine guidance of human activity. At the most, God could be conceived as a concept of Good, in the manner of Plato, and Christ was an inspired thinker and a courageous and socially minded man. My eyes had been opened to social and economic problems and my views slowly crystallized in favour of socialism. I was greatly influenced by a seminar at a summer conference of the Student Christian Movement in Muskoka in 1932. Professor Eric Havelock, a theologian from Victoria College, working from the ideas of Jesus, presented a detailed argument in favour of a collectivist approach to the problems of society. I was aware of the formation that same year of the League of Social Reconstruction (LSR), by a group of professors from Toronto (including Havelock, Underhill, and some of my own teachers) and others, such as Frank Scott, Eugene Forsey, and King Gordon from Montreal. Their initial program advocated a radical reconstruction of society and the economy, and was documented in the book *Social Planning for Canada* (1935). In the same spirit, in November 1932 I had taken the lead in reorganizing the Fabius Club, hitherto a student discussion group, into an avowedly socialist organization dedicated to establishing a "cooperative economy, with production primarily for use, not for profit." It was hoped that the club would counteract the influence of the Marxist Student League of Canada, which immediately issued, in its new organ, *The Spark*, a scathing denunciation of our club.

I expounded my socialist convictions in several speeches inside and outside the university. In early 1933, speaking to a church group on "Youth and the Depression," I waxed grandiloquent on the crisis of our civilization, comparable to the fall of Rome and the French Revolution. I blamed this crisis on the "business system," which had shown itself incapable of functioning efficiently or justly. The religion of Jesus, I argued passionately, demanded "a sincere social conscience and a sentiment of neighbourliness." "Had Jesus been alive today, he would have condemned without hesitation a social system which was a perpetual incitement to selfishness and made the Golden Rule almost impossible."

Although I had some sympathy for Russia, I had little for Marxism or communism. In an essay on Marx and socialism, part of which was published in *The Undergraduate* (March 19, 1933), I argued that Marxism contained an essential truth about the great influence of economic factors on ideas and institutions and on the course of history. But I rejected the doctrine of historical materialism that predicted the inevitable collapse of capitalism. Marxism ignored the potential of human action to change these tendencies, and the role of race, religion or nationality in determining human thought and action. I recognized that a revolution might come but denied that it was inevitable or would necessarily succeed. In the Soviet Union competitive capitalism had given way to state and cooperative control of production and distribution, but its future could not be predicted. In other countries Marxist revisionism had produced the doctrine of social democracy as a peaceful, parliamentary route to socialism. In England the labour movement, which was not Marxist at all but Fabian, had adopted a gradualist and ethical approach to the establishment of socialism.

This major evolution in my views reflected my experiences in the summer of 1933. An offer of employment as a bellboy at the luxurious Jasper Park Lodge in the Rockies fell through because of the Depression. Instead I embarked on a trip across the continent, hitchhiking and riding the freight trains, with a view to attending the founding conference of the CCF in Regina, Saskatchewan. The Danforth CCF Club later appointed me one of its official delegates and sent me $10 to help defray expenses. In the company of a fellow student, Powell Smiley, I headed West, first by thumbing it on the highway via Chicago to Winnipeg, then "jumping the freighters": travelling on top of box cars, in the company of about a hundred other "professional bums," as I ungenerously called them. It was a windy, sooty trip through the night to Broadview, a division point, where the train stopped for refueling. There a young Mountie, unarmed and hardly older than we were, waving a riding crop, requested that we disembark and proceed to RCMP headquarters for questioning. He warned us not to travel by freight train again since, if caught, we could be detained for up to 60 days in Regina.

Hitchhiking along the highway in slow stages, we finally arrived at the convention, a few hours late, to find that we were "big news." The Regina *Leader Post* (21 July 1933), heralded our arrival with front-page photographs and a banner headline, "Hiking CCF Lad Bucks Police Net Convention Bound." The delegates welcomed me as the "voice of Canadian youth," and insisted I speak from the platform on the first day of the meeting. M.J. Coldwell, leader of the Saskatchewan Farmer-Labour Party, offered to pitch a tent for us in his backyard, and we spent the next few nights there. This gave us the opportunity to join the Coldwells and their guests, J.S. Woodsworth and his wife, at break-fast each morning, and — even more exciting — to attend the nightly gatherings of leading delegates in their living-room. Unfortunately, toward the end of our stay, Smiley absconded with my blanket and some of my belongings, and I never saw him again.

During the next three days, in the boiling heat of a prairie mid-summer, I listened to the sometimes stormy debates as delegates draft-ed the official platform of the first nationwide party of democratic socialism in Canada. Its purpose was to found a Co-operative Com-monwealth Federation, in which the guiding principle for production and distribution would be human need, not profit. Although the term "socialist" was not explicitly used, the program proposed a planned, socialized economic order, including the socialization of finance, the social ownership of industry, and a socialized health system. It was a melding of Christian socialism, British Fabianism, Marxism, and agrar-ian protest, where exponents of these diverse tendencies had suppressed their differences to forge a remarkable consensus. The document set forth, under 14 points, a detailed plan to "eradicate capitalism and put into operation the full program of socialized planning," as the final sentence proclaimed.

After the convention closed I continued my transcontinental trip, in the end covering some 9,000 miles. This journey confirmed my conviction of the need for drastic social change. On the first leg of my journey I had visited the World's Fair in Chicago, with its astonishing portrayal of recent advances in science, industry and transportation — the "Century of Progress." It was ironic, however, as I wrote at the time, that in the midst of a worldwide Depression the fair had nothing to report on humanity's social and intellectual failure to keep pace with material progress.

As I travelled across the Prairies and through the Rockies, then down the west coast of North America and back through the agricultural and industrial heartland of the U.S., I was constantly reminded of the Depression in industry and in agriculture, and of the poverty and social degradation which were its byproducts. I mingled with unemployed youths — victims of an unjust and inefficient system — in or atop the empty boxcars, in the "jungles," railway yards, sandboxes, flop-houses, missions and, more respectably, in YMCAs. Once I was even an overnight guest in a local jail. Thousands of men (rarely a woman), most of them young, but a few quite old, panhandled their way back and forth across the continent in search of an ever-elusive job. In the automobiles that picked me up on the highway and in the towns through which I passed, I met a wide cross section of society — salesmen, grain farmers, factory workers, and fishermen — and listened to their grievances and their ideas, often highly critical of the conditions of their daily lives. Every mile seemed to confirm societal ills that Roosevelt, with his New Deal and the National Recovery Administration, and the CCF, with its goal of social reconstruction, were seeking to correct. In my mind the sheer extent of deprivation seemed to justify the more radical recipe proposed by the CCF: that of a cooperative commonwealth, a planned society.

Back at the university in the autumn of 1933, my first step was to help organize a CCF club on the campus, and I was elected its first president. After some opposition we decided to affiliate directly with the Federation. Speakers included J.S. Woodsworth, William Irvine, Alberta's CCF leader; Graham Spry, advocate of public broadcasting, and Frank Underhill, who urged abolition of the Senate. We put out a little newspaper, modestly entitled *Change* and selling for two cents —

"small change," as Professor Morgan contemptuously called it. The first issue published my report on the CCF convention. In a talk to the club it became clear that I had replaced my earlier ethical approach with a more concrete political conception of socialism, one owing more to Marx than to Jesus. I accepted the idea of the conflict of two classes, the rich and the poor, the owners and the workers, and the view that certain classes had used government in Canada to secure their class objectives. The cause of exploitation was the capitalist system, and the solution lay in the abolition of private enterprise, private profit and property; and in state planning of the economy, as advocated by the CCF. Representative democracy offered a device for avoiding revolution and a peaceful constitutional method of securing power. There might, however, be a backlash of the ruling classes, who would resort to force to defend capitalism; the socialist party itself might become a support of capitalism as in Germany and in England.

In Hart House debates I spoke on several occasions in favour of the CCF. On 29 November 1933, with Arnold Smith, and in the presence of the guest speaker, J.S. Woodsworth, I opposed a resolution to the effect that there was no acceptable alternative to the two older political parties in Canada. Claiming that there was no real difference between these parties, united as they were in their defence of private enterprise, private ownership, and private property, and in their unwillingness to change the status quo, I argued that the CCF alone, using the methods of representative democracy, and eschewing the use of force, would be able to transfer ownership to the people. The defeat of the motion gave implicit endorsement to the CCF. In a foray to the McGill Mock Forum in Montreal, accompanied by Richard Bell, my conservative classmate, we left-wingers, with the support of William Irvine, carried the day for socialism and the CCF. At another debate, where the Prime Minister, R.B. Bennett, was guest speaker, some of us planned to give him "a lesson in economics," and with the advice of Professor Morgan, prepared a coordinated attack on Bennett's policies of imperial preference and protective tariffs. In my speech I advocated a flexible use of exchange mechanisms, including the dropping of the gold standard so as to achieve a balance of trade.

As an associate editor of the *Varsity*, I wrote a number of editorials on social and political issues. One such, entitled "Touching on Depression" (13 October 1932), rejected the doctrine of individualism on the basis that it reflected the unjustified view that human nature was egotistical. The tragedy of the Depression was rubbing away the false glitter of individualism, and people were recognizing the injustice of the present disparity of income and welfare. Under an alternative social system, I argued, people would be able to evolve a social consciousness, a "social-ism." In "Depression and Revolution" (6 January 1933), I lamented the misery and degradation of the unemployed and the socially deprived. "One generation lost and incapacitated in a Great War! Another, hardly matured, being ruined by a Great Depression!" I expressed the fear that a revolution, in the style of the Russian one, might be touched off by the inflammable conditions prevailing in every European and North American city. The only rational method of averting this was "a deracination of the causes of grievance."

While my attitude toward communism was still negative, I now held more positive views of Russia. In a debate at the University College Parliamentary Club, in the course of defending democratic socialism, I launched a vitriolic attack on communism and its use of violence. My fraternity, Psi Upsilon, was seeking to improve its image by having intellectual discussions at its weekly meetings, and in that forum I defended socialism against the species of communism present-ed by Stanley Ryerson, the communist student leader. He was a very able student in the French Department, who later headed the Quebec branch of the Canadian Communist party. In another debate, how-ever, I rejected the proposal that western powers should treat Russia as an outlaw state, and praised in glowing terms the economic, social, cul-tural, and even moral achievements of the new Communist state, as well as its peaceful foreign policy.

Despite my membership in the Foreign Affairs Club, my views were not clearly formulated and were sometimes self-contradictory. Capitalism and imperialism had produced worldwide Depression, with 40 million unemployed, and had helped to cause the Great War. I condemned the jungle ethics of international affairs and opposed rear-mament as benefiting only the arms manufacturers and promoting international tension. War would be eliminated only when capitalism was replaced by socialism. I expressed sympathy with the Oxford Union resolution in 1933, which declared that in no circumstances would its signatories support King and Country. I supported the League of Nations, but, in common with Woodsworth and the CCF, I believed that Canada should not become too much involved in inter-national conflicts. Canada had been drawn into the Great War by its imperial connections and in the future should follow its own indepen-dent policies.

Although for years I had been emotionally and morally opposed to war I was not an integral pacifist, that is, one who opposed war in all circumstances. However, in October of my senior year, I participated in forming an Anti-War Society, which grouped together about 50 persons of different outlooks — Christian, socialist, even communist — and sought to awaken students to the danger of war while advocating the stoppage of munitions manufacture and distribution. At its opening meeting I presented the ethical and economic objections to war, and declared it an unsatisfactory way of settling international disputes. When I requested that the Society be recognized as a university association, the university president, Canon Cody, an arch-conservative cleric, gave me a severe dressing down. I did not understand, he said, that when a mad dog was loose in Europe, all must resist, militarily if need be. In November we had planned to demonstrate against war at the Peace Tower on Armistice Day, but this was not permitted.

It is difficult to know why I felt impelled to be so active in student affairs and to seek office and power in so many organizations. In a *Varsity* editorial, I rationalized this striving as a search after "hidden values," the essence of a university education. In an interview I cast doubt on the view that students sought office so as to qualify for certain overseas scholarships. Whatever my motives, and perhaps despite my rather unorthodox political views, I did become a Big Man on Campus and candidate for a Rhodes Scholarship. I seemed to qualify for the somewhat dubious label of "all-round man," one who possessed a quite exaggerated set of virtues. I applied in my third year, as a trial run, without success, but was chosen in the autumn of 1933, along with John R. Baldwin of McMaster University, for the province of Ontario. The competition involved writing a three-hour essay on a chosen topic (I selected fascism) and a final interview by the selection committee. Headed by the Toronto financier J.M. Macdonnell, a former Rhodes Scholar, the committee included Roland Michener (later governor general), then Canadian secretary of the Rhodes Trust. I remember little of the gruelling ordeal other than the question, "Does not socialism require a moral rebirth of society, and if that were achieved, would socialism be necessary?" I have no idea what my answer was, but I am sure that I defended socialism as embodying moral principles. Although a committed socialist, I apparently felt no compunction at receiving a fellowship financed through the ill-gotten gains of the arch-capitalist and imperialist, Cecil Rhodes.

When I received my degree in convocation hall in June 1934 from the hands of the venerable, white-bearded chancellor, Sir William

Mulock, then 90 years old, in the presence of my parents, I felt very proud of what I had accomplished. At the graduation dinner in the great hall, it was an honour to sit at high table with the prime minister, W.L. Mackenzie King. After the formality and ceremony and a very busy year, it was a welcome relief to "retire" to Muskoka for summer work. This time I was a busboy at Bigwin Inn, resort for the wealthy, on the Lake of Bays. Once again I enjoyed the amenities of what amounted to a paid summer holiday in the company of my friends and fellow students, including Eileen. It was a happy summer, spent in anticipation of the forthcoming experience of study at Oxford.

What did I gain from my four years at the University of Toronto? In the fall of 1931, speaking as sophomore president at the soph-frosh banquet for incoming freshmen, I tried to define the value of a university education. I found that it had contributed to a heightening of ideals, a deepening of convictions, a breadth of sympathy for people of different background, class, race and religion, and to greater influence in later life. We "young men" [sic] would be expected to exercise a leadership role not only within our nation but in the world as a whole. And if we were not to be leaders, then we would occupy "the humble, unrecorded position of worthy members of society." These were the high-faluting and somewhat naive words of a young student, but perhaps they do capture something of what a university might optimally give its graduates in the course of their education.

4

MOVING TO THE LEFT: OXFORD

WHEN I SAILED FOR ENGLAND on 19 September 1934 aboard the *Empress of Britain*, I was leaving Canada for what I thought would be two or three years. My brother Don had left in wartime to meet his death in Flanders in 1917; I set out in a time of peace and returned safely, after six rich years. An appeal to Sir Edward Beatty, head of the CPR and chairman of Quebec's Rhodes Scholarship selection committee, got me a reduced fare, and I sailed in the company of fellow students — John Baldwin, Jean Chapdelaine, Sam Hughes, Max Patrick, Lorie Tarshish, and others — heading for Oxford or Cambridge. During the trip we were entertained at tea one day by Sir Edward Peacock, a Canadian, who was governor of the Bank of England, and we also met W.L. Mackenzie King, who, I reported home, was charming but "scrupulously avoided all politics."[1]

My first encounter with my "ancestral land" was in Southampton, where we docked. In London I was under the experienced guidance of Lorie Tarshish, who was returning to Cambridge for his second year of economics. He introduced me to places that would soon become favourite spots of mine — the Charing Cross bookstores, the Tate Gallery, and Bertorelli's restaurant. After a brief visit to Stanwell Moor, the village of my parents, I proceeded in great excitement to the famed city of spires.

My Rhodes scholarship required that I study at Oxford, and it was good for at least two, and probably three, years. I had already made two crucial choices — a college and a "school." First, after long discussions with former Oxonians and consultation of Oxford handbooks, I had placed Queen's College as my first preference, because it was strong in my proposed fields of study, and it was relatively small. When it turned me down, I appealed to J.B. Bickersteth, warden of Hart House and onetime undergraduate at Christ Church, for assistance in securing admission to this much larger college. Second, I had also decided to

Rhodes Scholar, 1934

take the interdisciplinary "school" of philosophy, politics and economics (PPE) or "Modern Greats," which also included modern history and international relations. Somewhat disillusioned by my intensive study of economics at Toronto, I was anxious to buttress my study of political theory with empirical knowledge of modern history, political institutions, and foreign affairs. It opened up the panorama of world affairs, of which I had been but dimly aware at Toronto; it also gave me a good basis for my later postgraduate study in history and for teaching political science.

The choice of Church, or "The House," was fortunate in some respects, less so in others. It gave me the chance to study with outstanding dons, including Michael Foster and A.J. Ayers, in philosophy; Roy Harrod, in economics; Keith Feiling, in British history; and the Hon. Frank Pakenham in politics and international relations. Two weekly tutorials, for which I had to prepare essays, gave me a rare and unique kind of instruction — discussion in a one-on-one session with a tutor. In political theory I wrote a host of papers on Plato, medieval political thought, Hobbes and Locke, Descartes and Hume, and Mill and Hegel, modern pluralism, as well as one on Pareto, for which my tutor had to seek a qualified reader outside the college. Lectures were less important. Each term I tasted some of them and continued with those that proved valuable, such as those by Professor G.D.H. Cole on socialism and the labour movement and by Professor (later Sir) Alfred Zimmern on international institutions.

The House was an architectural gem and rich in tradition, but it was aristocratic in tone, and it was hard for me, as a "colonial," to adjust. The "hunting set," the "hearties," the English "Scholars," and those of high birth and wealth showed no interest in me (nor I in them). But the college was so large that one could find and cultivate friends from less exalted or less unfamiliar circles and from other parts of the world. Apart from Canadian Rhodes scholars, such as George Ignatieff, Arnold Smith, and John Baldwin, my closest friends were the Indian and "old Etonian" Gopal Kumaramangalam (Kumara), a communist who later became prominent in Indian politics; Francois Lafitte, illegitimate son of Havelock Ellis, an erudite Marxist who became a leader-writer for *The Times* and later professor of social sciences at Birmingham University; Harold Crowther, from Rhodesia, a student of French and lover of music; and John Evans-Lawrence, a well-off Englishman from Gloucestershire, who was educated at Eastbourne, a lesser public school. There was no room in my life for girls; I wrote home that those at Oxford were "uniformly ugly." For the next year or more I led a "celibate life" and looked forward to a visit in the summer by Eileen Woodhouse, my Toronto girlfriend.

I was required to live in college and had rooms at first in the Meadows Building, on the top floor of staircase 5, which I described in my first letter home as "positively palatial," with a view out over "the green, mist-covered meadow, with its grazing cows." When the fire was lit in my big living-room, there was warmth only in its immediate neighbourhood; the bedroom was "like a refrigerator," the bed "like a snowbank." Conveniences were minimal, with a hot-water bottle in my bed, a commode underneath, and a jug of hot water brought in every morning. The toilets and baths were in the basement of the next stair-case, so that taking a bath necessitated a quick scoot through the damp air and then a long climb back up my staircase. My "scout," Lee, was "a giant, somewhat domineering." His services embarrassed me, unused as I was to having a servant. During my second year, I changed to smaller and less expensive rooms on the top floor in Peckwater Quad. They were warmer and cosier but lacked the lovely view. I felt more at home, however, with my new scout, Sims, "a very small and rather timid" man, who had been at "The House" for 44 years.

The day began at seven-thirty with a roll-call ("roller") in hall three times a week, a procedure that involved appearing, in dressing gown if preferred, circling a table once, and then returning to one's room to sleep or to have breakfast. The morning was devoted to occasional lec-tures and sometimes an hour with a tutor, with students always having to wear or carry a tattered short gown. I had a simple lunch, served in my rooms by the scout, or in the Junior Common Room. The after-noon was taken up entirely by athletics; the libraries were closed. Tea every day, either at home or with friends, was the occasion of endless discussions of politics, society, and culture. One was required to dine, once more in gown, in the great dining hall, with its huge fireplaces and portraits of the illustrious. I often passed the evening at the "flicks," or taking in a play, concert, or political club meeting. At 9:05 at night the great bell in Tom Tower, which pealed every hour on the hour during the day, rang out its deep tones 105 times, to mark the closing of the gates at 9:20. Thereafter, admission required payment of fines escalat-ing, according to the lateness of the hour, from threepence to two shillings and sixpence after midnight. Although the cathedral, a part of Christ Church, was only 50 yards from my rooms, I seldom attended the services (and certainly not the morning one) in spite of the beauti-ful choral music to be heard. I studied in my free hours, usually in the Radcliffe Camera, occasionally in the Christ Church library, or in the cold of my rooms.

My sports were rowing and ice hockey. I devoted every afternoon in the autumn to learning the difficult and unaccustomed art of row-ing, at first in a fixed "tub" at the college boathouse on the Isis (Thames) and later in a boat with full crew. As the weather deteriorat-ed in late autumn and winter, this was a rigorous and not-too-pleasant routine. A fortnight of "training" involved walking once or twice around the Meadows before breakfast, daily practice on the river, and a heavy dinner in hall. No drinking or smoking was permitted — bedtime was at ten-thirty. In December, in a trial race, I suffered the humiliation of "catching a crab" — allowing my oar to go deep in the water and thus braking the boat to a standstill. These preparations culminated in early spring in Toggers or Torpids, the bumping races, in which all boats were strung out in a long line on the river and each boat sought to draw even with the stern of the next boat. Our boat, the third house crew, dropped ignominiously from 36th to 38th place on the river, the position from which it would start the following year.

Ice hockey was also energy-consuming. As there was no rink in Oxford, we had to make a weekly trip by bus each Sunday to Richmond, near London. Most men on the two Oxford teams were Canadians, with an added American or Scot. The second team, on which I played defence, had no real proficiency. The climax came at Christmas, when we toured Switzerland, playing Cambridge and local Swiss teams in Caux, Gstaad, Kandersteg, Zermatt, and Zurich. We scored few victories but enjoyed the wonders of the Alps. I felt a tinge of regret that I took this pleasure trip instead of travelling in Spain, where civil war was soon to break out.

During the spring and summer terms it was a relief to enjoy the beautiful weather by long walks on the river, bike trips in the countryside, or punting on the Cherwell. I enjoyed music, sometimes playing the piano in Crowther's rooms, and later in my own rooms on a rented piano. There were luncheons or teas with friends or tutors or at Rhodes House with the warden. Evans-Lawrence invited me several times to attend a dance or for an overnight visit at his family's beautiful mansion in the Cotswolds.

Vacations — six weeks at Christmas and at Easter, almost four months in summer — were intended as times of study and travel, with examinations on one's return. My first Christmas, apart from the two weeks in Switzerland, I spent in London, combining study every morning with a busy social program which afforded me a taste of English life and society. A program arranged by Lady Francis Ryder gave us "colonials" and Americans a brief entrée into the life of the well-to-do. There were lunches, dinners, and balls offered by the great city companies (Drapers, Goldsmiths, Grocers, Merchant Tailors, and so on), lunches at private homes, meetings with members of Parliament, and visits to the House of Commons, the BBC, *The Times*, and the *Daily Herald*. My second year of "Ryderism" included lower reaches of society, with a dockers' at-home at Toynbee Hall and a tour of London at night, including the markets at Billingsgate and Covent Garden and shelters for the unemployed.

I was also able to visit my many relatives, all of whom lived in the modest circumstances of the lower middle class, mainly in London or nearby in the Stanwell area. I spent my first Christmas away from home at my Aunt Ruth's in Stanwell Moor. Two of my cousins, Bob and Nellie, both school teachers in London, "adopted" me; they came up to Oxford during Eights Week and took me to London on excursions, where I learned a little about English housing and schools.

My Easter vacation in 1935, and the early part of the summer vacation, I spent in Germany, where I went to improve my German, one of the two languages required for the B.A. At Easter I lived for six weeks with the family of Frau Pfarrer Simon, the widow of a pastor, and her son and daughter, in Freiburg im Breisgau in the beautiful Schwarzwald, or Black Forest region. There I enjoyed the coming of spring, often in the company of the daughter, Gretl. She was a very attractive girl but, alas for my German, spoke good English. In early summer I stayed a month in Berlin, in the residential district of Charlottenburg, in the home of another widow, Freifrau von Türcke, whose husband had been killed on the Eastern Front in the First World War. Her daughter was less attractive but spoke little English, so that my German improved. With her I drank in the sights of the then-great and undivided city. I went on to Munich, where I lived for one night in a private home but was driven out by a siege of bedbugs, which the landlady charged I had brought with me. I sought refuge in a larger *pension* inhabited mainly by young American girls. This did not help my German much. During these visits I devoted much of the day to German history and language and to my Oxford studies. During my leisure hours I sampled German food and beer and began to experience German art and music. I also became vividly aware of the evils of Nazism.

During the summer of 1935 I first encountered Central Europe and the Balkans. I spent a wonderful week in Salzburg, Austria, at the festival of music and theatre, listening to the music of Arturo Toscanini, Bruno Walter, and Felix von Weingartner and to a performance of *Faust* directed by Max Reinhart. After a week in Vienna I proceeded by boat down the Danube, alone, travelling fourth class at an absurdly low fare, due to a special student reduction. I got my first glimpses of Czechoslovakia as we passed the Castle in Bratislava. I stopped over for several days in Budapest and Belgrade, then went on through the Iron Gates to the Romanian port of Giurgiu, whence I took a train to Bucharest, with a side-trip to Braşov in the Transylvanian Alps. I continued my tour by Romanian ship through the Bosphorus and the Dardanelles to Istanbul; by Greek ship to Athens, from which I made side-trips to Marathon, Delphi, and Corinth; and finally by train through northern Greece and Yugoslavia, with stopovers at Salonika, Skopje, Sarajevo, Mostar and Dubrovnik. This trip introduced me to the ethnic complexity and the politics of this region, with which I was to concern myself for the rest of my life. By this time war was threatening and I felt that I should hurry home. A brief visit to Geneva gave me the opportunity to witness the League of Nations in session and by chance to hear the concluding address to the Assembly of its president, Edvard Beneš, the president of Czechoslovakia. Unfortunately, I did not take advantage of the cheap excursions to the Soviet Union available at this time, but rather foolishly decided to postpone such a visit until I had learned Russian.

Late in the autumn of 1935 (2 November to be precise) came an event that changed my life. One morning, as I was walking through Tom Quad on my way to the buttery, attired in dressing gown and slippers, I met my good friend Kumara. With him was a young American, Sally Bright, and he introduced us. It is a scene that remains engraved on my consciousness. Sally was a student at the London School of Economics (LSE), whom he was escorting around Oxford at the request of her American boy friend, Peter Rhodes, a communist too busy with political activity to look after her (Peter was to become an organizer of volunteers to Spain and a United Press correspondent). Sally and I hit it off from the start. We had dinner that night with Peter, Kumara, and François, and tea the next day alone in my room.

Sally had been a student of sociology and economics at Barnard College, in New York City. She was a student leader and had graduated with the highest honours and membership of Phi Beta Kappa. She had been elected by the student body to a scholarship for study abroad. The daughter of a carpenter from Norristown, near Philadelphia, and a Quaker by upbringing, she had studied at the Friends' George School, where she had been active in student affairs and listed on the honour roll. In London she was not taking a degree but was studying sociology under the eminent sociologist Morris Ginsburg, and the demographer R. Kuczynski, and attending the lectures of political scientist Harold Laski, a left-wing socialist. During the autumn she had gone to public lectures given by G.D.H. Cole and John Strachey,

George Lansbury and William Gallagher, and, like me, she had become a believer in socialism and an admirer of the Soviet Union.

I spent Christmas "vac" in London because of Sally. For four weeks we were together almost daily, absorbing the sights and the politics of London and spending many hours of companionship in her digs or mine. This was the beginning of our love, and it continued with a rendezvous almost every week in the next term in London or Oxford. In London I stayed in her tiny attic room on Tavistock Place in Bloomsbury. We studied together, explored London, attended political rallies and demonstrations, and went to films and concerts. In Oxford I once smuggled her into my room in The House for the night, and another night I sneaked out of college after hours, climbing down the ivy of the Meadows buildings and crashing to the ground when the ivy broke. I suffered no serious injury and spent the night at her bed-and-breakfast place. In both cases I risked being "sent down" for my escapades, but fortunately I was not detected. In January we spent a weekend in Brighton, searching out the places where my father and my grandfather had lived and worked.

During my Easter vac in 1936 we spent five weeks in Chepstow, in Monmouthshire, in the beautiful Wye valley. It was an idyllic spring, and we cherished every spare moment, taking long walks, exploring nearby castles and Roman ruins and visiting Cardiff and the Severn. At the end of the vacation Sally and I paid a visit to Abertillery, one of the dying coal-mining valleys of South Wales, a sharp contrast to the beauty of Chepstow. There we lived in the home of a miner who had been out of work since 1927; a Communist party member, he was active in the radical unemployed workers' movement. We walked through the drab town and on the bare, slag-covered hills, and learned of the difficulties of miners' lives. This personal contact with workers strengthened our belief in socialism. When some of the miners came to a summer camp near Oxford for a holiday, they marvelled at the beauty of the countryside, with its unbelievably green hills and valleys.

Before Sally left for the United States, we were able to meet several times in Oxford and London and again in Paris for a final, ecstatic weekend, which remained in our minds as "a wonderful dream." We lived together in a little hotel, the Fleurus, and later in the Paris-Dinard. We were exhilarated by the left-wing political atmosphere of France under the newly elected Popular Front government. We visited the Père la Chaise cemetery and the Chambre de députés and attended a massive trade union meeting in the Vel d'Hiver. When the time came for her departure, we almost missed the boat-train at Gare St Lazare. Sally had left her purse, containing tickets and passport, in the restaurant where we had our last lunch. With literally only seconds to spare, we bade a tearful farewell as she fell up the stairs onto the train.

Politics, both in Oxford and in England generally, was now absorbing my attention. Oxford politics mirrored the national scene, with strong Conservative, Labour, and Liberal clubs. Kumara took me to the opening meeting of the Labour Club, attended by some four hundred people, and addressed by its president, G.D.H. Cole, in his annual "state of the union address." My fellow Canadian David Lewis was a leading figure in the Labour Club and introduced me to others. I joined the club at once and at its weekly meetings heard party "greats" such as Clement Attlee, Arthur Greenwood, Herbert Morrison, and George Lansbury and the more radical Sir Stafford Cripps, R.H.S. Crossman, and Harold Laski. At informal weekly gatherings in Cole's rooms, this renowned scholar and writer of mysteries reclined on a couch because of serious illness and conducted a vigorous discussion.

I soon stood on the left wing of the Labour Club and was more sympathetic to the Communists than to the Labourites. I regularly attended the Communist-led October Club, listening to Maurice Dobb; William Gallagher, MP; Arthur Horner, miners' union leader; and John Strachey. I was a devoted reader of the *Daily Worker* and the *Labour Monthly* (as well as *The Times*) and had nothing but scorn for the Labour Party's *Daily Herald*. I became a subscriber to the Left Book Club and an avid reader of its publications, such as books by Laski and Strachey, and of Marxist literature in general. At Christmas 1935 I used a gift of money from my mother to purchase Emile Burns' *Handbook of Marxism*, Trotsky's *History of the Russian Revolution*, and the huge tome by Sidney and Beatrice Webb, *Soviet Russia: A New Civilization?* The Webbs convinced me that the Soviet Union had "solved some of the most important problems which capitalist governments have confessed themselves unable to solve" and was indeed "a new civilization." The question mark in the subtitle seemed unnecessary.

In a conference at Oxford on Canada I made a radical critique of the CCF and urged a United Front with the Communist Party. My political views had moved far to the left and were a far cry from the Regina manifesto. In this I parted company with David Lewis, who was strongly anti-communist and opposed any link with the October Club. (When Lewis returned to Canada he became a leader of the CCF, later renamed the New Democratic Party.)

In November 1935 I did some door-to-door canvassing for the Labour party in the Oxford municipal election, and a year later, in the national election, I did the same for Patrick Gordon-Walker, Labour candidate in Oxford. In May 1936 I distributed leaflets during a bus strike in Oxford that had been caused by the arbitrary dismissal of a driver.

In national politics, none of us on the left had any liking for the National government of Ramsay Macdonald, or for the Labour opposition, headed by George Lansbury; although Mayor Simpson of Toronto had given me letters of introduction to both Macdonald and Lansbury, I did not present them. I was more impressed by Strachey and Laski, even by Bill Gallagher and especially by Harry Pollitt, the boiler workers' union and Communist party leader. Economic conditions in England, especially the existence of two million unemployed, shocked me. Hugh Dalton's exposition of "gradual socialism" seemed less persuasive than the urgent need for drastic changes. When King George V celebrated his silver jubilee in May 1935, I deplored it as a mere stratagem to strengthen the empire and prepare for war. When the king died in January 1936, my letter home expressed my view, as "a republican," that the attempt to "idolize" this "ordinary man" was "ridiculous and shameful," and in the interests more of the upper classes than of the people. Sally and I were of the same mind on this issue and on politics in general. During my visits to London we marched together in great demonstrations on behalf of the unemployed, against war, and in favour of independence for India.

Since politics dominated the Oxford Union I had joined it immediately upon arrival in England, thereby gaining admission to its weekly debates, as well as the use of its library and dining-room and an all-Oxford messenger service. The Union was not, as often charged, a nest of radicals: its presidents alternated between conservatives and socialists, and its resolutions between conservatism and radicalism. At the end of November 1934, David Lewis, a Rhodes Scholar from Quebec, "one of the best speakers and finest minds here," as I called him, successfully defended socialism as an alternative to the National government and was elected Union president by six votes. His election was "a tremendous achievment," I wrote home, for "a very radical socialist, a Canadian, and a Russian Jew by birth" (1 December 1934).

In my second term I finally mustered enough courage to speak from the floor, in a debate of 2 February attended by Megan Lloyd George and Stafford Cripps. The resolution, "that this House prefers

Mr. Lloyd George's New Deal to Socialism," was carried by five votes. According to Union President David Lewis,[2] I "made an excellent maiden speech, wherein he pointed out that private enterprise and planning were mutually exclusive. Mr. Skilling must speak more and often." On 21 February I intervened again in a debate on the hereditary principle in government, and condemned the principle as "contrary to democracy."[3] In March I rose to the exalted heights of serving as teller, wearing the customary dress suit. On this occasion, Lewis, on a motion "that this House envies its grandchildren," delivered a brilliant farewell speech, in which he "lamented the smugness and respect for tradition of the Oxford attitude."[4] I did not speak on that occasion, or later, and soon dropped away from regular attendance. Incidentally, the Union remained a man's preserve. Although a motion admitting women to lunch and dinner was passed in 1935, a poll in 1936 overwhelmingly rejected the proposal that women could become elected debating members.

My main tutor, Frank Pakenham, was the son of an Irish peer who was not many years out of New College (1927) with a first in PPE. He was appointed to Christ Church as fellow (1932) and then as "student" (1934) and was responsible for teaching international relations, international history, and political institutions. Not yet 30 years old, he was an attractive person and a stimulating tutor. Diffident in manner, awkward and shy, he hardly seemed an aristocrat. Although he was still nominally a Conservative, he disagreed more and more with their policies and swung steadily to the left, ultimately joining the Labour party. Some of his students claimed that this was because of our influence, but it was more probably the result of his several years of teaching in the Workers Educational Association in the Midlands, and of a meeting in Oxford, addressed by fascist leader Sir Oswald Mosley, which we attended together. It ended in violence and Pakenham suffered serious injuries. (Elevated to the peerage as Lord Pakenham, he held a number of posts in the Attlee government and later, as the Earl of Longford, was Labour Party leader in the House of Lords.)

During my second year at Oxford, 1935-36, the Italian invasion of Ethiopia and the danger of German aggression brought the threat of war closer and dominated our thinking and conversation. I had become highly critical of Hitler and doubted his supposed conciliatory attitude. At a banquet for Rhodes Scholars in the autumn of 1934, I had regarded the toast to heads of state, including Hitler, as German chancellor, as "hypocritical." At a dinner the following year some of us refused to raise our glasses and remained in our seats. My attitude to Hitler and to war was ambivalent, however. In spite of increasing misgivings about Hitler and Nazism, I had no compunctions about spending my Easter and part of my summer vacation in Germany, whereas some of my fellow students refused to visit the country. Hitler, I wrote, was regarded by citizens as a "saviour" who had rescued Germany from the depths into which it had been plunged by the Allies at the end of the war. Germany "did not want war," I thought, but war would come as a result of competing nationalisms and imperialisms; every country was to blame. Although Hitler was not to be trusted and was planning to attack the Soviet Union, we must nonetheless seek to come to terms with him — "anything to keep off war for a while." I felt that some of Hitler's demands should be accepted, including even plebiscites in Memel, Danzig, and Austria, and the militarization of the Rhineland, in return for Germany's rejoining the League and the signing of an Eastern mutual assistance pact, which would guarantee the Soviet Union against attack. In a letter to Sally (April 1936) I naïvely called this "revisionism by consent" the "only hope of preventing war."

As a result of my studies under Alfred Zimmern and attendance at a discussion group in his home, I came to view the League of Nations as an instrument that could stand in the way of aggression only if it were used as such by the member nations. When Italy invaded Ethiopia, I favoured strong economic and financial sanctions and was critical of measures that did not cover nickel and oil. At the same time I feared some kind of compromise with Italy and opposed the Hoare-Laval pact. But, like some Labourite critics such as Cripps and Lansbury, I opposed a "League of Nations war," which would in reality be no more than a struggle of rival imperialisms. Yet British withdrawal from the League, as advocated by Lord Lothian, would be a retreat into isolation; rather Britain should fulfill all its League obligations, even at the risk of war. At the same time I opposed British rearmament, as threatening the beginning of a new arms race, and favoured granting Germany equality in armaments.

The outbreak of civil war in Spain in July 1936 was a constant preoccupation in my conversations with friends and in my correspondence with Sally. The steady advance of Franco's forces and the increasing military intervention by Germany and Italy led me at first to support non-intervention. When German, Italian, and Soviet troops and arms poured into Spain in spite of the agreement, I came to doubt its value. I was increasingly critical of the policy of the British Labour party, especially its support of non-intervention and its refusal to accept the affiliation of the Communist party. I was more than ever convinced that the only solution lay in a government of the People's Front, in Britain, if peace were to be preserved and fascism countered. In July, when I met again some of the Welsh miners at the Oxford summer camp, I began to lament my "political lethargy" and was more than ever determined to do something useful in politics. As a result I wrote several articles — on the Popular Front, the League of Nations, and the Edinburgh conference of the Labour party, of which I was very critical.

The show trials in Moscow during the summer also disturbed me greatly but did not shake my conviction that the Societ Union was a real democracy and the only reliable defender of peace. Relying on the testimony of the left-wing Labourite Denis Pritt, I felt that there must be "good reason" for the verdict but regretted the lack of independent evidence to convince public opinion and to refute the critics of the Soviet Union. I admitted that the trials had done irreparable harm to the Soviet Union, at home and abroad, and to the cause of socialism. I was critical of the one-party system for preventing any political opposition, but I was naive enough to believe that the new constitution would remove these defects.

In spite of many other activities, my studies remained my chief preoccupation and were squeezed into every available minute in term and during vacations. At my first "collections," a brief interview, hardly more than two minutes long, which was held in hall, at the end of term, my work was rated "very good." A private report from the House to the warden of Rhodes House described me as "a little bewildered by the amount of work to be covered." Later reports waxed less than enthusiastic about my efforts in economics and philosophy but described my work in politics as very promising and at the end of the second year called it "very good indeed." The written "collections" in October 1935 — examinations based on work done during the summer — netted me the honour of the Boulter Exhibition and a prize of £40. During the second year Pakenham discussed with me a strategy for getting first-class honours in Schools. During the Easter vac in Chepstow I spent five weeks ploughing through some 25 books and hundreds of pages of notes.

In June 1936 came the big test — Schools — a whole series of written papers in many subjects — a physical and mental ordeal lasting six days. I was not pleased with my performance. The "*viva*," or oral exam, lasted only five minutes and was not used by the examiners to decide whether I should get a "first." The final result, which I learned only in late July, was a crushing blow to my hopes and my pride — second-class standing. My tutors later comforted me that it had been a "distinguished second" and that most of my papers had been marked Beta++. This hardly consoled me for what seemed to be my first academic failure, likely to hurt my aspirations for graduate study and a teaching career. Yet I was not completely discouraged — I had done my best, and grades and marks seemed less important here than they did in Toronto. Following the curious Oxford custom, I eventually received the M.A. degree by keeping my name on the college battels for two years and paying the appropriate fees. Averse to graduation ceremonies, I received both B.A. and M.A. degrees *in absentia.*

The summer after Schools was filled with travel in Britain and on the continent with my mother and father. We took two long trips by car to the north of England and into Scotland, then one south into Devon and Cornwall. These forays gave my parents their first opportunity to see something of their native land since emigrating so many years before. I also joined a "reading party" in Cornwall with two New Zealand fellow students, Ian Milner and Jack Bennett. I indulged in an orgy of reading: modern English, French, and Russian literature, and the war memoirs of Tomáš Masaryk and Edvard Beneš. (Milner was a Marxist, and during the Cold War gave up a high post in the United Nations and defected to Czechoslovakia.)

At the end of the summer I took two trips to the continent. In early September I went to Brussels, to attend a conference of the International Peace Campaign (IPC), which, under the patronage of Lord Cecil of Great Britain and Pierre Cot of France, brought together the most diverse political viewpoints. Among the 6,000 delegates were the Soviet trade union chief, Nikolai Shvernik; distinguished Britishers Philip Noel-Baker and Lord Lytton; the French communist Marcel Cachin; the Second International trade unionist La Brouckère of Belgium; the Spanish communist La Passionaria, whose eloquence drove the audience to a fever pitch, and the Canadian communist leader Tim Buck. The conference, predominantly left-wing, resounded with appeals for a united front against war and fascism, "arms for Spain," resistance to Nazism and fascism, and the defence of Ethiopia. Pacifists, such as Aldous Huxley and George Lansbury, were unable to accept the draft program and held a separate counter-conference.

My second trip to the continent, this time with my parents, took us to Geneva for the annual Assembly of the League of Nations. We witnessed a double crisis caused by Western appeasement. The efforts of the Spanish foreign minister, del Vayo, to put the Spanish question on the agenda, and of the Negus of Ethiopia to do the same for the Italian war against his country, both failed. It was clear that the League, from which Germany and Japan had already been expelled, was in deep crisis and that a new war was looming. On our way back to Paris we visited the grave of my brother, Don, in the tiny village of Aubigny-en-Artois, where 650 Canadians were buried. Nearby were Vimy Ridge and other huge cemeteries in which tens of thousands of French and German dead lay buried.

In my personal life there were worries and tensions, intensified by my long separation from Sally. On her return to her homeland she had secured a wonderful job at the Millbank Memorial Fund, working in the field of population statistics. In our long and passionate letters we recalled our seven months of intimacy and wrote of our loneliness and our yearning to be together again. We found that our thoughts on politics followed increasingly parallel lines. When Eileen Woodhouse came for her planned visit I had to break to her the news of my love for Sally.

I also had to wrestle with another problem, this time academic. In early 1936 my interest in Czechoslovakia had been awakened by historical reading and my admiration of its role in world affairs. It was the only truly democratic country in central and eastern Europe and was a linchpin in the Franco-Soviet security system. Its democratic traditions, personified by T.G. Masaryk and Edvard Beneš, and its struggle for independence during the First World War, had kindled in my mind the idea of doing graduate work, even a doctorate, on modern Czech history. Academic specialists in Oxford and in London suggested that Oxford was a logical place for my studies. C.A. Macartney, specialist on Hungary and central Europe, who was coming to All Souls in the autumn, told me that he was willing to supervise my work for a B.Litt degree. This would have required, he said, regular visits to London for research and for the study of Czech and eventually a research trip to Vienna and Prague.

In September 1936, I settled down in comfortable digs outside college on St Aldate's Street, but I was still haunted by doubt. I was sorely tempted by an alternative plan of moving to London, where the materials for research in the British Museum were rich, far better than those in the Bodleian in Oxford. R.W. Seton-Watson, noted specialist on central and southeastern Europe at London's School of Slavonic and East European Studies, was ready to supervise a thesis for a doctoral degree and thought that I could finish my work by June 1938. In my letters to Sally I discussed the pros and cons of the two approaches and the effect that each would have on our determination to be together soon.

By the end of October I made up my mind to go to London. The successful completion of a PhD and a recommendation from Seton-Watson might counterbalance my second class in Schools and help me in the search for an academic job. Seton-Watson held out the hope of some financial assistance from the Czechoslovak government. The Rhodes Trust, having received a strongly favourable letter from Pakenham, had approved a third year of study under the scholarship and accepted the idea of my moving to London. In her letters to me, Sally expressed full approval of my decision and her readiness to sacrifice her job in New York so that she could join me in London at the earliest possible date.

NOTES

1. Words in quotations are from my weekly letters home. Where necessary, I give dates of letters in brackets.
2. *Oxford Magazine,* 14 Feb. 1935.
3. *Ibid.,* "D.L.," 28 Feb. 1935.
4. *Ibid.,* 17 March 1935.

with out weight with[?] bones
with out body, walked through the dark
for two hours
this afternoon while writing

in my head

EMBARKING ON CZECH STUDIES: LONDON AND PRAGUE

I WENT DOWN FROM OXFORD in October 1936 and took up residence in an old boarding-house at 63 Torrington Square, in the heart of Bloomsbury, not far from where Sally had lived the preceding year.[1] A few minutes away, at no. 40, was the University of London's School of Slavonic and East European Studies, also located in a former boarding-house. Its facilities were quite inadequate — no common room, no lecture hall, and inadequate space for the small library. It was cold and dank, heated by gas fires; the only telephone was in the director's office. Despite niggardly budgets, however, the school had built up a strong staff of experts on the Soviet Union and the eastern European nations, and three in particular were to be my mentors.

I registered there in early November at the office of the secretary, Dorothy Galton. She had once worked with Count Michael Karolyi, former Socialist premier of Hungary, and had made no secret of her socialist convictions when she was appointed. She spoke excellent Russian, was an admirer of the Soviet Union, and was left-wing in her politics, so that we were kindred spirits and soon became close friends.

The director, Sir Bernard Pares, was a long-time student of Russian history, who had introduced Russian studies in England at Liverpool University and had come to the school in 1922. He worked passionately for the development of regional or area studies that combined a language with history and the social sciences. As chief editor of the school's *Slavonic Review*, he made it a major scholarly journal and also published articles more political in content. Having an undying affection for things Russian and a close acquaintanceship with the more liberal prewar leaders, he had been devastated by the Bolshevik Revolution and had made the school and its journal a refuge for Soviet émigré scholars. After the rise of Hitler his hostility to the Soviet regime abated, and he received a visa for travel to the USSR. He was 70 when, in 1936, he made his first visit there since the revolution. On the basis of his experiences he published a little paperback *Moscow Admits a Critic*, which balanced praise and criticism of the new communist system. He became a vigorous advocate of Anglo-Soviet friendship and of an alliance of the two powers against Hitler. Sir Bernard was a bachelor, with no one to care for his needs. Unkempt in dress, he was most untypical of the British elite and endeared himself to me for that as well as for his political stance. When I first met him for an interview as a beginning student, he drew my attention to the requirement of the syllabus that a doctoral thesis must be a contribution to human knowledge; looking over his *pince-nez* glasses and puffing his ever-present pipe, he warned me that this did not mean a contribution to British ignorance.

My supervisor was to be Professor R.W. Seton-Watson, specialist on the affairs of central and southeastern Europe, then 65 years old, shy and diffident, but dynamic. A Scot, he had become enamoured of all the small nations of central and eastern Europe and made a name for himself (sometimes writing under the pseudonym *Scotus Viator*) by his pre-First World War books on Hungary and the South Slavs. He had worked actively for the creation of a School of Slavonic Studies within King's College at the University of London and became a lecturer when it was formed in 1915.

In 1914 Seton-Watson had become a personal friend of Masaryk, then a professor, and he had supported him when he went into exile to work for the liberation of Czechs and Slovaks. He was instrumental in securing Masaryk's appointment as lecturer in the newly formed London school in 1915; the latter gave his inaugural lecture on the theme of the problems of small nations in Europe. After the war, in honour of Masaryk, the Czechoslovak government established a Masaryk chair, financed a Czech lectureship, and later generously supported the building of a new headquarters for the school. In 1922 Seton-Watson was appointed Masaryk Professor of Central European History. A man of some wealth, he often dispensed with a salary and contributed it to the school's activities. During the years of my study under him, Seton-Watson published several books in which he bitterly criticized Western appeasement of the dictators and advocated solidarity with the Soviet Union against the Nazi German threat.

My other major tutor was René Wellek, a young Czech scholar who in 1935 had been appointed to the Czechoslovak lectureship as teacher of Czech. In my earlier conversations with Seton-Watson, before I had decided to come to the school, he had, surprisingly, suggested that I could do my work with the use of German only, without knowledge of Czech. However, when I arrived at the school he encouraged me to learn Czech. His understanding was, he said, that he was to feed me books on Czech history, and Wellek was to stuff Czech into my head as fast as possible. I came to know Wellek as a friend. He later emigrated to the United States and became a renowned specialist in comparative literature.

Another friend was the 50 year-old Bill Rose, a Canadian and Rhodes Scholar, who had been appointed reader in Polish language and literature in 1936. Interned in Silesia during the First World War, he had used the time to learn Polish and later took a doctorate at the University of Cracow and taught for some years at Dartmouth College in New Hampshire. A sociologist and historian, and a fine scholar, he was the third member of the school's leading trio and shared the editorial duties of the *Review*. After Pares's retirement in 1939, he became director — a post that he occupied when I secured my doctorate in 1940. He took me under his wing, often inviting me to his home for dinner. Our relations were marred somewhat by the anti-semitic views of his wife, which he, though a devout Christian and an active YMCA worker, did not openly challenge. Our paths later crossed again when he returned to Canada for his retirement.

In the months following my arrival in London I saw Seton-Watson every week in his little office, lined from floor to ceiling with books, and with an autographed photo of Masaryk looking down upon us. He was not very punctual, and I often had to wait hours for him in the hallway. Although he had a prodigious knowledge of central and eastern Europe, he was not an inspiring teacher, and our weekly tutorials were often limited to his giving summaries of books, often using his yellowed notes as sources. He sometimes deprecated his knowledge and once told me that he was a fraud, as he did not know the Czech language. In my first year he conducted a small seminar on the national renaissance in central Europe.

In addition to meetings in his office, Seton-Watson sometimes invited me to his home in Wimbledon, where we talked in his study, with books piled high on the floor and on every chair or table. We usually went for a long walk, with his dog, on the Commons and in Richmond Park, during which we discussed historical questions and the issues of the day. As a socialist, I did not share his liberal viewpoint, but I admired him for his scholarship and for his strong advocacy of resistance to Hitler and sympathized with his criticism of British foreign policies. Sometimes I was invited to stay for dinner with his wife and his family, including his young sons, Christopher and Hugh, who were later to become distinguished historians. He joked that Hugh favoured Harry Pollitt, the Communist leader, as prime minister of a united front government.

My program of work was not easy, and I sometimes wondered whether I was intellectually equal to doctoral work and was bothered by my abysmal ignorance of central Europe. In Oxford, in a conversation about my plans with Sir Alfred Zimmern, I had felt humiliated when I could not answer his simple question as to the date of the Battle of the White Mountain, which ended Bohemian independence. Day after day I went to the British Museum and searched in its catalogues — then in huge, heavy, mostly hand-written volumes. Under the great dome of the Reading Room, where the spirits of former readers, such as Marx and Lenin, hovered, I wrestled with massive tomes in German and French on the history of Austria-Hungary and of Bohemia and began to prepare a long summary of the entire history of the Czech nation. There were moments of acute discouragement with this preparatory work, and I found the initial stage of learning Czech hard going.

As for the topic of my thesis, I was interested in the prewar nationality question and social democracy and had hoped to work particularly on the ten or fifteen years immediately prior to the First World War. This would be a test case for the validity of Marxism, I thought. Seton-Watson initially approved this choice but eventually pushed me further into the past, so that I ended up focusing on the Czech-German national conflict in the 1880s under Count Taaffe, then Austrian prime minister. This gave me a good knowledge of a crucial phase of the Czech national movement, but I sometimes regretted that I had not chosen a later period and, in retrospect, that I had not concentrated on the role of T.G. Masaryk in prewar Czech politics (on which I prepared a book more than 50 years later).

Life in London was very different from Oxford. I had a room on the top floor of my boarding-house, heated only by an electric heater fed by pennies, and shared the bath downstairs with other boarders. There was no scout or landlady to prepare my breakfast, so I usually had a cold meal of bread and jam, with milk. The days were as grey and as damp that first year as only an English winter can be. But my work kept me occupied, and I led a busy cultural life, attending plays, operas and concerts, films, and lectures.

Oxford friends, such as Kumara, Francois Lafitte, Ian Milner, and Arnold Smith visited me when they were in London. There were new friendships with two fellow graduates of Toronto, Henry Noyes and Harold Taylor. Noyes was doing a doctorate in English literature, and with him I attended concerts and meetings. (In later years he gave up a normal U.S. academic career to join the progressive Abraham Lincoln School in Chicago. Born in China, he became an ardent supporter of Communist China and ran a successful firm for the distribution of books from the People's Republic.) Harold Taylor was a graduate student in philosophy, whose centrally heated apartment I sometimes used for study or for a bath. He was short of funds and eked out a living by playing the clarinet and writing for the *Melody-Maker*, a popular musical magazine. (Our paths crossed later at the University of Wisconsin; he left there to head up Sarah Lawrence College in Bronxville, NY — the youngest college president in the country.) We scrambled eggs for lunch in Henry's room and chatted endlessly about literature and politics. Under my influence, both later told me, they became more radical and left-wing in their views.

Before Christmas I made two new friends: Pepa, a Polish doctoral student, and her friend, Henri, a Swiss engineering student. Over the holidays we embarked on a walking tour on the South Downs, but I fell ill and ended up spending a week in bed in a hostel and then in London, during which Pepa looked after me. She was stimulating intellectually, but a militant communist and so conspiratorial that at first she refused to divulge her last name. I spent much time in their company talking and reading and, at Henri's suggestion, started learning Esperanto.

As international tensions increased, I became more active politically. I took part in a big political demonstration in favour of arms for Spain and a later one welcoming the hunger marchers who had arrived on foot from all over England. I also attended mass meetings, including one in Albert Hall, when 10,000 people heard speeches not only by the usual Popular Front advocates but also by Winston Churchill, and another at Friends House, where G.D.H. Cole, Harold Laski, Francis Acland of the Liberals, and Robert Boothby of the Conservatives, spoke in favour of the Popular Front. I also wrote an article for the *Canadian Forum* (February 1937) in defence of the People's Front policy, and another for the *New Commonwealth* (7 November 1936) bitterly criticizing the Labour party conference in Edinburgh. The latter drew a letter of sharp rebuke from the general secretary, J.S. Middleton. I had some fears that this article would damage future work in the CCF or even my job chances in Canada.

By the end of October 1936 I began to consider joining the Communist party of Great Britain. Although I did not feel myself to be a Marxist or a Leninist, I saw value in the Marxist approach to history and politics. Sally wrote me that she had voted the straight Communist party ticket in her first vote in a U.S. national election and had filled out an application for joining the party. On her return home that night she found my letter reporting that I was contemplating the same step. She did not join until July the following year, and I still hesitated. When Kumara urged me to join, offering me the assignment of teaching a course on Marxism, I argued that I did not know enough about the subject and was not even a convinced Marxist, nor did I feel inclined to give up an evening or two a week to this task. However, after the Friends House meeting, I overcame my doubts and decided to join. Despite our separation, therefore, Sally and I were entirely in tune politically, and we had both committed ourselves to a radical approach to politics.

This was the time of the constitutional crisis created by the government's disapproval of the marriage of King Edward VIII with the twice-divorced American Wallis Warfield Simpson. I was disgusted that so much was being made of a relatively trivial matter, diverting attention from the more serious events in Spain. The ruling classes, I believed, were filled with panic that this marriage would impair the dignity and authority of the monarchy; this was not only a great asset to their rule and a guarantee of the unity of the empire, but also a part of the defence against communism and fascism. When the king chose abdication, I welcomed it as a shock to the very foundations of the monarchy and imperial unity and to the entire social system. I lamented the failure of the Labour party to take an independent stance. Only five members of the Commons supported the Independent Labour party's amendment for establishing a republic.

As the situation in Spain deteriorated I became increasingly uneasy with the British government policy of non-intervention in the face of ever-mounting German and Italian support of the rebels, and with the failure of the Labour party to mount a campaign against appeasement. I warmly supported the United Front campaign by the Communist party and the left wing of Labour, represented by the Socialist League, headed by Sir Stafford Cripps, and deplored Labour's ban on any cooperation with the communists. At a public meeting in Kingsway Hall called by the Second International, and addressed by passionate advocates of the United Front, I joined in the chanting of "Arms for

Spain" which made it difficult for Sir Walter Citrine, the chairman, to speak. At one point a lady in the row in front of us turned and plaintively begged us to desist — she was Lady Citrine!

In February 1937 I attended another mass meeting in Albert Hall; enthusiastically applauded speeches by advocates of the United Front such as Francis Acland, Harold Laski, Harry Pollitt, Denis Pritt and John Strachey; and contributed money to the cause. I was impressed by the support of the Spanish People's Front government shown by distinguished intellectuals, such as W.H. Auden, Pablo Casals, J.B.S. Haldane, André Malraux, Heinrich Mann, and Stephen Spender. Hundreds of young English intellectuals and workers volunteered for service in Spain; one well-known writer, Ralph Fox, had already died in action. I wondered whether I should follow their example, but I did not feel myself to be enough of a revolutionary and was unwilling to sacrifice my academic work or my eventual marriage with Sally.

I was greatly concerned with the danger of a new general war, and especially upset by Hitler's speech in late January 1937, attacking Czechoslovakia as "the spearhead of Communism." Rearmament was necessary, I thought, but too dangerous to be placed under the control of the present government. Would Britain use the arms against Germany or against the Soviet Union? I was solidly behind the policy of the Soviet Union and in March attended a Congress of Peace and Friendship with USSR, where Dr. Hewlett Johnson, the "red dean" of Canterbury, and the Russian writer Alexei Tolstoi, as well as G.D.H. Cole and John Strachey, sang the praises of the Soviet Union. When the trial of Trotskyites took place in Moscow, I deplored the damage that it had done to the reputation of the Soviet Union and to the campaign for a united front, but I was convinced that their guilt had been established and that the sentences were justified.

In early 1937, disturbed by the worsening international situation and fired by my friend Pepa's example, I finally decided to join the Communist party. My party duties were to include attending a study course for candidates and a branch meeting each week, participation in a Holborn committee surveying living conditions, and work for both the Labour party and the Communist party in the London City Council (LCC) elections. This involved addressing envelopes and canvassing door to door.

I began work on an essay on the early history of the Czechs, to 1867, and in March 1937 presented it to Seton-Watson. I also intensified my study of Czech. I decided to go to Czechoslovakia for the summer, but in view of increasing German aggression, wondered sometimes whether the country would continue to exist. I began to realize, too, that writing the thesis would take a full year at least, and applied for several fellowships.

I felt very much alone at this time, especially as I was living in an area filled with memories of Sally. I found it difficult to concentrate on my academic work. I had other women friends, like-minded in politics, but I remained faithful to Sally and ever hopeful of an early reunion, perhaps in the autumn. In our letters we poured out our love for each other and exchanged ideas about marriage and our future life together. We were both buoyed up by the conviction that our common feelings of love would overcome the difficulties and dangers of separation.

Unable to bear continued separation, I decided to go to North America during the Easter vacation, and on 27 March I boarded the *Queen Mary*. Six days later Sally greeted me at the West River dock, and I stayed at her apartment near Columbia, as her "husband." We had a happy two weeks together, attending plays and meetings, discussing politics and our future life. Sally was able to take two weeks off to accompany me to Toronto. She stayed with my family in our flat above the store on the Danforth. (My mother was very upset when she found out about our intimate relations.) Ma arranged a reception for many of my friends, and I met others separately. I had a chance to discuss future job prospects with Alex Brady and other professors. I refreshed my connection with the CCF by meeting with Graham Spry, and also met Tim Buck, head of the Canadian Communist party. I gave several talks, including one at a CCF club, on the situation in Europe. Back in New York we enjoyed another two weeks together, with more plays and political meetings, including a May Day demonstration of 200,000 in Union Square and a meeting that evening in Madison Square Garden, at which Earl Browder spoke to an enthusiastic crowd of 20,000. My six-week stay in North America had been more than worthwhile, and it had cost me only £20 in addition to the fare of £34.

My return to London coincided with the coronation of King George VI and Queen Elizabeth on 12 May 1937. Weeks of preparation through the spring reached their climax on coronation day. People began to assemble the night before, in heavy fog, some even succumbing to fatigue, cold, and hunger. Because London bus workers were on strike, traffic was heavy, and many people had to walk miles to reach central London. I walked along at the back of the crowds, watching hawkers selling cheap souvenirs and periscopes, and noticing how poor and unhealthy people looked. Some £20 million was spent on pomp and ceremony surrounding one very ordinary man, while other ordinary men, women, and children throughout his country were living with poverty, ill-health, and unemployment. I hoped that this would be the last king crowned in England!

Dorothy Galton offered me the use of her large flat on Mornington Crescent in north London, while she was away. It was palatial compared to my previous lodgings, with a bright and airy living-room and a view out the back window to a large garden with big trees. For the next six weeks I lived there with Fred Lasserre, a Canadian architect of Swiss origin, a graduate of Toronto who shared my political views. As I walked in the neighbourhood I felt that I was living in a community of ordinary English people. I concentrated on my studies, pressing forward with the Czech language and completing a 50-page essay on the Czech historical background up to 1907. It was a pleasure to present this to Seton-Watson in June. I visited Oxford to request an extension of my scholarship for a fourth year from C.K. Allen, the warden of Rhodes House. Help from the Czechoslovak government had not materialized.

Politics remained depressing, especially after the resignation of Prime Minister Stanley Baldwin and the forming of what I considered an unabashedly reactionary government under Neville Chamberlain. The situation in Spain deteriorated daily. The farce of non-intervention continued, with increasing intervention by German and Italian forces and no real opposition from either the British government or the opposition. I was disheartened by the purge of the armed forces in the Soviet Union, which, I thought, would temporarily weaken its military strength.

In early June I joined in a mass rally for Spain in Hyde Park and a march on the House of Commons in Westminster to lobby MPs on the Spanish situation. Later that month I attended a meeting for Spain in Royal Albert Hall, chaired by H.G. Wells. Paul Robeson, who had flown in from Moscow, sang "Ol' Man River" in his rich bass voice. He made an impassioned appeal to all intellectuals to choose sides in the worldwide struggle. He had made his choice, he said, in favour of the only country in the world where his people were not oppressed.

I spent four months in Czechoslovakia, from June through September 1937, travelling the length and breadth of the republic, and began my research. The cost of my first journey was hardly exorbitant

— the train fare was $15. I stopped off en route in Nürnberg, which had retained its flavour of lovely antiquity despite Nazi rule. But everywhere one was reminded of Hitler: his picture hung in every office and shop, and every other person wore a Nazi lapel badge. The ostentatious "Heil Hitler" salute grated on my ears and eyes. One day, when I went for lunch, I was sickened by a small notice on the door of the café, "Jews not desired."

After a thorough customs examination at the frontier, I arrived at the old and once lovely town of Cheb (Eger), located in a predominantly German-speaking region of Czechoslovakia. It was a quiet, sleepy town of 35,000 people. Its main street was drab and colourless; the houses were small and dilapidated; water came from pumps in the streets. Several times I was accosted by begging children, and I noticed a family of dark and long-haired "Roma" (gypsies). Of the total population, only about 10 percent (3,000) were Czech, but these seemed very conscious of their nationality. The offices of the pro-Nazi Sudeten German party were large and prominent. The party newspaper, *Die Zeit*, was hardly distinguishable in content from the newspapers of the Nazi Reich.

My arrival in Prague coincided with a three-day holiday weekend, which I spent wandering the streets, guidebook in one hand, dictionary in the other. First came the celebration of the victory of the Czech Legions at Zborov, in 1917, in the great Masaryk Stadium on Petřín Hill. Before a crowd of about 30,000, there was a re-enactment of the battle and a dramatic presentation by peasants in national costume of the building of the republic. Over the loudspeaker an announcer appealed to everyone to defend themselves and to fight if necessary: "Our allies are with us. The whole democratic world is with us; we believe in them and they in us." The crowning point of the spectacle was the unexpected arrival of T.G. Masaryk, the president. In an open car he made a complete circle of the whole field and was welcomed by cheering and the waving of white handkerchiefs. He acknowledged this ovation by slowly raising his hand to his hat-brim. I saw him very clearly as he passed — a tall figure, all in black, even to his hat, his thin, sharp-featured face stern and severe. This 87-year-old philosopher-statesman evidently commanded the respect and the love of his people. Monday was another holiday — the anniversary of the death of Jan Hus, the great Czech religious reformer of the fifteenth century who had been burned at the stake by the Catholic church. In the evening there was a service in his memory in the fine Old Town Square, with its imposing statue of Hus. The service opened with a hymn played by brass instruments from the Town Hall tower and continued with choral music and speeches.

During that summer I lived in a student dormitory, the Švehlova kolej, in a bare and uncomfortable room, at what seemed to me the absurdly low rent of 15 cents per night. At eight o'clock one morning, in the Parliamentary Library, I met Professor Zdeněk Tobolka, the chief librarian and a distinguished historian. Day after day thereafter I worked steadily on my research there or in the Klementinum, the old university library, its huge reading room heated by a single gigantic porcelain stove. I was able to discuss my work with Professor Otakar Odložilík of Charles University, who was to become my lifelong friend, and with other professors. René Wellek guided me about beautiful Prague and took me to Karlštejn Castle, constructed as a summer residence by Charles IV, the fourteenth century Bohemian King.

Following the central European custom I sat for hours at a time each morning in one of the innumerable cafés, studying Czech and reading the newspapers that hung on the walls. I was anxious to find someone with whom I could exchange English and Czech conversation and finally spent a week or two with Zdeněk Prokop and his family in Brandýs nad Labem. This was a small country town at the centre of a fertile agricultural region, which Zdeněk and I explored on foot or by bicycle. Harvest was in full swing, and we witnessed a picturesque festival procession, with the peasants dressed in folk costume. Zdeněk, a graduate of the Commercial Academy in Prague, seemed very American in his approach to life. His father, a civil servant, was an intense Czech nationalist, anti-German, anti-semitic, and anti-Bolshevik. Everyone in the family was convinced of the necessity of rearmament and was ready for war should it come. They all hated Hitler, as well as Stalin, and had a profound respect for Britain and the United States. In their pleasant and spacious villa I had my first taste of typical Czech food, with vast quantities of *knedlíky*, or dumplings, and a variety of tasty cakes.

A scholarship gave me food and lodgings for two weeks at the Summer School of International Affairs in Tatranská Lomnica and covered my travel from Cheb to Poprad. I pursued a circuitous route eastward, passing through the Ostravsko-Karvinská industrial region. I stopped off in Kroměříž, with its magnificent archbishop's palace; at Olomouc, with its vast square and huge cathedral; and at Zlín, the home of the Bat'a shoe works, with its striking modern architecture.

Most interesting, however, were my four days in Silesia in the predominantly Polish town of Bystřice nad Olzou. I was the guest of a Polish Lutheran pastor, Jan Karpecki, with whom Professor Rose had lived during his wartime internment. We walked for miles in the neighbourhood. On one occasion we illegally crossed the Polish border, which ran along the crest of the mountains, and went down on the other side to have a look at the splendid palace of the Polish president. The pastor spent much of the time describing the sufferings of the 80,000-strong Polish minority, which, he claimed, the Czechs were trying their best to denationalize.

At the summer school the program dealt with the problems of central Europe and Czechoslovakia, with many lectures by Czech and Slovak political leaders, including Kamil Krofta, the foreign minister; Ivan Dérer, minister of justice, a Slovak; Wenzel Jaksch, German Social Democratic leader; and diplomats, politicians, and scholars from Czechoslovakia and abroad. There were about 150 participants — young scholars, journalists, and politicians from almost every country of the region as well as from Britain, France, and Italy. I was one of two people from North America, and the only Canadian. We had a surfeit of the official Czech and Slovak points of view, but I had a chance to talk privately to a Slovak autonomist and a German Henleinite. At one point, while expressing my strong support for the republic, I reported what I had learned about the complaints of the Polish minority. The chairman rebuked me, as a foreigner, for putting forth what he called a list of second-hand complaints. Apart from the official program, we had a chance to climb in the Tatra Mountains and to visit Kežmarok, with its beautiful wooden Protestant church, and Levoča, with its splendid gothic church and its exquisite carved wooden altar by the sculptor Pavol.

I returned to Prague by way of Bratislava and Brno. In Bratislava I met a number of leading Slovak personalities, including Dr Anton Štefánek, a close friend of Seton-Watson's; the latter was regarded as a kind of national hero for his contribution to the liberation of Slovakia from Hungarian rule. The people I met were Czechoslovak in orientation, not separatist, but they had a distinctive Slovak point of view. Two young Slovaks, Vladimír Houdek and Josef Šoltes, who had been at the summer school, took me on excursions to Děvín, a ruined castle on a rocky cliff overlooking the juncture of the rivers Morava and Danube and the border with Austria, and to Bradlo, to see the gigantic monument in honour of Gen. Milan Štefánik, co-founder of the

Czechoslovak republic. In several Slovak villages we were invited inside the houses to see the beautiful hand-painting on the walls. The climax of one day was dinner in a little garden, where we drank wine and ate cheese and bread that we had brought with us. It was a good introduction to Slovak drinking habits, but left me very sick the next day.

Brno, the largest city in Moravia, with a population some 20 percent German, was rather drab and dirty. There were some fine old buildings, including the Cathedral of Peter and Paul on one hill and the ancient Austrian prison of Špilberk on another. My hostess, Sylvia Eltz, who had also been at the school, was a German-speaking lawyer and a Social Democrat who supported the Czechoslovak state.

At Tatranská Lomnice I made several new Czech friends, including Olga Schieszlová. The daughter of Dr Schieszl, head of the chancellery of President Beneš, she had studied at Mount Holyoke College in the U.S. and spoke perfect English. She was Social Democratic in outlook. I saw much of her at the conference and later for five weeks in Prague. We explored the city together, walked in the Šárka valley and to Bílá hora, and made an excursion to the Sázava River. It was a beautiful summer romance, and we fell in love. Thus my worst fear materialized, and on the very eve of my reunion and marriage to Sally. I still felt bound to Sally by our shared love and our almost identical interests and views, so there could be no question of abandoning plans to marry my first love. In farewell letters Olga and I professed our affection for each other and our sorrow that we had to part. In fact, apart from a brief meeting with Sally and me in England the following April, we did not see each other again for ten years. I told Sally about Olga in letters before her arrival but did not reveal the depth of my affection.

I returned to Prague a few days before the death of Tomáš Masaryk, the president-liberator, the title given him by law. His death was considered not a tragedy, but rather the natural conclusion of a long and productive life. Masaryk personified the achievement of independence and was the embodiment of the national ideals. Outside the country he had became a world figure of great moral influence and had won respect even from political enemies, such as the Germans and the Magyars. The city and the republic were in deep mourning for a week. People poured into the city from all over the republic. Black-edged newspapers, with pictures of Masaryk on his death-bed and on his catafalque, were on sale at every news-stand. Each shop window contained a bust, a picture, or a small statue, draped in black and decked with flowers. Huge black banners flew from buildings. At the castle in

Lány, which had been Masaryk's favorite retreat, thousands of people visited the room where his body lay in state. Later in the Prague castle, Hradčany, high above the city, the residence of Habsburg emperors, Bohemian kings, and Czechoslovak presidents, there was a queue of mourners, miles long, day and night, waiting for hours to view his bier.

The day of the funeral was a public holiday, and the route of the procession was lined with great crowds from early in the morning. I was disappointed not to get a reserved seat at the window of a building along the route and had to satisfy myself with watching from behind the lines of people. The cortège included President Beneš, public dignitaries and foreign guests, and many soldiers and wartime legionaries. The coffin was carried on a gun carriage and six soldiers walked beside it — one from each of the nations living in Czechoslovakia. Overhead, military planes flew back and forth. The procession wound through the city to the Wilson railway station, from which the body was carried by slow train for burial in the cemetery in Lány.

I had purchased tickets for Smetana's *The Bartered Bride* at the National Theatre and exchanged them instead for a special performance of Smetana's *Má vlast* (My Country), in honour of the late president, put on by the Prague Symphony and conducted by Václav Talich. At beginning and end the orchestra rose and turned to the large bust of Masaryk at the back of the stage. The audience, most of whom were dressed in black, stood in complete silence at the conclusion. It was a moving demonstration of the pride and affection, almost worship, that the Czechs felt for Masaryk.

I attended other meetings in tribute to Masaryk. At one, a university professor gave a eulogy, poetry was read, and personal recollections were given in German by Professor Seton-Watson. He spoke of his relationship with Masaryk during the war in London and quoted from some of Masaryk's letters to him. On another evening Seton-Watson spoke on the radio, this time in English, with a translation by the announcer.

For days the press devoted many pages to Masaryk's life and work; everyone tried to find in him an embodiment of their own particular ideals and principles, however different. The nationalists saw him as the person who raised the Czech nation from a political sleep of three centuries to a position of independence and world significance. The liberals saw him as the defender of humanist and liberal values — peace, democracy, tolerance, and social justice. The conservatives honoured him as one who built and defended the Czechoslovak state and saved it from the postwar danger of Bolshevization. The Social Democrats praised him for guaranteeing the Czech working class political freedom and social justice. The Communists saw him as the symbol of the struggle against the threat of fascism at home and abroad. The militarists lauded him for the formation of the Czechoslovak army during the war and his rejection of the policy of pacifism. The Slovaks considered his greatest deed the signing of the agreement in Pittsburgh, PA in 1918, which promised them political autonomy. Even the Sudeten German fascists of the Henlein party honoured him as the one Czech who had sought the abandonment of the ancient hostility of German and Czech. There was hardly a break in the united front of the nation — hardly a voice raised even in mild criticism. This confirmed the words of the prime minister, Milan Hodža, who had declared: "Masaryk is us — he is Czechoslovakia."

It was almost a relief to hear a discordant note struck in the Communist press, which dared to voice its philosophical and political differences with Masaryk. While giving him full credit for his revolutionary deeds in freeing the Czech nation from Habsburg rule and his recognition of the need for democracy and social justice, it criticized him as a defender of the bourgeois social and political system against the revolutionary workers' struggle and as a barrier against communism. He sought to achieve his aims by progressive means, but, when necessary, he had resorted to violent means to crush the workers' struggle for economic justice.

In our correspondence during the summer Sally and I had often discussed the possibility of her joining me in Prague and our marrying there. For her it meant the sacrifice of a wonderful job and leaving her friends in Manhattan for an unknown country and an uncertain future. For her family, and for mine, it was disappointing that we would wed away from home and in their absence. A grant of £200 from the Rhodes Trust solved the financial problem of our living for another year in Europe. We were at first afraid that this might require celibacy, as the Rhodes Scholarships did, but learned to our relief that there were no conditions attached. Sally sailed in September on the German liner *Europa*, bound for Bremen; after a 17-hour trip by train through Germany, she arrived at Masaryk Station in Prague at six a.m. on 6 October. I had rented a spacious room in downtown Prague, where, in the early mornings, we awakened to the noise of horses and carts passing along cobbled streets. This hardly disturbed the dawn of our new life together. Our long separation was at last over.

I had begun to fulfill the requirements for a civil marriage to be held in the Old Town Hall. After registering at the police station on the day of her arrival we went to the Old Town Hall the very next day, only to learn that it would take several days for us to secure a special certificate of exemption. The next morning we learned that we must provide official Czech translations of our birth certificates and that the next possible marriage day would be the following Thursday. But when we presented ourselves, attired in our best clothes, for the great event, we were informed that we needed a court interpreter to translate the service and two witnesses.

Finally, on Saturday, 16 October 1937, the ceremony took place in the ancient Marriage Room, a beautiful gothic chamber with arched ceilings and wall paintings with floral designs and Czech sayings. Ours was one of several weddings and lasted but a couple of minutes. A handshake sealed the bargain (no rings were exchanged), and a high official proclaimed its legal validity. After lunch with our two witnesses, Czech friends of mine, Antonín Paleček and Jaroslav Valenta, we walked on the Hradčany (Castle Hill). During the next weeks we enjoyed a honeymoon in beautiful Prague, walking on the Malá Strana, the Hradčany, and Vyšehrad, and listening to glorious music, including Smetana's *The Kiss* at the National Theatre and, at the Estates Theatre (Stavovské divadlo), attending the 150th anniversary of the première of *Don Giovanni,* which Mozart himself had conducted in the very same theatre. After that performance we walked through the old squares of Malá Strana, enjoying the beauty of the palaces at night and the lovely views of the Charles Bridge and the Old Town. Ascending to the Castle, we looked out over the lights of Prague and its illuminated towers.

One Sunday we made an excursion to the quiet country town of Kutná Hora, once a silver-mining centre and the residence of the Bohemian kings. There were countless fine buildings, including the gothic church of St Barbara, with extraordinary flying buttresses. Nearby, in a tiny village, was the large farmhouse where Paleček's parents lived, which I had visited several days earlier. Like them, Antonín was a member of the conservative Agrarian party, so that politically we had little in common. Meanwhile I resumed my research in the ancient Klementinum and other libraries. Sally began to adapt to life in Prague and to study German. She also met several Czech demographers and did some work on Czechoslovak population in the library of the Statistical Institute.

On 28 October 1937 Czechoslovakia celebrated the 19th anniversary of its declaration of independence. The city was gay with red, white, and blue flags, a striking contrast with the black banners of six weeks earlier. We spent the afternoon walking on the Vyšehrad, a high, rocky promontory above the river where a fortress once stood; within its walls was a great cemetery filled with the graves of many great personalities of Czech history. In the evening we attended a meeting in memory of Masaryk organized by the Workers Academy. There was music by Smetana, recitation of Czech poetry and Kipling's *If*, and a speech by Professor Zdeněk Nejedlý, a communist scholar who was writing a massive biography of Masaryk.

Back in London in November 1937 for a few months of research before returning to Prague, we found a comfortable room with the use of a kitchen in a little house at no. 2, The Vinery Villas, in St John's Wood. We enjoyed the fine spring weather and walked in Regents Park. We shopped in an open-air market not far away. Sally's good food soon caused me to regain the weight that I had lost during my months alone. Here we celebrated Sally's 25th and my 26th birthdays. Our landlady was Leosia Robson, a friend of Pepa's, a tiny Polish-Jewish lady who, though hampered by a club foot, was nonetheless a bundle of energy. She was a communist, and had separated from her former husband, an editor of the *Daily Worker*. Sally kept busy with household tasks, our social and political activities, and the study of German. She joined the London Consumers Cooperative and became active in the St John's Wood Women's Guild. We found time for excursions to Hampton Court and Hampstead Heath and to visit the Regents Park Zoo — a beautiful structure designed by Fred Lasserre's firm. I set to work at once, making daily trips to the School of Slavonic and East European Studies for Czech lessons and frequent trips by "tube" to the British Museum's newspaper collection in Hendon, where I went through the available Czech newspapers up to 1893.

In my letters home I expressed alarm at the threat of a second world war. In an article in the *Canadian Forum* ("The Czech Front," February 1938) I warned of a fascist offensive centred on Czechoslovakia. The British government, I wrote, was refusing to take a firm stand in defence of this endangered country. British prestige had never sunk so low and Britain would have to be considered an accessory to the crime if war broke out. The invasion of Austria on 15 March led to a wave of protest, and public figures such as Wickham Steed, Sir Norman Angell, R.W. Seton-Watson, Lord Cecil and more importantly, Lloyd George and Winston Churchill, urged support for

Czechoslovakia. All these events confirmed our belief in the urgent need for a new government in Britain, preferably based on a People's Front led by the Labour party.

The worsening situation in Europe led Sally and me to devote more time to political activities. We were both active in door-to-door canvassing on behalf of the Tenants' Defence League and gained an insight into the appalling living conditions of poorer Londoners. We even tried our hand, in preparation for May Day, at speaking at street corners — a daunting task, as we started with no one present and often ended the same way! We took part in many protest demonstrations in Trafalgar Square and Hyde Park, including a march for the freedom of India (in which, side by side with us in the ranks, were Professor Gregory Vlastos, Queen's University philosopher, and his wife, Val). When the Nazis occupied Austria we joined a massive demonstration of 50,000 outside the House of Commons and then marched to the German and Czechoslovak embassies under the slogan "Stand by Czechoslovakia."

On 2 May 1938, a red letter day, I began to write my thesis, and I managed to complete 50 pages in draft before leaving for Prague. On my final visit with him, Seton-Watson confessed that he had read only five pages. He was busily engaged in writing his books on Europe and the dictators and a history of Czechoslovakia. My discussions with him at his club, the Athenaeum, at his home in Wimbledon, or at the school, were devoted more to the international situation than to scholarly matters. I launched another letter campaign in search of a future academic job in North America, and even in England, but without success. The only bright spot was the offer in May of a job in Prague with the Czechoslovak Broadcasting Corporation. It was in that capacity that I was able to observe and comment on the catastrophic events of 1938-39 that seemed to end, forever, Masaryk's dream of a free and independent Czechoslovakia (see chapter 1).

NOTES

1.   I base this chapter in part on my correspondence with my parents and others between 1936 and 1940 (UTAS, Boxes 8 and 9). I give the dates of letters quoted, and some of these were published in English in *Kosmas* and in Czech in *Listy z Prahy*.

II

WAR AND COLD WAR

6

THE WAR YEARS:
THE MIDWEST AND MONTREAL

CHAPTER 1, THE DEATH OF A COUNTRY, described our experiences in Prague during the dramatic years 1938 and 1939. During that period we were observers of the gathering crisis that culminated in the Munich betrayal of Czechoslovakia by France and Great Britain. We were eye-witnesses to the subsequent Nazi occupation of Bohemia and Moravia and the break-up of the Czechoslovak Republic. The western powers acceptance of this Nazi aggression was one more step in their policy of appeasement, which had already been initiated by non-intervention in Spain and the toleration of the Nazi invasion of Austria. It was the opening movement of the prelude to war.

We decided to return to England by a somewhat circuitous route — by way of Vienna (now part of the German Reich) for some final research and then to Brittany for a few days holiday. In Vienna I worked away for a month in the State Library, ironically having to read the nationalist and pan-German newspapers from the 1880s, in a city now belonging to the German Reich. Every day Sally visited museums and churches, gardens and parks. But her enjoyment was marred by the signs that she saw at every entrance: "Entry forbidden to Jews." She seized the opportunity to visit the Jewish community and was taken to one of its 16 soup-kitchens. She was saddened by stories of the suffering of Jews since the Nazi takeover. I took time off from my work to join her for excursions to Schönbrunn Palace, the Prater, and the Kahlenberg. We spent our last Sunday on a wonderful trip by train and boat to Melk, the beautiful abbey on the Danube.

The next day, laden with three heavy bags, we proceeded to France by train, breathing a sigh of relief when we at last crossed the frontier into Switzerland. After two nights in Paris we headed for the little village of Santec on the coast of Brittany. We arrived at the end of a festival, la Kermesse, and were delighted to observe the Breton women wearing their black embroidered dresses and little lace caps. We were the only foreigners in the Hotel de Gulf Stream. The sea stretched out before us — a glorious blue, broken by huge wild rocks that at low tide rose out of the sand along the shore. After our exhausting time in Prague, it was a relief to relax and to enjoy sun and fresh air and good food. We were isolated from the world and were only dimly aware of the crisis over Danzig.

Ten days later came the sensational report of Molotov and Ribbentrop's non-aggression pact between the Soviet Union and Germany. The hotel emptied overnight, and after a tense twenty-four hours we joined the exodus. We took the first train to Paris, crowded with tourists and soldiers called up for military service. At each station on this long and tiring trip we witnessed what seemed a kind of repeat of the Prague mobilization in September 1938 , but this time there was no enthusiasm — the women accompanying the men and carrying their bags were in black, and many were weeping bitterly.

After a night in Paris we set out on the boat-train to Boulogne and caught what turned out to be the last Channel steamer before the outbreak of war. The boat was crammed to capacity with passengers, cars, and baggage. We had been lucky to pass through the months of crisis unscathed and to reach the safety of England one day before war was declared. The next morning we listened as Chamberlain announced on the radio that a state of war existed between Britain and Germany.

LONDON

We stayed for a few nights in our old home at no. 2, The Vinery Villas. There we experienced the first air-raid warnings, right after Chamberlain's speech and then twice during the night. These were false alarms, but each time we ran across the street in our pyjamas to our air-raid shelter, located none too safely beneath a garage and right beside the railway tracks and a canal. The next day we learned that the School of Slavonic and East European Studies would have to evacuate to Oxford immediately to give space to the Ministry of Information. (The school had just moved into splendid new quarters in the university's Senate House, behind the British Museum.) Pares, Rose, and Seton-Watson were to work in Oxford with the Royal Institute of International Affairs. We had lunch with Bill Rose, the new director, and helped him and Dorothy Galton move the school library to a temporary wartime location in Gordon Square.

Sally and I were not anxious to stay any longer than necessary in the war zone, but we were also not keen to run the risk of crossing the Atlantic in wartime. For the next eight weeks we stayed with my cousin Eric Coffin, his wife, Peggy, and their little boy, Gordon, on their small farm in Dorset. In the peace and quiet of rural England the war seemed remote. Sally and I devoted all our time to writing and typing the thesis and finished a complete first draft. During a one-day trip to London I worked in the British Museum, where readers had to carry their gas masks and open their brief cases for inspection at the entrance.

We were still on the farm when the Nazis invaded Poland on 1 September 1939 and the Soviet army marched into eastern Polish territory. We were both convinced that the Soviet Union was justified in taking this defensive action against German aggression in Poland. The Soviet Union, an ally of Czechoslovakia and France, had been excluded from the fateful decision at Munich. Chamberlain had sacrificed democratic Czechoslovakia in order to steer German aggression to the east, ultimately against the Soviet Union.

In November 1939 we went back to Oxford so that I could fulfil the requirement of spending a final term at the school and talk about my work with Seton-Watson and Rose. Seton-Watson had not read one word of my thesis, which I had sent to him chapter by chapter. Sally and I continued what seemed the never-ending task of writing and typing, and finally completed a final draft at the end of the month. We had the good luck to meet Jan Masaryk, Czech ambassador to Britain, at a tea held in his honour, and were impressed by his engaging American-style personality.

Suddenly, I received an offer of employment with the British Broadcasting Corporation (BBC). This satisfied my desire to do some useful war work and saved us from bankruptcy. My work consisted of editing a daily digest of German foreign broadcasts for government departments. When I contracted German measles, we jokingly ascribed this to my work! In April 1940 I was promoted to the research department, where I was given the more challenging task of analysing the content of German home broadcasts, starting off with a study of the anti-British hate campaign.

This job meant moving back to London, to our old place, The Vinery Villas. For the next few months we experienced wartime London — blackouts, gas masks, rationing, air-raid shelters, sandbagged buildings, uniformed people rushing about, and rising living costs. There were frequent bus accidents because of the heavy fog and unlit streets. The expected air-raids on London, however, had not yet materialized. The winter was unusually snowy and cold, and everywhere outside pipes (a British tradition) froze and burst. I was able to walk to Broadcasting House through Regents Park, sometimes in the inky dark of the blackout, with a torch (flashlight) in my hand or, in the brief hours of foggy sunlight, under the silvery barrage of balloons overhead. It was a relief when spring came and we could enjoy walking in the park once more. Although we had no time for political activities, I managed to write a weekly column for the *Tribune*, a new left-wing Canadian newspaper edited by A.A. McLeod. We began to pack and ship our books and unneeded clothing home to Canada.

I worked at the BBC on three rotating shifts, sometimes at night, so that during the daytime I could prepare for the examiners a copy of the thesis, which Sally typed. We were both under great strain and suffered several severe colds. Dorothy Galton took each chapter up to Oxford for safekeeping and once gave us the encouraging news that Seton-Watson had praised the thesis to her. At last, at three o'clock one Sunday morning at the end of April, we completed the huge manuscript of 579 pages and had it bound for the examiners. It was entitled "The German-Czech National Conflict in Bohemia, 1879-1893."

In early May Nazi forces occupied the Low Countries and France, thus creating the danger of an invasion of England. Our holiday on the South Downs was interrupted when I was suddenly ordered to move to the Midlands. There, in the small town of Evesham, I was asked to listen all day long to German home broadcasts for any clue of an impending invasion. I often worked at night, but I could still enjoy the beautiful springtime, taking long walks and canoeing on the Avon. Sally remained in London and began to prepare for our departure from England. On my return from Evesham for a few days off, I was alerted to the possibility of the BBC's evacuation to some safer location.

Sally informed me by telegram on 20 June that the examiners had approved my thesis and recommended its publication. Because of the pressure of war work, they were dispensing with the oral examination. I was disappointed not to have the chance to defend my work before three illustrious scholars — Professors Seton-Watson, Sir Alfred Zimmern, and C.K. (later Sir Charles) Webster. In spite of many crises and the coming of war, I had successfully accomplished my academic aim. Unfortunately the thesis was never published, but copies were placed on deposit in the school's library and in the U.S. Library of Congress.

I secured exemption from British military service as a Canadian permanently resident in Canada and then obtained an exit permit. We had some problems in securing ocean passage, since Sally, an American citizen, was not permitted under U.S. law to travel on a belligerent ship; she gave up several chances to go home on American liners so that we could return together. In the end Sally acquired a Canadian passport, as the wife of a Canadian, and when space at last became available, we sailed, on 24 July, on the *Duchess of Richmond.* Shortly before this date, the *Arandorra Star,* crowded with German refugees, had been torpedoed and sunk in the Irish Sea. Escorted by a destroyer into the open ocean, our good ship, painted battleship grey, its name erased, and blacked out at night, sailed across the Atlantic by a zig-zag course. The ship was full of British children being evacuated to Canada; they were unaccompanied and were attended only by the stewardesses. No preparations were made to care for their fate in case of an emergency.

Fortunately we reached Quebec City without mishap. We were soon with my parents in West Hill, near Toronto. Back in England just a few days later, the German air offensive, which had up to then been directed against port cities, was concentrated on London, and the blitz began. My anabasis, begun six years earlier, was ended. Sally and I, having shared with many others the hazards and crises of the prewar years, had escaped the trials and suffering that Europeans were doomed to endure as war unfolded.

A TORONTO SUMMER

For the first weeks back in Canada we settled down in the peace and quiet of West Hill, in the small cottage to which my mother and father had retired in 1939. My parents had worried about Sally and me for months as war seemed to track me down relentlessly. My mother was especially cast down by the failure of the League of Nations, whereas my father felt great relief that war had been averted by Munich. Both were devastated by the outbreak of a new war only a generation after the first one that had killed my brother and brought them such personal suffering.[1]

After the years of tension and turmoil in Europe, West Hill in August 1940 was for us a haven of tranquillity. Sally could explore the city of my birth, and I visited the library of the University of Toronto only to discover its woeful inadequacy vis-à-vis central Europe. I published an article on the economic consequences of the German occupation for the *Monetary Times.*[2] I also wrote a pamphlet for the Canadian Institute of International Affairs (CIIA), whose general secre-

tary was my fellow Rhodes Scholar John Baldwin, on the development
of democracy from its origins up to 1914.[3] I prepared another pamphlet for them analysing the ills of the capitalist world and political
democracy, and argued that the only solution was full-fledged socialism
combined with democracy. This was turned down as too controversial.

Sally was deluged with letters from anti-Nazi German refugees,
many of them Jewish, who, in the panic of an imminent invasion,
had been rounded up by the British Home Office and sent over to
Canadian internment camps. Eventually the injustice of this action was
recognized, and they were gradually released. They became Canadian
citizens, and some of them achieved great distinction in various walks
of life. Meanwhile many of them, having obtained Sally's name from
refugee groups in England, appealed to her for help in securing things
that they needed, such as books and writing materials, and once even a
violin. Sally was rewarded for her efforts (after our departure) by a visit
to West Hill from an RCMP officer who inquired about her relations
with "subversive elements!"

At the end of the summer of 1940 the prospect of getting work for
the ensuing academic year did not seem bright. I was a candidate for
a position at the Canadian Broadcasting Corporation (CBC) as news
commentator, but I lost out in the competition. Suddenly, two academic jobs materialized. One was at the University of Alberta, and it
offered what seemed to me a munificent salary of $2,500 per annum.
There I would have taken part in the highly regarded adult extension
course and would have no doubt gained a deeper insight into the
Canadian West. The other was a makeshift job, or jobs, at United
College in Winnipeg, where I would be assistant to two professors, in
history and in economics, at $700 per annum ($350 from each department). My father was astounded when I turned down Alberta and
accepted the Winnipeg offer. For me the choice was clear: the latter was
the first step to a real academic career.

WINNIPEG

We journeyed west by train. Our immediate financial problems were
eased by invitations to stay as guests for a couple of weeks at the home
of Professor Arthur Lower, of the Department of History, and then
later to live with Professor Bus Woods for seven weeks, while his wife
was absent for the birth of a baby. Sally was to act as housekeeper and
cook. For the balance of the term we rented — for $16 per month,

including heat and light — a large attic room in a house within walking distance of the college. There we set up our first real home, borrowing furniture from friends and putting up our Prague pictures. One of our pleasures was to prepare two large scrapbooks on our time in Czechoslovakia. (These were later stolen from our apartment in Montreal.) We acquired a cheap radio so that we could follow the news of the world. We also began to prepare for the notorious Winnipeg winter, with its very low temperatures and heavy snowfall.

My teaching duties were heavy but interesting. I was to assist Professor Lower, a distinguished historian of Canada, in his course on world history. This introduced me to periods of history that I had not studied since high school. In economics I was to assist Professor Woods in a subject closer to my previous work — the economic history of modern Europe. Each week I conducted 14 one-hour discussion groups and graded essays. To earn extra money I also gave a few lectures at the University of Manitoba. The position brought me into contact with two distinguished scholars and with bright and interested students, mostly from Manitoba.

Winnipeg turned out to be informal and hospitable. Sally and I were invited to dinner at the homes of Professor Lower and of Professor Arthur Phelps, of the English Department, both ardent Canadian nationalists. These were always evenings of fierce discussion and debate. We also were guests of George Ferguson, chief editor of the *Winnipeg Free Press*, a vigorous defender of Canadian national interests and Liberal policies. This opened my eyes to a Canada of which I had been only dimly aware during my trip out west in 1933. We found kindred spirits in Edwin Eagle, professor of classics, and his wife, who shared our views of the Soviet Union and of world politics. Professor Lower questioned me on my reported left-wing sympathies and warned me that I should not allow them to influence my teaching, but this did not seem to affect our academic or social relations.

Winnipeg had for me a certain aura as the city of J.S. Woodsworth (a graduate of United College) and the General Strike of 1919 and as the home of central and eastern European immigrants. We made excursions to the Icelandic settlement of Gimle on Lake Winnipeg, the historic Hudson's Bay Company post of Fort Garry, Portage la Prairie, and the French suburb of St Boniface, and we explored the Polish and Ukrainian areas of Winnipeg. I made a trip in the dead of winter to two small farming towns near the American border, where I lectured in a schoolhouse. A second lecture was cancelled because of a heavy blizzard, and I holed up for a couple of nights in the homes of farmers who were CCF members. I got a taste of rural life and listened to their stories of the effects of the drought on the community.

We were both invited to give lectures on Czechoslovakia and central Europe by various local groups. Sally attended meetings of the Women's International League for Peace and Freedom, with which she had been associated in Europe. I sat in on a CCF convention and watched the intense activity of David Lewis, my Oxford friend. We were much taken by the views of Mrs Neilsen, a radical, progressive MP, who warned in her speeches that the defeat of Germany was not the only goal. There were serious problems at home that needed solving, but people seemed afraid to voice their opinions about them. When the British trade union chief Sir Walter Citrine spoke in Winnipeg, we were saddened that he spent so much of his time attacking the Soviet Union, not Germany, and we distrusted his claim that the war would sweep away privileges and classes. In a speech at the Winnipeg Youth Council on "England at War," I raised questions that were freely discussed in England but that Canadians seemed to be afraid to raise — What are we fighting for? Who is to lead the nation at war? How are civil liberties to be safeguarded?

I prepared a long article on the problems of central Europe for the student magazine *VOX*, of which Marshall Crowe, later Canadian diplomat in Moscow, was an editor.[4] I gave a 15-minute talk on the CBC national network on 28 October, Czechoslovak independence day. I quarried my thesis materials for an article on the Austrian roots of Hitler's thinking, discussing his life in Austria and the influence exerted on him by Georg von Schönerer, pan-German nationalist, and Karl Lueger, the anti-semitic mayor of Vienna.[5]

For the next year Dr Graham, the principal, could offer me only a renewal of my post as assistant at a salary of $1,200. It was a delightful surprise to be invited to the University of Wisconsin to be interviewed for a post in the Department of Political Science. This was the result of a recommendation from my good London friend Harold Taylor, who was a lecturer in philosophy there. Wearing a brand new suit, a heavy overcoat, and a rough fur hat (purchased at the Hudson's Bay store for $1.25), I cut a somewhat exotic figure but felt nervous under the scrutiny of members of the department. Professor John Gaus, the chairman, was strongly interested in the common regional interests of the U.S. Midwest and the Canadian Prairies and was an admirer of the British political system, on which he had written a book. I was filled with respect for the high scholarly standards of this great Midwestern university and overwhelmed by the friendly reception and by the beauty of the Madison campus.

I was desperate to get the job but returned, exhausted and depressed, convinced that I had failed to make a good impression. Much to my relief, after a long, agonizing wait, I received an invitation to join the faculty as assistant professor at a salary of $2,500 per annum. I was to fill the vacancies of three senior professors — one had died, and Grayson Kirk and Walter Sharp had left for positions in the east. I was to teach primarily international relations and international organization and, in accord with Gaus's wishes, a new course on Canadian government — the first of its kind in North America.

During the summer of 1941 Sally and I returned to West Hill. We bought a cheap second-hand car in Detroit and managed to get it into Canada, as Sally's property, without duty. Once again we enjoyed the pleasant semi-rural environment of West Hill, with an occasional trip into the metropolis. I spent much time preparing my new teaching assignments and fulfilling the requirements for securing a permanent immigration visa for U.S. residence and employment. I took advantage of the opportunity to attend the annual meetings of the Canadian scholarly societies, the so-called "Learneds," and of the CIIA, which were held in Toronto. On 22 July we heard on the radio the shocking news of the German invasion of the Soviet Union and rejoiced in Winston Churchill's immediate declaration of solidarity. This removed all our doubts as to the justice of the war and assured us that it would be prosecuted with vigour. We learned with sadness of the bombing of London, including direct hits in the Marylebone district, where we had lived, and on the monitoring service of the BBC, where I had worked.

WISCONSIN

In August 1941 we embarked on our life in the United States — home for Sally, and for me a new adventure. On our way west we spent almost a month in Norristown, Pennsylvania, Sally's home town — her first visit in four years and my first chance to meet her family and friends and to see the historic sites of Bucks County. Our car laden with books, boxes of china, and assorted luggage, we journeyed westward to Madison, a beautiful city built on hills and four lakes in the heart of the Wisconsin farmland. We set up our new home in a comfortable apartment in Norris Court, and for the first time we had our

With Sally in Madison, ca. 1942.

own kitchen, a study, and a guest room. In due course we received the rest of our belongings, which had been stored in a cellar in Winnipeg; some of our books had been badly damaged by the spring flooding of the Red River.

The University of Wisconsin was a progressive institution, with a distinguished faculty and a mixture of students from the farms and towns of the state and from the east. My department had been headed for years by Frederic Ogg, the author of major texts on American and comparative government, editor of the *American Political Science Review*, and president of the American Political Science Association. John Gaus, urbane and well-read, was a leading figure in American political science and later became APSA president. Bill Ebenstein, Austrian-born, was a stimulating lecturer and author on Germany and foreign governments.

During the first two semesters, as a novice instructor in political science, I taught a large course on world politics and a smaller one on international organization. I was able to use my knowledge of Europe and the League of Nations to good advantage but had no chance to deal with central and eastern Europe. The course on Canada was difficult, as I had never studied this subject, but I had as a guide the lecture notes of McGregor Dawson, loaned to me by Brough (C.B.) Macpherson, my classmate at Toronto, then a professor there. I managed to keep one step ahead of the class by preparing each lecture the day before.

We first heard of the Pearl Harbor attack while we were listening to a Chicago Round Table Discussion on "Canada at War." The next morning some thirty to forty students and professors gathered in the reading room in South Hall to hear Franklin Roosevelt's address to Congress. At the close everyone stood for the national anthem. It was a moving introduction to our time in the U.S.

Once again we were involved in a country at war, although the conflict seemed remote in our Midwest asylum. Having lived for two years in belligerent countries, the adjustment was not as difficult for us as for most Americans. Moreover, Wisconsin had been a seat of isolationism for some years, divided by controversies over American involvement in world affairs. In the ensuing months there was much discussion of how to adapt the program to wartime and postwar demands. The department introduced a new course, "Government and War," given by several professors and broadcast on air. My contributions were lectures on Canada and Latin America, the League of Nations, and the transition to peace. I started a senior course of my own on war and postwar international problems. I served on a committee of the Teachers' Union, which sought to plan an interdisciplinary course on "Problems of the Postwar World." As a result of differences of opinion, nothing came of it, but it did lead to a more ambitious course on "Trends in Contemporary Civilization," taught by specialists in science, arts, economics, and political science, in which I took part. In January 1942 an unofficial faculty group was established to discuss postwar reorganization and to affiliate with a similar body at Harvard.

In my lectures in the classroom and outside, I stressed the common interests of the Western allies and the Soviet Union not only in the defeat of Germany and Japan but also in creating the conditions for a lasting peace. I had an abiding faith in the democratic character of the Soviet system and in its foreign policy and rejected the wave of anti-Soviet opinion in the West. In a lecture to the large Freshman Forum, in which President Dykstra had invited me to speak, I expounded these views, citing in support speeches by U.S. Vice-President Henry Wallace. I dismissed out of hand the "bogey of Bolshevism" and the much-touted threat of Red imperialism. While I had no real confidence in the Western governments and was critical of Anglo-American dominance over war policy, I also urged an early opening of a second front in western Europe to relieve the military burden on Russia. I was also highly critical of the report of the Teachers' Union committee on postwar problems, in June 1943, which called for cooperation with the Soviet Union but coupled this with a vicious attack on communism as a social system and on the Communist parties of the West. I was able to convince the committee to endorse the idea of a United Nations Political Council to elaborate a war strategy and to draft common peace aims.

My own position at the university was uncertain. As a junior member of staff I would likely be among the first released if the faculty were cut. I was eligible for military service. I had watched conscription at work in Czechoslovakia and England and did not hope or expect to escape the obligation so many had to assume. On 16 February 1942 I registered for the draft, but for the time being I anticipated deferment as an alien and a married man. By September 1942 it seemed as though deferment for married men would soon end. If I did get called up, I expected to serve in the ranks at first but hoped to seek later promotion and transfer to the Canadian armed forces.

My status would be affected by the Army Specialized Training Program (ASTP), which was to be introduced by the War Department in certain selected universities to provide training for soldiers assigned to military government duties in liberated areas. Wisconsin was selected for programs on Germany and southeastern Europe, including Czechoslovakia. I had some misgivings that the War Department would exercise strict control of the program in the universities and that military government might be used to suppress popular revolution. Nonetheless, on balance, I thought that the program was positive and participated in it during the academic year 1943-44. I gave six lectures to five hundred students on the German republic and, to a smaller group of sixty, a series on the history and politics of Czechoslovakia. By virtue of this work I was exempted from the draft, at least until April 1944.

In the autumn of 1943 Sir Bernard Pares, former director of my old school in London, was sent by the British government as an "envoy" to the U.S. and was invited to stay at Wisconsin for four months. I was given the complicated task of looking after him, his schedule, and his still-pressing sartorial needs, during his visit. His lectures were impassioned if conservative appeals for cooperation with Russia and Britain, but it was the old Russia and not the Soviet Union that he seemed to hearken back to.

During my first year at Wisconsin in 1941-42, my busy schedule gave me little time for research except during summer. Dr Alex Brady, of the CIIA's Research Committee, invited me to prepare a study of the growth of Canadian diplomatic representation. In early summer I spent a few days in Ottawa exploring the feasibility of this project. Norman Robertson, permanent under-secretary of state at External Affairs, was not enthusiastic and declined to promise access to confidential files. My former professor George Glazebrook, head of the research department at External Affairs, was more encouraging. I decided to take it on and, with much help from Sally, did research in my spare time and during summer vacation. I made further trips to Ottawa and Washington and had valuable interviews with Hume Wrong, Lester B. Pearson, Escott Reid, and other leading Canadian diplomats, some of whom made comments on my draft chapters. *Canadian Representation Abroad: From Agency to Embassy*[6] became, I was told, compulsory reading — a kind of Bible — for members of the Department of External Affairs. It was highly praised in reviews by leading Canadian scholars, and I was pleased to learn later that it even sold well — almost one thousand copies in the first year.

Other work on Canada developed from my participation in the Wisconsin Teachers' Union committee on postwar problems. This group eventually published a book, edited by Professor T.C. McCormick, of Sociology, which included my chapter, "Canada: Good Neighbor to the North."[7] I based it on a paper that I had delivered in a panel on Anglo-American-Canadian relations at the annual meeting of the American Political Science Association in January 1942. At the meetings of the Canadian Historical Association (CHA) in the summer of 1943, I gave another paper, "The Development of Canada's Permanent External Representation." Another offshoot of my teaching on Canada was my supervision of a Wisconsin thesis by William Willoughby, a young American from Kentucky, on the impact of the United States on Canada's foreign policy. He received his doctorate in

November 1942. After completing his military service he went on to teach in a Canadian university for the rest of his life.

I kept closely in touch with Canadian academic life by attending the "Learneds" every year. The meetings of the CHA and the Canadian Political Science Associations (CPSA) overlapped with those of the CIIA and provided an unequalled opportunity to meet and hear the leading figures of Canadian scholarly life. The CIIA meetings were organized in the form of panels, so that I could take part in discussions of Canadian foreign policy. I always combined these meetings with a visit to my parents in their rural retreat. Dad was busy as a "farmer," as an instructor in repairing shoes for the Royal Canadian Air Force (RCAF), and later, as an employee of a war factory in Ajax.

I also wrote three more popular articles on German war propaganda and on the conduct of the war. "Organizing Hatred" was a study of a German hate campaign based on my research with the BBC in London; it was turned down by the *Public Opinion Quarterly* but published by the *Dalhousie Review*.[8] "Will November 1918 Repeat Itself?," about Nazi propaganda and based on official instructions that I had had access to in London, came out in the *Public Opinion Quarterly*.[9] "Who Runs This War?" argued that the Anglo-American concentration of power in wartime strategy should be replaced by a Supreme War Council representing all the Allies.[10]

Sally and I took on other activities. Early in my stay in Madison I became involved in the Teachers' Union, which was a local of the American Federation of Teachers (AFT). It was a rather quiet and academic organization, weak in membership and leadership. As chairman of its membership committee I tried, with only a modicum of success, to broaden the ranks. In November 1942 I spent three days in Milwaukee at the convention of the Wisconsin Federation of Teachers (WFT). In his address, the president of the AFT envisaged an important role for the federation in exerting, through the American Federation of Labor (AFL), an influence on postwar educational and social organizations — I was frankly sceptical. However, I was drafted as a member of the WFT's Committee on Education and War and went to Milwaukee again in February 1942, when we discussed the teaching of democracy and of war and postwar problems.

Both Sally and I spent many hours working for Russian War Relief (RWR). We tried hard to broaden the RWR committee so as to make it more representative of labour, students, the university, and churches, but our success with labour was limited. Our chair was Helen White, distinguished professor of English and prominent Catholic laywoman. I was in charge of radio publicity and arranged weekly programs on all three Madison radio stations, for a total of 170 by August 1943. We took an active part in the War Chest drive for funds, even soliciting on the street for donations from passers-by, and our total contribution came to $6000. I was also in close touch politically with left-wing students and often spoke at meetings of the Wisconsin Liberal Association, condemned by some as communist-controlled. Even worse for my "reputation" was my role as "adviser" to the avowedly left-wing American Youth for Democracy. Somewhat ironically, I also served on the university's Discipline Committee, which had to deal primarily with the problem of cheating.

Sally helped in the planning of a Consumers' Information booth at the Wisconsin State Fair. She also joined a study group of the League of Women Voters on the war and economic welfare. In our second year in Madison, 1942-43, she took on a full-time job with the Travelers' Aid Society, working at a booth in the bus and railroad stations, to give help to travellers and soldiers. Sally and I celebrated our fifth wedding anniversary — 16 October 1942 — by studying in the library together and then having lunch in the Students' Union. I bought her a wedding ring, which we had both thought an unnecessary formality in Prague. We began to pay off debts that she had incurred for her college education.

OTTAWA AND MONTREAL

Meanwhile I was offered a number of other challenging wartime assignments. The first was an invitation from my former Toronto professor, Wynne Plumptre, to work with him in the Washington, DC, office of the Canadian Wartime Prices and Trade Board. I declined this and several less attractive offers from the BBC and the CBC but seriously considered a position as wartime assistant in the Department of External Affairs. Gerry Riddell, a young historian, who held such a position, told me that the salary was so low that I would have to go into debt! Since there was little likelihood that I would be able to use my specialized knowledge of central Europe, I declined.

More tempting was an urgent and mysterious invitation from John Grierson, head of the Wartime Information Board, to come to Ottawa to discuss an undefined assignment. It turned out that this was to head up a special section of the board to promote support for the war among

Canadians of foreign origin. I was to replace the incumbent, Professor Watson Kirkconnell, a talented linguist and translator of literature from many foreign languages, who was strongly anti-Soviet and closely associated with right-wing ethnic groups. Presumably my own positive attitude toward the USSR was regarded as an asset. I accepted a definite offer from Grierson's assistant, Davidson Dunton, but five months later I was informed that the board had not been able "to clear up problems of personnel and departmental organization," so the job fell through.

Finally, in May 1943, I did accept a position with the CBC as director of European short-wave radio broadcasts in its newly created International Service (IS). I spent some months that spring and summer in Ottawa with the Wartime Information Board (WIB), which had already mounted a modest program of what was called "political warfare" by broadcasting to occupied Europe. There were daily transmissions in French by a talented young Québécois, René Garneau, and in German by a young German Jewish refugee, Helmut Blume, who had been released from internment camp in Canada. In charge was Don Brown, a likeable fellow, who lacked any special knowledge of Europe or international affairs and worked in a haphazard and erratic manner.

During Brown's frequent absences I made several trips to New York, visiting the Office of War Information (OWI) and the WIB offices, as well as the American networks, and was thus introduced to the world of international shortwave broadcasting. In Ottawa I also made myself familiar with WIB radio operations, reading the files on the background of Canadian Political Warfare (PW). On the very first day I was surprised to be invited to read a broadcast in German. After five years the PW had not really accomplished very much and was just beginning serious activity on the eve of the invasion of Europe. I became a member of the PW committee, under the chairmanship of George Glazebrook, of External Affairs. At its first meeting I learned that neither he nor External had a high regard for political warfare or for the German broadcasts and were quite willing to accept American and British policy directives in these operations.

Peter Aylen, director of the IS, seemed quite ready to accept without question the authority of External Affairs. He believed that our program should focus on English and French for Britain and France, respectively, and for the armed forces abroad; other languages would play a minor role. He did not favour the continuation of German broadcasts after the end of the war. By dint of hard lobbying in government departments I won what I considered a major victory in early November 1943, when it was decided to continue the German broadcasts during and after the war.

We moved the IS to Montreal in November 1943 and at last, on Christmas Day, started daily transmissions over its brand-new transmitters in Moncton, New Brunswick. According to reports from England and later from the continent, our signal came through loud and clear, the strongest from North America. French-language broadcasts remained in the competent hands of Garneau and his associate, Gérard Arthur. English-language broadcasts were supervised by temporary staff until Arthur Phelps, my old colleague at United College, Winnipeg, took over. Another valuable colleague was Stuart Griffiths, an experienced CBC broadcaster, who was in charge of publicity. My main task was to prepare for broadcasting in other languages. I built up a small staff, including Helmut Blume as the mainstay of German broadcasts, assisted by Erich Koch, another "graduate" of the internment camps, and an Austrian, Karl Renner, as a free-lancer. A little later I appointed a Czech, Walter Schmolka, one-time lawyer and singer, to head the Czech program. My aim was gradually to add Slovak, Dutch, Flemish, and perhaps Norwegian. I myself did only occasional broadcasts in German and in Czech — for instance one on Masaryk's birthday in March 1945.

The Department of External Affairs, through the person of Terry MacDermot, of its Information Department, sought to interfere directly in our work. At one point he even tried to censor a talk that I prepared on Canada's Good Neighbour policy, but I went ahead anyway without making changes. I was determined not to allow our broadcasts to escape from our control and sought a clearly defined authority recognized by Ottawa. This required me to go to Ottawa from Montreal twice a week for liaison with External Affairs and the intelligence agencies, as well as to Toronto to familiarize myself with CBC domestic broadcasting. Closely connected with our German broadcasts was the question of the role of German prisoners of war (POWs) who had been taken in combat in Europe and were interned in camps across Canada. The internal life of the camps had been under German military control, with Nazi indoctrination prevailing and the "Heil Hitler" salute used. Prisoners who were anti-Nazi were in some danger, and few of them were willing to take part in German-language broadcasts. Slowly, in the sixth year of the war, a program of reorientation or re-education of prisoners began to take shape, hampered by lack of funds and by the ignorance of the Canadian officers concerned. It seemed to me that a campaign of reorientation was needed among the Canadian personnel, too!

We were anxious to use German POWs in Canada for our broadcasts to Germany, but we were hindered at first by the policy of External Affairs that we should limit ourselves to Canadian news and avoid political commentaries. Even Peter Aylen rebelled at this restriction, and we began to conduct limited PW, using the services of a German officer, Col. Walters, a former submarine commander, who was released from camp on parole and began to broadcast strongly anti-Nazi speeches. Only in early 1945, in the climactic period of the war, with Soviet forces standing before Berlin, did we reach an agreement with External Affairs that we should put less emphasis on Canadian affairs in our German programs and that we would be permitted to use more POWs in our broadcasts.

Meanwhile, the re-education of POWs was proceeding very slowly, partly because Prime Minister Mackenzie King was slow to approve it. We found the Canadian intelligence agencies more understanding of the need for such a program. In a memorandum in March on the relation of our radio work to reorientation, I urged the need for segregation of anti-Nazi prisoners in so-called "white camps," and an active anti-Nazi propaganda program in all camps. Only after VE-Day, in May 1945, did the PW committee finally decide to create a "white" camp, to which 120 anti-Nazi prisoners from camps across Canada would be transferred. At a meeting with German camp commandants from all camps, the committee outlined the principles of a reorientation program of lectures and publications. Meanwhile, at the invitation of Canadian military intelligence, Blume and I had made visits to nearby POW camps in Farnham and Sherbrooke, Quebec, where some prisoners had agreed to send messages to their loved ones at home in our broadcasts. At the end of May we made our first visit to the newly established "white" camp, in Sorel, where 15 prisoners were willing to work with us. We were dismayed, however, by the strongly anti-Soviet and often militarist attitudes of even anti-Nazi prisoners.

An interesting interlude during the summer of 1944 had been our two-week stay in Quebec City, where I covered a meeting of the governing body of the International Labour Organization (ILO). Our job was to produce a daily program of 40 to 50 minutes for the IS and a daily commentary for the CBC national network. I had a desk on the floor of the meeting room and had to follow the proceedings closely and to nab delegates for talks. We broadcast some 50 speakers, in seven or eight languages. It was an exhausting daily routine, and I was vexed by running interference from Peter Aylen, back in Montreal.

As a student of international organization I found it fascinating to observe the proceedings and to listen in to the discussion of the relations of the ILO with the United Nations, which was just concluding its founding conference in San Francisco. There were some 50 delegates from 19 countries; these included, in addition to government delegates, representatives of employers (a rather undistinguished group), and of labour. Among the latter were such charismatic figures as Léon Jouhaux, head of the French Confédération générale du Travail (CGT), recently released from a concentration camp, and Lombardo Toledano, the radical Latin American trade unionist. Notable was the absence of representation of the USSR, which had little use for the ILO at that time.

From 1 May 1945 we were on the alert to broadcast a special program on victory in Europe, often reporting to work at three a.m. On 7 May came the early unofficial Associated Press report of the German surrender, which was enough to bring the people of Montreal onto the streets in celebration. Finally on 8 May we listened with joy and relief to Churchill's announcement of victory. We were disappointed that fighting was still continuing in Prague, but it was clear that the Allied coalition had won over Nazism. In August came the surprising surrender of Japan. In this case, too, there was an early false announcement, which produced uncertainty and nervous waiting at our office until it was made official by the newly elected British prime minister, Clement Attlee. After seemingly infinite suffering the Second World War was over, thank God, and the way was open for a world at peace. This would be fraught with difficulties, but the formation of the United Nations gave us hope for the future.

We were in Canada during the final, climactic months of the war and at the time of ultimate victory. My work kept me in close touch with the Canadian government, and our broadcasts linked me once again with central Europe, including Czechoslovakia. I had helped to set up the Canadian international short-wave radio system, an important development in Canada's external relations. I had built up a good staff of eight people and laid the groundwork for the IS's expansion into a large, multilingual service. I was even tempted to stay on for another term, to further the development of our operations and of the German reorientation program. But my department in Wisconsin was urging me to come back for the first semester. And I had often been frustrated by the niggardly treatment of our service by the CBC, and the unimaginative and ill-informed attitude of External Affairs personnel, and the petty interference of Peter Aylen. I was therefore happy to go at this point and to leave the "Voice of Canada" in Europe in the good hands of Stuart Griffiths, as acting director; Earl Birney, distinguished poet, the new director; and the staff.

NOTES

1. This and following chapters are based on a diary that I kept during the war years.
2. "How the Czechs Lost Control," 12 October 1940.
3. "How Did We Get That Way?" *Democracy and Citizenship Series* [CIIA] no. 1 (1 Oct. 1940).
4. "From Munich to Sofia," *VOX* 12, no. 2 (March 1941).
5. "Austrian Origins of National Socialism," *University of Toronto Quarterly* 10, no. 4 (July 1941): 482-92.
6. Toronto: CIIA 1945.
7. T.C.T. McCormick, ed., *Problems of the Postwar World* (New York: McGraw-Hill, 1945), 490-513.
8. "Organizing Hatred," *Dalhousie Review* 33, no. 1 (April 1943): 11-22.
9. "Will November 1918 Repeat Itself?" *Public Opinion Quarterly* 7, no. 2 (summer 1943): 258-66.
10. "Who Runs This War?" *Queen's Quarterly* 44, no. 3 (autumn 1942): 220-29.

THE "WISCONSIN IDEA" AND THE UNITED NATIONS

BY MID-SEPTEMBER 1945 we were in the Midwest again, back in our apartment in Norris Court. We bought a piano, which became a great source of pleasure to us. Sally resumed her work with Travelers' Aid. My teaching program was heavy and included the demanding gateway course in world politics, where enrolment jumped from 115 to 315 in the second year. An initial disappointment was the cancellation for one term, for budgetary reasons, of my course on international organization. When the course was given the following semester the enrolment was high — 39 students — and in the second year, 60. The number of students in my course on Canada, which I had come to look forward to so much, was very low — only five — but it jumped to 15 the following year. I felt that I was able to awaken interest in this unknown northern neighbour. I was particularly glad to give a course on eastern Europe, since I was planning to resume research on Czechoslovakia. There were 18 students in this course at first, 20 in the second year. I felt that some of them began to grasp the complexities of this area so remote from their consciousness. In the second year I introduced a graduate seminar on international relations, with ten or twelve students. We discussed the role of labour and socialism in international relations, including Marxism, Leninism, Stalinism, the Second International, the Communist International, and the International Labour Organization. The many returning veterans, who had been away from books for a long time, were serious students and our discussions were enriched by their experience.

During these two years, 1945-47, I was active in the Teachers' Union, and although I was not yet an officer, I was asked to draft a statement of purposes and activities. According to this, the union should press for improvement of faculty salaries and act as a watchdog for academic freedom. The union ought to set out a policy for university education, including curriculum revision, and should seek closer relations with local labour and with the students. Most controversial was the idea of seeking to influence faculty and public opinion by taking a stand on public issues, not only state and federal but also international.

I was dissatisfied with the local's leadership and with the slow pace of action. The poor turnout at meetings was discouraging, as was the low membership. I organized a caucus of some of the new and younger members to promote greater activity. After a campaign for new members we reached a high of 115 in March 1947. In my department there were 19 members, including all the assistants. Our greatest achievment was our campaign for higher salaries. A report drafted by Professor James Earley of the Economics Department called for a 25 percent increase in salaries of $3,000 or less and smaller increases for higher salaries. At a faculty meeting, the historian Professor Knaplund, one of the most conservative members of the faculty, spoke on behalf of our proposals and paid tribute to the union's work. We scored a signal victory when all our proposals were adopted. This was a high-water mark in the history of the relations of union and faculty at Wisconsin.

We also pressed for increased housing for both students and new faculty and presented a statement to this effect to the state legislature. We also sought curbs to rises in prices and rents by urging restoration of the recently abolished Office of Price Administration in Washington. In connection with congressional elections we took part in the Political Action Committee of the local unions and endorsed our colleagues, Bill Rice and Howard MacMurray, as candidates. At a well-attended meeting in January 1947 the union adopted a strong resolution in support of MacMurray in an academic freedom case.

In the second year I became a somewhat reluctant president, and attended the AFT's annual meeting in St Paul, Minnesota in that capacity. The membership was abysmally small in contrast to the number of U.S. teachers and was particularly weak in colleges and universities. An independent caucus was formed to express the discontent of many delegates with the conservative leadership of the union and to press for more liberal policies, as well as for democratization of the AFT and its relationship with its parent body, the American Federation of Labor (AFL). This group, of which I was a member, drew up a statement of principles and objectives and had a considerable influence on the proceedings.

The main issue before the convention was federal aid to schools, especially whether non-public (including Catholic) schools should receive such aid. Certain locals, including ours, opposed any form of aid to parochial schools. The AFT compromise proposals, eventually adopted by the convention, included some aid to them. Another issue was the question of the relationship of the AFL to the World Federation of Trade Unions (WFTU). AFL spokesmen argued that it was impossible to cooperate with the WFTU, which included the Soviet trade unions. Our Wisconsin local had recommended AFL affiliation with the WFTU, and, in cooperation with other delegates, we won a surprise victory in the Resolutions Committee. Although we had considerable support on the convention floor, we were in the end defeated.

A week later I attended a meeting of the Madison Federation of Labor. I had been impressed at the convention by reports as to how closely some teachers unions cooperated with their local labour councils and regretted that our local did not have better relations with Madison labour. I was discouraged, however, by the conservative character of the federation in this small, not heavily industrialized town.

Broadcasting on WHA, the university radio station, took much of my time. I was appointed a member of the university's Radio Committee, which served in effect as the "dean" of radio work, controlling personnel, finances, and programs. I was disturbed when the dean of commerce, Professor Elwell, condemned a statement, critical of private enterprise, made by a professor in a broadcast course. This seemed to be a direct infringement of freedom of discussion in the classroom. A statement of policy for WHA, which I was asked to draft, placed responsibility on the director for choosing speakers and on the speakers to discuss issues objectively. This was approved without change and was, I thought, a victory for academic freedom. I organized and moderated weekly sessions on the United Nations, which involved interviews with campus specialists on the World Court, the World Bank, the ILO, the UN Relief and Rehabilitation Administration (UNRRA), the World Health Organization (WHO), the Economic and Social Council, and UNESCO.

Meanwhile I was able to find some time for writing and research. In the early autumn Sally and I worked on the proofs of my book, *Canadian Representation Abroad,* and Sally composed an excellent index. I wrote two articles on the Canadian diplomatic service, one on the trade commissioners' service, and another on the veto power in the United Nations Security Council, and a pamphlet on the United Nations.[1] But I was anxious to get back to research on central and eastern Europe, particularly to revise my thesis by extending it to cover the period up to 1914. During the summers of 1946 and 1947 I made a good beginning and continued to work on the project after leaving Wisconsin, but it remained unpublished.

There were discussions of the possible formation of an Institute of Central Europe at Wisconsin. I was interested in the project, but I had some misgivings. Hans Gerth, a sociologist, and Chester Easum, a historian, both specialists on Germany, wished to see the institute focus on Germany, although Easum was willing to include Austria, Czechoslovakia, and Poland. I believed that the institute should include the Soviet Union and eastern Europe. At this time I began to study Russian.

Anti-Soviet hysteria mounted after Winston Churchill's "Iron Curtain" speech at Fulton, Missouri, in 1947. I associated myself with the Council of Soviet-American Friendship in Madison, drafting a resolution on relations with the Soviet Union. I spoke on Russia at meetings on the campus and across the state as well as in classroom lectures, such as the large Freshman Forum. I was openly critical of the bipartisan American foreign policy of opposing the Soviet Union and was sympathetic to the challenge to this raised by former vice-president Wallace. In the spring of 1947 I condemned the "Truman Doctrine" of aid to Greece as an American intervention that would, I thought, sharpen the division of the world into two camps and ultimately lead to war. When Truman made a major speech in Canada, I felt that he was seeking to enlist Canada in this crusade. In a talk on the CBC I urged an independent Canadian course, one which would moderate the sharp division between the two blocs. When Washington advanced the Marshall Plan of aid to Europe it was, in my view, designed to make the Truman Doctrine more palatable to Europe. I had grave doubts as to whether it was meant to help all of Europe, including the Soviet Union.

I was concerned by the danger of the atomic bomb and supported its control by the UN Security Council. I welcomed the sane and responsible attitude taken by many scientists, who pressed for development of the bomb through UN agencies. I was convinced that this most destructive weapon would inevitably be used in a future war, so that the main task was to eliminate war by dealing with its causes through the United Nations.

THE UNITED NATIONS

I received several invitations from the CBC to cover early sessions of the UN's principal organs. This opportunity to watch the UN at first hand contributed a great deal to my teaching of international organization. The work took me back to the hectic world of broadcasting that I had known in Prague and Montreal. I had to prepare daily news reports of the day's sessions for the International Service (IS) in Montreal and longer interpretive commentaries for the national network. My broadcasts drew favourable comment from the Department of External Affairs.

The UN Security Council was fascinating, as we watched the controversial debate on the Iranian question around the arc-shaped table in the hastily prepared but beautiful Council chamber in the Hunter College gymnasium. The real issues of the conflict were hidden beneath what seemed to be a discussion of procedural issues. The Soviet Union had continued its wartime occupation of northern Iran, which was inhabited mainly by Azerbaijanis, and at first tried to block discussion by the United Nations. The Americans, however, demanded immediate discussion and defended the right of a small nation to be heard. I was afraid that this would alienate the Soviet Union, split the "Big Three," and foment anti-Soviet public opinion in the United States and Western countries. The real issue was not Soviet pressure on a small country, but rather the conflict of interests between the Soviet Union and the other great powers in an area of great strategic importance to all. This rift was a threat to peace and to the future of the United Nations. Moreover, Iran was far from being a parliamentary democracy and denied all semblance of autonomy to the northern region. In my broadcasts I tried to present the situation objectively but was highly critical of Western policy and sympathetic to the Soviet position. In a talk at the Political Science Club in Madison my presentation aroused a controversial discussion in which I found myself completely isolated, with all my colleagues opposing my stand.

In May 1946 I returned to New York for meetings of the UN Economic and Social Council (ECOSOC), also held in Hunter College. The press and radio paid little attention to these dull and technical proceedings. It was exciting, however, to watch Eleanor Roosevelt present the report of the Human Rights Commission. I also observed meetings of the Security Council on the Spanish question. The subcommittee's report, after six weeks of investigation, *recommended* that the Security Council *recommend* that the General Assembly *recommend* to UN members a general break in relations with fascist Spain. The Soviet Union opposed this weak proposal, which sidetracked the possibility of effective economic sanctions against the Spanish regime. I also watched the opening session of the Atomic Energy Commission, where the first momentous discussion of the future of the bomb took place. Bernard Baruch, on behalf of the United States, proposed that an international authority, without a veto power, be established by stages. This meant that the United States would not relinquish its monopoly until the final stage.

In November 1946, I was at the UN again, this time in Lake Success, on Long Island, where provisional headquarters had been established in the former Sperry arms plant. Meetings of councils and committees took place there, but plenary sessions of the General Assembly were held in Flushing Meadow, also on Long Island. There an impressive hall had been created, with floor space for delegates from 51 member countries, galleries for the press, glass-enclosed booths for radio, a double-decked dais for the speakers' rostrum and chairman, and, behind, a great map of the world. I usually began the day by attending a press conference at the Canadian headquarters in the Hotel Biltmore and sometimes drove to Lake Success in an official Canadian car. I moved from committee to committee, depending on how interesting items on the agenda looked. In the Trusteeship Committee there was a sharp controversy over the proposal of Prime Minister Gen. Ian Smuts, of South Africa, for the annexation of South West Africa, a former German colony, which was sharply opposed by smaller countries, such as Czechoslovakia, Guatemala, and Haiti. A debate over the future of other dependent areas, such as the former League of Nations mandates and the Pacific Islands occupied by the United States in the Second World War pitted the United States and the Soviet Union against each other. John Foster Dulles, the U.S. Secretary of State, flatly declared that if an agreement on the Japanese islands were not reached, the United States would continue to exercise de facto control. The Soviet delegate criticized the efforts of the American and other mandatory powers to retain exclusive control of these territories and hit out at South Africa's proposal of annexation.

In ECOSOC, Eleanor Roosevelt spoke eloquently on the refugee question, disputing Soviet delegate Andrei Vyshinsky's concept of democracy. She urged that those who did not desire to return to their homelands should not be forced to do so. There was another sharp debate over the future of UNRRA, which Britain and the United States wished to terminate. New York Mayor Fiorella La Guardia spoke on the need for replacing it with a United Nations Emergency Fund. He made an eloquent plea for aid and a vigorous attack on the United

States for using food as a political weapon. In the plenary session of the Assembly there was a debate over the five great powers' veto in the Security Council, in which the Australian delegate gave a masterly criticism, ably supported by New Zealand. Canada remained silent. Senator Connally, of the United States, defended the veto but criticized Soviet use of it. Andrei Vyshinsky, in a fiery, improvised speech, defended his country's use of the veto and stressed the need for unity of action among the "Big Five."

The following year I covered the UN Special Assembly on Palestine. I also sat in on the opening meeting of the Sub-Commission on Freedom of Information, a committee of experts, at which my former classmate George Ignatieff was the chief Canadian delegate. A key figure was another Canadian, John Humphrey, head of the Human Rights Division of the UN Secretariat. He had earlier offered me a job in his department at a salary of $6,000, and he still held the offer open. George asked me if I were interested in a summer job with External Affairs; Peter Aylen, now head of the UN's Radio Division, inquired whether I was available for the post of permanent CBC commentator. Although these offers were tempting, I preferred to stay in academic work and to visit the UN from time to time. In January 1946 Sir Bernard Pares had urged me to apply for the post of director of the School of Slavonic and East European Studies. Although I did not feel qualified or ready for such a move, I sent in a letter of inquiry, which — I was not surprised — produced no results. In November 1945, I had somewhat reluctantly turned down the offer of a job with UNRRA, in Poland or Czechoslovakia, which would have given me the opportunity to get back to eastern Europe. My department, however, was not anxious to see me go on leave so soon after a year away.

WISCONSIN IN DECLINE

In Madison the university seemed to be entering on a period of decline. There had been a huge influx of students — 18,000 in 1945-46, who were admitted without adequate availability of housing or of faculty. Classes were huge, and classrooms were bursting. As union representative I joined students and veterans who met the president to urge the calling of a special convocation to counter the decline of faculty morale and the discontent of the students. Equally depressing was the faculty discussion on curriculum reform, based on the report of a curriculum committee, headed by Professor Ogg, presented in January 1946. The report was conservative and contained no general philosophy of education and no proposal for drastic revision of approach. A minority of the committee proposed an alternative curriculum, one offering students the option of a more integrated and imaginative program of studies. Both reports were approved by the faculty.

The retirement of Max Otto, the brilliant philosopher, seemed to mark the end of an era; the old spirit lingered on, but a new and more modern spirit would be required if Wisconsin's liberal reputation was to be preserved. At a dinner in his honour, Lloyd Garrison, former head of the Law School, noted that the "Wisconsin idea" — the phrase long used to describe the unique quality of the state and the university — was no longer much talked about. He warned that institutions never stood still; they either moved forward or backward.

The situation in my department became increasingly unpleasant. I was not happy with my salary, which remained at $3,000 per year, with a raise of only $200 for the next year. The cost-of-living bonus amounted in my case to 15 percent of my salary, quite out of proportion to the 35 percent jump in the cost of living. The department, in spite of a democratic façade, seemed to be quite undemocratic. As an assistant professor I was excluded from decisions on salaries and new appointments. It irked me that I had no part in planning the international relations field. As early as April 1946 I was beginning to feel that I must move elsewhere at the first opportunity.

The so-called MacMurray case severely damaged the reputation of the university. The Department of Political Science recommended the permanent appointment of our colleague, Howard MacMurray, a lecturer in extension. Although approved by the dean, this nomination was not accepted by the Board of Regents, presumably because he was a Democratic candidate for the U.S. Senate. While the snub represented a clear infringement of academic freedom, our department at first acquiesced in the regents' decision. I was almost alone in questioning the decision but was excluded from further discussions in the budget committee. In the end the department did reaffirm its recommendation and asserted the right of a teacher to be active in public affairs.

Most professors showed reluctance to sign a public statement of protest, which was ultimately endorsed by 24 townspeople. As a junior member of the department concerned I was in an awkward position. I was president of the Teachers' Union, which had declared its support for the MacMurray's senatorial candidacy. When the regents finally rejected the president's recommendation for the appointment, the union committee issued a strong statement, drafted by me, which hit the headlines. The union proposed that the faculty express its regret over the decision and that in the future, if the regents rejected a faculty recommendation, they should do so only for extraordinary and compelling reasons and after prior consultation. This proposal was signed by ten other full professors, most of them non-union members. In the end it was modified so as to avoid any reference to the MacMurray case and to amount to a mere statement of principles — a sad outcome of the long controversy. This confirmed my views of the unreliability of the faculty and the president in the defence of academic freedom. I aired my criticism of the whole affair in several of my classes and was warmly applauded.

During all this turmoil I was awaiting with impatience a departmental decision on my future — whether, as I hoped, I would be promoted to associate professor, with tenure. I felt increasingly out of step with the department, not only as a result of the MacMurray affair, but also because of discussions of our future program. There was little hope of an appointment of a Soviet specialist, as I had urged. John Gaus revealed to me that the department was likely to place less emphasis on international relations and more on local, state, and American government. He had no sympathy for my views on the Iranian situation as expounded at the Political Science Club but said that he did not think that the precedent of the MacMurray case would have a negative influence on my appointment.

I was more and more inclined to seek a post elsewhere. While I had not closed the door to the UN position, I preferred to remain in the academic world. There were some nibbles from Canadian universities, but none attractive enough to merit consideration. Meanwhile a favourable alternative presented itself at Dartmouth College, in Hanover, New Hampshire. In late February 1947, the dead of winter, I visited Hanover, without Sally. Delayed by a blizzard en route, I arrived by train 24 hours late, quite exhausted. The visit gave me a very good impression of the department and the position. The president, John Dickey, who had formerly served with the State Department, had a strong interest in international relations and in Canada. Nonetheless I came away discouraged, feeling that the visit had not gone well. But after waiting in agony some seven weeks, I received an offer of an assistant professorship at an annual salary of $4,500.

We might have been tempted to stay on at Wisconsin for a year or two if I had received a promotion and tenure. The chairman, Llewellyn

Pfankuchen, remained silent on my future prospects. Gaus told me that it would be difficult for me, as a Canadian citizen, to handle American foreign policy in the Republican atmosphere that was likely to prevail in the U.S. The fateful decision came on 19 March 1947: I was denied a promotion and permanent tenure and offered a one-year appointment as assistant professor at a salary to be determined at budget time. This seemed unjust in view of my record of teaching, research, and outside activities during my years at the university. Although the decision was justified officially by the uncertainty of the departmental program, I suspected that it was a result of my radical political stance on university and public issues and my sympathetic attitude to the Soviet Union. My friend Merle Curti later confided that he had heard that the department considered that I was a follower of the Communist line.

I still had some reservations about Dartmouth — the difficulties of fitting into a small college and community and teaching several courses jointly. Dartmouth had the image of being a college for students of wealthy background who were interested more in the outdoors than in academic work. Older members of the faculty had a similar reputation. But, according to all reports, younger members of faculty were actively involved in scholarly research and in public affairs. The classes were small, the teaching burden relatively light, and vacations were long. The program of teaching fitted into my interests — international relations, international organization, and eventually a course on eastern Europe. Hence in April, with Sally's full support, I accepted the Dartmouth offer. When the press reported my decision, I gave an interview where I linked my departure with the MacMurray case. John Gaus's decision to leave had also just been released to the press and explained by him in similar terms. Many of my good friends thought that I had chosen the right path and welcomed my statement.

The birth of our first child took place in 1947, after almost eight years of postponement because of the war and the uncertainty of the future. On 3 April, after a false alarm that lasted a day, the baby was born at one-thirty a.m. An hour later I saw for the first time David Bright Skilling. For the next week or two I did little work and spent much time at the hospital and dining out with friends. Six days later came the offer from Dartmouth; a week later I accepted it, and Sally and David came home. What a new life was beginning for us — with a baby in the house after nine years of being alone! For a week or two I was busy with shopping, washing dishes and clothes, feeding the baby, and sleeping during the day. Then my mother came to Madison to be with Sally for a couple of weeks. By the latter part of May Sally was back to normal, and I thought it safe to leave her alone while I travelled.

I made two separate trips that spring — one to the United Nations and another to the Canadian Learned Societies. The latter held their conclave for the first time at Laval University in Quebec City. Laval seemed a strange place, with its clerical and medieval appearance, its forbidding grey walls, its robed instructors, and the crucifixes in each classroom. However, it was clear that the university, and Quebec, were undergoing great changes. There was an unusual air of friendliness between the French and English Canadians at the meeting. At the CIIA meetings I introduced the discussion on relations with the Soviet Union, suggesting that Canada might have a mediating influence. The defection of the Soviet diplomat Ivor Gouzenko and the resulting spy case in Canada had created an atmosphere of anti-communist hostili-ty. I disputed the notion that the solution of the world's problems lay in social democracy and urged a coalition of socialists and communists with other decent elements of centre and right — on the Czechoslovak pattern.

I stopped over a couple of nights in Montreal, to see old friends at the CBC and give several broadcasts in English and Czech. The IS now gave broadcasts in the Scandinavian languages and was soon to intro-duce Russian. I was not, however, tempted to return to the madhouse of international broadcasting. Teaching and research looked more attractive. In West Hill with my parents I enjoyed a real holiday, with swimming, riding, reading, and nostalgic visits to the University of Toronto.

Now the time had come to get ready to leave Madison, our home for the past six years. Most precious of all the attachments that we would miss were the close friendships with more progressive faculty members and graduate students that transcended political differences. Among the former the rarest was Merle Curti, noted scholar of American intellectual history, a lifelong socialist and pacifist, whom I admired for his open-minded and liberal outlook and for his scholar-ship, which he managed to continue despite caring for his bedridden wife, Margaret. Fortunately we would see them in New Hampshire, where they spent summers at an old farmhouse close to Hanover. The worst loss of all — just before we left Madison — was the sudden and tragic death after a heart attack of my close friend the anthropologist

Scudder Mekeel. At a memorial meeting, I praised his progressive concept of scholarship based on action within the community.

During August, in sweltering heat, we packed our belongings for the move east and purchased a second-hand 1939 Ford, for $875. David was already five months old, and both Sally and he were in good shape for the long journey. We had managed to save about $3,000, including $800 in the state retirement fund, and in addition some investment in the generous state insurance scheme. True, as the day of departure approached, we began to run out of money, but we had enough to manage the move east until my salary began at Dartmouth.

The years at Wisconsin had been a fullfilling and challenging time for both of us. I was proud of what I believed were substantial contributions to academic and political life and of the radical position that I had stuck to at some cost. In retrospect I would criticize my continued admiration of Soviet policies, but these were my firmly held beliefs, which Sally shared and fully backed. At a farewell dinner, attended by some 30 of my students, I was praised for my devotion to the Wisconsin ideal of progressive action for a better and more preaceful world.

NOTES

1. "The Rise of a Canadian Diplomatic Service," *Journal of Politics* 9, no. 2 (May 1947): 211-25; "Canada's Foreign Trade Service," *International Journal* (autumn 1947): 325-37; "The Canadian Diplomatic Service," *Public Affairs* 60, no. 1 (Dec. 1945): 23-37; "The Weapon of the Veto," *Public Affairs* 10, no. 2 (March 1947): 109-14; "A Chance for World Security," *Canadian Affairs* 2, no. 8 (May 1945).

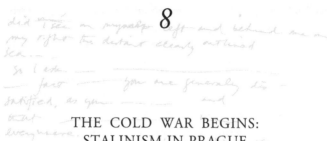

8

THE COLD WAR BEGINS: STALINISM IN PRAGUE

FOR THE NEXT TWELVE YEARS Hanover, New Hampshire, with its five thousand inhabitants and three thousand students, was to be our home base. Located on a plain high above the Connecticut River, Hanover was within a short distance of the hills of New Hampshire and Vermont, which were a riot of autumnal colour at the time of our arrival. We soon discovered, however, that there were rural slums as well as the picturesque New England postcard villages. White River, five miles away, was the nearest shopping centre and had the main railway station and airport. Our new apartment was in Dow House — a large, old mansion in a park-like setting, with a view across the Connecticut to the mountains.

The academic setting was very different from Wisconsin — Dartmouth was a liberal arts college that had no graduate students and small classes. The students were carefully selected — 650 in the freshmen year had been chosen from 6,000 applicants. My first impression was that the students were brighter and better-informed than our graduate students at Wisconsin. In effect I was a member of three departments — Government, International Relations, and later, Russian Civilization. We soon made friends within the college community: Dayton McKean, a specialist on political parties; Elmer Smead, an expert on government and business; Robert K. Carr, who had just completed a tour of duty as chief of staff of the (U.S.) President's Commission on Civic Rights; John Masland, a specialist on Japan; another colleague, Don Morrison, who had just become dean; and Arthur Wilson, a fellow Rhodes Scholar and professor of biography.

My chief assignment was to teach, together with John Masland, the course on world politics and to give my own course on international law and organization. I took the students in that course on what was to become an annual field trip to the United Nations. I was also expected to take part in a seminar of students specializing in international relations, which was devoted that year to the German peace treaty. It was conducted by a former Hungarian diplomat, John Pelényi, who had resigned from his post when the communists took over and was not in any sense a scholar. My task was to prepare a bibliography on the theme of the seminar; for this purpose I spent much of my time in the Baker Library, which allowed open access to the stacks. On the lower level were the colourful murals by the radical Mexican painter Orozsco.

A unique feature of the curriculum was a course called "Great Issues," which had been conceived by President Dickey as a means of acquainting graduating students with public issues and cultural questions through lectures by distinguished guests. It was required of all seniors — close to six hundred in all — and came to be resented by many students precisely because it was compulsory. During the first year I attended most of these lectures and thus heard the challenging views of speakers such as Dean Acheson, Robert MacIver, Archibald MacLeish, Lewis Mumford, Nelson Rockefeller (a graduate of Dartmouth), and Lester Pearson, Canada's minister of external affairs.

I did not teach Canadian government or continue with research on Canadian foreign relations. I turned down several job offers from Canada in 1947, including one from Dalhousie University, in Halifax, where I was offered the chair of political science, previously held by Professor R.A. MacKay. This was the long-hoped-for chance to return to Canada, but it would have required me to specialize in Canadian affairs. My refusal seemed to mark a choice between Canada and eastern Europe and to put an end to my idea of going back to my native land.

Because of my low rank and my foreign citizenship, I initially decided to avoid public espousal of unpopular causes. I was favourably inclined to Henry Wallace's campaign against current American foreign policy. I soon began to feel that I could not continue to lie low politically just for the sake of promotion. On a trip to Oberlin College in the spring of 1948, I shared the platform with Dean Acheson and Lewis Corey, a socialist from Antioch College, both of whom were strong defenders of the Marshall Plan and bitter critics of the Soviet Union and communism. I condemned the Marshall Plan as similar to the Truman Doctrine in using aid as a means of establishing American hegemony in Europe. I warned against the use of force to deal with the Soviet Union and urged a new attempt at compromise. In order to meet the challenge of the Soviet social system there must be profound social and economic changes at home to improve the appeal of the United States in the world. I came away greatly impressed by the atmosphere at Oberlin, especially the intense political interest and the liberal attitudes of the students. I began to look at Dartmouth through somewhat more critical eyes, and became slightly depressed by the political apathy of the students and the weakness of progressive thought among the faculty. I was alarmed at the administration's constant talk of economy and wondered what it might mean for my own salary and my promised promotion.

I resumed research into Czech history, starting with an article based on my thesis about the founding of Charles University in 1348. I also drafted a proposal for a course on eastern Europe. The course was eventually approved, and in the second semester of 1948-49, some 18 students enrolled. As early as Christmas 1947 I began to lay plans for a return to eastern Europe for the first time in nine years, although my enthusiasm had been somewhat dampened by events in Prague in February 1948. I distrusted the reports in the Western press, however, and wanted to go and see for myself what was happening.

This time we were resolved to go together and were fortunate to be able to arrange for Romie Koopman, a friend from Madison then living in New York, to come up to Hanover with her two children and look after David. At first the Social Science Research Council hesitated about giving me a grant in the light of the political changes in Czechoslovakia, but it finally awarded me $1,000, subject to my securing a visa and a passage. At the last moment I received a visa and a re-entry permit, and Sally got her passport and visa.

CZECHOSLOVAKIA, 1948

We had left Czechoslovakia under Nazi occupation and returned to it under Communist rule. The February coup in 1948 brought the Communists to power in Czechoslovakia and launched the country on a new Stalinist course. In spite of great changes in the Soviet Union after Stalin's death, Czechoslovakia maintained the Stalinist system more or less unchanged until well into the 1960s. I had an opportunity to observe it first-hand at three stages of development: the initial establishment of Communism in the summer of 1948; its consolidation into full-blown Stalinism in the summer of 1950; and its slow, systemic relaxation in the summer of 1958.

In June 1948 Sally and I travelled by sea from Montreal to Liverpool and then by air to Prague. A stay of two weeks in London gave us an opportunity to observe postwar England. We lived in our old digs, The Vinery Villas, and had a happy time visiting favorite places and seeing old friends. On the surface, apart from the bomb damage everywhere, little seemed to have altered. But the changes were both subtle and profound — the strain of years of warfare and bombing and the shabbiness of people and buildings were counterbalanced by improved living standards under the social security policies of the Labour government. We were struck by the vibrancy of parliamentary and academic life and of the press, and felt that Britain was more democratic than the United States. Labour was in power and prewar radicals, such as Sir Stafford Cripps and John Stachey, held high posts. My Oxford tutor, Lord Pakenham, was minister of civil aviation and a member of the House of Lords.

The School of Slavonic and East European Studies, now comfortably housed in the Senate building behind the British Museum, was under the direction of Philip Bolsover, former British diplomat in Moscow. R.R. Betts, successor to R.W. Seton-Watson in the Masaryk Chair of Central European history, had a balanced view of developments in Czechoslovakia. Doreen Warriner was warmly sympathetic to the moves toward planning in Central Europe. My old supervisor, Seton-Watson, now professor of Czechoslovak history at Oxford, looked old and ill, a shadow of his former self. He was highly critical of events in Czechoslovakia and believed that in 30 years the Russians would prove themselves to have been "arrant fools," for their action in February 1948. As for the death of Jan Masaryk, he had at first accepted the official verdict of suicide but came to believe it was more likely that he had been murdered. The school had no relations with the Soviet Union but had established summer schools and student exchanges with Czechoslovakia and Poland.

On July 4 we touched down at the Ruzyně airport nine years almost to the day since we left occupied Bohemia in 1939, and eleven years, also to the day, since my first arrival. Once again, we were welcomed by our old friends the Rudingers, and shared their apartment in Vinohrady, on the corner of Stalinova Avenue (which we had known as Fochova). Both Rudingers were still convinced Communists and expressed favourable, though often critical views of the political situation. Zdeněk was assistant general manager of the nationalized engineering industry, and Lisa worked with an international agricultural institute. Prague itself was almost undamaged by the war, but buildings were shabby from years of neglect. People looked pale and undernourished. Rations were meagre, and not many fruits or vegetables were available. Everywhere there were plaques, decorated with bouquets, in memory of those brave individuals who had fallen during the Prague uprising in May 1945. The Old Town Hall, where Sally and I were married, had been badly damaged but was under reconstruction. The statue of Woodrow Wilson in front of the Wilson station was gone. On the Malá Strana, opposite the Kinský Garden, a Soviet tank stood on a pedestal as a monument to the liberation of Prague.

By chance we witnessed two events similar to those that I had seen in 1937 and 1938 — the celebration of the birthday of Jan Hus and the Sokol Slet. In the Old Town Square, speakers, including Zdeněk Fierlinger, deputy premier, linked the ideals and traditions of Jan Hus with Czechoslovakia's "new democracy." The Slet preserved many of the features of the traditional Sokol gymnastic display. The Revolutionary Trade Union Movement made a dramatic presentation of "the defence of the achievements of the workers." On Army Day the stadium was filled with workers brought in from the factories, who remained in their seats during a deluge of rain and welcomed as a good omen a magnificent double rainbow. Prime Minister Klement Gottwald, standing in a box just above our seats, received a tremendous ovation. We were later told of anti-Communist demonstrations by Sokols, but we did not witness them.

The new rulers lost no opportunity to boast of the regime's achievements, to assert its links with past traditions, and to proclaim its close ties with its Soviet and other allies. A great Slavic Agricultural Exhibition, in the fairgrounds, presented the achievements of the Slavic countries and, incongruously, non-Slavic Romania. The huge Soviet display was dominated by an enormous sculpture of Lenin and Stalin. Another exhibition, "Vlastní silou" (By Our Own Strength), portrayed the achievements of Czechs and Slovaks through successive phases of their history.

We listened to similar boasts of achievment by high-ranking members of the regime. The former diplomat Zdeněk Fierlinger, a one-time Social Democrat who had favoured union of this party with the Communists and eventually joined the latter himself, described the February crisis as the result of efforts by reactionaries to establish a government without Communists. Both Edvard Beneš and Jan Masaryk, he asserted, had been sympathetic to the new regime, although the former had had some reservations. There would be no terror or violence, he declared, but there was a need for strict vigilance against foreign agents. On another occasion, a meeting of Czechoslovak-Soviet Friendship held in the Hvězda Castle, Zdeněk Nejedlý, historian and long-time Communist, currently minister of education, put the blame for the danger of war on American imperialism and on Czech and Slovak exiles abroad and declared that war would be avoided through the strength of the Soviet Union, Czechoslovakia's most reliable ally.

In private conversations our friends offered conflicting interpretations of everything. Some of my prewar friends, such as the Rudingers and Hanuš (Heinz) Frank, concurred with official views but criticized mistakes and weaknesses and admitted that the regime faced great difficulties. They endorsed the seizure of power in February as a victory for the workers, were critical of Beneš and his reluctant acceptance of the new regime, but regarded Jan Masaryk as a full supporter of it. In contrast, Antonín Paleček, my prewar colleague, still employed by Czechoslovak radio, and his wife, bitterly opposed the system and equated it with the Nazi regime. According to them the Jews dominated all spheres of life, and Jan Masaryk had been murdered. Zdeněk Prokop, with whom I had exchanged language lessons in 1937, was in the export-import business and was equally vituperative. So was our former landlady, Kadrnožková, who was still making corsets in her apartment in Žižkov. She dwelt on the horrors of the Soviet occupation and said that the regime was worse than that of Nazi Germany. She told of visits by the Gestapo who were searching for me after our departure in 1939.

My good friend Olga Haningerová's husband, Bošek, still held a position in the office of the prime minister. They both tried to be fair, acknowledging the good features of the regime but criticizing its defects. The nation, Bošek said, was divided into two camps, one looking for inspiration to American political democracy, the other to the Soviet Union. At the university, Josef Polišenský, a young historian, former Social Democrat, was reluctant to express his opinions openly. He minimized the changes at the university since February but seemed uncertain and worried about his own future and that of the university. There was no younger generation of historians, he lamented, to teach new courses and to handle the huge postwar influx of students.

My conversations with two of his distinguished senior colleagues, philosopher Dr J.B. Kozák, and literary scholar J.B. Čapek, both non-Marxist followers of Masaryk, seemed to confirm his assessment. Kozák said that personnel changes since February had been few and expressed regret that the British universities had refused to attend the anniversary of Charles university. (Seton-Watson also regretted the British decision and planned to publish a book of historical essays in the university's honour.) Čapek thought that the situation since February was not so bad and declared that he would continue to lecture in the spirit of Masaryk and Beneš. One student leader, a Communist, also minimized the purge of faculty and emphasized progressive changes; students were now represented on the faculty council, a body dealing with important matters such as appointments and promotions. These talks led me to conclude (quite wrongly, as events later showed), that there had been no wholesale purge and that the university remained a place of relative intellectual freedom.

Sally and I made an excursion by car to the villages of Lány and Lidice. In Lány we visited the peaceful little cemetery where Tomáš Masaryk, his wife Charlotte, and his son Jan shared a common grave in a large grass-covered plot, without gravestones, but marked with a large M. In sharp contrast was Lidice; in 1943, as a reprisal for the assassination of Reichsprotektor Reinhold Heydrich, the community had been razed to the ground and then buried under three feet of soil. The site was now being excavated, so the foundations and basements of the buildings could be seen. Where 173 men had been shot to death there stood a 30-foot wooden cross, formed by two rough tree trunks, with a wreath of barbed wire at the top, a Soviet memorial, moving in its simplicity. There was to be a park of remembrance, to serve as "an indictment of racism and the policy of appeasement." A new Lidice was to be built, with modern homes for the surviving widows who wished to return. We came on a brigade of young people, including some 40 Canadians, sweating away on the construction site. This solidarity in reconstruction counteracted the tragedy of the past and made Lidice seem a place of the future, a phoenix rising from the ashes. In one of the basements I picked up a rough chunk of fused glass as our own souvenir of the tragedy.

Sally and I made longer trips to the transformed, formerly German-speaking border areas of the so-called Sudetenland. The district around the resort town of Karlsbad, or Karlovy Vary, once 90 percent German-speaking, was now 99 percent Czech and Slovak as a result of the transfer of the Germans to Germany and settlement by Czechs and Slovaks. Former communists who had been refugees in England or inmates of concentration camps dominated local politics. Škrlant, district party secretary, and his wife, Barbara, a member of Parliament, whom we had met before the war in Kladno, had survived underground activity and years in prison. Our friend Hanuš Frank, a native of the city, had been one of the few Sudeten Germans permitted to return and was manager of the Grand Hotel Pupp, now the preserve of the few remnants of the Czech and Slovak bourgeoisie, Soviet officers and other foreign guests, and members of the emerging party elite. In Cheb, which I had visited in 1937 and 1938 when local Nazism was at its height, was now a town of 30,000, almost entirely Czech and Slovak, with only 700 Germans. The back streets were veritable slums. Czech settlers regarded their empty houses as unfit for human habitation. Many parts of the town, including the airfield, had been bombarded during the American advance in 1945 and were still in ruins. There were two monuments to the American First Army, and we could hear the radio blaring forth programs from the U.S. zone of occupation in West Germany a few miles away.

Bratislava, Slovakia, once trilingual, was now almost exclusively Slovak, with its German population gone and its Magyar minority greatly reduced. Most of the Jews had perished during the war. Above the city the old castle stood in ruins, as it had since the Napoleonic Wars. St Martin's Cathedral, once the coronation place of Hungarian kings and queens, was undamaged, and a well-attended service was in progress. The narrow streets of the old town seemed almost like slums, with a few dilapidated baroque palaces and the old synagogue in ruins. The statue of General Milan Štefánik, co-founder of the Czechoslovak state, still stood on the *quai* in Roosevelt Square. Across the river were the workers' suburbs of Petržalka, which could be reached only by a tiny ferry or the temporary pontoon bridge constructed by Soviet army engineers.

Other cities offered a pleasant contrast. Bat'ovany was a modern town of about 4,000 people, many of them young workers from the neighbouring countryside. It was modelled after the original Bat'a community in Zlín. In its factories the Communist pattern of strict regulation was superimposed on the traditional Bat'a discipline. The historic town Turčiansky Svätý Martin, now called simply Martin, was still the home of the Matica Slovenská, which performed its traditional role of fostering Slovak culture through research and publishing.

Back in Prague I continued my historical research, studying late-nineteenth century Czech politics again in the Klementinum Library. I also worked in the Historical Seminar in the Philosophical Faculty, to which I secured access, even when it was officially closed, through the good offices of my friend Polišenský. Thanks to him also, I was able to enter the Historical Seminar of the former German University (now forever closed) and could take some of the books that the Germans had confiscated. I took time out from my studies to prepare several broadcasts for the CBC — one on Cheb and the frontier districts, another on Lidice, a third on the May Revolution in Prague, and a fourth (which unfortunately was lost in transit) on Charles University since the war. In preparing the one on the May Revolution I visited scenes of the five days at the end of the war when Prague rose in revolt and tried to recapture the spirit of that brief moment of Czech heroism.

On 2 September 1948 came the death of former President Beneš, a dramatic event that symbolized the end of the democracy of Masaryk and the complete triumph of the Communists. The press paid tribute to the former president for the part he had played in the liberation in both wars, his struggle for peace, his resistance to Nazism between the wars, his recognition of the place of the Soviet Union during the war and afterward, his endorsement of the revolutionary changes since 1945, and finally "his acceptance of the will of the people" in 1948. For two days his body lay in state in the National Liberation Monument on the hill of Vítkov. The funeral ceremony took place in the Pantheon in the National Museum, with a brief address by Prime Minister Zápotocký, the reading of poems by Hora and Seifert, and the playing of Dvořák's New World Symphony and the Hussite chorale.

I was able to witness the procession from the window of a building on Václávské náměstí. The cortège moved slowly down the avenue — political dignitaries, churchmen, and professors in robes, soldiers, Sokols, and peasants in folk costumes. In front came the coffin on a gun-carriage, followed by Hana Benešová, on foot, in black mourning dress and veil, escorted by the president's brother, Vojta, from the United States. As the coffin passed, crying and sobbing were audible. In front of the crowds stood the workers' militia, ordinary workers in rough overalls, each with a rifle; they played a key role in the Communist takeover in February and were deployed now to prevent any possible demonstrations. The parade wound through city streets to the Square of National Heroes in Pankrác for a municipal ceremony and then by car to the Beneš residence in Sezimovo Ústí for burial.

Thus both the Communists and their opponents paid farewell to the second president. Each claimed his heritage, neither with full justice, since Beneš was neither a complete friend nor an open foe of the Communists. For me this seemed like a re-enactment of the funeral of Masaryk, which I had witnessed in 1937, and marked the symbolic termination of the democracy of Masaryk and Beneš and of the Czechoslovak Republic in its postwar form.

After my return to North America, in an article summarizing my impressions, I tried to preserve a certain ideological detachment. For some the 1948 events had represented a victory for democracy over the forces of reaction. For others, however, February ended the efforts to find a common ground for liberal democracy and communism within a single state, and marked the transformation of Czechoslovakia from a parliamentary, multi-party democracy into a people's democracy, in fact a thinly veiled Communist dictatorship.[1]

OUT OF STEP

When I returned to Dartmouth in October 1948 I found it difficult to adjust to this small New England college after the excitement and tension in central Europe. Dean Morrison, in a report to the American Association of University Professors (AAUP), envisaged only a slow process of faculty retirement that would keep the "dead wood" — i.e., professors who did no research and were often not even good teachers — around for some 15 years longer. The AAUP struck me as moribund, especially compared with the Wisconsin Teachers' Union; its officers seemed satisfied with the status quo and made no recommendations for improvement of salaries. The Faculty Council, to which I was elected in December, as a representative of the lower professorial ranks, did not inspire me with confidence.

Meanwhile, the atmosphere in the country as a whole was alarming as a result of growing anti-communist hysteria and the witch-hunt against communists in Hollywood, at the universities, and in government departments. This was promoted in particular by the U.S. House Committee on Un-American Activities and its investigations of alleged subversives. Richard Nixon (Rep.-Calif.), a member of the committee, lecturing in the Great Issues Course in January 1949, defended it as necessary and justified the loyalty purge in government departments and the need for legislation against the Communist party. Even Robert Carr, in a lecture prior to Nixon's visit, conceded the need for control of "subversives," although he warned of the threat to civil liberties involved. In my view the committee was being used as a weapon of thought control and to terrorize individuals for their beliefs.

This danger came closer to home when a bill was introduced into the New Hampshire legislature that would have forbidden the "teaching" of communist doctrine, required a loyalty oath by all teachers, and created a committee to conduct a probe of 'communistic' teaching at the University of New Hampshire. At a meeting in Dartmouth Hall, Rep. Hart justified his proposal in highly emotional terms (communists were "rats" and "termites") and seemed quite unaware of the dangers to academic freedom involved. Bob Carr spoke strongly against the bill, arguing that there was no real threat of communism in the state and that a loyalty oath and investigations were of doubtful value. Alas, the legislators passed the bill and established a committee under Attorney General Louis Wyman.

The situation in Canada, as I discovered during a visit to the Learned Societies in June 1949, offered a sharp contrast. There was no campaign against "reds" or investigations in the universities, and academic freedom seemed more secure. I was also interested to learn that Soviet studies were being encouraged at the universities of Toronto and British Columbia, both of which had received Carnegie grants to this end. As my own future did not seem to be assured in the United States, I began once again to think of a possible return to Canada.

Although my attitude toward the Soviet Union and communism was gradually changing, it continued to be quite out of harmony with the prevailing American consensus. The coup in Czechoslovakia had shaken my beliefs, but I rejected the outright condemnation of communism that was so common in Western political and academic circles. I still believed that there were certain aspects of democracy in the Soviet system, though hampered by the rigidity of the Marxist framework of analysis and by the party's control. The key to peace still lay in recognition of the equality of the two great powers and mutual concessions and in the granting of aid to the Soviet Union.

I was not convinced of the justification for the new North Atlantic Treaty, which did not, I believed, address the real problem. The expansion of Soviet influence in Czechoslovakia, for instance, had not been the result of armed attack, and there was little likelihood of such an action by the Soviet Union. When Lester Pearson visited the campus in January 1949 I was disturbed by his strongly anti-Soviet attitude and concluded that Canada did not have the will or the capacity to try to bridge the gap between Moscow and Washington. At CIIA meetings in Montreal in June 1948, I had been shocked that many speakers placed the emphasis almost entirely on preparations for a war against the Soviet Union.

By April 1949 I had more specific reasons for thinking of leaving Dartmouth. When, in January 1949, the department recommended my promotion, with two people opposed, this recommendation was turned down by the committee advising the president. It was not clear whether this was for financial reasons, for purported weaknesses in my teaching, or because of my politics, as evidenced by my speeches at Oberlin and on other occasions. President Dickey was becoming increasingly nervous about communists in colleges and universities and fearful of criticism by alumni.

Meanwhile, Don Morrison was becoming interested in developing Soviet studies and set up a committee to examine this move. At his request I drafted a plan for such a program, taking as a model the interdisciplinary studies of the Russian Institute at Columbia University. Discussions in the committee became bogged down in a conflict with Dmitri von Mohrenschildt, Professor of Russian Civilization and editor of the *Russian Review*, the only Russia specialist on the campus. His antipathy to the Soviet Union was so great that he was opposed to its serious study. For him Russian history had simply stopped with 1917 and would eventually be resumed after the fall of the Soviet regime. His chief supporter, ironically enough, was John Adams, a historian, who was equally anti-Soviet but considered Russian and Soviet history a seamless web of authoritarianism.

The committee eventually approved a partly historical, partly analytical orientation course, of which Dmitri would be chairman. It recommended only one new course in the social sciences, on Soviet foreign policy; a course on Soviet literature; and intensive Russian-language instruction. In a memorandum I was highly critical of this report and suggested the addition of a course on Soviet politics, which would include lectures on Marxism and economics. The final report offered a somewhat more balanced program, with courses to be given in Soviet politics (to be taught by me in place of my eastern European course) and on Soviet geography. I was surprised, in view of the inadequacies of the program, that Dartmouth received a three-year grant of $50,000 from the Carnegie Endowment. The funds were to be used for the appointment of a sociologist, for payment of a newly appointed lecturer in Russian, and for library books. In the end the post of sociologist was filled by René Fülop Müller, who was not a trained sociologist but had lived in the Soviet Union in the 1920s and published many books on subjects ranging from Rasputin to Dostoyevsky and Lenin. It was decided to send a young anthropologist, Elmer Harp, to Harvard for training in the Soviet field. When the program started in October 1951, it had only five majors, and they were joined by one senior.

I devoted most of my time during the summer of 1949 to the revision of my thesis and also worked on the Russian language. We took frequent breaks for swimming and for picnics and walks in the countryside. But the big event of the summer was the birth, on 8 August, of our second son, Peter Conard, as we named him. He was born at three p.m., after a long wait the previous night. Sally was at first seriously ill, but she recovered and rapidly regained her strength. Although Peter was able to breast-feed for three months, Sally had to give this up when she developed an infection. My sister-in-law, Jeanne, came down to help us for several weeks. David, who was by then almost two and a half, seemed to accept his new brother easily.

MANHATTAN, 1949-50

Don Morrison had talked to me more than once about becoming the college's authority on the Soviet Union and urged me to apply for a senior fellowship at the Russian Institute at Columbia University. I was tempted but did not want such an appointment to interfere with my research on eastern Europe. Following an exploratory trip to New York after Christmas I concluded that if I were to go down to Columbia I would do research in politics, preferably under the supervision of John Hazard, whose unbiased approach attracted me. A chance meeting with my old mentor Sir Bernard Pares elicited from him advice to stick with Czechoslovakia and to specialize on Czech-Russian relations. When an offer of a senior fellowship arrived, it was impossible for me to decline such a wonderful opportunity, which would facilitate a transition into the Soviet field while retaining my primary focus on Czechoslovakia.

My fellowship at Columbia, originally for one year, was extended a further semester and allowed me to devote my time to study and research without teaching duties. During the first semester I attended the lectures of a distinguished team, all American-born, who had worked in U.S. government departments during the war years. I was soon convinced that I had made the right choice of John Hazard, who was warm and friendly and a stimulating supervisor. A lawyer and political scientist, he had studied law in the Soviet Union in the 1930s and worked with U.S. Lend-Lease during the war. His lectures on tsarist law and government, Soviet political institutions, and public administration were models of the art of lecturing. I found another kindred spirit in Ernest Simmons, specialist in Russian literature, who at Dartmouth had given a fair and unbiased lecture on the Soviet concept of democracy. His courses on Russian and Soviet literature were enlightening. Geroid Robinson, historian and director, had studied in the Soviet Union in the 1920s and had conceived the idea of the institute as early as 1943. His lectures were dull and traditional and revealed a complete lack of sympathy for the system. He was succeeded as director by Philip Mosely, distinguished specialist on eastern European history, who had played an important role as U.S. government adviser in wartime and postwar diplomacy. His lectures were rambling and uninspiring, and his attitude to the Soviet Union was extremely hostile. Abram Bergson, an economist, had never been in the Soviet Union, but his analysis of the Soviet economy was precise and objective. A series of special lectures on Marxism by the philosopher Herbert Marcuse filled in a serious gap in the institute's offerings. In my study of the Russian language, I found immensely valuable a course on Russian translation given by Leo Gruliow, editor of the *Current Digest of the Soviet Press*. Other senior fellows included three distinguished historians — Cyril Black, of Princeton; Bob Byrnes, of Indiana; and Oliver Radkey, of Oklahoma. There was also Bertram Wolfe, well-known writer on Marx, Lenin, and Stalin and on the Soviet Union. A one-time Communist party member, he was bitterly hostile to the Soviet Union. At a dinner of the fellows we clashed when he asserted that war with the Soviet Union was inevitable.

During the second semester I attended fewer lectures and concentrated on research and writing. By the time I left New York I had completed several articles on the Soviet and eastern European theories of people's democracies. One, prepared at the request of John Hazard, was published in the *American Slavic and East European Review*, of which he was editor. I embarked on a comparative study of Soviet and Czechoslovak Communist institutions and published an article on this in the *Political Science Quarterly*.[2] A more general analysis of Soviet influences in Czechoslovakia in the two years of communist rule appeared in the Canadian *International Journal*.[3]

Our apartment on Riverside Drive was shaped like a railway car, with three bedrooms. It was only a few steps away from the park on the high banks of the Hudson, where we enjoyed many walks and picnics. We went to plays, movies, concerts, and dance performances, and Lynn Turgeon and Jack Hardt, two Russian Institute graduate students who lived in an adjacent apartment, frequently babysat the boys. New York was a crossroads, so that we had many reunions with old friends of Sally's days at Barnard and at the Millbank and other friends from our times in Wisconsin, Oxford, and London, including Ian Milner, and Harold Taylor. We were happy to see our Prague friends Otakar Odložilik, now an exile teaching at Columbia, and Chitra, the Rudingers' daughter, who had married an American professor and was living in the Midwest. We had visits from my parents, on their way to and from Florida, as well as from Andy and his wife, Jeanne. Once in a while Sally's parents and her sister, Tacy, and her children, came over for a day or two, and we spent Christmases with them in Norristown.

I managed to do some preliminary research in Manhattan on the theme of Czechoslovakia under Communist rule, an inroad I hoped would lead to a book under the auspices of the Russian Institute. I explored the Library of Congress, the New York Public Library, and the Columbia Library and interviewed a number of exiled Czech political leaders, including Vladimír Bušek and Hubert Ripka (National Socialists), Štefan Kočvara (Slovak Democrat), and Ivo Ducháček and Adolf Procházka (People's party). These conversations did not prove very fruitful, and it was clear that further academic progress would have to await my next trip to Prague. This time, unfortunately, it was too expensive for Sally to come with me, and the children were too small to travel so far. In May 1950 I sailed on the Polish ship the *Batory*, via Copenhagen and Gdynia.

CZECHOSLOVAKIA, 1950

My second visit to Prague took place under the less favourable conditions produced by the consolidation of Communist power, the quickening pace of communization and the introduction of full-blown Stalinist practices and values. Still more disturbing was the ever-increasing international tension after the outbreak of war in Korea in late June. This time I approached Czechoslovakia by way of Poland. I was unable to secure more than a three day transit visa and thus had only a glimps of the terrible destruction and the initial reconstruction of Gdansk (formerly Danzig), and Warsaw.

An overnight trip from Warsaw took me to the Czech border early in the morning, just minutes before the expiry of my visa. We crossed at the railway junction of Bohumín, where Polish and Czech border officers did not examine my bags, although each counted my foreign currency. I was at once made aware of the political atmosphere by the banner headlines in the Czech and Slovak newspapers, announcing the end of the Slovak party congress and the opening of a show trial in

Prague. The pages were filled with abusive, anti-Western statements by party leraders and with the charges against the accused. Every railway station was decorated with posters, slogans, and pictures of Gottwald and Stalin.

In Prague I stayed at the Flora, a modern but simple hotel on Stalinova Avenue, near the Olšany cemetery and almost across the street from my friends the Rudingers. I had a comfortable room where I could study in the morning. One night, at three a.m., two men in civilian clothes came without warning to check my passport and my currency exchange certificate. They found everything in order and left with apologies. It was difficult to contact scholars and others in the new atmosphere of international conflict, but living conditions in Prague appeared better in 1950 than they had in 1948. More food was available in stores and restaurants, and many things were no longer rationed. Meat and butter could still be bought only with coupons, and prices were often high. People looked better dressed and better shod. In striking contrast to Warsaw was the almost complete absence of destruction, and hence of construction, in central Prague. The renovation of the Old Town Hall had been completed; the marriage room was more simply decorated than in 1948. Retail trade was nationalized, and each store bore the name of the enterprise above the entrance — for example Zdar (shoes) and Pramen (groceries). Bookstores were everywhere, not only for Czech books, but also for books and arts and crafts from Slovakia and from Poland, Hungary, and other people's democracies. A palatial Soviet bookstore looked more like a library. In the windows of what used to be the American information office was a display of the horrors of the American way of life — strikes, lines of unemployed, blacks being beaten, and so on.

I set to work at once on my research, this time on a new topic — the emerging Communist system of rule, as mirrored in the new constitution and in the hegemony of a single party. With Polišenský's help I was able within several days to arrange a meeting with Professor Vladimír Procházka, vice-chairman of the National Assembly, who had been chairman of the Constitutional Committee that drafted the new fundamental law. Although he promised me access to some of the unpublished materials from the committee discussions prior to February, in the end I had to content myself with published materials only. He was never available again — he was always reported to be busy or ill! Promised interviews with other officials and with the national committees did not materialize. Within those limits I made satisfactory progress with my research in the Klementinum and in the Municipal Library, and I searched in the *antikvariats* for books that I needed.

The difficulties encountered when I tried to extend my visa for a few days gave me an instructive lesson in the ways of the new democracy. I was sent back and forth between the ministries of Foreign Affairs, Information, Education, and National Security, with each passing the buck to the other. After days of persistent effort, and after my original visa had expired, I finally got an extension at the district National Committee. I spent many hours changing my travel arrangements, which necessitated at least two trips to the National Bank. I had squandered the better part of a week on these struggles with the new bureaucracy.

Even more revealing was the political show trial that lasted for a week in the Pankrác courthouse. The daily proceedings were fully summarized after the evening news and in greater detail in the press. Charges of treason and espionage had been laid against a number of prominent non-Communists, including Miláda Horáková, a leading National Socialist; Z. Kalandra, an avante-garde writer, and former communist, later a Trotskyite; Professor Zdeněk Peška, an expert on constitutional law; several leading social democrats; and some former businessmen and high officials. The chief prosecutor, Col. Viest, a Slovak, gave a damning indictment of the prisoners, who were accused of seeking, through war and with outside help, the destruction of the people's democracy and the restoration of capitalism. All had confessed their misdeeds, but none received any leniency in return. The verdict — at ten one night — was the death sentence for four of the accused and long prison terms for the others.

A month later I had an even more shocking experience — listening to a report on the trial by Col. Viest to a mass open-air meeting in Stromovka Park. Viest, a young man in uniform, spoke for an hour and three quarters, summing up the evidence of the trial; he pointed out the treachery of the émigrés and their willingness to wage war, the baseness of the West and its diplomats and journalists, and the need for caution and vigilance (*bdělost a ostražitost*). The audience, predominantly proletarian, applauded repeatedly. Shortly after this macabre meeting the appeals of the condemned were rejected, and the four were immediately executed. During my stay a militant campaign was mounted in support of the Stockholm resolution calling for a ban on the atomic bomb and the destruction of all stockpiles. A grotesque feature of this peace crusade was a campaign against the potato bugs, or Colorado beetles, allegedly dropped in the frontier regions by American planes, and the mobilization of volunteers to fight this pest.

Equally frightening was the campaign against the United States after the outbreak of war in Korea. The mass media took up the cause of North Korea as a struggle for national freedom and unification, comparable to the U.S. Civil War, with the American intervention equated with the British support for the Confederacy in the 1860s. In the factories and in the mountain villages of northern Bohemia through which I passed during a holiday weekend, there were posters in support of North Korea. People in the Prague factories, we were told, were working at high speed and under great stress. I myself doubted that war would come unless the Soviet Union intervened directly in Korea, and I thought this unlikely. I was concerned about the warlike mood in the United States, about which Sally wrote, and the mobilization of American military and economic resources for possible war. On my last day in Prague I visited the Czechoslovak Parliament and listened to a statement on "the aggression" in Korea by "my professor," Procházka. Since the Czechoslovak and Soviet press concealed and distorted the real situation, I tried to get a clearer picture by reading the British *Daily Worker*. It was only in Trieste and Venice, on my way home, that my careful reading of *The Times* and the European edition of the *Herald Tribune* made me aware of the full seriousness of the crisis.

Another striking feature of the Prague atmosphere was the adulation of the Soviet Union and the constant stream of propaganda and information about the Soviet pattern of life and politics. An extraordinary example of this was a meeting in the Philosophical Faculty of Charles University devoted to Stalin's statement on linguistics. Before a capacity audience of students and professors, Gustav Bareš, member of the Central Committee and party secretary (and my former Czech instructor!), spoke for two hours on the epochal significance of the article not only for philology and language, but for scholarship in general. The slogan enunciated by Gottwald "The Soviety Union our Model," was obviously being taken seriously.

Every possible institution and medium was used to extol Communism and its objectives. The Congress of Youth celebrated the creation of the Czech League of Youth (ČSM) and its attainment of one million members. Emblazoned on banners all over town were slogans such as "A Million Members of the ČSM — A Million Builders of Socialism," or "The Komsomols — Our Model." The delegates, some two thousand in number, cheered every mention of Stalin or Gottwald and chanted "We are the New Youth, We are the Gottwald Youth." The climax was a parade through the city that lasted three hours and carried huge pictures of Stalin, Gottwald, Široký, Slánský, and Zápotocký, not to mention Marx, Engels, and Lenin. The marchers chanted slogans of all kinds — "We Are for Peace — Produce More and Better Goods" and "Long Live the Soviet Union and the Red Army." It was announced that a new children's organization was to be named the Pioneers, on the Soviet model, and would serve as an instrument of the Communist party in mobilizing young people for greater production and the defence of peace.

Coupled with this worship of the Soviet Union was the teaching of the official ideology. In an old palace on Celetná ulice there was a study and consultation centre of Marxist-Leninism. Bright, clean, and well-furnished, the main reading room had walls decorated with the usual portraits of Lenin, Stalin, and Gottwald, Marx and Engels, alongside Stalin's slogan: "Theory becomes useless unless joined with revolutionary practice." The Higher School of Political and Social Science, located in another fine palace on the Malá Strana, served to train journalists, public servants, and party functionaries in Marxist politics and economics.

After pressing hard for permission I was allowed to attend several sessions of the National Assembly. It was located in a modern building between the Municipal Theatre and the museum and represented, it was jokingly said, a combination of the two. The parliamentary chamber was square and lofty; behind a raised tribune for government members was a huge replica of the Bohemian lion, the state's symbol, in its new form, without crown or cross. The main subjects on the agenda were the new criminal and penal administration codes and the draft law on nationalized industry. The proceedings were cut and dried and bore no resemblance to a genuine parliament. Little did I realize that the new criminal codes were those under which the later trials of the 1950s were to be conducted. The men on the tribune were to be the agents of these judicial murders, and one of them, Ladislav Kopřiva, the minister of national security, a victim of this travesty of justice.

None the less there remained at least some vestiges of Czechoslovakia's past traditions. The name of Masaryk was still used to designate the main railway station and an embankment on the Vltava. In the Hall of Fame of the National Museum stood statues of Masaryk and Beneš and of other great Czechs and Slovaks. There was a special exhibit devoted to the seventeenth century Czech pedagogue and exile Jan Amos Komenský. In the Masaryk Chata (chalet), where I spent the holiday weekend, there were pictures of Tyrš and Fügner, founders of the Sokol movement, as well as (of course), Gottwald. The anniversary of Jan Hus was celebrated on a hilltop by women in Sokol costume in an old-fashioned, traditional ceremony without contemporary political allusions.

Finally, on July 13, my work done, I departed from Prague and went by air, via Vienna, to Trieste, under allied occupation. I had no trouble with my exit from Czechoslovakia although I carried with me many books (including some that were forbidden) and my notes and research materials, all buried deep at the bottom of one of my bags. I spent a week travelling by steamer on the Dalmatian coast, and used the days remaining for a trip to Florence, Rome and Naples. Leaving Naples on the *Saturnia* on August 4, I completed my circular voyage to Europe by sailing through the Mediterranean and passing through the Straits of Gibraltar. During the trip I had something of a shipboard romance with Claire Fontaine, a young American woman from Bronxville, NY, where she ran a flower shop; for some years thereafter we enjoyed the occasional rendezvous in New York and New England.

After this second visit to Prague I realized more clearly how fundamental were the changes which had taken place in Czechoslovakia. Whatever the differences between the forms and principles of the Soviet and the Czechoslovak systems, there was clearly an essential identity, derived from the dominant position of the Communist Party and its control of all institutions of government. It was impossible, however, to tell whether in the long run the present pattern would become permanent and what form communism would take in Czechoslovakia 30 years hence.[4]

NOTES

1. See "Journey to Prague, 1948," *Kosmas* 5, no. 1 (1986): 139-56. See also *International Journal* 4, no. 2 (spring 1949): 119-36. I also published a pamphlet for the CIIA's *Behind the Headlines* series, entitled "Eastern Europe in Flux," 19, no. 4 (Sept. 1949).

2. "People's Democracy, the Proletarian Dictatorship and the Czechoslovak Path to Socialism," *American Slavic and East European Review* 110, no. 2 (April 1951): 100-16,

3. "The Czechoslovak Constitutional System: The Soviet Impact," *Political Science Quarterly* 67, no. 2 (June 1952): 198-224;

"Czechoslovakia: The Soviet Impact," *International Journal* 6, no. 2 (spring 1951): 109-17; "The Soviet Impact on the Czechoslovak Legal Revolution," *Soviet Studies* 6, no. 4 (April 1955): 361-81; "Czechoslovakia: Government in Communist Hands," *The Journal of Politics* 17, no. 3 (Aug. 1955): 424-47; "The Formation of a Communist Party in Czechoslovakia," *American Slavic and East European Review* 14, no. 3 (Oct. 1955): 346-58.

4. See "Journey to Prague, 1950," *Kosmas* 6, no. 1 (summer 1987): 127-43.

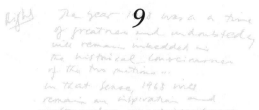

9

THE COLD WAR DEEPENS: McCARTHYISM IN THE U.S.

IN CZECHOSLOVAKIA I HAD BEEN SHOCKED by the severe political repression and the rapid communization of all institutions on the Soviet model. But I did not feel any more kindly to Western capitalism as an alternative or to U.S. policies toward the Soviet Union. I was driven more and more to a position in the middle, which became increasingly difficult to occupy as the world situation deteriorated. Back in New York I faced the question of what we should do for the balance of 1950. There were various job possibilities, such as the post at the UN offered me by John Humphrey, work at the institute in an eventual army training program, appointment as CBC commentator at the UN, and a teaching assignment at Sarah Lawrence with Hal Taylor. In the end none of these materialized, and when my fellowship at Columbia ended, we returned to Hanover in February 1951. Just before going back I learned that my department had unanimously recommended me for promotion to full professor, with a $600 increase in annual salary. The chairman, Dayton McKean, told me that it had been strongly supported by my Columbia colleagues Ernest Simmons and John Hazard. In April I received the appointment. In May 1952, at a private ceremony in the president's office, I was surprised to be presented, along with five other colleagues, with an MA from Dartmouth. This was granted to all full professors who were not graduates of Dartmouth. Thus was I admitted to the Dartmouth fellowship!

I had a relatively light teaching load in 1951 and was able to press ahead with my book on Czechoslovak Communism. I had a study on the tenth floor of Baker Library, where I could work without interruption. I made the occasional trip to Cambridge and to New York and Washington for research. In February 1951 I gave a lecture in Great Issues on the "Eastern European Revolution," in what I thought was a balanced fashion — to my delight, I was congratulated by John Dickey.

In Russian Civilization, of which I was now a member, departmental meetings were the scene of constant battles; these, to my surprise brought me together with John Adams in an effort to prevent Dmitri's domination. The orientation course, an uncoordinated series of lectures given by members of the department though usually by von Mohrenschildt, had an enrolment of 72 students. In a final symposium we engaged in a battle royal. As often happened, the extreme hostility to the Soviet Union by the other participants provoked me into presenting the Soviet viewpoint more strongly than I really believed.

I began to have doubts about the situation in the college as a whole. When the Reserve Officers Training Corps (ROTC) was introduced, it had a marked effect on the tone of the college and on the curriculum. One thousand students registered in the ROTC, which saved them from the military draft, and the college from financial collapse. I felt that the army program, though taught by officers, was of low quality, and I opposed participation in it by civilian professors. In October 1950, at one particular faculty meeting, President Dickey espoused a distinctly grim vision for future education and academic freedom.

Happily, just before my leaving Columbia John Hazard had broached the surprising and exciting idea that I return for a semester in 1952-53 to replace him while he went on sabbatical. In July 1951 I accepted an offer from the Russian Institute to take over his duties for a semester. The salary was to be relatively high — $9,000 per year, of which $1,500 would be tax-exempt moving expenditures. Dartmouth was willing to grant me a further leave of absence, so we moved back to New York in the autumn of 1952 and returned to Hanover in early 1953.

We lived at the Hazards' brownstone mansion on East 94th Street, acting as house sitters during their absence and paying a nominal monthly rent of $100. Central Park was close at hand and a great place for walks. Sally had no easy task in looking after this five-storey house and caring for two lively boys. Our friend John Hardt (later chief economist at the U.S. Library of Congress) lived in, so that we were able to go out often in the evenings, using the Hazards' subscription tickets to the symphony and theatre. We had occasional dinner parties in the almost-baronial splendour of the Hazards' dining-room. During our year in New York we celebrated the 15th anniversary of our marriage and Sally's 40th birthday. My parents, who were both in their eighties, visited us twice and on one occasion were joined by the Brights, so that all four grandparents and the four grandchildren were together.

At the university I occupied Hazard's spacious top-floor office in the old building on 112th Street. I taught Hazard's course on Soviet political institutions, with an enrolment of about 60 students, and a course of my own on the Soviet Union and eastern Europe — the first given at Columbia. Although it met at eight a.m. on Saturdays, 45 students attended. I also conducted a seminar, with 13 students, devoted to Marxist and Leninist theories of state, law, and revolution. Although I was becoming more critical of the Soviet system, I tried to avoid polemics despite the prevailing spirit of the Cold War. It was difficult, however, to occupy a middle ground on controversial issues, and I was accused of lack of objectivity by a student of Latvian origin. Even more disturbing, back at Dartmouth Don Morrison told me that unidentified colleagues at the Russian Institute had said that, in my effort to be objective, I had leaned over backward to avoid criticizing the Soviet Union. This hurtful news was balanced to some degree by praise from graduate students and from John Hazard, who talked of my coming back for a repeat performance in 1958.

Sally and I watched the 1952 American election campaign on a rented TV set. General Dwight Eisenhower, we thought, was better than his Republican rivals for the presidential nomination but was likely to fall under the influence of the more reactionary General Douglas MacArthur and Senator Robert Taft. The Democratic nominee Adlai Stevenson represented a continuation of the New Deal in a moderate form. Neither candidate, we were sure, would bring about a marked change in foreign policy. The final result was depressing; the defeat of Stevenson, an intelligent and able man waging an enlightened campaign, and the victory of a war hero represented for us a triumph of reaction. It opened a new era in American politics that boded ill for the United States and the world.

DARTMOUTH, 1953-56

Back in Hanover, we rented a comfortable small college house on South Balch Street. Hanover was an almost idyllic environment for the two boys, who began school in September 1954. During summer we had swimming, excursions, and picnics, and for me there was tennis and even some mountain climbing. During the severe winters, comparable only to Winnipeg or Moscow, the boys and I did a good deal of skating and skiing. At an early age the boys took lessons in the Ford-Sayre ski program, and I participated in it as a volunteer instructor, with guidance from a professional skimaster. With our neighbour John Stewart, professor of English, and his wife, Joanne, we formed a chamber music group, the Corbett Society, which played regularly in each other's homes. In February 1953 we traded in our '39 Ford (the "Blunder bus," as we called it), for a 1949 model, at a net cost of $950. We enjoyed many an excursion in neighbouring Vermont, several holidays on the coast at Cape Ann, and one on Nantucket. In June 1954 we took a trip to Tacy and Tom's farm in Oaks, Pennsylvania, and attended the annual reunion of the Conard family. Later that year came the tragic news of the death of my mother, who had meant much to me and had been such a strong and kindly influence in my life.

The Hanover and Dartmouth scene had changed somewhat for the better. The annual town meeting and meetings of the school board were filled with emotional argument about the building of a new high school. Sally was elected a member of the finance committee and was active in the League of Women Voters. The faculty meetings were also scenes of stormy debate over proposed curriculum reforms. Our own department had been rejuvenated by the appointment of younger men of scholarly bent.

As always, the Russian civilization program caused me much grief. In May 1953 Dean Morrison told me that I was reported to be less than balanced in my treatment of the Soviet Union in my courses. My chapter on Soviet government and politics, in a book based on lectures in the Department of Russian Civilization's orientation course, was severely criticized, and later the book as a whole was turned down. Worse still, when I finally submitted the manuscript of my own book on Czechoslovak communism to the Russian Institute, I was asked to cut the manuscript from 500 to 350 pages. Having accomplished this task, the book then lay on Philip Mosely's desk for many months until the final negative verdict in March 1956. I had attempted to write objectively, with the balance of an E.H. Carr or a John Hazard, but came into conflict with the emotionally charged atmosphere of the Cold War. It was a crushing blow. Some of the chapters were later published as articles in major journals.

During the summer of 1955 I took a job at summer school at the University of Vermont. For the first few weeks I commuted from Hanover each week, driving north to Burlington early Monday morning. Later the family joined me in a rented cottage on Grand Isle, on Lake Champlain — a delightful spot, where we could swim and fish and enjoy something of a holiday. My teaching was in world politics and international administration. Disappointingly, only four students registered for the first course, and two for the second. I supplemented my light teaching load by chairing a special public seminar under the auspices of the Warren Austen Institute in International Understanding, which offered a series of lectures by outstanding public and academic figures.

I continued my annual field trips to the UN and spoke often on the UN around the state, including at the governor's conference celebrating United Nations Day in Concord. Sally had her turn to go to the UN, escorting two high school students who had won an essay contest. A seminar organized by the Woodrow Wilson Foundation on the UN took me to New York four times during the winter of 1954-55. On the basis of reports by experts we discussed specific case studies of UN activity, including the administrative aspects of technical assistance, the admission of China to the UN (favoured by most participants), the right of nationalization, and the problems of Somali independence.

In early 1954, I joined a group sponsored by the World Federalists to discuss revision of the UN Charter. This was headed by Dave Bradley, my neighbour and friend, an Olympic skier during his undergraduate days at Dartmouth, who had written an excellent book on the atomic danger, *No Place to Hide*. Our discussion centred on Grenville Clark's plan for total disarmament and a federal world government. In the end we concluded that world federation was not feasible but that there should be some revision of the Charter in regard to the veto and membership of the Security Council.

Another conference of interest was a New England seminar on the Soviet Union held at Tuft College, in Medford, Massachusetts; a number of leading Soviet specialists, including Merle Fainsod of Harvard, Henry Shapiro, long-time United Press correspondent in Moscow, and Robert Tucker, just back from nine years in Moscow, with his Russian wife, took part. I also met Fred Barghoorn, of Yale; George Fischer of Brandeis; and Marshall Shulman, new head of the Harvard Russian Research Centre.

In 1956 we decided to build our own house — a move made financially feasible by a substantial increase in salary, my pay for summer teaching, a college mortgage covering 90 percent of the price of the lot, and a small loan from the college to cover the balance. We were fortunate to secure from the college, at a moderate price ($1,300), a large lot on the hillside on Kingsford Road. Over an acre in extent, it included many large trees and flowering bushes, and two stream beds, which became raging torrents in spring. We put up a prefabricated Techbilt house, a split-level structure of modern design, with large windows on all sides. We sited the house so that it would have solar heat from a southern exposure and a screen of trees to give maximum privacy. It was a great thrill when workers first broke ground and when, at eight-thirty a.m. on 29 May, the house arrived on a huge truck from Concord, Massachusetts. In September we moved in and discovered that our lot was a bird's paradise; Sally revelled in identifying the birds and spotted grouse and pheasants.

Alas, just before leaving for a second summer session at Vermont, I was diagnosed as having cancer and was operated on for a colostomy at the Mary Hitchcock Memorial Hospital in Hanover. Thanks to immediate action, and excellent surgery, I survived and, at age 44, lived to continue a full "second" life, marred only by certain serious and continuing after-effects. I had a long convalescence through the summer and autumn and had a reduced teaching load.

Hysteria concerning so-called subversives was sweeping the country. Senator Joseph McCarthy (Rep.-Wisc.) was waging an unrelenting campaign against such imagined agents in the U.S. State Department and other government agencies. The witch-hunt even extended to the United Nations, where communists, or those who pleaded the Fifth Amendment (refusing to testify on the grounds of possible self-incrimination), were dismissed — a policy that drew biting criticism from other member countries. A similar search for subversives was already underway in New Hampshire through a committee headed by Attorney General Wyman. President Dickey was obsessed with the danger of communism; although he proclaimed his belief in the free marketplace of ideas, he vitiated this by excluding communists from it. He denied the right of anyone to plead the privilege of the Fifth Amendment, except to refuse to incriminate another person. Otherwise, he argued, this would be tantamount to evidence of Communist party membership and would necessitate dismissal. Thus an individual who was called before the committee had to face the dilemma of incriminating himself or herself either by answering questions or by refusing to answer and could expect no help from the administration.

In May 1952 our AAUP local had taken a very weak stand on this issue, declining to denounce the congressional investigation. In October 1954, however, it set up four committees — on faculty participation in governance, curriculum, salaries, and, at my suggestion, academic freedom. Chaired by John Finch, of the English Department, the last committee presented to the faculty a report on academic freedom and a longer report opposing the continuance of the Wyman Committee. Four of us, headed by Finch, went down to Concord to present these findings to the state's House Appropriations Committee. We described the investigations as a threat to academic freedom and a waste of taxpayers' money, as there was no danger of subversion in New Hampshire. We also presented our report to the state's Senate Judiciary Committee, but to no avail — the Wyman Committee continued its destructive work.

In October 1955 it was a surprise and a shock for me to become a victim of this system. Without warning, I was visited by an agent of the U.S. Immigration Service, who interrogated me for more than two hours. I admitted that I had been briefly a member of the Communist party of Great Britain and that I had been associated in Wisconsin with the Student Liberal Association, American Youth for Democracy, and the Council of Soviet-American Friendship. I saw no reason why these early associations should cause problems ten or fifteen years later. But in April 1956 I received a subpoena to appear before the Wyman Committee in Concord. Provost Morrison called me in to inform me that the college was cooperating with what it regarded as a legitimate undertaking and would offer me no legal counsel. He himself showed no sympathy whatsoever with my predicament. I learned shortly thereafter from another investigator that I could come voluntarily, but if I came under subpoena my expenses would be paid. I chose the latter course, and he slipped me an envelope with $8 in expense money. He gave me a copy of the rules of procedure of the hearing — it would be an executive, or closed meeting, but the state's attorney general could publish the transcript at his discretion. He also warned me that information obtained might be transmitted to federal agencies. On the advice of a young lawyer, Joe Ransmeier, a former colleague at Dartmouth, I decided to cooperate with the investigation.

In April, Sally and I drove down to Concord for what turned out to be a short and rather perfunctory appearance before the committee. The attorney general, who presided, seemed to be on the defensive, perhaps because of a U.S. Supreme Court decision, announced in that morning's newspaper, which invalidated state sedition laws, and hence presumably the New Hampshire statute. At the hearing I admitted once again my membership in the British Communist party between November 1937 and April 1938, but denied membership in its American counterpart at any time. When Wyman later left the chair and talked to me privately, I told him that these matters could be dealt with best by established federal and state authorities and did not require special committees of investigation. I came away angered at this invasion of my right to privacy but also certain that the whole thing had been a tempest in a teapot.

How wrong I was! In the autumn of 1956, just after we had moved into our new house and while I was still recovering from my operation, we were notified by the U.S. Department of Justice that my permanent immigration visa, the so-called green card, had been cancelled, presumably on the basis of information provided by the Wyman committee. The reason given: that in returning from my mother's funeral in late 1954, I had crossed the border "illegally"! According to the federal McCarran-Walter Act, no one who had been a member of a subversive organization was permitted to enter the United States. This was in my opinion a travesty of justice, since my affiliation had been years earlier and I was not a member of the Communist party or any so-called subversive organization at this time.

We faced, however, the prospect of my having to give up my post at Dartmouth and leave the country at short notice. I sought advice from the Canadian embassy in Washington and from Judge McLane, a liberal-minded lawyer and member of the Dartmouth College Board of Trustees, who belonged to the progressive wing of the New Hampshire Republican party. McLane learned from Rep. Perkins Bass, also a liberal New Hampshire Republican, in Washington, that I could seek a new green card while remaining in the country. I decided that the wisest policy was to apply for another immigration visa. Under the McCarran-Walter Act, however, I was required to provide evidence not merely that I was not a communist or a sympathizer but that I opposed communism. I had to submit an affidavit of my own to this effect and similar affidavits from other persons.

There followed a trying time during which I was unable to leave the country, even to attend the funeral of my brother Andy, who died in 1958. I consulted frequently with McLane and Bass; with President Dickey; with friends such as Alex Brady, Merle Curti, John Hazard, and Harold Taylor; and with colleagues at Dartmouth. Six of the latter — Elmer Smead and Arthur Wilson, Jack Gazley, Jim Cusick, Charlotte Morrison, with whom I had been associated in United Nations activities, and Dave Bradley, now a member of the state legislature — were ready to prepare the necessary documents. They praised my service to education and the community and documented my "anti-communist" views by citing my scholarly publications on Czechoslovakia and the Soviet Union. Some others disappointed me by failing to write letters of support. At last, in June 1958, nine months after my application, I received the welcome news that I had been granted a new visa, and one month later I journeyed to Toronto to pick it up. The ordeal was over, and I could continue my career in the United States.

In spite of these personal crises I decided to carry out my plan of visiting the Soviet Union, for which I had already received a grant from the newly formed University Committee on Travel Grants, headed by Professor Robert Byrnes of Indiana University. This program facilitated month-long visits to the USSR by specialists who had had no previous chance to travel in the Soviet Union. It gave me some satisfaction, in August and September 1958, to "thumb my nose" at the Wyman Committee and the U.S. Department of Justice by travelling to the country of which I was considered an agent. It was exciting to visit for the first time the land that had fascinated me for so long and about which I still held many illusions. It also gave me the chance to visit Poland and Yugoslavia and to go back again to Czechoslovakia after an absence of eight years – this time, alas, without Sally.

CENTRAL AND EASTERN EUROPE, 1958

It was a shock, twenty-four hours after leaving Montreal, to observe the contrast between the glitter of a modern North American city and the dilapidated appearance of Prague. The city had the same run-down and shabby look as in 1950. There had been little rebuilding, and scaffolding still covered many structures. Traffic was disrupted on Václavské náměstí by construction of an underpass. Parks were neglected, lawns not mowed, flower-beds wild and unkempt. Soldiers were everywhere. The stores seemed full of supplies and were crowded with shoppers. I was struck by the absence of party buttons, which ten years ago had been on almost every lapel or blouse.

Symbolic of the new order was the gigantic statue of Josef Stalin on the Letná Heights, which could be seen from the city below. This monument showed the Soviet leader, with his wooden features, standing at the head of a line of soldiers, workers, and farmers, which was nicknamed the bread line. It seemed a grotesque obscenity in the beautiful city of spires. Up on the Vítkov heights, on the other side of Prague, was the splendid equestrian statue of Žižka, the Hussite general, with the Czechoslovak red, white, and blue flag waving beside it. The former Museum of National Liberation had become the Mausoleum of Klement Gottwald. The interior, of multi-coloured marble, was the repository of several biers for top communist leaders. The place of honour was occupied by Klement Gottwald, whose body, attired in a dark dress suit, with head and shoulders slightly raised, lay preserved, under a glass cover. A bright light illuminated his head and made his hair seem somewhat reddish, and his skin white and pink. As in the Lenin Mausoleum in Moscow, visitors moved quickly around the tomb, without apparent emotion.

The display of Gottwald's corpse was a hideous imitation of the Soviet practice of embalming and displaying the bodies of Lenin and Stalin and was in striking contrast to the simple grave of Masaryk in Lány. A close friend of mine, Joe Rudinger, a prominent chemist, told me of being summoned, with other chemists, in the middle of the night to the Central Committee on the embankment of the Vltava. They were informed of the alarming decomposition of Gottwald's body and ordered to take immediate steps to arrest it. The body remained in place until its removal in 1961.

In the same spirit of the cult of personality was the Klement Gottwald Museum, which portrayed the life of the Communist leader in the context of Czech revolutionary tradition, from Jan Hus onward. The final room was dedicated to "The Soviet Union, Our Model," with a citation from Gottwald's statement of "the law of ever increasing approximation" of Czechoslovakia to the Soviet pattern. Equally absurd, in Prague, was the Lenin Museum, located in Lidový Dům, once the headquarters of the Social Democratic party, which Lenin had visited once in 1912. The exhibits documented every detail of Lenin's life and showed Josef Stalin in a picture or two, but Leon Trotsky was nowhere to be seen.

I spent much of my short time in Prague with my dear prewar friends Lisa Rudinger and Olga Haningerová. Both had suffered greatly, with their families, during the terrible 1950s, but each embodied diametrically opposed traditions. Lisa's husband, Zdeněk, was still in prison, a victim of one of the lesser trials following the Slánský trial. One night in October 1952 he had been arrested without warning, and 22 months later, after constant interrogation, he had been tried and sentenced to 21 years in prison. Lisa, a long-time Communist, had been expelled from the party and, having lost her previous work, was employed as an assistant in a laboratory in the hospital at Krč. She recounted in detail the travail of their lives during those years. Zdeněk had been jailed in Slovakia, often in solitary confinement, and engaged in occasional hunger strikes to protest his sentence. Lisa, and their son, Josef, visited him at rare intervals and expended every effort to secure his release, writing letter after letter to the Central Committee and to party leaders, without success. Their good friend Karel Kreibich, one of the founders of the Czechoslovak Communist party, had secured the intercession of the British Communist party, which Lisa and Zdeněk had joined during their wartime exile, but to no avail. A new secret trial in 1958 had changed his sentence to seven years, but did not cancel or mitigate the charges against him.

My friend Olga and her husband, Bošek, survived the horrors of war and German occupation although countless friends and colleagues of theirs had been executed or had died. They were still living in Olga's parents' beautiful villa on Tichá ulice on Petřín, which I remembered so well from 1937. Bošek had been dismissed from the office of the prime minister after February 1948 and was working as a manual labourer in a milk bar, at a monthly wage of 900 crowns (the average workers' wage was 1,600). Olga was working in the Medical Library, at a wage of 1,100 crowns per month, and was giving private lessons in English. She worked 50 or more hours per week and had to care for her three children, Milan, Olga (Gina), and Jelka, and all four of their aged parents. Bošek spoke bitterly of the *prověrka* (purge), which had cost him his job, and complained of the constant discrimination against non-conformist opinions, especially religious views. As a socialist, he was in favour of a planned economy, he said, but he asked me to tell friends in the United States that "we want political freedom."

Josef Polišenský had experienced quite a different fate. A former Social Democrat, he had joined the Communist party and kept his post at Charles University through the 1950s. He was a full professor, earning a monthly salary of 3,000 crowns, and was able to travel, this year to the Netherlands, Sweden, England, and Austria. He was cautious in his comments and expressed the view that non-Marxist professors who had stayed on in 1948 were more or less secure but that the appointment of non-Marxists was not likely.

I travelled by air to Košice, in Slovakia. On the flight to Košice, on a Soviet-made Ilyushin 12, I was surprised to be invited by the pilot to join him in the cabin — "strictly forbidden but you are our guest," he joked. He insisted on my staying in the cockpit during the landing. I was equally surprised in the Hotel Slovan to find a large shortwave radio on which I could listen to the BBC. Košice was a clean and well-kept city. People were well-dressed and more sophisticated than I had expected. Stores were full of goods, including luxury articles such as glass and antiques. I saw hundreds of peasants in their Sunday-best folk costumes, or in ordinary work clothes, some of whom crowded into the largest church for communion. I gazed at the buildings where the Košice Program of the postwar government had been proclaimed. In the Square of Liberation there were graves of many Red Army soldiers and a monument to the fallen in the Slovak Uprising

The next day I crossed the border at Čierna nad Tisou, which was to become famous ten years later as the meeting place of Soviet and Czechoslovak party leaders during the Prague Spring. As we chugged across the border I surreptitiously photographed the two parallel lines of barbed wire fences, with two watch towers and soldiers patrolling on foot and on horseback. Kiev was a modern city of wide boulevards and substantial modern public buildings. In striking contrast were the great blue-domed Cathedral of St. Sophia, crowded with worshippers, and the monastery of Pechersk, where the bodies of monks were still preserved in the deep tunnels below.

From Moscow I flew down to Stalingrad and to Tbilisi in Georgia. The city of the great battle of World War II was a miracle of restoration, but in a classical style that seemed quite inappropriate to modern Communist Russia. On the way to Georgia I stopped for one day in the resort town of Sochi, beautifully set on the Black Sea, with tropical vegetation but repellent in its ostentatious luxury and ugly monumental architecture. Tbilisi was a delightful city, its architecture and atmosphere distinctively Georgian, showing evidence of its Byzantine and Christian past. I took a bus to Stalin's birthplace in Gori where a great museum was dedicated to the career of the native son. The cottage where he was born was encased in a marble building and bore on the doorway the inscription, "here was born the leader of the toiling people of the world."

I spent most of my five weeks in Russia, in August and September 1958, in Moscow and Leningrad. It was thrilling to walk on Red Square and in the Kremlin in Moscow, to visit the Hermitage and the fortress of Peter and Paul in Leningrad and the Imperial Palace at Pushkin, and to admire the churches, monasteries, and art galleries in both cities. I was travelling *de luxe*, at $30 per day, which entitled me to the services of a guide and the use of a car for two or three hours daily. The guides were usually intelligent and well-informed; although they were thoroughly loyal to the Soviet Union, conversations were often stimulating. These services were a great boon in making excursions, such as one to Yasnaya Polyana, where Tolstoi had lived for many years; his simple grave, without inscription, lay in a birch forest near the main house.

In Moscow and Leningrad I had a busy program of interviews with scholars and officials at the institutes of Economics and of World Economics and Politics in the Academy of Sciences, at the Institute of Marxism-Leninism, and in the faculties of Law and of Economics at the universities of Moscow and Leningrad. I also had an interview with the editor-in-chief of *Voprosy filosofii*, Mikhail Kammari. I had a long meeting at the Higher Diplomatic School with Professor Eugene Korovin, specialist in international law; he expounded familiar Soviet views on sovereignty and international law and on the United Nations, and he defended Soviet intervention in Hungary in 1956. At the University of Leningrad I was also received by the Chair of the History of the Communist Party. High-ranking officials of the Leningrad and Moscow city soviets and of the Leningrad Sovnarkhoz expounded at great length the structure of the system of regional soviets and defended the current doctrine of decentralization.

The views expressed by all these people followed the official line and defended the democratic nature of the Soviet system. When I plied them with questions about democracy, decentralization, and Marxism-Leninism, they responded with the standard arguments. They emphasized the change in atmosphere and in opinions since Stalin's death and openly admitted his "errors." Kammari was critical of the cult of personality but explained it as a product of economic and social forces and said that it could not occur again. Yet Stalin's works were still being studied, he said. Marxism-Leninism, the experts told me, was the exclusive and obligatory framework of scholarship and politics because it "was the only correct philosophy." There were, however, great differences in the ways in which it was interpreted and applied, they assured me. Vladimir Kotok, one of the leading authorities on the "people's democracy," on which I had written several articles, explained this doctrine in quite orthodox terms. The idea of national communism was unconditionally rejected, but individual countries, it was said, would advance to socialism along their own paths. The Yugoslav interpretation, which refused to recognize the universal laws of the building of socialism, was beyond the pale.

It was refreshing to hear more independent views in private conversations, away from places of work, with individual scholars whose names had been given me by friends at home. In addition to two economists at the Institute of World Economics and Politics (IMEMO) — Vladimir Kazakevich and Zalman Litvin — there was also Yurii Zamoshkin, a sociologist, who had spent a year in the United States and had visited Dartmouth College; he was doing an advanced degree at the Institute of Philosophy. In Leningrad I met with Yurii Kovalev, a university instructor in American and English literature, and Yurii Borshchevsky, a specialist on Persian literature of the twelfth century, in the Academy of Sciences. None of them opposed the Soviet system or its fundamental policies, but they often expressed unorthodox opinions and were sometimes quite critical of official attitudes.

I came away from my first visit to Russia full of conflicting and confusing impressions and suspicious of clichés and oversimplifications and of propaganda pro and con. I became painfully aware of my own ignorance and found myself unable to draw hard and fast conclusions. The Soviet Union was a land of contradictions and paradoxes, of old and new, of communist and non-communist, of much that was distressing and much that was appealing. Perhaps the most starling example of paradox was at the Moscow airport, where a young woman calculated the charges on my excess luggage on a calculating machine and then checked it on the ubiquitous "*schoty,*" or abacus. I felt that Russia could not be understood in terms of institutions and doctrines but had to be seen in human terms, in a setting of almost-infinite complexity.

I did not realize until near the end of my stay that a new international crisis was brewing over Formosa and that war threatened. Then came reports every day in *Pravda* of factory meetings denouncing American aggression and proclaiming solidarity with China. Some people admitted that they were seriously worried by the possibility of war, but no one was willing to admit that the blame lay anywhere else but on U.S. shoulders. No one criticized Soviet foreign policy — why should they?" they asked; "It is correct."

STOPOVER IN WARSAW

On my return journey I stopped a few days in Warsaw. Part of the city was still in ruins, but the Old Town, and many churches, had been splendidly renovated, and the Royal Palace was under reconstruction.

The monstrous Palace of Culture in the city centre — "the gift of the Soviet people" — was an ugly excrescence on the skyline but served as headquarters of the Academy of Sciences. The best panorama of Warsaw, people joked, was from the top floor, since the palace could not be seen from there.

Although it was the holiday season, Orbis, the travel agency, arranged meetings for me with a number of persons, including Julian Hochfeld, a sociologist, head of the Polish Institute of International Affairs, Czesław Bobrovsky, deputy chairman of the Economic Council; and Sigmund Broniarek, editor of the party newspaper *Trybuna Ludu*. None of these criticized the fundamentals of the existing Polish system or rejected the close relationship with the USSR, but all were somewhat critical of things official and were flexible in expressing their views. Bobrovky had written a book on the controversial Yugoslav system, although it had to be published in France.

More orthodox was Broniarek, who laid stress on the great changes introduced by 1956 — the end of collectivization, the autonomy of the church and the changed relationship with the Soviet Union — and he argued that there had been no retreat by party leader Władysław Gomułka. Poland had common interests with the Soviet Union, but it had its own national interests, too. The events of 1956 had produced, he admitted, great ideological confusion, and Poles were still groping their way along a national path to socialism.

Jan Strzelecki, a sociologist, editor of the independent newspaper *Nowa kultura*, was a man of independent mind. He stressed the value of empirical studies by sociologists and polling of public opinion. There was a great desire for real democracy within the party (of which he was a member), but it was recognized that the international situation set limits on freedom of utterance and action.

My short stay was sufficient to reveal that there was a much freer and more open atmosphere and great differences in theory and practice with the Soviet Union. Poland, although it professed to be, like its neighbours, a people's democracy, and rejected the independent Yugoslav course, represented de facto a national brand of communism.

RETURN TO PRAGUE

My travels in the USSR and Poland whetted my appetite for a return to Prague. I was able to secure a new visa in Warsaw and later to extend my stay a few more days. Although I got no help from Čedok, the official travel agency, Dr Vladimír Soják, head of the newly formed Institute of International Politics and Economics (UMPE), arranged a number of meetings for me. Soják had recently spent a year at Northwestern University in Illinois and was fascinated by Western concepts of international relations. Through him I met several scholars at the Faculty of Law, and Pavel Eisler, an economist at the Higher School of Economics; V. Tlustý, a philosopher at the Charles University; and Professor Jiří Hájek, deputy minister of foreign affairs. I also had interviews with several officials of the Prague City National Committee and a borough committee, but their comments were stereotypical and not very informative.

Although these conversations gave me some insight into intellectual life and the workings of local government, they were much more official in tone than those in Warsaw and were marked by only cautious criticism. Some people argued that much had changed since 1956 and that there was a more open atmosphere of free discussion. Jiří Hájek told me that Marxism in Czechoslovakia had moved from its earlier abstract generalizations to the recognition of special conditions in different countries and had become more flexible and independent. Tlustý, however, conceded that Marxism-Leninism was the dominant doctrine and that no distinctive Czechoslovak philosophy had emerged. There was continuing respect for some of Stalin's achievements and writings, and there was general condemnation of Yugoslavia, but neither viewpoint was stated so uncompromisingly as in the USSR. It was clear, however, that Czechoslovakia had a long way to go to approach the level of openness in Poland.

Through Soják I received an invitation to attend a 20th-anniversary conference on the Munich crisis of 1938, which the institute was sponsoring from 25 September to 2 October in the former Palffy Palace on Valdštejnské Náměstí. It was limited almost entirely to scholars from eastern Europe, with a few Dutch, French, Italian, and other delegates, many of them communist in outlook. The only English delegates were Lord Stansgate, formerly Anthony Wedgwood Benn, left-wing Labour MP, and Andrew Rothstein, a Soviet citizen and Marxist. Some Western scholars, such as J.W. Wheeler-Bennett, of Britain, had refused to attend. English was not used, and speeches were translated into French, German, and Russian only. The session was very one-sided, and there was almost no criticism or discussion. Professor Hájek gave a long historical review, quoting from many documents to prove German aggressiveness and Western appeasement and some American responsibility. He praised the Soviet policy of support of Czechoslovakia and rejected arguments that Soviet military assistance was unlikely. The chief Soviet delegate was the venerable historian A.N. Mints, who gave a generalized and highly political report on Soviet support of collective security in the 1930s and its readiness to defend Czechoslovakia in 1938, but he offered no documentary evidence.

The only critical remarks were made to me privately by Julian Hochfeld, of Poland, who placed blame on the Soviet Union for its policies in 1939-40, which were just as responsible for war as the British policy in 1938. The fear of the Soviet Union by Western governments had played a role, as had the mutual desire of Britain and the USSR to get the other involved in a war against Germany. He thought that Poland, reactionary as it had been, might have consented, under Western pressure, to the entry of Soviet troops on its territory and joined a common front that would have averted war.

I managed to escape from the conference from time to time and looked in on the much more interesting conference of political scientists held under the auspices of UNESCO. Its purpose was to improve mutual understanding between East and West by studying the relations between planned and non-planned economies. During intervals I showed some of the sights of Prague to two delegates, Brough (C.B.) Macpherson, of Toronto, and the British professor, Morris Ginsburg, with whom Sally had studied.

The weather was rainy and dull and seemed to reflect the drabness and mediocrity of life in Prague. I saw much of Olga during my two visits. Although she and I had experienced such different lives in the 20 years since we first met in 1937, we recaptured — as though by a miracle — the closeness of our prewar relationship. In spite of her busy life she stole many hours for brief meetings, and even the occasional opera. I was sad to leave her again when I left for Belgrade.

At last, much later than planned, I set off for home via Belgrade. We touched down in Budapest, where I was asked by the stewardess, who spoke only Hungarian and German, to inform an Albanian, who knew only Turkish and Czech (he had been a student in Prague for a year and worked in a large automobile factory) that we had unexpectedly to change planes. At the airport in Belgrade I was greeted by my old college friend, the Canadian ambassador, George Ignatieff. In less than a week, with his help, and that of the Yugoslav Information Office, I was able to meet an extraordinary number of people in positions of authority. These included the editor of *Borba*, a secretary of the Central Trade Union Council, the chief of the secretariat of the Federal Executive Council, the mayor of Belgrade, the rector of the University of Belgrade, the dean of the Faculty of Law, and the heads of several research institutes, two of whom were members of the Central Committee.

Conversations were frank and open, although they often expressed an official viewpoint based on the recently published Yugoslav party program. This, they argued, was a kind of codification of policies already being pursued that were anathema to the Chinese as well as to the Soviets. The program represented their own version of Marxism, which they valued as a method of analysis. It had to be revised to meet new conditions and to reflect facts established by scientific study. Stalin and Stalinism were rejected without reservation, and — although no one said so openly — Lenin's revision of Marxism was not fully acceptable. Soviet scholarship, some of them said, was of no use in their own studies, whereas Western sources were valuable and frequently cited.

It was refreshing to hear their strong criticism of Soviet centralization and dogmatism, but they were united in defending their own Yugoslav institutions of workers' self-management, local autonomy, and decentralization. Their system was not a multi-party system and was not, they admitted, a perfect democracy, but it was on the way to democracy. The party had a new role – to persuade and to educate, not to order or control the government and industry. I left Yugoslavia with the conviction that its people had evolved a distinctive form of communism, both in theory and in practice, which marked them off sharply from the Soviet Union and Czechoslovakia and even from Poland. Although they did not use the term "national communism," it seemed to me that this was the best way of describing a country that not only rejected diplomatic and military association with the Soviet bloc and was independent in defending its national interests but also insisted on ideological originality and its own conception of communism.

TORONTO BECKONS

I returned to Dartmouth for what turned out to be our last year there. Some years earlier (in 1952) I had been tempted by an offer from Harold Innis, dean of the graduate school at Toronto, of an appointment as associate professor of political science, at a yearly salary of

$5,400, to teach comparative government and international relations and to play some role in the Slovic Studies Department. It would have been tempting to return to Canada at last and to enjoy the higher intellectual standards of the leading Canadian university and the greater academic freedom of the country. It would, however, have meant spreading my interests even more widely than at Dartmouth, with new courses in Canadian diplomacy and comparative government, and it would not have permitted the greater specialization in the Soviet and eastern European field for which I had hoped. After much soul-searching, Sally and I had decided that the answer must unfortunately be no. This decision seemed to mark a turning point in my life and to signify that I would remain a permanent expatriate. I seriously contemplated an application for U.S. citizenship.

Now, in late 1958, came a new and more attractive offer from Vincent Bladen, head of the Department of Political Science and Economics — a full professorship, at an annual salary of $12,500. My teaching would be entirely in the Soviet and eastern European field, and I would participate in the development of Russian studies in the university as a whole. This offered me an opportunity for greater specialization and an escape from the unhealthy political atmosphere of the United States. It would be wrenching to leave the beauty and comfort of Hanover and for Sally to emigrate to a foreign country. It would also be difficult to take the two boys out of the almost ideal conditions of the little village, but we hoped that at their age they would benefit from life in an urban environment and from better schooling. The offer was too attractive to refuse; Sally and I decided to accept the challenge and to leave New England for Canada in mid-1959.

III

CHANGING FACES OF COMMUNISM

10

RUSSIAN AND EAST EUROPEAN STUDIES: TORONTO

WHEN WE ARRIVED IN TORONTO in 1959, the university, like the city, was opening to the world. The Toronto that I had known as a youth and on occasional visits since had transformed itself from a provincial Canadian city to a world metropolis. The scores of languages of new Canadians could be heard everywhere. After living many years in a town of five thousand people, we were moving to a city of more than a million and a quarter. We were trading our modern Techbilt house, with its acre and a quarter of trees and shrubs, for an old-fashioned brick house, fortunately in an old tree-clad area of the city. With the substantial sum realized from the sale of our place in Hanover we eventually purchased a big, 30-year old house in North Toronto for $59,000. It had a large garden and was close to a relatively wild ravine; it was within walking distance of the grade and high schools that David and Peter were to attend.

The University of Toronto had changed beyond recognition since my student days. It had mushroomed to 14,000 students and was expected to reach a maximum of 23,000 in ten years. It still maintained high standards, and most of the top administrative posts were held by active professors. For me the main attraction was the opportunity to specialize in Russian and Czech studies and to take part in the development of an interdisciplinary program of Slavic studies.

The Department of Political Economy was still located in the old red brick gothic building on Bloor Street West where I had studied in the 1930s and that had previously housed McMaster University (now in Hamilton). Since the department was soon to move into the new Sidney Smith Hall, no one wanted to change offices. Hence, as a newcomer, I fell heir to the spacious office of the McMaster principal that had been occupied by departmental chairmen Harold Innis and Vincent Bladen. After Bladen's promotion to dean of the Faculty of

Arts, the acting chairman was W.J. Ashley, a shy man, very English in manner, who specialized in economic history and statistics. He endeared himself to me at the first (and only) departmental meeting that year by first introducing new members and then asking if anyone wished to prolong the meeting further.

BUILDING A CENTRE

The University of Toronto was undergoing a sea change in its attitude to the outside world. When I was a student in the 1930s, no one there had paid attention to the Soviet Union or to China, Africa, and Latin America. For many years thereafter Toronto had remained in this respect a kind of backwater; it was a great university in many fields but failed to match American and British universities in its international programs. The Department of Slavic Studies, established in 1949 under a grant from the Carnegie Endowment, was oriented primarily to Russian and Ukrainian languages and literatures and, to a lesser degree, to history and politics. My old Department of Political Economy offered nothing in the Soviet field. Several professors in history were interested in the Soviet Union but offered no courses.

Harold Innis, first as chairman of Political Economy and then as dean of the Graduate School, was keenly aware of these inadequacies. After a trip to the Soviet Union in 1945, he had developed a keen interest in the development of Russian studies at Toronto. As early as 1949 he had asked me if I was interested in a position in the Department of Slavic Studies. In September 1951, he requested, during a visit of mine to Toronto, that I submit a memorandum on the future development of this field. I recommended an interdepartmental area program comparable to those I had known in London and New York. Students would learn Russian and work in several disciplines, but with specialization in one. The program would require a number of Russian/Soviet specialists in several departments, including an economist and political scientist. Financial limitations impeded action in this direction, as did the university's preoccupation with the flood of returning veterans. In 1952, Innis offered me a post in political economy, but I reluctantly declined.

After Innis's untimely death in 1952, Vincent Bladen, his successor as chairman, took up the cause and, with Moffatt Woodside, dean of the faculty, sought funds — without success — from the Canadian government to assist in preparing specialists in the language and society of the USSR. Bladen's effort to raise the level of international studies at Toronto, he told me, met with "glacial hostility" in higher circles. In 1958 he conceived an ambitious plan to develop the study of certain previously neglected foreign areas. He invited me to take part in the development of Russian studies and at the same time offered positions to Cranford Pratt, then of McGill, a specialist in African studies, and to Nathan Keyfitz, distinguished populationist and sociologist, formerly of the Dominion Bureau of Statistics, who had travelled and done research in various parts of Asia and Latin America. Our arrival in the Department of Political Economy in the autumn of 1959 indicated that the university was at last taking a decisive step in the study of foreign areas.

Even more important, Bladen at once appointed a Decanal Committee on Russian and East European Studies to examine their future at Toronto. Acting as chairman at first, he brought together the handful of people at Toronto who had some interest in the study of the Soviet Union and the Slavic world. These included:

- George Luckyj, distinguished scholar of Ukrainian and Russian literature, after 1954 chairman of the Department of Slavic Studies (renamed in 1968 the Department of Slavic Languages and Literatures);
- Harold Nelson, a specialist in foreign policy and international relations, from History;
- Ross Macdonald, who specialized on Japan and Korea, also from the Department of History;
- Edward McWhinney, an expert on Soviet law, of the Law School;
- Leonid Strakhovsky, a Russian-born historian, from Slavic Studies;
- Ali Tayyeb, a young geographer from Pakistan;
- Stephen Triantis, an economist who had learned Russian and written several book reviews on Russian topics; and later,
- Neil Field, a geographer who had worked on Soviet affairs with the Canadian intelligence service.

We received an initial planning grant of $5,000 from the Rockefeller Foundation and spent over a year examining possible courses of action. We sent out exploratory missions to survey Russian studies elsewhere — Luckyj to England, France, and West Germany; Triantis to Austria, France, and West Germany, Harold Nelson to U.S. Midwestern universities (Indiana, Illinois, Ohio State, and Wisconsin); Strakhovsky to Columbia and Harvard; and me and the newly appointed chairman of Slavic Studies, Professor Herbert Bowman, to the west coast, to visit the universities of British Columbia, Washington, and California and Stanford University.

We also engaged in a lobbying and public relations exercise by inviting to Toronto five distinguished specialists in Russian studies — three from Columbia, E.J. Simmons (literature); P.E. Mosely (history); and Zbigniew Brzezinski (politics); Alexander Gerschenkron from Harvard (economics); and R.F. Byrnes (history) from Indiana. Each gave a public lecture and a seminar in his field and, in meetings with the president, the dean, and the appropriate chairmen, expressed his views of the best way to organize Russian studies.

On 18 July 1961, after many meetings, the decanal committee (now under George Luckyj), issued a report that recommended establishment of a graduate Centre for Russian and East European Studies and development of studies in the appropriate departments. It would embrace not only the USSR and pre-1917 Russia, but also eastern Europe, with special emphasis on the Slavic nations. The centre would have a distinctive pattern, based in part on European and American models but also reflecting the needs and conditions of Toronto. In accordance with Toronto's strong tradition of departmentalism, the centre would offer no courses of its own, and the web of cross-departmental studies would cover not more than three disciplines. It would have no staff other than the director and a secretary and would serve as a liaison with the departments.

In November 1962, during my absence in Europe on sabbatical, a new committee (chaired by Herbert Bowman) submitted a concrete proposal of such a centre to the president, Claude Bissell, and recommended that I be its first director. Prior to my departure I had talked to Bissell — my former classmate at the university in the 1930s — and found that he, unlike his predecessor Sidney Smith, was receptive to the unorthodox idea of an interdisciplinary centre. He accepted the committee's recommendation and, in a letter to me in Vienna, invited me to become director. On my return I found that he had forgotten to submit the committee's recommendation to the board of governors. But this was a minor oversight and was soon rectified.

The Dean of the graduate school, Professor Andrew Gordon, a natural scientist, regarded the idea of such a centre as anathema and felt that he had been by-passed by Bladen and Bissell. However, the associate dean, Ernest Sirluck, who was to succeed him, was warmly sympathetic to our plans. There were frequent heated discussions, in which Gordon used strong expletives to emphasize his views. He also insisted that I draft a constitution of the proposed centre as a basis of consideration by the graduate school. After long and tedious negotiations with various committees the centre was finally approved in April 1963. This, and the establishment that year of a Centre for Medieval Studies, marked the first steps in the university's creation of many other interdepartmental centres in succeeding years.

Thus the Centre for Russian and East European Studies (CREES), as it came to be called, came into existence with an initial roster of 20 faculty from several departments and with the committed support of the president and the new graduate dean. The director was not to be the equal in authority to a chairman but was responsible directly to the president's office and to the School of Graduate Studies. The Centre would not have its own teaching program and would not be entitled to appoint faculty members, which remained the prerogative of the departments. Its annual budget would be, for administrative purposes only — $5,500, which rose by 1967 to $22,500. It was expected to raise funds from outside the university. Within these limitations the formation of the centre was a historic step, laying the foundations for the university's eventual emergence as a major centre in Russian and eastern European studies.

I thus entered on my term as director, which was to last for 11 years, until 1974. During this period I carried a heavy administrative burden, although, unlike a departmental chairman, I was not responsible for faculty appointments, teaching assignments, or salaries. I was, however, deeply involved in fund-raising and in administering special centre programs. I enjoyed strong support and sympathy from Jack Sword, the assistant to the president, to whom I was responsible on budgetary and other matters. I carried out my duties with the advice of an executive committee and with occasional meetings of all centre members. Our accommodations were limited — four offices in Sidney Smith Hall, but with no reading room, library, or seminar room. I had the good fortune to have excellent secretaries, at first Mary Sosula, Russian-born, who spoke fluent Russian and knew German and Serbo-Croatian, and later Ahnna Lowry, a Canadian of Ukrainian origin, whose lack of knowledge of Russian was balanced by her personal charm and administrative skill. Both were particularly good at giving counsel to our students, and especially the Russian exchange students.

One of my foremost early tasks was to secure the appointment of Russian and eastern European specialists in the departments. This proved to be surprisingly easy, since Toronto was then riding a wave of expansion. In short order our ranks were strengthened by the appointment of Kathryn Feuer as chairman of the Department of Slavic Studies, and from the same department, of Bohdan Budorowicz, a specialist in Slavic history and bibliography, and others in Polish and Serbo-Croatian literature. In Political Economy new appointments included two Canadians — Ian Drummond, economic historian, who completed a PhD in Russian studies at Yale, and Franklyn Griffiths, an international relations specialist —   and an American, Richard Judy, a specialist in Soviet economics and in the then almost unknown field of computers. In History new members included British-born Peter Brock, a well-known historian of eastern Europe; the younger Andrew Rossos, a Canadian of Macedonian origin, who received his early education in Czechoslovakia and completed a thesis on Russia and the Balkans; and an American, R.H. McNeal, whose interest was primarily Bolshevik theory and practice.

We also had to concentrate on building up our library resources. In April 1961 a report on the university's library holdings in our field by a Slavic librarian at Columbia revealed serious weaknesses and recommended expenditure over a five-year period of $150,000 for Russian and Ukrainian, and $50,000 for other languages of eastern Europe. In fact at this time the library was spending less than $10,000 a year on our field, but within a couple of years we were spending some $50,000 annually. Budorowycz served as the centre's bibliographer and contributed greatly to the building of the strongest Russian and eastern European collection in Canada.

We immediately introduced an interdisciplinary program for an M.A. and diploma in Russian and eastern European studies. This was designed to prepare journalists, diplomats, and others for work in the area and to serve as a gateway to doctoral studies. Over the next years, it attracted some half-dozen outstanding graduate students, almost all of whom went on to academic positions in the field in Canada or the United States. However, the program did not attract a large enrolment and it fell into disuse, only to be revived many years later, in the 1990s.

In 1967 we set up a summer language program for the intensive study of Russian — the first school of this kind in Canada. The centre had hitherto given financial support to students for language study at Indiana, Middlebury, and elsewhere. Our school provided an eight-week course of accelerated study of Russian and proved very successful, enrolling each year some 50 to 75 students from all over the continent — in total we had over five hundred students in the program. The course was directed by Sergei Kononoff, a member of the Department of Slavic Languages and Literatures, and most teachers were members of that department. But the department had no great sympathy with a program in its field administered by the centre, and I endured frequent conflicts with it. After a decade budgetary reasons forced its cancellation.

An action that brought me special pleasure was that designed to ensure continued teaching of Czech, which was also threatened by budget reductions. In 1967, Josef Čermák, a lawyer, raised $30,000 from the local Czechoslovak community to support for three years the appointment of a professor to teach the Czech language and Czech and Slovak literature. Slavic Languages and Literatures committed itself to continuing this appointment after three years, thus assuring a permanent place for Czechoslovak studies.

One of our major projects was an exchange program with the Soviet Union. During a trip to Moscow in 1961-62 I had prepared the ground for this endeavour in discussions with the State Committee for Cultural Relations with Foreign Countries. In a later exchange of letters with the Soviet Ministry of Higher and Specialized Secondary Education we reached agreement on the annual exchange of four scholars in each direction. The Soviet nominees were mainly mature scholars, usually in their forties, drawn from many institutes and universities from all parts of the country. Ours were younger PhD students at Toronto in the humanities and the social sciences, with the addition of several Canadians studying elsewhere.

In 1966 I made a special trip to Moscow and other parts of the USSR to negotiate continuation of the program. It was somewhat anomalous that I, a university professor, had to deal with a Soviet ministry responsible for all Soviet universities and other advanced institutes of specialized education. We had, however, the blessing and the practical support of Canada's Department of External Affairs and its embassy in Moscow. In these negotiations I confronted six officials, headed by Vladimir Rastatourov, who turned out to be a tough negotiator. We had a second meeting in a private dining room in the Hotel Praga where, under a mural of the Hradčany, we drank toasts to the future of the exchange. Later I enjoyed a friendly reunion, over a luncheon at the Hotel Minsk, with some of the former Soviet students in Toronto. In Leningrad I had lunch with Gennadi Zaitsev, who had spent a year in Toronto; he had finished his thesis and got his candidate's degree.

The Russian officials showed great appreciation of the existing exchange with Toronto and welcomed the idea of an exchange of senior professors. They were, however, somewhat uneasy at our request to include in the latter Toronto professors who were not Canadian citizens. They welcomed the prospect of a national Canadian exchange, which, I told them, might provide each year for as many as 20 people in each direction. They spoke of the unique character of our relationship, since it was not based on a written agreement and was between one university and the ministry. This gave Toronto a privileged position, as compared with other Canadian universities. They broached the idea of an exchange with a single university, such as Moscow or Minsk, and pressed me hard on a Toronto-Minsk agreement. At the insistence of the Ministry I made a one-day trip to Minsk, where I was an honoured guest at a meeting with pro-rectors and professors At a table laden with fruit we drank innumerable toasts with Armenian cognac. I was then given a whirlwind tour of the university and although nothing was said about an exchange, that was clearly the purpose of the visit. I was convinced that few, if any of our students would want to spend a year in Minsk, and this exchange never did materialize.

We devoted much of our time to provisions for future exchanges and difficulties that had arisen from our previous ones. The Soviets could not guarantee acceptance of all topics, since some of them were studied not at their universities but in government departments or the Academy of Sciences. Nor could they assure visitors access to archives, since each archive would have to decide independently on requests. We agreed on dates for submitting names of candidates, and they assured me that there would no longer be delays in approving nominees. They requested a letter from me by the end of the year confirming the terms of our agreement and agreed to consider each non-Canadian nominee separately.

Administering this program was time-consuming and often frustrating, and it taught me much about Soviet bureaucracy. We had to press hard for the assignment of our scholars to appropriate institutions in the Soviet educational system, usually at Moscow University, although two studied at the Timaryazev Agricultural Academy. We often had to wait until the last minute for approval of our nominees, who were forced to cool their heels for some months in Canada or Europe. The Soviet scholars usually arrived without warning, sometimes long after the opening of our term. It was an ongoing battle to win Soviet acceptance of the idea that our scholars be accompanied by their wives. Soviet wives were not, however, permitted to come to Canada. Only in one case was a wife given permission to visit her husband during the Christmas holidays.

In Canada we had to negotiate the admission of the Soviet scholars, almost all of whom were natural scientists, to the appropriate departments of the university or, in several cases, to the Ontario Agricultural College in Guelph, later the University of Guelph. We also had to place them in university residences; each year one fortunate person enjoyed the luxury of Massey College at Toronto. We soon found out that they were unaccustomed to making decisions on their own, even on ordinary matters of living or travel, and my secretary had to help them. Sally and I tried to make them feel at home by entertaining them and arranging for them to visit other Canadian homes.

We had to brief our Canadian scholars on the difficulties and dangers of life in the Soviet Union — a sensitive task, which we carried out at an annual meeting attended by a member of the Department of External Affairs. I was strongly opposed to the RCMP's efforts to participate in this briefing and to interview our candidates before their departure. I felt that this might create serious problems for them if they were interrogated by the Soviet security police. In resisting this pressure, I had the firm support of the president of the university.

We benefited greatly from the experience of the American exchange program operated by the U.S. Inter-University Committee for Travel Grants and sponsored and financed by the U.S. State Department. It was a huge and costly undertaking that each year exchanged about 40 or 50 students in each direction. As director of our program, I attended annual meetings of the committee in Madison, Seattle, and Stanford. They were somewhat amazed to hear of our tiny but inexpensive program.

In the course of ten years we received some 30 Soviet scholars and sent the same number of Canadians. We developed a strong cadre of Canadian specialists on Russia and the Soviet Union, many of whom were appointed to Canadian or American universities. The experience had an intangible but important effect on the thinking of Soviet scholars about the West and gave the Canadians a taste of Soviet reality. We were dependent financially on outside funds, notably from the Laidlaw Foundation, whose chairman, Rod Laidlaw, developed a strong personal interest in our efforts and entertained Soviet participants at his home in Toronto and his château on Lake Simcoe. They were astonished to meet a capitalist who was young and informal and did not wear a top-hat and smoke a big cigar.

The exchange was inevitably dogged by politics. One of our students was expelled from the Soviet Union, and another subjected to prolonged questioning. Our protests were fruitless, but did not preclude the continuation of the program. The entire relationship was, however, abruptly broken off when the Soviet Union, without warning, withdrew its scholars from Canada. The reason — a Soviet scholar who had been studying at the University of Alberta had defected and was living near Toronto, working as a research assistant for a University of Toronto scientist. The Soviet authorities were fearful that the defector might have an unhealthy political influence on their exchange students. This ended our exchange and precluded implementation of an agreement already reached for the exchange of two senior faculty members for three-month stays. Meanwhile, a Canadian exchange committee that I chaired had prepared a broader national program, based on an agreement between the two governments.

By 1966 our centre had achieved substantial dimensions, with a total of 28 scholars in the departments of Slavic Studies (fifteen), Political Economy (seven), History (five), Geography (one), Islamic Studies (one) and Law (one). By this time the university was already investing some $400,000 in Russian and eastern European studies, for salaries, library staff, library purchases, and the centre's budget. The centre's activities were, however, severely handicapped by lack of funds. We made some unsuccessful efforts to raise money from Canadian magnates. We went first to Tomáš Bat'a, the Czech-born shoe manufacturer whose worldwide business had its headquarters in Toronto. As a result, I was invited to lunch with him and his wife in their palatial residence — otherwise no help was forthcoming. The same thing happened with Štefan Roman, the Slovak-born uranium magnate. At lunch in his luxurious business suite in a downtown skyscraper he revealed that he was not interested in giving aid to our university; it gave no instruction in Slovak, which he considered a Slavic language of crucial importance.

We next turned to the Ford Foundation, which had given major grants for Russian and eastern European studies to a number of American universities. George Luckyj and I made a visit to C.O. Swayze, a foundation director, in New York City as early as 1960, and he repaid this with a return visit in 1964. He indicated that a grant would be dependent on the development of international studies in general at Toronto. The Department of Political Economy had already appointed a committee on international studies, under my chairmanship. At the same time the university established an International Studies Program, headed by Cranford Pratt, which it hoped would stimulate this field by establishing various foreign-area centres, as well as one in international relations.

In 1966, after long preparation, we applied to the Ford Foundation for a grant-in-aid of $650,000, but this met with no success. Several years later, however, in 1973, at the initiative of the foundation, we were awarded $50,000 annually for a period of three years. This made it possible to make new appointments, to support research and travel by graduate students and faculty, to augment the library holdings, to award some graduate student fellowships, and to finance our exchange program. It was a major boost for the centre, which assured it a role of leadership in Canada and placed it in the front rank of such institutes in the Western world.

The development at Toronto was but a part of the growth of Slavic studies in Canada. Other centres were created at the University of British Columbia, Alberta, McMaster, and Carleton, along with several limited exchange programs. In 1954 the Canadian Association of Slavists (CAS) was established; it published the *Canadian Slavonic Papers* and held annual scholarly conferences. I made a special point of attending CAS meetings and contributing articles to the *Papers* and was eventually elected president. In a CAS symposium on Canada and eastern Europe I urged that Canada adopt a policy of "peaceful engagement" in that region so as to promote liberalization of the communist systems and the rapprochement of eastern and western Europe. This would require the expansion of economic and cultural relations with countries of that region and increased diplomatic representation, as well as the expansion of Slavic studies at Canadian universities and the further development of scholarly exchanges.[1]

By 1974 I had completed 11 years as director. At a celebratory farewell dinner I was given two striking paintings by the artist Ronald Brooks Kitaj. The existence of CREES was far from assured, however. Later directors Frank Griffiths and Gleb Žekulin had to fight for its very survival. In an article in the *University of Toronto Bulletin* entitled "Does Central Europe Exist?" I argued strongly for continued work on this region.[2] Fortunately, later directors of the centre, Tim Colton and Bob Johnson, with invaluable help from the Mellon Foundation, expanded the activities of CREES so that it became a focal point for a greatly increased number of graduate students in affiliated departments. It thus acquired a permanent place in the university and enjoyed a high national and international reputation.

TEACHING AND RESEARCH

My teaching program allowed me from the outset to concentrate exclusively on Soviet and eastern European politics. My main course was called "The Political Economy of the USSR" — a title selected by Vincent Bladen — and attracted an enrolment of several hundred. I was much happier in smaller courses; one, whose title and content evolved over the years, was always devoted to the comparison of the communist countries of central and eastern Europe or of the various forms of Marxism. I had a few graduate students under my wing: Bohdan Harasymiw, working on the *nomenklatura* system in the USSR, who was later professor at the University of Calgary; Stefania Miller, who studied the Catholic *Znak* movement in Poland, and later became a professor at McMaster; and three Americans — Paul Sanderson, working on economic reform discussions in East Germany; Fred Eidlin, studying normalization in post-occupation Czechoslovakia; and Edith Klein, who focused on educational autonomy in Yugoslavia. In 1978-79 a Japanese student, Gen Kikkawa, came to Toronto to work with me on interest groups and dissent in eastern Europe.

Although I had the burden of the CREES directorship, I managed to escape involvement in university committees and was able to devote much time to research and writing. I had worked for years revising my doctoral thesis and hoped to publish it with the University of Toronto Press. Their suggested changes would, however, have necessitated an enormous re-write, so that in the end it was never published. In 1970 I restated the essential argument of my thesis in a chapter of a book I edited with Peter Brock, entitled *The Czech Renascence of the Nineteenth Century*.[3] This was dedicated to my old friend and Czech historian Otakar Odložilík, and we presented it to him at a seminar in Toronto. I also published a number of articles and several major books on communism and the Soviet Union.

I spent a lot of time on the road giving lectures and seminars at many Canadian and American universities and attending conferences. I served on the executive committees of the American Association for the Advancement of Slavic Studies (AAASS), the Canadian Political Science Association (CPSA), and the Canadian Association of Slavists (CAS), as well as on the editorial boards of the *Slavic Review, Canadian Slavonic Papers, Soviet Studies,* and *Studies in Comparative Communism.* In 1968 Sally and I spent the whole summer at a conference in Palo Alto, California, devoted to change in communist systems. In 1973 and 1975 we enjoyed two sabbatical leaves away from Toronto. For the first I was a fellow at the Russian Research Centre of Harvard University and a guest of the Centre of International Affairs at the Massachusetts Institute of Technology (MIT). Since there was no real specialist on eastern Europe at Harvard, students of that area turned to me for advice — this led to several long-lasting friendships. In 1975, at the invitation of my friend Archie Brown, I spent two terms at St. Antony's College in Oxford as a "non-stipendiary visiting Fellow." It was good to be back in Oxford after so many years and occasionally to visit my old college, Christ Church. I gave seminars on Czechoslovakia at the Russian centres in Birmingham, Cambridge, Glasgow, London, and Swansea, and went further afield to the Free University in Berlin and the Hebrew University in Jerusalem. Finally in July, I went to Bob Tucker's conference on Stalinism and Political Culture in idyllic Bellaggio, on Lake Como, where I joined the distinguished company of Włodek Brus, Alex Dallin, Hélène Carrère d'Encausse from Paris, Leszek Kołakowski from Poland, Moshe Lewin and Marko Marković from Yugoslavia, T.H. Rigby from Australia, and others.

Sally and I found it difficult at first to shake off the spell of New England and returned to Hanover for several Christmases and summers. Once, in 1964, the short term in Toronto made it possible for me to teach in the spring term at Dartmouth. Sally and I took advantage of the cultural and intellectual life of Toronto and explored many corners of Ontario, including Stratford or Niagara-on-the-Lake, and Georgian Bay and the Lake of Bays in Muskoka. During the winters we enjoyed the occasional trip north to ski at Collingwood. Once in a while we splurged on a holiday in a more distant place — in 1970, to the Caribbean; in 1971, to Brittany and the Channel Islands; and in 1973, to Italy and Sicily.

As a citizen in my native land I was able to exercise the franchise for the first time in many years, but I took no part in university politics. As an American citizen, Sally did not have the right to vote and refrained from political activities. She was an active member of the University Women's Club and the University Faculty Wives Association, and took a deep interest in the activities of CREES, regularly entertaining students and professors in our home. Sally was a skilled editor of my writing and constructed indexes for several of my books. Thus we sank deep roots in our new home and developed a rhythm of life that was to last for more than 30 years.

Our sons came to Canada as "Returning Canadians," since they had been registered at birth with the Canadian embassy in

Washington, DC. They had dual citizenship but during the Vietnam
war they both chose to renounce American citizenship. Dave returned
to his birthplace, Madison, to attend the University of Wisconsin
during the Vietnam years. After returning to Canada he headed West,
earning a living by tree-planting on Vancouver Island. He fell in love
with the West and showed no signs of returning to the East. Peter did
not find high school challenging and at 17 he dropped out and left
home. This was during the tempestuous 1960s, and we were very concerned about our boy's whereabouts and his way of life. But he found
that freedom he could not find at school or at home. In 1969 he set off
alone for Asia, travelling through Greece, Turkey, Iran, Afghanistan,
Pakistan, and India. There he often lived in temples and shrines and
began to learn Buddhist practices and beliefs. During the war between
India and Pakistan in 1971 he left for Thailand where, as a Buddhist
monk, he studied ancient Tibetan, Pali, and Sanskrit, thus preparing
himself for what turned out to be a lifelong study of Buddhism. Like
his brother in the Canadian West, Peter fell in love with his new home.

In 1974 I had a heart attack, but I survived to enter what I called
my "third life." In February 1977 I reached my 65th birthday, and
retired. My 18 years in Toronto were busy and productive ones,
unmarred by the political difficulties that had dogged my work in
Wisconsin and New England. My years as director of CREES gave me a
sense of accomplishment, but I was glad in 1975 to resume the more
normal life of a scholar. There were to be many more years of personal happiness in Toronto, years filled with travel, research, publication,
and an ever greater involvement in the life and politics of
Czechoslovakia and central and eastern Europe.

NOTES

1.   Skilling, "Canada and Eastern Europe," *Canadian Slavonic Papers*
      8 (1966): 3-52. See also my "Canadian Attitudes to Change and
      Conflict in the Soviet Bloc," in Edward McWhinney, ed., *Law,
      Foreign Policy, and the East-West Detente* (Toronto: University of
      Toronto Press, 1964).
2.   February 9, 1987.
3.   Peter Brock and H. Gordon Skilling, eds. *The Czech Renascence
      of the Nineteenth Century* (Toronto: University of Toronto Press,
      1970).

Every room is covered in pictures of various sizes; perhaps they number many thousands ... in color bits of nature - animal in sunlight or shadow, sitting, standing in water, lying on the grass; near to a crucifixion by a ... who does not believe in Christ. However, human figures ... standing, walking, often they are naked ... all this is carefully ... in a book - name of artist - name of picture. People with ... books ...

II

PROBING THE ENIGMA OF COMMUNISM*

MY OWN ATTITUDES TOWARD THE SOVIET UNION and Communism were slow to change, but they were gradually shifting in the light of the changing face of Communism and the evolution of my own thought. In my student days at Oxford and London in the mid-1930s, I had pictured the Soviet system as a more or less perfect democratic model, one which had rigorously addressed, if not solved, all the major problems unresolved by Western capitalism. I found no fault in Soviet foreign policy and condemned Western policies toward the Soviet Union. The events leading up to the Second World War, especially the sell-out of Czechoslovakia at Munich, had seemed to confirm my viewpoint. During the early postwar years of deteriorating East-West relations and revived Western hostility to the Soviet Union I still gave the benefit of the doubt to Soviet actions and avoided outright condemnation of its system.

Even after the events of 1948 in Czechoslovakia I had searched for an approach that would avoid the spirit of the Cold War and the demonization of the Soviet and eastern European systems. Principal elements in my approach, which itself evolved over time, were comparative analysis; the emergence of distinctive national types of communism, including doctrinal divergences; conflict among interest groups in authoritative systems; and political culture and development.

This new approach first crystallized in a paper on the comparative approach that I gave at the American Political Science Association in September 1959 and published the following year in the *Journal of Politics*.[1] The predominant tendency of the analysis of Soviet politics to date had been to emphasize its uniqueness, either as a distinctive product of Russian conditions and Russian traditions, or as a special prod-

---

* Winston Churchill once spoke of the Soviet Union as "a riddle wrapped in a mystery inside an enigma." See my "Scholarship and the Soviet Riddle," *International Journal* 16, no. 3 (Summer 1961): 260-65.

uct of Soviet theory and practice. Needless to say, the Soviet system *was* different from others, but there were common elements. I argued that a better way to understand and interpret the Soviet system was to place it in a comparative context. What in the Soviet system was common to all governments? What was uniquely Russian? What in the Soviet system was common to all *Russian* governments? What was uniquely Soviet? What was common to all *Soviet* governments? What was unique to the Khrushchev regime? Such a comparative approach would not only contribute to the full development of comparative politics in general but also safeguard students against threats to objectivity represented by culture-bound assumptions and by Cold War prejudices. I made my first attempt to use this concept in a lecture at Carleton University in 1963, and expounded it more fully the following year at Yale University, where I proposed a theoretical comparison of the American and the Soviet systems. Only seven persons were present but one of those present, Karl Deutsch, described it as "a historic occasion when comparative politics and Soviet studies came together for the first time." This comparative approach met with sympathetic approval in the West and the article was translated into Italian and Portuguese (in Brazil), but it encountered outright hostility in the Soviet Union. One scholar, R.E. Kantor, writing under the title "Methodological Counsels for the Falsification of History," assailed it as illustrating the "bankruptcy" of bourgeois sociology, and as ignoring the principled difference between the Soviet and capitalist systems.

With a colleague, Steven Dupré, a specialist on U.S. government, I introduced a course at Toronto that sought to apply the comparative approach by dealing with the governments of the United States and the Soviet Union. Meanwhile, at Harvard, Zbigniew Brzezinski and Samuel P. Huntingdon, following similar lines of thought, published their path-breaking study of the American and Soviet systems in *Political Power, USA-USSR.*[2] I devoted a year-long seminar to this book and published a detailed review in the *Canadian Journal of Economics and Political Science.*[3] I praised it as the first major attempt to break away from the prevailing black-and-white approach to the two systems but criticized their analysis as nonetheless making too sharp a dichotomy between them. I used a similar argument in responding to the categorical denial of the theory of convergence by Bertram Wolfe and rejected his claim for the absolute uniqueness of the Soviet system and its total divergence from other systems. On the other hand I could not accept the theory of total convergence put forward by Pitirim

Sorokin.[4] I made a more systematic application of comparative concepts to the Communist states of eastern Europe in a book entitled *The Governments of Communist East Europe*.[5] Focusing on the eight smaller Communist systems, I did not follow the customary procedure of describing each one separately but instead analysed their similarities and differences under certain headings: "The Pattern of Power," The Holders of Power," "The Process of Governing," and "Implementing Decisions." I concluded that there was no noticeable trend toward a genuinely constitutional system in the Soviet Union, nor any sign of a diminution of the powerful position of the ruling party. However, there had been a marked decline in the use of force and terror as methods of enforcement and the rise of more voluntary means of achieving concurrence. Communism, I felt, should not be seen as unchangeable and monolithic but rather as variegated and fluctuating, like other systems, and just as unpredictable.

Increasing diversity among the Communist states resulted from Khrushchev's reconciliation with Yugoslavia, his recognition of the many paths to socialism, the open deviation of Poland and Hungary from the Soviet path, and the developing breach between China and the Soviet Union. Milovan Djilas, the Yugoslav dissident, had written that it was wrong to underestimate or even to ignore the significance of the inevitable differences in degree and manner between Communist states. This had produced what he called in 1957 the general phenomenon of "national communism." My travels in eastern Europe in 1961 and 1962 confirmed the view that national communism was a reality and was indeed a force that would be capable, in certain circumstances, of transforming the entire communist world. I became convinced that the picture of world communism as monolithic was not accurate. Beneath the appearance of conformity, communism was everywhere taking on national hues; each country was developing its own distinctive form. This was not to deny the continuance of Soviet influence and the persistence of certain common features, but all of them exhibited a certain distinctiveness in forms and practices and some degree of freedom from Soviet control. In a series of articles published later in book form I sought to differentiate the communist countries of Eastern Europe. In one article I attempted a more thoroughgoing analysis of these states in terms of the degree of freedom from Soviet control or influence. The "ex-satellites" such as Yugoslavia and Albania, were *independent states, entirely free of Soviet control.* Others — "unorthodox satellites," such as Poland and Hungary — were *semi-independent states, not entirely free of control, and subject to substantial Soviet influence, but exercising considerable autonomy of action in domestic affairs.* Yet others, the so-called "orthodox satellites," such as Bulgaria, Czechoslovakia, East Germany, and Romania, were *dependent states, subject to a high degree of Soviet control and influence, and exercising a much lesser degree of autonomy.* The lines between these several categories were not always sharp nor were they rigid and unchanging. The aftermath of the Twenty-second Congress of the CPSU in 1961 suggested that national communism was more likely to intensify than decline in the future.[6]

By the mid-1960s the image and the reality of world communism had been transformed. It was no longer a single Soviet bloc, dominated by Moscow, but at best a Sino-Soviet alliance, with two centres of authority, Moscow and Peking. In Europe the so-called bloc had lost some of its members entirely. Even its inner core of seven states, members of the Warsaw Pact and Comecon, were moving along markedly different paths. In the short history of a multi-state Communist system, not yet two decades old, there had been four open breaks by individual states — Yugoslavia, Hungary, Poland, and Albania. There was every reason to expect that there would be more such breaches in the future and a complete split between China and the Soviet Union. We might, I wrote, be witnessing the twilight of the world communist system.[7]

DOCTRINAL DIFFERENTIATION

Further evidence of differentiation among communist states was presented by doctrinal divergences. In the initial post-Revolutionary period, major Soviet doctrinal experts treated the various People's Democracies, as they were called, as following distinctive and unique patterns of transition from capitalism to socialism, differing in essential aspects from the course followed in the Soviet Union. After the formation of the Cominform, a new doctrine was enunciated by the Bulgarian Communist leader, Georgii Dimitrov, in December 1948. The central thesis was that the path followed by the eastern European Communist states was fundamentally the same as that taken by the Soviet Union. The view that each was following its own distinctive national path to socialism was branded as a deviation from the Leninist science of world revolution. With the exception of Yugoslavia, the Dimitrov doctrine was accepted by the leaders of the communist states and Czech and Slovak theorists obsequiously followed suit. In two long articles I gave a detailed exposition of the new doctrine, as developed by Soviet and eastern European scholars. Ten years later, in a second pair of articles, I demonstrated that a significant difference of interpretation had emerged among Soviet and eastern European theorists.[8]

These scholastic disputes represented, I concluded, not only an intellectual endeavour, in Marxist terms, to interpret and rationalize the past and predict the future, but also a political effort to mould coming revolutions in a certain desired direction. The examination of this esoteric theory served as a useful instrument for differentiating the views held by different scholars in different communist countries. This test cast further doubt on the idea that the communist world was homogeneous and emphasized the need to study these conflicts within the several communist states.

TOTALITARIANISM AND GROUP CONFLICT

Western analysis of communism had long been dominated by the concept of totalitarianism, which assumed that a single party, free of internal conflict, imposed its will on society and on all social groups. The uniqueness of the Nazi or the Soviet systems was thought to lie in the totality of their political power. This excluded, as it were by definition, the existence of any area of autonomous behaviour by groups other than the state or party and prevented any serious influence by such groups on the process of decision-making. The wide-ranging re-evaluation of comparative politics in Western political science largely ignored the Soviet political system and made no serious effort to test concepts derived from Western experience by applying them to Communist states.

Western scholars were thus not prepared for the extraordinary changes that occurred in the Soviet political system after Stalin's death and for the increasing diversity among Communist countries. Evidence steadily mounted that the Soviet system was not without conflict and that behind the façade of the monolithic party a genuine struggle was taking place among rival groups. These conflicts were not mere struggles among leaders for personal power but dealt with major issues of public policy. In the Soviet Union, Poland, Yugoslavia, and Czechoslovakia, some theorists openly recognized that interest groups were an important factor in policy-making.

In June 1965, in a paper at the annual meeting of the Canadian Political Science Association in Vancouver, I advanced the hypothesis that group conflict was important in communist political systems. In 1966 I gave a fuller version of this approach in an article which appeared in the journal, *World Politics*,[9] and was reprinted in a number of symposia on Soviet and communist politics. In 1966-67, while jointly conducting undergraduate and graduate courses at the University of Toronto on the interest group theme, my colleague Franklyn Griffiths and I conceived the idea of preparing a book on the subject. We had opportunities to test our hypothesis in discussions with colleagues and students in Toronto, in copious correspondence with other scholars, and at seminars in several American and British universities. Even in the Communist world I received a favourable response in seminars in Warsaw, Belgrade, and Bratislava. We enlisted a group of specialists in Soviet politics, and in January 1968 held a conference of the participants in Toronto to discuss a common framework of analysis.

The resulting book[10] included chapters on seven major groups — four of them official in character (party *apparatchiki*, security police, the military, and industrial managers), and three professional (economists, writers, and jurists). The case studies documented the fact that the Soviet system was passing through a period of transition. Although making of final decisions remained in the hands of a relatively small group of leaders at the top, there was a broadening of group participation in the crucial preliminary stage of policy deliberation and in the subsequent phase of implementation. Our approach assumed not that occupational groups such as writers expressed a single common interest but rather that within each occupational group there usually existed opinion groups with conflicting views on public policy. There were also criss-crossing alliances of these opinion groups.

At a critical point in our work, Griffiths, my fellow editor, told me that he could no longer accept the interest group approach and felt that he should withdraw from the project. He saw "conflicting tendencies" of opinion in Soviet politics; these cut across all group affiliations and brought together those of like mind in all groups. I persuaded him to continue as editor and to include his own approach, which was widely greeted by reviewers as a valuable alternative approach.

The ouster of Khrushchev in 1964, the reform movement in Czechoslovakia in 1968, and its reversal after the Soviet invasion produced drastic change in the role of interest groups.[11] In 1968 I classified the ten Communist systems into five categories:

• *Quasi-totalitarian*: Stalin's Soviet Union from 1929 to 1953, Mao's China prior to the Cultural Revolution, Yugoslavia prior to 1948, and the other eastern European states after 1947-48. These systems treated groups in theory as illegitimate and severely limited their capacity for independent action.

- *Consultative authoritarian:* In the GDR, Hungary, Poland, and the Soviet Union after Khrushchev, group activity was not autonomous and was repressed if it expressed any opposition. Professional groups were brought into the decision-making process as advisers and consultants.
- *Quasi-pluralistic authoritarian:* Hungary and Poland during the thaw of 1953-56, the Soviet Union under Khrushchev, and Czechoslovakia and Poland in the mid-1960s. The party leadership remained dominant in politics, and bureaucratic groups were powerful. Professional groups, however, advanced alternative policies, criticized official decisions and action, and in some cases challenged frontally a whole series of official policies.
- *Democratizing and pluralistic authoritarian:* This category included Yugoslavia after its break with the Soviet Union, and particularly after 1966, and Czechoslovakia between January and August 1968, when political groups were institutionalized and played a significant role in policy-making. Finally, there was
- *Anarchic authoritarianism:* This encompassed the unique Chinese experience during the Cultural Revolution, where group conflict was intense but the methods used by the groups were spontaneous and coercive, often violent.

I concluded that there was no automatic process of change in the direction of democratic pluralization as a result of economic development, as was frequently argued. The development differed from state to state and did not follow a fixed sequence. I illustrated this process of change in another article in 1970, "Leadership and Group Conflict in Czechoslovakia."[12] The relationship of groups and leadership evolved from the *quasi-totalitarian* stage of the first years of communist power (1948-53) to the subsequent stage of *consultative authoritarianism* (early 1953, early 1956). This was eventually followed (1961-67) by the *quasi-pluralist authoritarian* phase of sharp group conflict, when certain groups such as liberal economists, liberal writers, Slovaks, students, and scholars openly pressed their interests and opinions. The eight months from January to August 1968 — what I called the *pluralist authoritarian* stage — witnessed the crystallizing, institutionalizing, and legitimizing of many groups. After the occupation there continued to be constant and vigorous activity by organized and informal political groupings, though within stricter limits — a reversion to the *quasi-pluralist* model.

These ideas struck a responsive chord among younger scholars, some of whom were inspired to conduct research employing the interest group approach. It also produced a backlash by others, such as William E. Odum, who continued to defend the totalitarian conception of Soviet politics, and Andrew C. Janos, who argued that the authoritarian nature of Soviet rule by definition excluded interest groups. In 1979 in a symposium reassessing the role of interest groups, I argued that the question of whether interest groups existed in authoritarian systems could only be resolved on the basis of empirical research, not on the basis of abstract reasoning.[13] Fifteen years after the appearance of the original article on interest groups in *World Politics*, I reassessed its contribution in a major article in the same journal.[14] Critics had ignored the value of the interest group approach demonstrated in a number of case studies of the Soviet system. With the exception of Archie Brown and Jerry Hough, students of comparative politics had failed to incorporate the findings of research on interest groups in communist systems into their more general theories of politics. I restated the case for the validity of the interest group approach, not only for post-Stalin Soviet and eastern European politics, but even for the Soviet Union under Stalin and Russia under the Tsars.

RISE OF OPPOSITION

The rise of interest group activity in the Communist states led to the emergence of political tendencies that could be called "oppositional," in that they resisted policies presented by the ruling party and proposed alternative courses of action. There was a world of difference between this informal kind of opposition and the institutionalized opposition in democratic states. The latter took the form of competing political parties, organized pressure groups, and parliamentary and electoral procedures that guaranteed the expression of opposition views. In the Communist systems the party's monopoly of political power had not been relaxed, nor had there been any admission, in theory or practice, of the legitimacy of political opposition. But in spite of the appearance of changelessness, there had been an unmistakable change in the way in which these systems were in fact operating.

This dichotomy led me to analyse what seemed to be a contradiction in terms — namely opposition within one-party states — and to distinguish at least four different types of opposition.[15]

- *Integral:* This form involved opposition to the Communist system itself, expressing itself in covert or overt disloyalty, and taking the form of revolutionary conspiracies or underground activity.
- *Fundamental:* This type was opposition to, or severe criticism of, key policies of the regime, unaccompanied, however, by rejection of the system itself. It sought not to replace the leaders but rather to resist, or to influence, a whole range of policies pursued by them. This was often linked with ...
- *Factional* resistance: This was conducted by individual leaders within the highest organs of party and government, who challenged established policies or sought to gain power for themselves.
- *Specific*: Opposition to specific policies of the regime — a kind of "loyal opposition" — was usually conducted by professional interest groups, such as writers, lawyers, and economists.

The various forms of opposition might overlap or combine with each other and differed profoundly in individual countries and from one period to another. Needless to say, there seemed little likelihood, especially after 1968, of the emergence of a multi-party system that would guarantee genuine opposition and a fully democratic exploration of policy alternatives.

POLITICAL CULTURE AND POLITICAL DEVELOPMENT

In my study of Czechoslovak communism I found it useful to employ two other concepts of Western political science — political culture and political development. I had explored the problem of the relationship of communism to past traditions and to the political culture of the individual countries in several articles.[16] In 1975, in a paper entitled "Stalinism and Czechoslovak Political Culture" given at a conference in Bellaggio, on Lake Como, I posed the question as to why Stalinism, originating in the profoundly different conditions of Soviet Russia and deeply imbedded in the Russian past, could come into existence, and last so long, in a country of profoundly democratic and national traditions.[17] My hypothesis was that Stalinism in Czechoslovakia was a projection of the Bolshevization of the Communist party of Czechoslovakia after 1929, and the implanting of Bolshevik or Stalinist values after the seizure of power in 1948. These outgrowths reached their apogee in the political trials of the 1950s. Such developments were the work of Stalin and his protégé, Gottwald, but the Czech and Slovak people shared responsibility for this tragedy by their failure to resist. For almost a generation Stalinist leaders were successful in suppressing the traditional political culture and in introducing alien patterns of politics.

I pursued this theme in a paper presented at the congress of the International Political Science Association in Moscow in 1979 and ultimately published in shorter form as "Czechoslovak Political Culture: Pluralism in an International Context."[18] Taking the fate of pluralism as an example, I noted the remarkable degree of continuity in pluralist values and actions running through Czechoslovak history in the 80 years leading up to 1937 and reaching their greatest flowering during the First Republic. Even after their interruption in 1938, pluralist values were manifested again between 1945 and 1948, and especially during the Prague Spring of 1968. Yet it could not be denied that, during the German occupation and under Stalinist rule, pluralism had been destroyed. Thus, in the realm of actual political behaviour, discontinuity, not continuity, was the dominant feature of Czechoslovak political culture for almost 40 years.

Had the values of pluralism survived beneath the surface, in the hearts and minds of the people, as some argued? The enforced conformity with the official ideology, prolonged over 35 of the 40 years since Munich, had, it would seem, affected not only actual behaviour but also the values and beliefs themselves. I argued further that the international environment played a crucial role in the rise and fall of pluralism, which flourished only during the rare periods of complete or partial independence, such as the First Republic, only to succumb to external pressures from Germany and the Soviet Union. But domestic factors played their part. Czechoslovak leaders, for instance, Hácha and Tiso, and later Beneš and Dubček, and still later Husák, failed to stand up to foreign pressures. And there was popular resistance to outside dictate only briefly in the aftermath of the Prague Spring. The Czechoslovak tradition has been to yield to superior external force without a struggle.

While I presented my paper in Moscow to an audience of over a hundred people my words were being translated simultaneously into Russian. I ran into a storm of opposition. The chairman, Radovan Richta, a leading Czech sociologist who had played a positive role in the Prague Spring but had later recanted, lamented that my paper was more political than scholarly and reprimanded me, an outsider, for seeking to interpret events in a foreign country. This outrageous viewpoint was sharply rejected by the convenor of the panel, Richard Merritt, of the University of Illinois, who was himself a specialist on Germany. He later informed me that Richta had protested against the inclusion of my paper in the program. Three Soviet scholars and three Czechs joined in a clearly orchestrated campaign of condemnation of my analysis as unscholarly and filled with a Cold War spirit. Others in the audience rushed to secure copies of my paper, and several Soviet scholars, and even one of the Czech critics, assured me in the hallway that they had greatly appreciated my presentation. It was some satisfaction to have been able to present these heretical views in the heart of the Soviet empire.[19]

In spite of my commitment to the comparative approach, I was not happy with what I thought was the obsession of eastern European specialists with the concepts of modernization and development. Although some Communist countries did achieve economic and social modernization in certain fields, others, such as Czechoslovakia, were already modernized in 1945, and Communism had been profoundly demodernizing. Still more puzzling was the use of the concept of "political development," a term more ambiguous than modernization, and its linkage with modernization in a cause-and-effect relationship. I expressed this view as a commentator at a conference on political development at Stanford University in December 1975. I challenged the underlying ideas of the conference itself and later published my dissenting viewpoint under the title "Development or Retrogression?"[20] Almost all the countries of eastern Europe, prior to Communist rule, had to varying degrees achieved political development, for instance, in the form of political parties, interest groups, public organizations and elected representative bodies. Some, such as Czechoslovakia, and even Hungary and Poland, were substantially developed. Hence Communism, in its Stalinist phase, represented a significant reversal of political development and had led to what I suggested could best be called the "primitivization" of political life.

The collapse of the Communist system in the Soviet Union and in eastern Europe in the 1990s raised questions in the minds of some as to whether my efforts at theoretical analysis threw light on the real nature of these systems. In my view the totalitarian approach depicted the Communist systems as monolithic and unchangeable, while comparative analysis recognized the dynamic of change in these systems and the unique developments in each Communist state. It thus seemed more accurate than the attitude of those who disregarded the evidence of change and diversity provided by concrete research. Although the Communist systems were basically authoritarian in nature, the forms and degrees of authoritarianism clearly differed in each country and at different stages of development. Some were becoming less monolithic in their internal procedures, as various forms of interest group and dissident tendencies appeared. Although pluralist or quasi-pluralist elements did appear, the systems were not fully pluralist, nor were they likely to become so. Nor could they be considered politically developed in any meaningful sense of that word.

Similarly the "national communism" that I identified foreshadowed the possibility of increasing diversity and greater conflicts among these states and even the ultimate breakdown of the world communist system. In this respect my analysis proved more accurate than that of others who minimized the differences among Communist systems, even those between the Soviet Union and China, and persisted in believing in bloc unity long after it had disappeared.

In retrospect, my analysis seemed to have correctly focused on the points of conflict and the social forces within and among these states which eventually contributed to the collapse of world communism. Like most specialists on the Communist world, however, I did not foresee that these factors would be fatal for the systems. Although I recognized the existence of various forms of opposition, I did not anticipate the triumph of what I had called integral or fundamental opposition. Although I laid great stress on the role of dissent and independent activity in undermining the legitimacy of the systems, I did not realize their full potential in contributing to their ultimate collapse. In fact I assumed that the Communist systems might be stabilized and preserved through drastic reforms along the lines of the Prague Spring. The failure of the latter and the establishment of the state of war in Poland ten years later revealed the great obstacles that stood in the way of such reform and cast doubt on its ultimate attainability. The momentous events at the end of 1989 and in the early 1990s came therefore as a surprise to me and revealed the incurable inner weaknesses of the communist systems, which I had failed fully to understand.

NOTES

1. "Soviet and Communist Politics: A Comparative Approach," *The Journal of Politics* 22, no. (1960): 300-13.
2. New York: Viking; Toronto: Macmillan, 1964.
3. 31, no. 2 (May 1965): 273-80.
4. *The Humanist* (Sept.-Oct. 1968): 3-10, 32.
5. New York: Crowell, 1966.
6. For this, see my "Communism, National or International," *International Journal* 15, no. 1 (Winter 1959-60): 36-40; "Communism in Eastern Europe: Personal Impressions, 1961-1962," *Canadian Slavonic Papers* (1964): 18-37. Articles in *The Economist* and the *International Journal* in Toronto were republished in *Communism, National and International: Eastern Europe after Stalin* (Toronto: University of Toronto Press, 1964). See also "National Communism in Eastern Europe since the 22nd Congress," *The Canadian Journal of Economics and Political Science* 30, no. 3 (Aug. 1964): 313-27, also published in Skilling, *Communism, National and International.*
7. Richard Pipes, Alexander Dallin, Joseph S. Berliner, and Gordon Skilling, *The Changing Communist World* (Toronto: United Nations Association, 1963). See also Skilling, "The Crisis in Eastern Europe, Communism: National and International," *International Journal* 39, no. 2 (Spring 1984): 429-558.
8. "People's Democracy in Soviet Theory," *Soviet Studies* 3, no. 1 (July 1951): 16-33; *ibid.* 3, no. 2. (Oct. 1951): 131-49. See also, "People's Democracy and the Socialist Revolution: A Case Study in Communist Scholarship," *Soviet Studies* 12, no. 3 (Jan. 1961): 241-62, and *ibid.* 12, no. 4 (April 1961), 420-35; "Permanent or Uninterrrupted Revolution: Lenin, Trotsky and their Successors on the Transition to Socialism," *Canadian Slavonic Papers* 5 (1961): 3-30.
9. "Interest Groups and Communist Politics," *World Politics* 18, no. 3 (April 1961): 435-51.
10. H. Gordon Skilling and Franklyn Griffiths, eds., *Interest Groups in Soviet Politics* (Princeton: Princeton University Press, 1971).
11. "Group Conflict and Political Change," Chalmers Johnson, ed., *Change in Communist Systems* (Stanford: Stanford University Press, 1970): 215-34.
12. R. Barry Farrell, ed., *Political Leadership in Eastern Europe and the Soviet Union* (Chicago: Aldine, 1970): 276-93.

13. *Studies in Comparative Communism* 13, no. 1 (Spring 1979) for my comment; for Janos's reply, see *ibid.* 14, no. 1 (Spring 1980): 82-90.
14. *World Politics* 36, no. 1 (Oct. 1983): 1-27.
15. "The Party, Opposition and Interest Groups: Fifty Years of Continuity and Change," *International Journal* 22, no. 4 (Autumn 1967): 618-31; repr. in Kurt London, *The Soviet Union: A Half-Century of Conflict* (Baltimore: The Johns Hopkins University Press, 1968): 119-49; and "Background to the Study of Opposition in Communist Eastern Europe," *Government and Opposition* 3, no. 3 (Summer 1968): 294-321, repr. in Leonard Schapiro, ed., *Opposition in One-party States* (London: Macmillan, 1972), 72-103, and in Robert A. Dahl, ed., *Regimes and Opposition* (New Haven: Yale University Press, 1973), 89-119. A shorter version was published during the Prague Spring in Czech, in "Opozice ve východní Evropě," *Dějiny a současnost* (Prague) 11, no. 5, 113-16.
16. *Journal of International Affairs* 20, no. 1 (1966): 118-37; *The Canadian Forum* 49, no. 585 (Oct. 1988): 155-57.
17. Robert Tucker, ed., *Stalinism: Essays in Historical Interpretation* (New York: Norton, 1977): 257-80.
18. Archie Brown, ed., *Political Culture and Communist Studies* (London: Macmillan, 1981): 115-33. The original paper is available only in typewritten form. See "Prague 1968: The Aftermath," *International Journal* 33, no. 4 (Autumn 1978): 678-701. A leading Czech ideologist later wrote that my paper was not scientific and no more than a political pamphlet (*Nové slovo*, Oct. 18, 1979).
19. For a description of the congress, see my "Moscow Games," in the University of Toronto alumni magazine, *Graduate* 7, no. 4 (March-April 1960): 21-24.
20. *Studies in Comparative Communism* 16, nos. 1-2 (Spring-Summer, 1982): 125-30.

[Handwritten marginal notes across the top of the page, partially legible:]

...go away, neither richer or poorer ... when they came, and are absorbed once in their business, which has ... to do with art. Why did they ...? In each picture is a whole life to me imprisoned, a whole chain of fears, happ... and joys ...

..., and joys. Whither is this lifetime tending? What is the message of ... competent artist? To send light into darkness of men's hearts — ... in the duty of the artist," said Schumann. "An artist is a man ... he can draw and paint ... said ... ... to human ... souls go ... (W. Kandinsky: concerning the spiritual in art ...

12

JOURNEYS EAST FROM VIENNA

MY APPOINTMENT AT TORONTO in 1959 opened up possibilities for more frequent travel in eastern Europe, and I obtained an early sabbatical to make up for the one that I would miss at Dartmouth. Hence we were able to spend the entire academic year 1961-62 as a family in Vienna, and I was able to explore central and eastern Europe almost a decade after Stalin's death.

We crossed the Atlantic on the Italian liner *Homeric* and spent two and a half weeks in England — in London and Oxford, Stratford, Canterbury, and Dover. We took the old familiar Channel crossing to Calais, where we picked up our rented car, a brand-new Simca Chambord. Our first stop was Aubigny, in France, at my brother Don's grave. In the Netherlands we stayed for a week in a little hotel on a sleepy canal in the countryside, from which it was easy to drive into Rotterdam, Amsterdam, and The Hague. On a leisurely trip down the Rhine, we stopped for several days of walking in the Black Forest. During our few days in Bonn I interviewed diplomats in the Foreign Office about eastern Europe. Then on to Vienna by way of Salzburg — my first visit to this lovely city in 25 years.

In Vienna we found a comfortable and inexpensive place to live on a quiet street near the Türkenschanz Park. We had a small coal stove within a giant porcelain heater for heating the living-room, but there was no heat in the bedroom. Sally found it difficult to keep house with few modern facilities and to follow the local practice of shopping in many different stores; she later developed a bad shoulder as a result of carrying heavy bags home. The boys attended the American International School, where they studied French and German. For me this year provided a golden opportunity to travel in the neighbouring countries of central and eastern Europe, as well as the Soviet Union. I covered about 10,000 miles, crossing and recrossing the tightly controlled frontiers of the bloc countries. I was on the road for a total of five months — in East Germany and Poland in August, in the Soviet Union in November and December, in Hungary (with Sally) in the new year, in Bulgaria in March. I spent at least a week or two in each of the countries of the Soviet bloc except Albania.[1]

My purpose was to examine the impact on the European Communist world of the Twenty-second Congress of the Communist Party of the Soviet Union (CPSU) and of Khrushchev's renewed condemnation of Stalinism. During my travels I normally packed into one week conversations with many scholars, professors, journalists, party and government officials, foreign diplomats, and private persons. They could often speak English, but I could resort to French or German, Czech or Russian, and where necessary, I used an interpreter. I prepared for each trip by thorough study of eastern European materials in Vienna. In February, Sally and I travelled to Munich for ten days of research in the archives of Radio Free Europe and conversations with those in charge of the country desks.

GERMANY AND POLAND

On my first trip, in October 1961, I reached Berlin by air, flying over East German territory through the Allied air corridor and landing at the Tempelhof airfield, where a huge stone monument honoured the airlift of 1948. The Berlin Wall had been erected just one month before my visit, dividing this great city unnaturally into two parts. In the West, the Kurfüstendam typified the glitter and prosperity of the bourgeois world. New modern buildings contrasted sharply with those still in ruins. In East Berlin the famous Unter den Linden was gloomy and drab, and there were only a few buildings under construction amid the ruins.

The Wall was an ominous symbol of the division of Europe and of the Stalinist character of the German Democratic Republic (GDR). In the West this odious barrier was a magnet for Germans and for tourists, who were able to approach close and look over at the armed border guards on the eastern side. On Zinnerstrasse I stood within a few feet of the East Berlin workers who were strengthening the Wall with granite blocks. At Checkpoint Charlie, the main point of access, many West Berliners tried desperately to bridge the separation from loved ones by standing on a tall wooden tower and communicating with each other by shouts and through binoculars. It was at this point that I entered the East for a few hours. I returned by the U-Bahn, passing through police controls at the Friedrichstrasse station. On the eastern side the Wall looked grim and forbidding. At the Brandenburg Gate one could sit a hundred yards away and gaze through at the wide avenue leading to the Tiergarten in the West.

My conversations with diplomats and scholars in West Berlin revealed a sharp contrast of opinion on the Wall and the future of the East German state and the Oder-Neisse line dividing Germany and Poland. West German officials condemned the building of the Wall and rejected the idea of recognizing the East German regime, but they admitted that the border with Poland was a reality that would eventually have to be accepted. Other Germans strongly urged a policy of pressing for the unification of Germany. Some bitterly criticized American policy, fearing concessions that would endanger West Berlin's freedom.

Within a month I returned to East Germany, this time by car from Vienna. There was no opportunity to talk with officials or scholars, but I had a first-hand look at the towns and countryside. It presented a favourable contrast to the drab villages of Czechoslovakia but lacked the colour and prosperity of Bavaria or the Rhineland. The highways were much better than those in Czechoslovakia and were free of the heavy traffic of the West German autobahns. The Soviet occupation, including army bases and soldiers and officers in towns, was much in evidence, but it was not so blatant as the American military presence in West Germany.

In Dresden the city centre was still in total ruins after the devastating Allied air raid at the close of the war. The great Zwinger Art Gallery was restored and open to tourists. In Leipzig a new opera house had been constructed, and the famous World Fair was open. The courthouse, where Georgii Dimitrov, the Bulgarian Communist, had been tried in 1933 for allegedly burning the Reichstag, was now a museum in his honour. In beautiful Weimar, where Goethe, Schiller, Herder, Bach, and Cranach had once lived, the Goethe Museum presented a Marxist interpretation of the life of this great liberal and humanist. A few miles away the former concentration camp of Buchenwald was being used for propaganda not only against the Nazi regime but also in honour of the Communist resistance. My final stop on the way to Poland was the ancient town of Bautzen, near the border, where I was surprised to find street signs and other notices in the language of the Lusatian Sorb minority. The beautiful cathedral had been used from the time of the Reformation for services by both Catholic and Evangelical churches.

I crossed the Oder-Neisse line at the little German town of Görlitz (Zgorzelec in Polish) where the river Neisse (Nysa) was hardly more than one hundred feet wide. Like the other borders dividing the "friendly and fraternal" socialist countries, this one was lined with barbed wire and watchtowers. German officials were efficient and friendly; on the Polish side, in a dirty and primitive office, the officials were slovenly and unfriendly, and customs clearance took over two hours. There, as everywhere on my trip, my Simca was examined and admired by all: one border official knowingly identified it as a "Zimka," a little Zim, the official Soviet limousine for officials!

My drive through the former Silesia revealed almost no traces of its once German character, except in cemeteries and churches. Wrocław was still largely in ruins. Apart from the main square, with its splendid rebuilt gothic town hall and two magnificent churches, it looked drab and dreary. It seemed completely Polish; no one even understood German. The villages consisted of little old farmhouses, usually with thatched roofs, but many new rough brick houses lined the highway. The road to Warsaw was straight and flat, and I could travel at high speed, slowed down from time to time by slow-moving wagons and by chickens, ducks, geese, dogs, an occasional cow, and a few people on foot or on bicycle. Warsaw was a blaze of lights at night but presented a very depressing sight in the morning — widespread ruins, battered old buildings, and new jerry-built apartments, the ugly Stalinesque Palace of Culture towering over the city, and the apparent poverty of people in the streets. The Old Town had been carefully restored to its original form and beauty. In the ruins of the Ghetto stood the splendid monument to the Jewish fighters. There was no map of the city available, and only one gas station in the whole city that sold super-benzine.

It was easy to make contacts with a wide range of scholars, journalists, and diplomats, whose views confirmed the distinctive character of Poland as an "unorthodox satellite." Conversations testified to general hostility to Stalinism and determination to hold on to as many of the gains of 1956 as possible. Continuing fear and hatred of Germans were everywhere evident, but a sharp distinction was made between East and West Germans. A Polish diplomat argued the necessity of recognizing the full sovereignty of the GDR and of the Polish-German frontier.

The freer and more open character of intellectual life was evident. It was a surprise to be invited by Manfred Lachs, distinguished legal scholar and delegate to the United Nations, to address the Polish Political Science Association on teaching about the socialist countries in the West. At a meeting of the Club of the Crooked Circle, a Polish sociologist, Stefan Nowak, reported on the surprising results of opinion polls. These revealed that Polish students had a positive attitude toward socialism but a negative one toward Marxism; not many were non-religious, but few were actively religious. Talks with several other sociologists, including the "official" Adam Schaff and the independent Jan Strzelecki, indicated that although Marxism was the dominant doctrine in scholarly circles, there were many variants of the creed. Gone were the Talmudic discussions of the concept of People's Democracy. Marxism-Leninism had been replaced by sociology, which took the form of empirical studies and the analysis of public opinion.

I learned something of the uneasy relationship between the Catholic church and the Communist state in conversations with Catholic intellectuals and editors of Catholic newspapers. There was a readiness to accept socialism as a reality and, in some cases, even to take a somewhat positive attitude toward Marxism. In Lublin, in southeastern Poland, close to the Soviet frontier, I was the guest of Professor Leopold Seidler, rector of the official Maria-Skłodowska-Curie University. He claimed that there was "co-existence without cooperation" with the Catholic University in Lublin. At one point I slipped away from his ubiquitous tutelage and visited the latter institution. Although I was without introduction, I was warmly received by the rector, Dr Marion Rechowicz, who invited me to dinner with colleagues. They spoke openly of the limited autonomy of this, the only Catholic university in the Communist world, and of the great handicaps under which it conducted its work. My impressions of the strength of Catholicism were confirmed in the beautiful city of Krakow, which had escaped damage during both world wars. There were some 60 churches in the city, and on Saturday evenings and Sundays they were all crowded with worshippers. I had a meeting with Dr Jacek Woźniakowski, the noted art historian, who had been an editor of the leading Catholic weekly, *Tygoolnik Powszechny*, and was associated with Znak publishing house and the monthly *Znak*. He told me that they were greatly hampered by censorship and by the limits set on circulation.

THE SOVIET UNION

I flew from Vienna to Moscow in early November 1961 on one of the big new Soviet jets, the TU 104A. On my way in to the city I was impressed by the heavier traffic and many new apartment blocks, some much more attractive than those of the old Stalinist style. They were fast displacing the picturesque little log cabins (*izby*) of earlier days, although many of the latter remained in the outlying districts and some even in the centre. The streets were brightly decorated for 7 November, the anniversary of the revolution, and shop windows were more attractive in their display of goods. On the Sverdlovsk Square stood a massive new statue of Karl Marx, his head and shoulders hewn out of a monolithic piece of granite, with an inscription: "His name will endure through the ages." In the nearby Alexandrovsky Garden stood a great obelisk, inscribed with the names of the forerunners of the revolution from Marx to Plekhanov. At the Lenin Mausoleum people watched the ceremony of the changing of the guard every few hours. On the holiday, I strolled around central Moscow in the evening; the crowds were singing and dancing, a good many of them slightly tipsy. There were small knots here and there engaged in vigorous discussions. Classical and folk music was blaring forth from the loudspeakers on Manezhnaya Square — a gay scene!

Although it was Sunday, offices were open before a three-day break during the holiday. Intourist seemed friendlier and willingly agreed to let me divide my time between *de luxe* and the cheaper *pension* rates and spread out my use of a car and guide throughout the whole period. I was lucky to have as my guide a young man, Mark Gorelik, who was helpful and friendly. Although he spoke good English we often used Russian. Over the next weeks he spent much time in the Intourist office and other agencies trying to get them to satisfy my many requests for meetings and visits. I learned later that Amasasp Aratunyian, Soviet ambassador in Ottawa, had written a letter urging that every help be given to me. At times I despaired of results and resorted to direct approaches to various institutions and to individuals whom I knew by name. In the end I had a full program of meetings in academic institutions, sometimes with one or two persons, often in groups of eight or ten. The interviews took place in Russian, with the help of an interpreter, and sometimes in English. Each work day extended late into the night, as I made notes and tried to keep up with the daily *Pravda* and the *New York Times*. I was often utterly exhausted and suffered from a bad cough and diarrhoea. As the weather grew chilly and snow began to fall, I was glad to wear winter clothing.

Once more I was given a palatial room in the National Hotel over-looking the Manezhnaya Square and the Kremlin walls, facing toward Red Square and St Basil's Cathedral in the distance. Down the hall from me was my friend Harold Berman, professor of law at Harvard, who, with his wife, was spending the whole year at the Institute of State and Law and was to give 30 hours of lectures on American law. Their four young children were studying at Russian schools. It was good to be able to drop in on them in the evenings and to borrow the *New York Times*. My accommodation was a little too luxurious for my needs. As always, there was no plug in the bathtub, so that I was glad I had brought one with me. I got tired of eating alone in the large dining-room and frustrated by the slow service. None the less I was quite disappointed, on my return from Leningrad, to be placed in the vast and unfriendly Hotel Metropole, but I could do nothing about it.

My room and its balcony were ideal for viewing the military parade on 7 November. Early in the morning I watched the square fill up with tanks and trucks and soldiers. The central areas of Moscow were shut off by long lines of militiamen and soldiers. Access to Red Square and central Moscow was permitted only on presentation of passport and a special permit. At ten o'clock sharp, the military parade began, with Marshal Malinovsky and General Krylov standing in huge limousines and stopping at intervals to greet the crowds. The roar of many guns stirred up the birds from the Kremlin walls. Then came the workers, marching, to the music of many bands, in great columns about 25 abreast and carrying banners with political slogans. I was able to take many pictures from my balcony, although I was told it was strictly forbidden. When the parade ended, I joined the crowds streaming into Red Square. Everyone was curious to see the new grave of Stalin under the Kremlin wall.

On a later day I joined the long line of people waiting to enter the Lenin mausoleum, taking advantage of a foreigner's privilege of joining it well toward the front. The interior was unchanged since 1958, except for the removal of Stalin's body. Lenin was dressed in a blue uniform-like tunic, with a white shirt barely showing above the collar. His face looked shrivelled and old, and the reddish hue of the hair seemed unnatural. People were required to move through quickly, and there was no display of emotion or even respect. Afterward the queue moved to the Kremlin wall, where one could read the plaques dedicated to foreign communists buried there and view the graves of top leaders, including Stalin's. Unlike the others, his was not yet graced by a bust and was marked only by a tablet with the name I.V. Stalin and dates of birth and death.

The morning after the parade it was a great contrast to attend a church service at a small church, built in the baroque style, in a working-class district. It was jammed, with people standing close together throughout the two and a half hour service. The congregation included many old and middle-aged, and not many young people. A splendid choir sang the music of Tchaikovsky. The priest, in gorgeous robes, delivered a sermon on the theme of "love" and blessed the church, the patriarch, "Orthodox people," "our native land," and "the state authorities."

The following Sunday was sunny and cold. I attended the morning service at the magnificent Novo-Devichiy Monastery, then under reconstruction. The service was conducted in what had once been an imperial palace, richly decorated with icons. The bishop and the priests were in constant motion, swinging incense, waving long candles, bowing, praying, blessing, and changing robes behind the iconostasis. The powerful voices of the priests and of the choir were supplemented by the full-throated participation of the whole congregation. Many older women, in kerchiefs, knelt frequently and touched the floor with their heads. Afterward I wandered in the old cemetery and noticed the graves of Gogol and Chekhov, and of Alliliueva, Stalin's wife. Another day I went by car to the Zagorsk Monastery, founded in 1348 — a spectacular complex of domed churches, onion-towers, and a red brick Baroque tower, surrounded by a white wall. The churches were crowded with worshippers; robed priests and theological students walked back and forth in the snow-clad grounds.

At the famed Bolshoi, I occupied a front-row seat in a box seating 12. It was a splendid theatre, with its seven-tier horseshoe of gold-decorated galleries and brilliant red draperies. The superb performance included *Chopiniania*, danced slowly and gracefully by women to the music of Chopin; *City Night*, a tragic love story in "gang land" (New York City?) by Béla Bartok, and reminiscent of *West Side Story*, and *Paganini*, in which the main dancer took the role of a violin virtuoso who eventually met his death at the hands of his fellow fiddlers.

I also attended a performance of Mayakovsky's *Klop* (*Bedbug*), staged and acted splendidly and enthusiastically received. It was a story about the resurrection of a man frozen 50 years earlier and was a marvellous satire of certain aspects of Soviet society, especially in Stalin's time. It satirized the "nouveau riche," or "worker-turned-bourgeoisie," and culminated in a "red" but very "bourgeois" wedding and a huge drunken brawl.

In sharp contrast were two sessions of the Supreme Soviet, for which I secured permission to attend on the request of the chairman of Intourist. The first meeting, the Council of Nationalities, was held in the Grand Hall of the Kremlin, a long, oblong chamber, lined with great marble columns. Facing the audience were four or five raised tiers of seats for the members of the government and the officers of the Supreme Soviet. Behind in a niche stood a huge full-length statue of Lenin and, above that, in pure white, the Soviet coat of arms. The subject of debate was the budget for 1961-62; the speeches were dull and stereotyped. During a break we were able to wander through the magnificent Kremlin palace, including the private residence of the tsars and view the rich displays of the crown jewels. We watched the delegates file out — a very mixed group, some Oriental in appearance and dress, some rough and proletarian in appearance, but most were well-dressed in Western style. I spoke to one woman who said she was a milkmaid from a village near Brest. Another was a tractor driver from Mari in the far north.

Two days later I attended a joint session of both houses of the Supreme Soviet, attended by the entire party presidium, including Khrushchev, Brezhnev, Mikoyan, and Suslov and members of the Council of Ministers. We listened to the concluding speeches on the plan and on the budget, cut and dried performances without real debate. The voting took place by show of hand, paragraph by paragraph. Minor changes were made at the suggestion of committees.

Another "performance," this time with a greater appearance of reality, was a trial in a people's court in the Sverdlovsk *raion* of Moscow. An elderly man was charged with accepting a bribe of 100 rubles from a woman who wanted a better room in the building under his supervision. The poor woman, who had lived in a basement room without heat or light, was almost illiterate and wept throughout the proceedings. The judge tried to console her, saying, "There was no need to be afraid." He was well prepared and asked penetrating questions. It seemed that some kind of rough justice was being meted out, but I left before the verdict was given.

Some of the most interesting meetings were chance encounters. On my first evening a young woman, clad in a dressing gown, greeted me from the balcony next to mine. Excusing herself, she returned wearing a coat and brought two goblets of brandy. She was a chess player from Odessa, here in Moscow for a holiday. Another day I met two young Yakuts, an elementary school teacher and his wife, a radio engineer, who were in Moscow for 12 days of "schooling." In their hotel room we compared notes on Canada and Yakutia. They avoided politics but were very proud of the development of Yakutia. Another evening at dinner I met an Armenian engineer from Erevan. The son of a simple peasant, he was convinced that Marxism was "the most correct point of view" and that socialism was the best system.

It was interesting to be in Moscow just after the Twenty-second Congress of the CPSU, at which Khrushchev made a second frontal assault on Stalin and Stalinism and openly criticized Albania. I discussed the significance of this event with many people, including Arnold Smith, my classmate from Toronto and Oxford, who had been in Moscow for two months as Canadian ambassador. On one occasion he hosted a luncheon for a number of his fellow ambassadors and several Moscow correspondents of leading world newspapers. One guest expressed the view that Khrushchev's purpose was "to open up the way for new ideas and new ways and to discredit the old ways and those who still supported them." Another said that the attack on Stalin was designed to encourage local initiative and fresh approaches, though within strict limits.

I had a long visit in the beautiful apartment of Henry Shapiro, United Press correspondent, who had been in Moscow for 25 years. He believed that Khrushchev had not acted out of emotion; his was a calculated move intended to shock the Soviet people into realizing the necessity of completely rooting out Stalinism and to undermine continued resistance to his planned reforms. Soviet life had changed greatly since the first assault on Stalin in 1956, but the process of change would be slow, Shapiro thought. Compare the long evolution of the United States, he suggested, between 1900 and its present maturity.

I had an informative talk with the economist Vladimir Kazakevich, a member of the prestigious Institute of World Economics and Politics (IMEMO), who during the war had taught in the United States at the Cornell summer program on Russian civilization. He had no concern about coming to my hotel room and talking for four and a half hours in an open and uninhibited way. It was difficult to know how much one could rely on some of his statements. He made the point that Stalinism had appealed to ordinary Russians, many of whom had been ready to sacrifice their lives for Stalin during the war and who had wept at his death. Quite different was the attitude of the intellectuals, many of whom had been persecuted by Stalin and were relieved to see the end of his rule.

A good example of the interplay of Marxism and Western thought was Yurii Zamoshkin, a sociologist, whom I had met in 1958. He was a member of the academy's Institute of Philosophy and also taught at Moscow University. He had just returned from a six-month stay in the United States and was thoroughly familiar with American sociology. Although he was critical of its exclusively empirical approach and its lack of attention to theory, he was seeking to apply some of its methods to his own study of the relationship of the individual and the collective. Later we had a long discussion of my article on the comparative approach to the study of politics; he had read it and agreed with it. He acknowledged the need for a comparative analysis of American and Soviet institutions and practices in dealing with common problems, such as the role of the individual in industrialized society and the relationship of the individual to mass communications and bureaucracy. He was repelled by the individualism of American society. In the Soviet Union, he argued, the individual was an integral part of the whole and could and did influence the making of decisions. He shared my aversion to the "totalitarian" label as applied to the Soviet Union; he spoke of what he called "a self-imposed and inner-directed kind of disciplined participation of the individual in the affairs of society."

As in 1958, Zamoshkin took me to a meeting at the Institute of Philosophy. Several younger persons, such as V. Semenov and G. Osipov, were good examples of the sociological trend that he himself personified. Sociology did not exist as a separate field but was a part of philosophy. This did not exclude concrete sociological research, of which they gave a number of examples. Visits by Polish sociologists, notably Adam Schaff, had had an impact on their thinking. The discussion tended to be dominated by older persons, such as A.F. Okulov, acting director of the institute, and B.S. Mankovsky, well known to me as a specialist on the theory of people's democracy. The younger men were much more down to earth and practical and seemed bored by the theoretical and propagandistic views of their older colleagues.

My visits to the Institute of State and Law of the Academy of Sciences and to the Faculty of Law at the university confirmed for me that the old orthodoxies were still influential among older men but that younger scholars were thinking more independently. At a first visit to the institute I was greeted by two persons, V.P. Kotok and N.P. Farberov, whose names were familiar to me from their writings on people's democratic theory. I was depressed by their black-and-white and dogmatic approach. In discussing the discipline of state and law, they argued that the addition of the term "state" to the title of the institute meant that emphasis was being placed not just on law, but on the state, and that this included parties and social organizations. However, the internal structure of the party was ruled out; that was studied by party institutes and journals only. The role of the individual had been distorted by the cult of personality under Stalin, but this had not changed the system as such; it remained the most developed democracy in the world. Moreover, as I was to hear over and over, there could be no return to the cult of personality; that was excluded by Khrushchev's condemnation of Stalinism and by the new procedures of political life.

A talk with the elderly Professor S.S. Kravchuk, head of Soviet public law in the Faculty of Law at Moscow University, was similarly depressing. He did not expect that the party congress would bring changes in the teaching plan of the department, but there would, of course, be alterations in the content of lectures. I had some doubts about this when I later listened to a lecture by him on the Soviet system of government. It was extremely elementary and descriptive, based largely on his textbook on the subject, and was delivered in a dull and boring way. During an intermission, students crowded around me, asking me questions about our studies of the Soviet Union in Canada. Professor Farberov expressed even more orthodox and hackneyed views than Kravchuck. He admitted that there had been errors of interpretation in the past but the international communist conferences in 1957 and 1960 had set forth the correct combination of the general and the specific elements of the revolution.

It was a refreshing contrast to meet with Yurii Barabashev, of the Law Faculty, who had studied in Toronto for six months. He was a specialist on local government and was doing a comparative study of the United States, Britain, and Canada. With his wife we went to the famous Puppet Theatre and enjoyed a performance of *The Divine Comedy*, which combined actors and puppets. It was a good satire on God's creation of the Earth and of man and woman and of the fall of Adam and Eve. Mrs Barabashev looked quite smart in a fur coat and a Japanese scarf, both purchased in Canada, and she gave me a present for Sally — a pair of opera glasses.

In a later meeting with Yurii, in the restaurant of the Hotel Moscow, I summed up my article on the comparative analysis of political systems; he said that he was in full agreement. Then, as we looked out over Red Square and the Kremlin, we solemnly drank a toast in cognac to the comparative approach! He praised my lectures on the Soviet system in Toronto as objective. It was now possible, he said, for younger Soviet scholars to take a more balanced attitude to foreign governments. This was borne out in a meeting with one of his younger colleagues, Avgust Mishin, a specialist on bourgeois political systems, especially the American. Although he was a party member and head of the party bureau in the faculty, he expressed views that were often unorthodox. He did not reject the idea of a comparative analysis of the Soviet and American systems. "Men are men," he said, referring to common characteristics of political systems. He was at work on a large volume on bourgeois constitutional law that did not deal with each country separately but treated each function of government in a comparative framework. When I met him a few days later, Mishin had read my article and said that it was the best thing he had read in English on this theme. When I told him that a Soviet reviewer had condemned my article on the ground that the Soviet system was unique and superior, he rejected the view as non-Marxist. The two systems, capitalist and socialist, were not separate and unrelated as often argued — both worlds influenced each other.

The visit to the Law Faculty was discouraging in other ways — the propaganda posters everywhere, the absence of a single foreign book in the library of the Chair of State Law, and the mediocrity and conformity of a diploma essay on Czechoslovakia that I glanced at. The building and the library were run down, the toilets abominable.

Early in my stay I had an interview with Professor V.A. Zhamin, dean of the Faculty of Political Economy and a specialist on Chinese economics. The faculty was housed in an ancient building, not unlike my own department in Toronto. In a letter to Vincent Bladen in Toronto, I wrote that it was strictly an economics department, with seven chairs in specialized fields, including one on the economics of foreign countries. The students took a heavy program of lectures, mainly in economics; their class work ran to about 32 to 34 hours per week and dropped to 12 hours only in the final year. Of the 550 regular students, some 120 worked in foreign economics and were expected to study the language of the country of specialization.

A few days later I met with some of the fifth-year students working on Czechoslovakia, Poland, the GDR, China, India, England, and the United States. I met a specialist on Czechoslovakia, but she knew little Czech and did not seem to have much expertise. With her colleagues we had some discussion of the controversies over People's Democracies; they were familiar with the turns and twists of this theory in eastern Europe and seemed to accept the clichés and stock phrases with which I had had to cope.

Zhamin surprised me by inviting me to give a lecture on Canada, or on any subject I chose, and offering me a room seating one hundred. In the end I spoke to a regular meeting of the Chair of Foreign Economics, at which Zhamin was to speak after me on his recent visit to Poland. A large poster announced the time and place of the lecture on "The Study of the Soviet Union in Canada and the United States." Some 50 persons attended, including students and professors. I spoke in Russian, having worked on the text with my guide. I reviewed the postwar development of interdisciplinary Russian studies at Columbia and Harvard, their underdeveloped state in Canada, and our plans at Toronto. I presented the case for a comparative approach that would avoid the danger of ethnocentrism and of a Cold War mentality. No one later touched on these provocative questions. The dean thanked me warmly at the end and said that I was "the first bird that had flown in from Canada."

It was difficult for me as a Western political scientist to identify my opposite number in the Soviet Union. In fact political science did not exist as a separate academic discipline. Some aspects of what we would consider the discipline were studied as part of law, economics, history, and even philosophy, but not as components of a distinctive discipline. The Soviet Academy of Sciences had no institute devoted to political studies, nor were there faculties of political science in the universities.[2] When a Soviet Association of Political Science was formed a few years earlier, it was primarily designed to facilitate cooperation with the International Political Science Association and included in its ranks economists, jurists, historians, and philosophers.

Dr V.S. Tadevosyan, the president of the association, assured me that its establishment did not mean the recognition of political science as a separate subject. He regarded political science as a kind of master discipline, embracing all the social sciences and synthesizing the study of society in all its aspects. In some ways then Soviet political science corresponded with the doctrine of Marxism-Leninism, which suffused all the social sciences and was said to be the foundation of all policy. As Tadevosyan expressed it, "Our politics is based on science, on Marxism-Leninism and its application." In saying this, he used the Russian word *nauka*, which included both the physical and the social sciences and indeed was equivalent to the English word "scholarship." From this point of view the very term "bourgeois" political scientist, as the Western professor of that subject was inevitably dubbed, was almost a contradiction in terms. His professional study was deemed at best a biased system reflecting bourgeois values and interests, far removed from the allegedly scientific foundation of Soviet studies. The chief authority in political science was not merely the abstract doctrine of Marxism-Leninism, but its practical interpretation and application by the party and its leaders, at present Khrushchev. The authoritative study of politics was carried on not in the institutes and universities, but primarily in the higher levels of the party leadership, including the Central Committee apparatus. Its "professors" were primarily the party propagandists, including the scholars in party schools and universities and in the chairs of Marxism-Leninism at every institution of higher learning. All students were required to study this subject throughout their entire university career.

I had only one chance to penetrate the corridors of "party scholarship" — a visit to the Institute of Marxism-Leninism, where I was received by G.D. Obichkin, the deputy director. He questioned me about my study and teaching of Marxism-Leninism and presented me with an armful of the institute's publications. It was now publishing a second edition of the works of Marx and Engels in Russian in 36 volumes and a fifth edition of the works of Lenin in 55 volumes. It did not intend to publish any further volumes of the works of Stalin; his classic *Problems of Leninism* existed in many copies, and although it was still used it would no longer be published.

In this "holy of holies" I dared to ask about the relationship of Leninism and Marxism. Lenin was a continuation and follower of Marx, he asserted, but had developed Marxism further in the light of developments not known to Marx. When I asked the even more heretical question as to whether there was a similarity between Lenin's theory of the interrupted revolution and Trotsky's permanent revolution and referred to my article on this theme, Obichkin energetically rejected any comparison, declaring that Trotskyism was hostile to Leninism. He pulled down volumes from the bookcases to prove that Lenin himself had rejected the theory of permanent revolution. He urged me to revise my article before it was published and expressed willingness to advise me in future. It was clear that I had touched on a sensitive issue and that there had been no change of view on Trotsky.

I visited other institutes including the Institute of Economics, for the study of the Soviet economy, and the newly formed Institute for the Economics of the World Socialist System. At the latter the director, G.M. Sorokin, laid stress on the similarity in the process of development of the People's Democracies and seemed to be at a loss concerning the prevailing doctrine.

It was a relief to get away from ideology by meeting two geographers, both of whom showed a wide knowledge of the outside world, including Canada. Professor Yulian Saushkin, who had visited Canada, entertained Arnold Smith and myself at a lavish lunch in his spacious apartment in the main building of the University of Moscow. Afterward we sat in on the defence of a doctoral thesis by a middle-aged professor before an audience of 100 to 150 scholars. After four hours his thesis on urban planning was approved by secret ballot — a testimony to the democratic process in an academic context.

It was grand to go on to Leningrad, with its resplendent history as the former capital of Russia and the scene of the Revolution. I enjoyed wandering along the canals and the Nevsky Prospekt, examining plaques commemorating Lenin's activities and gazing at the splendid classical public buildings, such as the Admiralty and the Hermitage. The Kazan Cathedral, monumental but not beautiful, was now the Museum of the History of Religion, a vast propaganda exhibit of the Orthodox church as an institution of repression and an enemy of science and progress, of the evils of the Vatican and the Inquisition, and of the history of atheism in art, philosophy and science. The Museum of the Revolution traced the development of the revolution from 1861 on, featuring the role of Lenin in the events of 1917 but ignoring Trotsky. The director was busy removing pictures of Stalin from the walls.

My chief task in Leningrad in 1961 was the prosaic one of learning as much as possible about Soviet scholarship. As in Moscow, I was warmly welcomed by deans and professors of many faculties. Our discussions pointed to a general rejection of the comparative analysis of Soviet and Western systems and an emphasis on the essential differences between bourgeois and socialist governments. I had the dubious pleasure of attending lectures, some very elementary. However, the head of the Chair of Theory of State and Law, Professor D.A. Kerimov, gave an informed lecture on cybernetics and law. One of my most informative meetings was at dinner, entirely by chance, with a philosopher from the Herzen Pedagogical Institute who did not give his name. He was a lecturer in the required course on dialectical materialism, but admitted that his students were not really interested in compulsory subjects. He showed himself to be flexible and open to argument. Soviet Marxists did not accept a mechanical view of Marxism but recognized the role of ideas and of the superstructure in influencing development. At that point, having already said so much — perhaps, he thought, too much — he suddenly left, although our bottle of wine was still half full.

I explored the more practical side of politics by attending a meeting of the executive committee of the Kalinin *raion* soviet. My guide was a "senior instructor," one of 13 in Leningrad, a middle-aged woman and veteran Communist, tough-looking but friendly. The committee met in a large room decorated with pictures of Lenin and Khrushchev, with ten of the fifteen members present, plus 30 to 40 observers. On each of the eight items on the agenda there was a brief report, followed by limited discussion, with no great differences of opinion expressed — Soviet democracy in action!

It was wonderful to meet again my friends from 1958 — Yurii Kovalev, lecturer on American and English literature, and Yurii Borshchevsky, specialist in Persian literature. Kovalev entertained me at a sumptuous lunch at the *Vostochny* (Eastern) Restaurant and also at his home in a suburb. He was interested in Melville and H.G.Wells and was a huge admirer of the American writers Jack London, Theodore Dreiser, and Ernest Hemingway; *For Whom the Bell Tolls* could not be published in the Soviet Union, but Kovalev thought it was one of Hemingway's best novels. He had little interest in Soviet writers such as Sholokhov, Ehrenburg, even Gorky, and believed the best contemporary literature was the work of younger writers not yet known in the West. His wife, Licka, was a teacher of English in middle school and had been elected to the Vyborg district Soviet, where she served on its educational commission.

Borshchevsky entertained me one evening at the Caucasus Restaurant, and he and his wife twice had me home to dinner — spacious rooms in a former institute in the historic Vasilevsky Ostrov. They were distressed at having to move to a smaller, "faceless" apartment in a suburb. He was still studying and publishing on ancient Persian literature — "at the expense of the government," he smiled.

The Oriental Institute, renamed Institute of the Peoples of Asia, was now in close touch with the outside scholarly world but he himself had not been permitted to accept an invitation from Harvard to study for a year. Yet he rejected the notion that scholarship was not possible in the Soviet Union. "You cannot control the human mind," he said — "at least not fully." Like Kovalev, Borshchevsky had no interest in religion and regarded Marxism as useful primarily for uncovering economic and social influences. He was critical of the conclusions about Russia reached by various foreign "specialists:" "How could anyone understand Russia?" he joked, "even the Russians do not!"

I spent an unforgettable evening at the home of the sister of Galina Kruberg of the Slavic Languages Department in Toronto, with whom I had worked regularly on Russian conversation prior to my trip. With her husband and daughter, she lived in a single room in an old two-storied wooden house out in the suburbs, sharing the kitchen with other tenants. The father, a historian in the Naval Archives, arrived home from work a little tipsy. His wife was teaching history and political economy in a secondary technical school. She spoke feelingly of the terrible experience of the siege of Leningrad. Natasha, the daughter, was a very attractive young lass, with long blonde braids and a sweet smile. The conversation was a little strained; my hosts were friendly but clearly embarrassed, and refrained from making any political comments.

It was a great relief to leave wintry Russia in mid-December and return to my family in Vienna for Christmas. I came away as perplexed as ever by the difficulties of interpreting this great country and its Communist system. As I wrote to President Bissell at the University of Toronto, one saw everywhere the heavy hand of the past — not only of Lenin, whose statues were ubiquitous, but also of the tsars; the statues of Catherine, Peter, and even Nicholas I, still stood in Leningrad. How to preserve what was good not only from the pre-Soviet past, but also from the Leninist and Stalinist periods, and at the same time to shake free of what was regarded as the bad, including the evils of Stalinism so recently attacked by Khrushchev? Lenin was still treated as the source of all wisdom and the great leader, but Khrushchev was regarded as a worthy continuation of the Leninist tradition and the builder of a new and better Soviet Union, cleansed of the worst aspects of Stalinism. But how far had it really moved toward a more open and comfortable society?

HUNGARY

In January and February 1962, leaving our sons in the care of a young American couple, Sally and I spent a week in Budapest. The scars of the 1956 revolution were still evident. The lessons of that year had been so vivid that the Hungarian regime clearly had to tread carefully in order to avoid a repetition of those events. Under the slogan "Who is not against us is for us," Janoš Kádár seemed to have performed a miracle in winning the loyal participation and passive acceptance of the non-Communist population. As one non-Communist put it, Hungary was the second-freest country in the bloc. The Twenty-second Congress of the CPSU (October 1961), sounding the note of anti-Stalinism, had vindicated the cautious and somewhat "liberal" policy of the Hungarian party and had forged a bond between Khrushchev and Kádár.

With official blessing I was able to meet with scholars from the institutes of the Academy of Sciences and of the party and editors of major party journals and Magyar Nemzet, the organ of the National Front. At the Party History Institute I learned of the difficulty of writing a history of the Hungarian party, which required a reappraisal of leaders such as Béla Kun, Rákosi, and Nagy, and of course the revolution of 1956. At the Party School, teachers openly admitted that nationalism was still a serious problem, especially in relations with neighbouring countries, an opinion that was supported by many other conversations. Interviews with editors of party newspapers confirmed the positive effects of the Twenty-second Congress, especially in its attack on Stalinism and Albanian Communism. They admitted the difference between the Soviet Union and China, but, like others, they minimized its importance. One editor, Adam Wirth, a philosopher, confirmed the great changes in philosophy in Hungary and the rise of empirical sociology as the basis of official policies. This was also stressed by Sándor Szallai, of the Academy of Sciences, a strong advocate of the revival of concrete sociology. An interview with Erik Molnár, a leading historian and formerly active party politician, now something of a heretic, came to an abrupt end when he, after a very few minutes, excused himself. This gave me the opportunity, however, to meet his younger colleague, the distinguished historian György Ránki. I also met Tibor Szamuelli, nephew of the leader of the Red terror in Béla Kun's Communist regime. Educated in Moscow and fluent in English and Russian, he seemed to personify the merging of two worlds in one person. He described Hungary as a fundamentally Western country, with a deep anti-Russian and anti-Communist tradition, and without a real anti-German tradition. (Later he and his Russian wife were to defect to England, where he became a well-known conservative journalist.)

I met privately with a number of persons, including Tamás Daniels and his wife, who were relatives of my friend Andrew György, a strongly anti-communist American political scientist. His brother, I found, was a party member and sympathetic to the regime; he spoke quite positively about collectivization. I also met with two old friends from the 1937 Summer School in Tatranská Lomnica. In those days they had been staunch liberal journalists. Though Jewish, they had survived the war and the Rákosi period. One, István Gál, a writer, scholar, and for a short time a Hungarian diplomat, was employed by the British embassy in its information office and was able to pursue scholarly work to a limited degree. He felt that the West did not understand the positive sides of the Kádár regime; there had been a lessening of the role of the police and much greater freedom in literature and culture. The other, Gábor Biró, had joined the party and was an accountant in a large enterprise. The main features of Hungarian politics, he said, were the political indifference, the feeling of impotence among ordinary people, and the great uncertainty as to the future. He was more critical of the situation than others but conceded that it had improved much under Kádár. Both told me of the horrors of the great 1945 siege of Budapest, during which they had lived for months in cellars, with little food.

BULGARIA

In March, even though I had just recovered from a month in hospital with an infected pancreas, I carried out my plan of visiting Bulgaria. I had to be careful of my diet, eating mainly the grilled food that was a Bulgarian specialty. Even so I had a spell of diarrhea and had to spend a day and a half in my hotel room and eat only dry bread, tea, and cheese. The downtown streets were wide and devoid of traffic, but militiamen directed the few cars with dramatic flourishes. The sidewalks were crowded with pedestrians, who were dressed shabbily and looked rough and unsophisticated. Here and there were vicious anti-American poster displays.

The public buildings, including the party headquarters and my hotel, made of heavy stone, were ugly. In striking contrast was the gold-domed Alexander Nevsky church, erected in honour of the Russians after the war with Turkey. In the same spirit was a fine equestrian statue of Alexander II, the Russian tsar liberator. There were ruins of an ancient Byzantine church and of Roman buildings, a dilapidated mosque, and a bathhouse in the Turkish style. Further away was the mausoleum of Georgii Dimitrov, in a medium-sized stucco house, where the "leader and teacher of the Bulgarian nation" lay preserved under glass. His role in Bulgarian history was featured in the Museum of the Revolutionary Movement, which also sought to show that Bulgarian Communism had deep roots and a long Marxist tradition.

A Bulgarian professor in London had introduced me to Professor Christo Danov, an archaeologist, who took me to the Ethnographic Museum and the Archaeological Museum, and invited me to his home. His wife and two daughters spoke English well; they listened nightly to the BBC. The father elaborated the special factors that made Bulgarian Communism so strong, including the traditions of pro-Russian friendship and Bulgarian socialism, and the willingness of the small peasants to accept collectivization. He shared the widely held view, which my official guide strongly espoused, that the Macedonian language was but a dialect of Bulgarian. The mother and daughters were more openly critical of conditions in Bulgaria. They cited a gypsy saying: "Why build socialism in 20 years? Why not in one year and then go back to living in the old way?"

Danov told me that religion was weak in Bulgaria and that the Bulgarian church did not play a dominant role (Communists told me that religion was dying out!). At the Holy Synod of the Bulgarian patriarchate, my conversation with a young black-bearded priest, who had studied Christian ethics in Protestant seminaries in Berlin and Jena, partly confirmed Danov's view. The church, he said, was not a state organ, and did not interfere in political or economic affairs. He was proud of the origins of Church Slavonic in the Bulgarian tongue of Saints Cyril and Methodius.

Through the State Committee for Cultural Relations I arranged a number of official interviews. Most of these were conducted in groups, often in Russian, with the help of interpreters; coffee, chocolates, fruits, and brandy were served, and portraits of Dimitrov and Lenin always presided. At the State Committee those present seemed to waver between assertion of the national distinctiveness of Bulgaria, especially since the Twenty-second Congress, and their devotion to the general and common principles of the advance to socialism. They said that

V.V. Chervenkov, the former Stalinist leader, had lost all high positions, and they vigorously condemned his cult of personality. At the
Institute of Bulgarian History of the Academy of Sciences, the group
was joined by several scholars from the Institute of Party History.
When I inquired about Turkish influences on culture and politics, they
vehemently denied there were any except in the negative sense of reject-
ing the rule of a foreign conqueror. They were uneasy about admitting
the distinctive character of Bulgarian Communism but asserted that
the party had rejected the cult of Stalin long before the Twenty-second
Congress.

The deputy chief editor of the party paper, *Robotnicke Delo*, was
an old Communist who had lived in the USSR until 1948. Speaking in
German, he waxed enthusiastic over the beneficial impact of the CPSU's
Twenty-second Congress on Bulgaria. Since it had never been as Stalinist
as Poland or Hungary, de-Stalinization could take place gradually over
many years. But Bulgaria had deep emotional ties with the Russians and
had no sympathy at all for Albania or for Yugoslavia. At the offices of
Novo Vreme, the party's theoretical journal, I met the heads of the philosophy and other departments, about eight professors in all. They put
great stress on the long Marxist tradition of Bulgarian Socialism. They
admitted that there had been differences of view as to the nature of
People's Democracy, but in 1958 it had been decided that Bulgaria had
from the beginning been socialist and a dictatorship of the proletariat.
With Yugoslavia there were ideological differences but good state relations. The differences with China were not fundamental, they argued.

A meeting at the National Council of the Fatherland Front
brought together officials of the Front, a representative of the Agrarian
Union, a member of the former Zveno party, and a non-party man.
They did their best to persuade me that Bulgaria was highly democratic and that the people overwhelmingly supported the National Front
and Communist policy. They stressed the peaceful intentions of the
Soviet camp and were highly critical of American policies.

Boris Spassov, professor of public law at the state university, told
me that Bulgaria had attained socialism but did not require a new constitution yet. There would, however, be changes in the constitution in
the light of the Soviet Party's recent congress.

CZECHOSLOVAKIA

A trip with Sally and the boys at Eastertime afforded us glimpses of
Czechoslovakia.[3] It was a pleasure for us to drive through the beautiful

Bohemian and Moravian countryside, with its prosperous-looking collective farms and many handsome villas. The traffic was light, except in Prague, and everywhere we were greeted by smiles and friendly waves. But our first stop in Tábor made us aware of the serious shortages, especially of meat, with long queues waiting early in the morning. We were to see these everywhere, even in Prague.

We found that Czechoslovakia still occupied an unenviable position of uniqueness in its rigidity and its conformity to the traditional pattern of communism and in its loyalty, if not subservience, to Moscow. The gigantic statue of Stalin still loomed over Prague. Stalin's and Gottwald's names were everywhere, on squares, statues, and public buildings. Only Stalinova Avenue was suddenly, under cover of darkness, renamed Vinohradská (the old prewar name), to the surprise next morning of friends of ours who lived there. Some said that it should have been renamed "Avenue of Political Mistakes," but others quipped that the street was not long enough for that. Gottwald's body still rested in the mausoleum on the Vítkov hill, although it was closed for "technical reasons" in the spring.

The name of Tomáš Masaryk had been almost completely erased from public places, and his statues removed. Only in a tiny town in Moravia did I see a bust of him on the main street, with the slogan from 1937, "We shall remain faithful." And on Mickiewiczová — right opposite the Canadian embassy — was a small bust in relief of Charlotte, Masaryk's wife, on the outside of the house where they had lived until 1914.

Old friends and the occasional official interview confirmed our impressions of the backwardness of Czechoslovakia in the post-Stalin era and the lack of intellectual freedom. Our good friend Zdeněk Rudinger, after six years in prison, had been released in 1960 and talked openly about his ordeal. His wife, Lisa, still a Communist, spoke of the all-pervading fear — "fear of the people by the regime, fear of the regime by the people, and fear of everyone for each other." Their son, Josef, a prominent chemist, who was able to travel in both East and West, was still a party member but was even more critical of the party's policies and was full of jokes: "Why was there a much longer line outside the socialist hell than the capitalist hell?" Because it was a planned hell, and there was a scarcity of tar! Olga Haningerová's husband, Bošek, was back in a white-collar job as an accountant after years of manual work, but he earned less than an unskilled worker. Their greatest worry was uncertainty as to their children's future. Their son,

Milan, for instance, was not admitted to university because of his parents' background — as a result, according to the official report, "he had grown up in an environment which would influence his ideological development and political maturity." Professor Josef Polišenský was still a party member and earned well above the average wage. His wife, however, complained bitterly of their low income, their small apartment, and food shortages. Although a specialist in eighteenth century Czech history, Josef was forced to teach Latin American and working-class history.

Official conversations were difficult to arrange and were marked by caution and lack of frankness. Vladimír Soják, still director of the Institute of International Politics and Economics, claimed that the transition to socialism in Czechoslovakia had been more peaceful because the party was stronger and the country had deep democratic roots. He admitted that there had been few significant changes since the CPSU's Twentieth Congress in February 1956 and that there were serious economic difficulties. Pavel Reimann, director of the Institute for the History of the Communist Party of Czechoslovakia, served me coffee and cookies, and Russian vodka, in his office. A prewar party leader, and Jewish, he had not been a victim in the Slanský trials — some said because he served as a witness. He admitted that changes were taking place "more slowly" in Czechoslovakia than elsewhere. As to what distinguished domestic Communism from that of other countries, he repeated the usual litany of a developed industry and a strong working class, the strength of the party, and the absence of an anti-Russian tradition.

Through the good offices of Soják I was able to meet specialists on the esoteric theory of People's Democracy, on which I had written four articles. A high point was a meeting with editors of *Problems of Peace and Socialism*, the ideological journal of the Soviet bloc. Its central office was located in Prague, in a former Catholic seminary, which ironically retained a large green dome and, over the doorway, a cardinal's red hat. I was received by three Russian editors, who served me coffee, Hungarian wine, and apples. The editor-in-chief, A.I. Sobolev, was away in Moscow. The controversy over People's Democracy, they said, had been a conflict between dogmatist opinions, such as those of Farberov and Mankovsky, and even Sobolev, and what they called "creative Marxist views."

On our way to Slovakia, on the eve of May Day, we travelled through Moravia. In Jihlava a military officer reprimanded us for taking pictures of soldiers who were decorating their barracks. The main square of Telč, with its beautiful baroque façades, was still named after Stalin. In Slovakia the villages were poorer and more backward, with ploughing done by oxen, but there were many large farmhouses and villas, often built, we were told, with the help of Tuzex dollar coupons donated from abroad. In Bratislava the Castle was still under reconstruction, but some ancient buildings were beautifully renovated. The streets of the old town were dilapidated and dank with the smell of centuries. Outside St Martin's two or three beggars rolled their eyes and muttered prayers.

On May Day we watched from our hotel windows a parade of some 60,000 people — a highly organized command performance, we judged, with an apathetic crowd and unenthusiastic marchers. On the reviewing stand on Stalin Square, where a huge statue of the great leader gazed down on the scene, the party's first secretary, Karol Bacílek (who was to be removed from power a little more than a year later), waved with forced friendliness. The next day, as we drove homeward to Vienna, the Austrian countryside looked bright and fresh; the towns were colourful and prosperous, and the roads were crowded with automobiles.

YUGOSLAVIA

In May I flew down to Belgrade for a week of interviews with top officials, scholars, and foreign and Yugoslav diplomats. The city made a good initial impression, especially the new airport — an airy structure, mainly of glass — and the handsome skyscrapers for party and government offices in New Belgrade on the other side of the Save River. Central Belgrade was a medley of decayed old buildings and modern ones of mediocre style. There were many poorly dressed people, including tired-looking peasants, carrying great bundles, but there were also smartly dressed younger people. The entire city closed down at noon, and shops reopened at five p.m. During their free time people strolled in the usual *corso* in the main streets or sat eating and drinking in the many sidewalk cafés and open garden restaurants. I, too, enjoyed the wonderful Serbian food and drink and often sat in the sunshine after meals, making notes on my interviews.

The cult of Marshal Tito's personality was evident in the portraits hanging in all public buildings and in a modern museum that housed gifts presented to him on various occasions. During my stay his birthday, combined with Youth Day, was celebrated at the stadium. Attired in the resplendent light blue uniform of a marshal, Tito sat in his box and acknowledged the plaudits of the crowd. Two great banners proclaimed the main slogan of the day — Brotherhood and Unity — and other smaller ones bore words such as "peace," "youth," and "socialism." There were several major performances, almost ballet-like in quality, by young people and by the military — a beautiful display of precision and grace.

My hotel, the Toplice, was in the older part of town, near the huge Kalemagdan Park with its ruined fortifications; a military museum, portraying the innumerable wars of Serbian and Yugoslav history; and the striking statue to France by the sculptor Meštrović. I often went there for a walk or for a meal in a restaurant on the terrace overlooking the juncture of the Save and the Danube. Nearby was the main Orthodox cathedral, in baroque style, with tall, slender towers. Inside were the tombs of great literary figures, Serbian princes and tsars, and Orthodox patriarchs. Opposite the church stood the Patriarchate, an enormous square stone building, topped with the more usual Byzantine dome and an incongruous electrically lighted cross. I later saw the Serbian patriarch, at a reception in honour of the visiting Alexei, the Russian Orthodox patriarch, given by the Soviet diplomatic representatives. The 84-year-old Alexei sat with other bearded priests in their high hats and black robes, eating and drinking at a table piled high with food.

I received a warm welcome on arrival from the Canadian ambassador, Bill Crean, who entertained me at the residence several times and helped me to arrange meetings with high-level diplomats whom I had met in 1958. Leo Mates, Yugoslavia's assistant under-secretary of state for foreign affairs for the United Nations, western Europe, and the Americas, expressed serious worries about the effect on Yugoslav trade of the restrictive practices of the European Common Market. Yugoslavia did not intend to join the Common Market, however, nor was it dependent on trade with the Soviet bloc. The main goal must be to develop trade with Asia and Africa and with western Europe. Mates chose to talk mainly of rapid Yugoslav reconstruction and industrial development from 1950 onward and the present goal of achieving self-sufficiency by modernization of agriculture. He seemed to be arguing in a subtle way for gradual and partial collectivization. Ivo Vejvoda, assistant under-secretary for eastern Europe, was as suave and Western-oriented as Mates but spoke very positively of relations with the Soviet

Union. Under Khrushchev these had improved, but there could be no question of rejoining the bloc. Relations with Albania were bad, and there could be no rapprochement without a change in its aggressive attitude. He did not expect a break between the USSR and China, however; the alliance was too important for both. Milković, former ambassador to Athens and Sofia, had fought as a partisan in Macedonia. Relations with Bulgaria were not good mainly because of its refusal to recognize the reality of a Macedonian nationality. Albania's resistance to the Soviet Union was based mainly on the personal interests of a small ruling clique of criminals and assassins. There could be no improvement in relations with Albania under this leadership.

I also had meetings with scholars in several of the main research institutes and colleges. Dr Uvalić, director of the Institute of Social Science, was an economist — a specialist on Soviet socialist economic systems. With apparent regret he said that there were no scholarly relations with the Soviet Union or other socialist countries, except for Poland. In eastern Europe the original plan of rapid industrialization without regard for resources had been wrong. The present idea of a division of labour through Comecon was wiser but difficult to implement. Another economist, Janež Stanovnik, a Slovene, director of the Institute of International Politics and Economics, was interested primarily in economic development. Like others he was a Marxist, but not at all dogmatic. He strongly defended the need for a single economy in the country as a whole but was confident that the Yugoslav policy of decentralization would be proven right. He strongly defended Yugoslav policy and was highly critical of Bulgaria and Albania. Professor Radković, of the Higher School of Political Science, had written a book on the history of socialist thought and was preparing another on Austro-Marxism. There were two schools of Yugoslav Marxism, he said — the technocratic or bureaucratic, which emphasized expert knowledge and minimized the role of the people, and the humanist, which was abstract and remote from the realities of practical life. Branko Pribičević, deputy director of the Institute of the History of the Working Class Movement, was a younger man who had studied in England under G.D.H. Cole. His own special interest was the history of social democracy in western Europe. The work of the Institute on Eastern Europe and the Soviet Union was weak, and it had no relations with the party history institutes of those countries. He thought that the trend toward decentralization had gone too far but that recent government changes would not alter the system of workers' councils and people's communes — the "Yugoslav way."

I met also with Vlajko Begović, former director of the Institute for International Politics and Economics, and now principal of the Higher School of Political Science, and with Puniša Perović, former head of the Institute for the History of the Working Class Movement and now secretary of the Foreign Affairs Committee of the Skuptschina. The two were more politicians than scholars, but their views on the Soviet bloc and Khrushchev's policy were similar to the others. The effect of the Twenty-second Congress, they said, was mainly in the minds of men, including the leaders themselves. Basic changes would come eventually, however, not as a result of the leaders alone but as the result of social forces. They, too, thought that there was no likelihood of a complete breach with China. Begović had studied in Czechoslovakia in the 1920s, and was highly critical of the hesitancy of its Novotný regime to follow the lead of Khrushchev in introducing change.

These official meetings were balanced by conversations with Canadian, American, and British diplomats and with resident and visiting journalists, who were more critical of Yugoslav policy. The diplomats placed greater emphasis on the difficulties of the economy and the depth of the crisis in foreign trade. One thought that a recent speech by Tito in Split was a signal for greater centralization to meet these problems. Another linked the speech with the trial and imprisonment of the dissident Milovan Djilas for his book, *Conversations with Stalin.* A journalist ascribed the arrest to Tito's anger with Djilas for his breach with the League of Communists and to his suspicion that he still had political ambitions.

BALKAN JOURNEY

A family journey to the Balkans in June and July 1962 took us first to Hungary. We had a fascinating drive along the Danube to Esztergom, the seat of the archbishop, with its ancient fortress and its enormous basilica. In Budapest we explored the Castle heights and visited the galleries and museums. I had no official appointments but met again with the Daniels and with Biró and his family. I had a surprise meeting, the result of a mere telephone call, with the eminent Marxist philosopher György Lukács, in his apartment high above the Danube. He was a warm and alert old man, with white hair, piercing eyes, and a hooked nose. We discussed at length the nature of Marxism, especially the role of the individual leader, such as Hitler and Stalin, and of economic and social forces, which in his opinion were the dominant influences on historical development. He urged a creative effort to develop Marxism but found no evidence that this was being done in the Soviet Union or Hungary. He appreciated what was being written by Polish and Yugoslav Marxists, but some, such as Kołakowski, Kardelj, and of course, Djilas, had abandoned the fundamentals of Marxism.

After leaving Budapest, we made a brief stop at the Roman ruins in Acquincum and spent a day in the beautiful baroque town of Eger, once under Turkish rule. There the friendly curator of the castle, Béla Kovács, gave us a tour of the ruins and of the museum. One evening we were taken to one of the many private winecellars outside the town. Although we had no common languages, we drank and sang together for a good many hours. An older man was the life of the party, dancing the *czardas* with Sally. As we walked home through the deserted streets, he shouted anti-communist slogans.

During our last days in Hungary we drove through the Buk mountains and then, in intense heat, over the flat Hortobágy plain, or *puzsta*. In a shady spot we stopped to eat some of the enormous lunch given to us by the Eger hotel for the balance of our coupons — two bottles of wine, cold pork chops, chicken, salami, Debrecen sausage, cheese, bread, and turnips. We visited a state horse ranch where a "cowboy" put 150 horses through their paces for us. We spent the night in Debrecen, a city with spacious squares and wide streets and a huge, two-towered Calvinist church.

As we entered Romania at a border crossing in the middle of nowhere, we at once felt as though we were crossing from modern to medieval Europe, and also from an unorthodox to an orthodox satellite. At the border the customs inspectors examined everything we had and searched inside and underneath the car. On the Romanian side the highways were alive with people and animals, and we were often slowed to a snail's pace, sometimes by large herds of pigs or cows, including water buffalo, and at regular intervals by the police. We were struck by the poverty of the villages and of their inhabitants.

The city of Cluj introduced us to the complexities of the nationality problem, as we visited the Ethnographic Museum, with its Magyar, Saxon, and Romanian peasant art. The population of the city was now half Romanian and half Hungarian, with the German minority having been forcibly transferred to Germany by Hitler. There were two opera houses, Hungarian and Romanian, and two theatres, and there had been two universities. According to Professor Lescu, the dean of history, these were now fused into a single one, with Romanian the dominant language, but with chairs in Hungarian in some fields. In Braşov, set in the Carpathian Mountains, we had as a guide a young historian, a German-speaking native of the town. When I had visited Braşov before the war, its population had been about 30,000, with one-third each of Hungarians, Germans, and Romanians. Now it was an overwhelmingly Romanian city of 220,000, with only about 16,000 Hungarians and 6,000 Germans. The beautiful Black Church, which was German Lutheran, was the easternmost gothic church in Europe.

We were discouraged from going to Tîrgu-Mureş, capital of the Autonomous Hungarian Region, because, we were told, the roads were bad and hotels were not available (later we learned that neither was true). We passed along highways crowded with dilapidated wagons, occasional burros, and ox-drawn carts; we followed the local practice of honking constantly. We were astonished by the number of storks nesting in the chimneys. In one village we were greeted by a group of peasants in Austrian costumes, descendants of immigrants from Salzburg two centuries before, who welcomed us as coming from their "homeland"! In another village we met a group of people wearing typical Romanian national dress, who showed us their little church with frescoes on the exterior walls.

We travelled on through the Carpathians to Bucharest — a bustling modern city of broad avenues and large parks, with an Arc de Triomphe modelled after Paris. There were striking modern buildings, including the Hall of Congresses and new apartment houses, and on the outskirts the splendid Church of the Metropolitan. The older shops and houses were shabby and poor-looking. Our hotel was first class, but extremely hot and noisy, and we sometimes sought refuge from the heat in the swimming pool of the Hotel Lido across the street. We visited a fascinating museum of Romanian folk art in a turreted Romanian-style house, and also the Village Museum, where peasant houses from all over the country had been reassembled in a large park. Politically interesting to me were the Museum of Marx, Engels and Lenin, until recently called the Lenin-Stalin Museum, and the Museum of the History of the Romanian Communist Party, which made manifestly clear the lack of deep roots of Romanian Communism and revealed the beginning of the cult of personality of Gheorgiu-Dej.

Through the Institute for Cultural Relations with Foreign Countries I was able to have three official interviews, which were usually conducted in French and were not very productive. At the Institute of Juridical Research of the Academy of Sciences, Trojan Ionescu, although he was a member of the commission for a new constitution, was unable to give me any information about it (except that it would document the achievement of socialism) or about the new penal and civil codes in preparation. More instructive was a talk with Rausser, editor in chief of the journal *Probleme economici*, housed in the huge Stalinesque building of the party newspaper, *Scînteia*. He had been educated in Leningrad and spoke some English. The system of industrial organization had not been revised on the model of Khrushchev's, since it was already decentralized. The rapid industrial advance had been based on a balanced policy of investment and had assured a substantial rise in living standards. Collectivization had been completed rapidly because it had been relatively gradual and based on voluntary acceptance.

We had a short drive to the Bulgarian border through the flat Wallachian plain, with its vast fields of grain, tobacco, and sunflowers. The villages were extremely poor and primitive, with wells on their dusty main streets. The houses were often made of wattling and mud and had thatched roofs. Women were cutting wheat with scythes, and men were gathering it into stooks by hand. Only the occasional combine was to be seen.

We crossed the Danube on a newly built bridge and entered Bulgaria. The countryside was dry and rocky, and the fields were irrigated. The highways were crowded with oxen and burros, pulling small, low carts. Women were working by hand in the fields. The tiny houses were brick or white-washed plaster, with red tiled roofs. We saw several mosques, including a most beautiful one in Kolarovgrad where prayers took place daily. On the high cliffs in the mountains we visited the ruins of two of the ancient Bulgarian capitals, the first one from the seventh century. We spent a restful couple of days in the Golden Sands on the Black Sea — an attractive and well-designed resort, with its low hotels set into forested hills. The long, sandy beach was alive with human forms, including women in bikinis, and with a Babel of many tongues, especially Czech, German, and Russian. Dr Dimitrii Petrov, in charge of health facilities in the entire area, was quite proud of this, and the neighbouring resort of Druzhba. He escorted us to the nearby port of Varna, which had been successively a Greek colony, then Roman, Byzantine, and Turkish, and finally Bulgarian.

On 1 July we drove through the mountainous countryside, where there were many herdsmen of sheep, cows, and horses. Farm equipment seemed ancient, often rusted and unused, and was replaced by human labour. The ancient town of Tarnovo had a spectacular location, built tier upon tier on the side of the steep cliff above a meandering river; the streets were picturesque, the houses Turkish or Byzantine in style. With a young student as guide, we visited the Preobrazhensky Monastery, high on a rocky hillside where we were welcomed by a priest in black robe and stove-pipe hat. Our guide was not religious and was quite fascinated when I told her of my teaching of Marxism-Leninism in its various versions. Here only one interpretation was accepted, she said, but she thought that there should be discussion of differing viewpoints.

Driving through the Balkan Mountains we viewed the battlefields of the Shipka Pass, at about 1,300 metres, where the Bulgarians, with Russian assistance, had defeated the Turks in 1877. Here were gravestones and a monument to eternal Russian-Bulgarian friendship, and down below, in the village, was a great domed Orthodox church built by the Russians in memory of the battle. On our way to Sofia we visited the interior of a tumulus, or large mound, which contained the tomb of a Thracian prince from the time of Alexander the Great. Then to Sofia through the Balkan Mountains and the valley of the Maritza, with the snow-covered Rhodope Mountains in full view. Our hotel was located on Mt Vitoshe, high above the city, with spectacular views of Sofia and the mountains, but there was no running water in our room. We stayed only briefly. On the morning of our departure we drove out to view the tiny thirteenth century Boyana Church, with its ancient interior frescoes and Byzantine dome. Near the border with Yugoslavia, in the mountains, we visited the imposing fortress-like Rila Monastery, now a workers' rest home, where we were turned away in a rather frosty manner. We spent the night in a nearby hotel above a rushing mountain stream. When we told a waiter we were proceeding to Macedonia, he vigorously asserted that it was Bulgarian, not Macedonian.

We entered Yugoslavia on a gravel road, high in the mountains, driving through a wild and desperately dry and rocky region. There were tiny thatched cottages, often made of plaster or mud. In the fields, women were cutting grain with sickles or hoeing fields by hand. On the roads there were men on horseback or on mules, with women riding side-saddle. We met one woman, in colourful national dress, with a baby on her back, strolling along, knitting as she walked. We could not talk to her as she spoke only "Macedonian!" Other women in similar costumes seemed to testify that this was indeed a Macedonian region.

When we approached Skopje, capital of the Macedonian Republic, we felt we were leaving biblical times and entering the twentieth century. From the ruined castle and a big mosque on the hill one could look down on the skyscrapers of the modern city and on the old city, with many minarets and mosques, and a multi-domed Caravanseraj, an ancient hostelry for merchants. Our guide, Tomovski, himself a Macedonian, an editor of the newspaper *New Macedonia*, told us that the city was mainly Macedonian, but with substantial Serbian, Turkish, and Albanian minorities, as well as gypsies. We spent much of our time in the old Turkish part of town, a fascinating dip into another civilization. Many of the men wore the fez, the women pantaloons. The houses were mere hovels, the shops tiny holes in the wall. The gypsy town was even more primitive, with dozens of people clustered around the well.

Officials had been forewarned of our arrival from Belgrade and had already arranged meetings for me with the director of the Institute of Economics, a professor of economics at the university, and officials in the Secretariat of Legislative Affairs and the Secretariat of Enlightenment. These interviews offered me a short course on the nature of socialism in this agricultural territory, the complexity of the national question in a heterogeneous region, and the structure of government in an autonomous republic in a federal state. Since most of the arable land was in private hands, socialism really amounted to the development of those farms that were under "social ownership." Through cooperation the private farmers would learn the superiority of "socialism" and voluntarily join cooperative farms. Discussions were underway about a new constitution that would maintain the advantages of decentralization but would recognize the need for greater centralization to protect the all-national interests. As for the nationality question, the educational system recognized the equality of all nationalities, assuring them schools in Albanian, Macedonian, and Turkish. Mixed schools existed only in mixed areas, but all children were required to learn Macedonian, and even Serbian. Several people waxed indignant at the refusal of Bulgaria, even under Communist rule, to recognize the Macedonian nationality.

We gained a first-hand illustration of the nationality policy by visiting the Kosmet Autonomous Region (Kosovo Metohija). Why go to Priština (the regional capital)? Tomovski asked me; he had never been there himself! It was not far from Skopje but was reached only by a very rough cobblestone highway, where one had to keep to about 20 or 30 miles an hour. The landscape was rugged and dry and surrounded by bare, tawny mountains. We passed a gypsy encampment and saw many Albanians, the men in their characteristic dress, including homespun jodhpur pants and a white felt skullcap. In the middle of nowhere was a beautiful fourteenth century monastery, Gracanica, with a central and four smaller domes and magnificent frescoes inside. A few kilometres from Priština was the battlefield of Kosovo polye, a bare, deserted plain sacred to the Serbs as the place where they had lost their independence to the Turks in 1389.

Imagine our surprise when we first saw Priština, a modern city, with fine buildings, factories, apartments, and a hotel of striking design. As elsewhere, there was a sharp contrast between the new city and the old, with its narrow, cobbled streets and the open shops of artisans, making tin-ware, shoes, or hats. In the afternoon *corso*, many Shiptars (Albanians), gypsies, and Turks wore national dress and contrasted with the young people who were attired in Western style. I had a long talk with Fadil Hoxha, president of the Kosmet region, an Albanian, who was dressed in a light suit, a tieless sport shirt, green socks, and orange suede shoes. For an hour or two he talked, in Serb, with a poor interpreter, about the rights of the region and of its nationalities — 67 percent were Shiptars, 23 percent Serbs, the rest Montenegrins, Turks, and others. Before the war the Albanians had no rights and no schools — now they were assured full equality and formed the majority of Kosmet representation in the elected organs of Yugoslavia, the Macedonian republic, and Kosmet. The Albanians, he assured me, were satisfied with conditions and had no desire to be united with neighbouring Albania. Nationalism and national conflict, he said, were dying out! (How much alive it was became clear in the Balkan wars 30 years later!)

We went on through the Kosmet, passing a large animal and grain fair and stopping briefly to see another beautiful monastery, Dečani, with an extraordinarily beautiful Christ in its central dome. In Peć we admired the monastery of the patriarchate, with several round domes and rich frescoes and the sarcophagi of the patriarchs of the Orthodox church from the thirteenth century on. The streets were unpaved, with fountains at the side; many old houses in Turkish style were near collapse.

Then on to Montenegro through rugged mountain roads, with many hairpin curves, through wild mountain valleys, gorges, and tunnels. One had to be cautious at every curve as the trucks rounded them fast, honking their horns, leaving little space between us and the cliffs at the edge of the road. Signs were few, so that we sometimes lost our way. At the Cakor Pass, 1,900 metres high, we had a magnificent panorama of majestic snow-clad mountains. The houses were often built of logs and looked Alpine, with steep, grey-shingled roofs. We followed the border with Albania all day and could see the vast ranges of the mountains on the Albanian side and Lake Scutari, which looked deserted and mysterious. We did not linger long in Titograd, the modern capital of Montenegro, located on a flat plain and dominated by hideous official buildings. We pushed on over more serpentine roads to Cetinje, the ancient capital, high up in the mountains. It was quite small and sleepy but seemed to wake up in the corso. It had the castle of Njegoš, former monarch, who had been a bishop and a poet, and a museum portraying the wartime struggle for liberation.

The next morning we ascended on a rough mountain trail to the peak of Lovćen, through a rocky countryside that resembled the surface of the Moon. Each tiny village was built of grey stone, and the fields were surrounded by walls of the same rock. We were rewarded at the summit with a spectacular view of the Adriatic and the great Gulf of Kotor below. Rounding 26 serpentine curves we descended to the charming little town of Kotor, with stone houses and a Romanesque church. It had been successively under Byzantine, Serbian, Venetian, Turkish, Austrian, and now Yugoslav rule.

The Dalmatian coast, part of the republic of Croatia, was like another world. We drove along the beautiful shore, lush with tropical vegetation — cypresses, palms, and oleander — the arid Karst mountains behind, and the green and blue sea in front of us. At twilight we approached the ancient walled city of Dubrovnik, outlined against a magnificent sunset. We stayed in a low, modern hotel built right on the rocks of the shore, where I suffered a 24-hour bout with diarrhoea. In spite of a plague of foreign tourists we revelled in the beauty of what had once been the independent city state of Ragusa. It formed a harmonious whole of splendid churches and residences in white stone, and the broad main Placa had shining marble pavements. Walks along the walls gave us panoramic views of the mountains and the crystal-clear sea and glimpses of the private villas within the walls.

We experienced another change of civilization as we left the Italianate and Venetian Dalmatian coast and entered the former Austro-Hungarian provinces Hercegovina and Bosnia, long under Turkish rule. We passed along grey, rocky hillsides, a patchwork of walled, irrigated fields. The roads were once again precipitous as we climbed the Karst range, everything getting hotter and dustier. At a waterfall we swam in the clear, cold water and quenched our desperate thirst. We stopped at a necropolis of so-called Bogumil tombs, great monoliths from the thirteenth or fourteenth century. The Turkish influence was once more evident, with mosques and Turkish-style buildings everywhere. The main city of Hercegovina, Mostar, was a lovely sight, with its arched, stone footbridge; its shuttered houses, in blue, purple, pink, and yellow; and its mosques and bazaar and a Turkish café (all to be demolished by war 30 years later!).

Following the rushing Neretva River and the narrow-gauge railway track, we went on to Sarajevo, capital of Bosnia-Hercegovina, which I had visited 27 years earlier. From our hotel room we had a splendid view of the Turkish quarter and the bazaar, the main mosque and minaret, and the hillsides beyond, dotted with mosques and Turkish cemeteries. Twice a day we could hear the high-pitched shriek of the muezzin calling the faithful to prayer. We gazed at the corner on the quay where Gabril Princip, a traitor to some, a hero to others, had assassinated Archduke Ferdinand and his wife. As the plaque declared, here was fired the "shot that expressed national resistance to tyranny" — and incidentally marked the beginning of the Great War!

Here I had two interviews, assisted by a young Serbian who spoke good English. Professor Hamdija Čemerlić, professor of constitutional law, a Moslem, but Serbo-Croatian by nationality, told me that Serbs and Croats spoke the same language and differed only in the use of Cyrillic and Latin scripts and in history and culture. Serbs tended to be Orthodox, Croats Catholic, but many Serbs were Muslim. Bosnia and Hercegovina had been given autonomy as a kind of balance between Serbia and Croatia. Its autonomy was, however, limited, and it had no independent legislative power. A member of both federal and republican constitutional commissions, he told me that the new constitution would not make fundamental changes in the position of the republics.

I also met with Professor Fazlija Alikalfić, vice-rector of the university, a Moslem. The university, founded in 1949, used the Serbo-Croatian language, and most of the students were Serbo-Croatians from Bosnia. The use of either script was a matter of personal preference, and both were used interchangeably at the university. The Commission on Religious Affairs, of which he was a member, advised the government on matters relating to the three main religious communities, Orthodox,

Catholic, and Muslim, which were roughly equal in number and, he said, lived together in diversity and in brotherhood. There was an increasing number of non-believers. The government encouraged the development of non-belief, but there was no anti-religious propaganda.

After leaving Sarajevo, still in Bosnia, we passed through well-cultivated, rolling country, but we soon entered rough mountains again. Jajce presented a singular sight, with a castle, old gate towers, a waterfall right in the city, and unique, whitewashed houses, with steep shingled roofs, tumbling down the hillside. Most fascinating was the market, to which peasants came from far and wide on foot or on horseback and with pack-mules. It was an extraordinarily primitive scene, taking one back centuries, as was the huge cattle market outside the town. The women wore long white dresses, vests of black or red, hand-woven aprons, and sometimes long jackets of white wool reaching to the ankles. The men wore brown homespun trousers and white shirts, black boleros, black or brown fur hats, and moccasins with turned-up toes. Jajce was also noteworthy as the headquarters of the partisan movement and the site of the first wartime Yugoslav assembly.

The road to Zagreb was being repaired by hand, hundreds of men working with shovels and picks. At the bank of the river women were washing clothes, beating them on the rocks. As everywhere in Yugoslavia, children rushed to the roadside to wave to us, perhaps to beg. We entered Croatia on a fine highway through flat farm land and soon reached Zagreb. There we moved from the realm of Turkish civilization to the sphere of Austro-Hungarian culture proper. The Croatian capital was quiet and old-fashioned, with spacious parks and nineteenth century public buildings, but also with modern factories and apartment houses. The old city was located in the Upper Town, on a hill rising from the city centre. It seemed like a bit of the eighteenth or early nineteenth century, with baroque buildings and the lovely gothic Church of St Luke. In the interior were beautiful statues by Meštrović, whose works also graced the parks below.

As always, I sought out information through official meetings. Professor Dušan Sabolović, dean of the Faculty of Economics, received me in his office, serving vermouth, open-faced sandwiches, and coffee. The disparity in levels of development of the Yugoslav republics was decreasing, he told me, but there was a continuing controversy as to whether the more developed republics should aid the others by transferring funds or rather should concentrate on their own further development — an alternative that he seemed to prefer. Nikola Seculić, vice-president of Croatia, spoke rather formally and expressed what seemed to be highly correct views. He repeated what others had told me — that there would be no fundamental changes in the new constitution, but only a more exact definition of the rights and powers of the federal government, the republics, and the communes.

The last lap on our Balkan trip took us to Slovenia, through fertile farm valleys, which resembled Austria in many ways — large villas, onion-shaped church towers, baroque statues, houses of pastel-coloured plaster — a far cry from Bosnia or Macedonia. We crossed the border into Austria in flat country: there were no examinations on either side. We were relieved to have safely completed our long journey through Communist countries and to be back in "the West."

We had another short visit to Slovenia in July when we left Austria for Italy. This time we crossed the frontier in the mountains, at the Loibl Pass (3,168 metres), surrounded by the jagged, rocky peaks of the Julian Alps. The border post was engraved with the date of the St Germain Treaty in 1919. On the other side we descended precipitously, at a gradient of 34 percent, to the Yugoslav customs post. Just beyond was an impressive monument to French victims of Mauthausen — a metallic skeleton, with hands and arms raised above the head, standing between four huge plinths.

In Bled, hotels were full, and we spent the night in the private home of a worker's family. We drove around the tiny jewel of a lake, with a romantic castle on one hilly shore, Tito's walled residence on another, and a little church on an island. In the morning we drove on fast to Ljubljana, the capital, a large modern city in the plain, with many baroque buildings and an ancient castle on a high hill in the centre. A statue of Napoleon reminded us that he had once conquered this city and made it the capital of Illyria. The trip to the frontier led along good roads for a while and then round more hairpin curves in the mountains. We crossed into Italy about ten miles from Trieste; from the height of land we could look down on the Adriatic and the port and the city that I had visited in 1950.

Our peregrination through Yugoslavia had given us a vivid impression of the heterogeneity — linguistic, national, cultural, economic, and yes, even political — of the land of the South Slavs. In particular in the southern regions we had perhaps the last chance to see backward regions on the verge of modernization. And we witnessed what seemed to us the relative stability and unity of a Yugoslavia that, three decades later, was to be torn apart by war and violence.

The year of travel throughout central and eastern Europe confirmed once more the existence of what I called "national communism." One could not but be impressed by the extraordinary diversity among states that called themselves Communist and supposedly hewed to a more or less single line of theory and practice. The Twenty-second Congress of the CPSU had had different consequences in each of the states and had a long-run potential for modifying profoundly the shape and content of Communism in central and eastern Europe.

We drove homeward to the Atlantic by way of Venice, Florence, and Rome — and then through France. As a result of our travels David and Peter developed a lifelong wanderlust.

BACK TO THE USSR FIVE YEARS LATER

In 1966 I returned to the Soviet Union, this time to hold discussions on our exchange program. This time I entered the Soviet Union via Romania, and had my first visits to Kiev, Minsk and two Baltic cities, Riga and Tallinn. I completed my round trip by leaving Russia by train to Helsinki.

In Kiev I was struck by the spanking-new airport of modern design and the vast areas of new apartment houses. There were new hotels now, and more restaurants and cafés; the service was better, and the waitresses were attractive and efficient. But there were still signs of the old bureaucracy, such as defects in construction and frequent official bungling. Buses were cheap, though sometimes very crowded, and taxis were readily available. Best of all was the new metro; the stations, unlike the ornate Moscow subway, were simple and attractive in design, I took several long trips, once out to the beaches on the Dniepr and several times to the end of the lines, where I was surprised to see mile after mile of new apartment buildings and only a few remaining *izby*.

It was impossible to arrange a visit to the Ministry of Education to talk about exchanges — these things were decided in Moscow, I was told. I did have an interview at the university with several professors in the Juridical Faculty. They did not accept political science as a separate discipline and were quite unfamiliar with the idea of interest groups. With a younger lecturer I discussed the question of whether sovereignty in the Ukraine and Canada was real and how limited it was by the influence of Soviet Russia and the U.S., respectively.

In Moscow I was disappointed to be placed in the second-rate hotel Ostankino, on the city's outskirts. It was located near the high aluminum spire honouring the astronauts, the huge National Exhibition, and the Museum of Peasant Art in the Sheremetev Palace. There were many new apartment houses, but also very poor districts of ancient wooden houses. The back streets were full of potholes and there was a common pump for water at every corner. By going to the central Intourist office and bearding a high official in his private den, I was able to transfer to the attractive Hotel Minsk on Gorky Street, close to the centre of Moscow.

Before leaving Ostankino I paid a visit to the Timiryazev Agricultural Academy to see our exchange student, Bob Stuart, and his wife. They were living in a dormitory, in one small room, and used a tiny washtub for washing and for bathing and a hot plate (illegally) for cooking. Bob, a geography student, whose research was focused on the collective farm system, had been fortunate to receive permission to visit and, with his wife, to stay overnight, on several collective farms in the Krasnodar region. The Stuarts took me on a trip by *Raketa* (rocket) on the Moscow-Volga Canal, a waterway connecting five seas: the Black, Azov, Baltic, White, and Caspian.

The Canadian Ambassador was Robert Ford, a distinguished poet who had translated Russian and Serbo-Croatian poetry into English. He had great admiration for the courage of the Soviet writers who expressed broad currents of opinion and wielded a good deal of political influence, he thought. Ford gave a luncheon in honour of officials of Air Canada who had negotiated an agreement with Aeroflot for direct flights between Montreal and Moscow. I seized the opportunity to visit George Kastaki, a Greek citizen long employed at the Canadian embassy, who was well-known for his collection of avante-garde art. His priceless collection ranged from icons of the fourteenth century, abstract works by Kandinsky, Chagall, Popova, and others from the prewar years and the 1920s, to contemporary paintings. He surprised me by presenting me with one of a large number of unframed canvasses by his friend, Anatol Zverev, a young abstract painter, who was not permitted to exhibit publicly.[4]

As usual, I sought out friends and acquaintances in the scholarly fields, to find out about new developments, especially in comparative politics and sociology. These areas seemed to me to be a kind of litmus test of the degree to which Soviet scholarship was being influenced by the West. At the Institute of State and Law I was shown several new books on the political aspects of society, but political science was still not recognized as a distinct discipline. Yurii Barabashev told me that the work of his faculty remained primarily legal, with little or no emphasis on political studies. I heard a lecture by his colleague, Avgust Mishin, on political parties in bourgeois systems, which was comparative in approach and dealt with specific aspects of government across several countries. Yurii Zamoshkin now had his doctorate and was a full professor in the School of International Relations, which trained people for the Foreign Ministry. At a marvellous dinner at the House of Journalists, he reported that there had been a more rapid development of sociology, especially in Leningrad, and expected that there would soon be a separate Institute of Sociology. There was still a conflict of opinion among philosophers as to whether sociology should be regarded as a discipline. He favoured concrete sociological research and his own work focused on the social and psychological aspects of personality.

Minsk, which had been almost completely destroyed by war, was a brand-new town, and clearly owed almost everything to Soviet rule. The main public buildings were massive, Soviet-style structures. There were, I learned, 28 institutions of higher education, 30 institutes of the Academy of Sciences, and 10 hotels. The University, established only in 1929, now had almost 15,000 students, mainly Belo-Russian in nationality. Sixty percent of professors were Belo-Russian, but Russian was the main language of instruction; the choice of language depended on the national origin of the professor. All professors were appointed by *konkurs* (competition) and reappointed every five years — it was rare, however, that anyone was *not* reappointed. I explained that our practice of permanent tenure was designed to protect individuals from dismissal because of their political views. That could never happen here, they said — all decisions were made on the basis of scholarship. The faculty were united in their Marxist-Leninist viewpoint, I was assured — there were no substantive differences of opinion. When they asked, I told them that we had Marxists and even communists, on our faculty.

Unlike Minsk, Riga and Tallinn had rich historical and cultural traditions of their own. Riga was mainly Latvian in population, but with a Russian minority of perhaps 30 percent. The narrow, winding streets were poor-looking and ill-kept. Many churches were boarded up or in ruins — some were used for storehouses; only a few served religious purposes. The magnificent domed Lutheran Cathedral was now a concert hall and a museum portraying the evils of Catholicism and

Lutheranism. In the Orthodox cathedral there was an exhibit on Lenin. The huge Palace of Culture, in classical style, constructed in the 1960s, already looked old. The University was named after Petr Ivanovich Stuchka, lawyer and Communist political leader of 1919, whose statue stood in a nearby park. I was received by the pro-rector, Jansen, and three professors of law, all of whom were Latvian. Most of the 6,000 students were Latvian, I was told. Those from the countryside often knew little Russian and had to take special language courses. Most of the professors were also Latvian — eight of nine in the Law Faculty. Lectures were given in Latvian or Russian depending on the nationality of the professor, they said.

My stay in Tallinn, Estonia, for one day only, was purely a tourist visit, with no official meetings. My young Estonian guide, a strikingly beautiful blonde, said Estonia was "midway between Europe and the Soviet Union." The city, 60 percent Estonian, stood on a high rock, surrounded on all sides by steep cliffs and was fabulously beautiful. On the narrow, winding, cobbled streets and open squares there were two gothic cathedrals, one Orthodox and one Lutheran, and historic old dwellings and palaces. From several lookouts one could view the city below, a panorama of tiled roofs and gothic church spires, and beyond, the harbour and the Baltic Sea.

In Leningrad I stayed in a wonderful old hotel, the Astoria, on St Isaac's square, with a full view of the cathedral from my window. In my spare time I visited the Museum of the History of Leningrad, devoted to the 900-day siege of the city, and the Lenin Museum, which displayed every event in Lenin's life, including a map showing 206 places where Lenin had lived, worked or spoken in or near Leningrad. The Hermitage and the Imperial Palace were overwhelming with their fantastic collections of priceless paintings acquired over centuries by the tsars. The Russian Museum, with its wonderful collection of nineteenth century Russian art, was also impressive. Paintings from the Soviet period were uniformly bad, and there were hardly any viewers.

By chance I was able to witness several weddings in the House of Marriages, located in a gorgeous old Romanov palace. The couples were married in rapid succession by a trim, blonde matron on behalf of the Leningrad soviet, and they then enjoyed lavish refreshments and champagne — all most unproletarian! In the Church of St. Nicholas I watched baptism ceremonies — one after the other naked children were dipped in a tin tub by the priest, who made the sign of the cross over each one. On the other side of the church was a row of coffins with the lids removed and the corpses of old women lying in full view — a gruesome sight!

Also by chance a charming woman, a ballerina of the Bolshoi ballet sat down at my table in the hotel dining-room. She presented me with a signed copy of a biography she had written of the great ballerina, Semenova. She invited me to join her on a shopping tour; in each shop she pushed through the huge queues and purchased something, while others stood patiently in line. On the way home by taxi she hopped out and bought one egg; she also bought me some cough drops for my cold.

I spent an evening with the Borshchevskis, who were now living in their new three-room apartment, quite far from the city centre. As the librarian at his institute, Yurii was in charge of the largest Asian library in the world. Since "the thaw," he reported, much better books were being published and people somehow managed to get hold of books published abroad, such as *Dr. Zhivago*. The trial of the two writers, Sinyavsky and Daniel, the proceedings of which he had read, was politically stupid and morally unpardonable, he thought. I met with the Kovalevs — this time separately, as they were divorced. Yurii was still teaching at the university and had had a two month lecture tour in Australia. His wife, Licka, was still teaching English and was busy with broadcasting and writing.

I met once again with Professor Kerimov, who was now pro-rector and had become a corresponding member of the Academy of Sciences — a lifetime appointment with no real duties but substantial privileges, such as an apartment, the use of a car and chauffeur, funds for travel, and access to rest-home facilities. He was editor of the *Political Science Yearbook* but did not agree with the Western recognition of political science as a separate discipline. The most radical change at the university was the establishment of a new Institute of Complex Social Research, with a staff of 150 from all relevant disciplines, to study the relationship of the individual to society and of the individual and society to nature. Its purpose, the director, Yurii Emelianov, told me, was to unify the social sciences in the study of social questions.

I seized the opportunity to discuss the theme of interest groups in Soviet politics with scholars in Moscow and Leningrad. Barabashev accepted the notion and distinguished between groups expressing private and public interests. As examples of the former, collective farmers defended their private plots against Khruschev's effort to abolish them, or teachers opposed government's efforts to reduce salaries. As illustrations of the latter, he cited a working group, of which he was a member, advising the Soviet Presidium on local government. He also cited the permanent committees of the Soviet and their subcommittees and informal groups of professors working on proposals for changes of legislation. His colleague Mishin also recognized the existence of pressure groups but thought that their influence depended on the level at which they operated. At the topmost level the Academy of Sciences was powerful and exerted great influence over policy. The trade unions, however, were not so influential, except at lower levels. He gave as an example the organization of dwarves (*lilliputi*) — mainly circus workers, who tended to die at a younger age — which had been able to change pension policies in their favour. Yurii Kozlov, another legal specialist, spoke of trade unions or Komsomols, groups who often espoused quite different conceptions of the public interest, and of advisory bodies who recommended new legislation. There were also voluntary organizations of fishers and sportspeople, and associations to protect the environment. Kazakevich, of IMEMO, told me of a new Society for the Preservation of Historical Monuments, of which he was a member, which sought to preserve and restore historic buildings. Zamoshkin, the sociologist, endorsed my analysis of private and public interest groups and agreed that the totalitarian concept was no longer applicable. He stressed the role of experts in public policy-making; differences of opinion were often expressed. In Leningrad, Emelianov agreed about the importance of interest groups and their influence on government but spoke only of formal political organizations: trade unions, the Komsomols, the Academy of Sciences, and the Union of Writers and Union of Artists. The legal specialists, Tadevosyan and Farberov, were ready to acknowledge a certain role for organized interest groups in Soviet society, e.g., the Academy of Sciences, and its institutes, but they were reluctant to define a role for personal or group interests. These could give rise, they feared, to contradictions between social and group interests and the public interest.

I left the USSR in 1966, as in 1961, with mixed feelings and uncertain conclusions. I had the general impression that most scholars were feeling freer and had a growing familiarity with Western scholarship. The grip of Stalinism had lessened and new ideas, including those from the West, were more widely accepted. Some scholars were ready to embrace political science and sociology as non-party methods of study, but others, clearly, were not. The Soviet Union was far from becoming an "open society," but it was no longer the "closed society" of before.

The effects of de-Stalinization would, however, be known only after ten or twenty years; it was difficult to predict the results of the intermixture of the dominant Marxism with competing ideas from abroad. The Soviet Union was still far behind other communist countries in terms of degrees of political freedom and was ill-prepared for the burst of popular dissent which was soon to arise in Czechoslovakia and elsewhere.

NOTES

1. See my "Communism in Eastern Europe: Personal Impressions, 1961-1962," *Canadian Slavonic Papers* 6 (1964): 18-37.
2. See my "In Search of Political Science in the USSR," *Canadian Journal of Economics and Political Science* 24, no. 4 (Nov. 1963): 519-29.
3. "Journey to Czechoslovakia, 1961-1962," *Kosmas* 7, nos. 1-2 (Summer-Winter 1988): 219-39.
4. See Peter Roberts, *George Costakis: A Russian Life in Art* (Ottawa: Carleton University Press, 1994).

hat, the more wondrous the ——, the more clearly that reliable ——— arises: and then what? what more? what else, what next? if it is to be done with it and what will become of it all is, I would ,—— experience of the limits of the

—— ; one has approached the ——— most limits of the meaning his finite, worldly existence can offer him and for this very reason —— for this very reason ——— an abyss —finite, of uncertain——

13

A SUMMER OF FERMENT: PRAGUE AND BRATISLAVA

A TRIP OF SIX WEEKS TO CZECHOSLOVAKIA in the summer of 1967 was my longest and most fruitful since the war, and we also visited East Germany and Poland. In Czechoslovakia, the ideas of reform were everywhere expressed, and conversations were open and frank. That country, once lagging behind Poland and Yugoslavia, and even the Soviet Union, was now in the van of the Communist camp in open and controversial debate.[1]

We were abroad from May to September. Our first stop was in England, where I was a visiting scholar at SSEES, my old school, and spent a pleasant weekend with staff and students at Cumberland Lodge in Great Windsor Park. I presented my interest group analysis there and at LSE, and in Glasgow, Birmingham and Oxford. In London I met my Oxford tutor, Lord Pakenham, now the Earl of Longford, and heard him speak in the House of Lords. We also met our old friends, Dorothy Galton and François Lafitte.

Our travels on the continent began in Bonn, where I had meetings with West German and Canadian diplomats and also with several West German Social Democrats. These conversations were dominated by the recent formation of the Great Coalition of the Christian Democratic Union (CDU) and the Social Democratic Party (SDP) and its adoption of the Ostpolitik. This policy of "building bridges," as the Americans called it, was designed to develop economic, social, and cultural relations with the eastern European Communist states. The avowed purpose was not to separate eastern Europe from the USSR but rather, it was hoped, in the long run to encourage more independence and liberalization. Although the eastern European states, except for Romania, had rejected diplomatic relations with West Germany, they would, the diplomats hoped, eventually follow suit. The German Democratic Republic (GDR) had to be treated differently, as it turned on the all-

German question; there could be absolutely no question of recognizing this state at the present time. But there was no desire to isolate the GDR from the bloc, and there could be practical relations with it. Unification of the two Germanys was not an immediate prospect, but this would come in the long run.

We continued our journey to the east in a brand-new Opel, rented in Bonn, which took us from West Germany through the GDR to Prague for six weeks in Czechoslovakia and then from Slovakia through Poland for a seaside holiday, and then to the GDR and back to West Germany. At the border of the GDR we entered what a poster declared was "the land of freedom, democracy and humanism"; we had to submit to no less than ten separate immigration and customs checks! Elections were in progress, with 581 candidates for 434 seats in Parliament.

In Weimar, the city of Goethe and Schiller, the streets were dimly lit at night, and there were very few people and no traffic. It seemed even more drab and run down than in 1961. There was a statue to the prewar German Communist Ernst Thälmann, who had perished in the nearby Buchenwald concentration camp, and there were streets named after Marx, Engels, Karl Liebknecht, and William Pieck, another leading Communist. We visited Buchenwald in fog and blowing rain, which added to the atmosphere of horror surrounding this vestige of Nazi terror.

We proceeded north and east through towns celebrated in the history of German Social Democracy — Erfurt, Eisenach and Gotha, where party conferences had been held in the late nineteenth century. In dilapidated Erfurt a young priest in the magnificent cathedral called on the congregation, in a world of hatred, conflict, and lies, to work daily for Christ and his message of love. Gotha had a splendid red-brick town hall, fine old buildings, and a dilapidated castle. Tivoli, where the socialist congress had met in 1878, was, somewhat ironically, closed on Sundays. In Eisenach, the birthplace of Bach, the socialist congress had met in the Golden Lion, where the museum portrayed the victory of communism in the GDR as a logical development of socialism.

In Jena, there was the church of St Michael, where Luther had preached for 30 years and where he was buried. Here, too, was the university where a great bust reminded one that Marx had once studied there. We also saw the giant Zeiss works, founded in 1846, to which the Communists had fallen heir. In Dresden we found the core of the old town still in total ruins, a grim symbol of the destruction of the city by Anglo-American bombing raids at the end of the war, as posters reminded us. Several of the ancient buildings, including the Hofkirche, had been reconstructed, but the domed Frauenkirche was still a hollow shell. Everywhere were banners calling for friendship with the USSR and for support of the National Front in the elections. In a side-trip to Meissen, on the Elbe, we saw the lovely old houses of this medieval town, the great porcelain works, and a magnificent cathedral housing pictures by Dürer and Cranach.

On the Czechoslovak side of the frontier[2] we passed through territories formerly inhabited primarily by German-speakers, but there were few traces of Germandom left. Villages and towns were no longer empty as they had been 20 years earlier, and were repopulated by Czech and Slovak settlers from elsewhere. Terezín, the old Austrian fortress, which had been a concentration camp for Jews, was open as a museum of propaganda against Nazi brutality. The village of Lidice, razed by the Germans as a reprisal for the assassination of Heydrich, served a similar purpose, but also as a reminder of Soviet "liberation." The new town was an architectural monstrosity of uniform, dull brown houses. There was a lovely rose garden, but no plaque indicated the donors.

In Prague we lived in Vladislavova ulice, in the heart of the city, in a two hundred-year-old house in which Jan Neruda, the poet, had lived and died. Since it lacked a refrigerator we had to shop daily in the small local shops or in one of the few self-service groceries and delicatessens. We soon learned to follow the saying, "If you see a queue, join it"! As foreigners, we could enjoy better facilities — for instance, many attractive restaurants, with good food and service and, at our rate of exchange, low prices. Popular eating places offered simple fare, often only *knedlíky* (dumplings) with gravy. Shops, at least in the city centre, looked smarter than several years back and had attractive window displays. Here we were joined for ten days by our son, David, who was making a journey to Europe and Israel with a Vienna schoolmate.

We learned from our old friends the Rudingers the difficulties of life for ordinary people. Housing was one of the most serious problems, as construction and renovation were not keeping up with demand. They themselves, after waiting for two to three years, had found an apartment in a distant suburb, Spořilov, where 14,000 people lived. They had no elevator for many months, only one self-service store, and no private phones; the few public booths were often out of order. People commuted two hours daily by bus and streetcar. Shopping involved standing in long lines at many different stores. Work was long, 44 hours weekly, and wages low, ranging from 800 to 1,500 crowns (Kčs) monthly (the real exchange was roughly twenty Kčs to one U.S. dollar).

Golden Prague was spoiled by the terrible state of decay, the result of 30 years of neglect. In the Old Town and Malá Strana there were scaffoldings everywhere, but renovation was slow and construction shoddy. On the outskirts were huge white apartment complexes (so-called settlements, or *sídliště*), which were distant from the city centre and, we were told, often lacked shopping places or even a cinema. There were signs that Czechoslovakia was escaping from the thrall of the Soviet Union and returning to its own traditions. The grotesque monument of Stalin was gone from the Letná heights above the city; its enormous underground base now stored potatoes. The embalmed body of Gottwald no longer lay on public display and had, we were told, been burned because of its deterioration. Franz Kafka, who had been rehabilitated after years of condemnation, was honoured by a bust on the house where he was born. And in Vinohrady there was a tablet on the gate of the villa where the Masaryks had lived in the 1880s. But there was no plaque to mark the birthplace of Karl Kautsky, the Social Democratic theoretician.

There were many places of art and entertainment, such as Laterna Magika, whose black humour and tales of frustration and absurdity were far removed from socialist realism and were closer to Kafka and the prewar avant-garde. At the Černé dívadlo, performances were some-times pure comedy, but some skits portrayed sadness and alienation. In the Jazz club Reduta, young folks listened to raucous, improvised music. The Suchý and Šlitr cabaret offered gentle, satirical skits. At the Alhambra night club the show was based on North American Indian and cowboy motifs, with the added attraction of semi-nude girls. The tiny Theatre on the Balustrade offered a brilliant pantomime by the French artist Fialka, which satirized everyday life or tragically portrayed alienated man. There were excellent films of the "new wave" and splen-did performances of Czech and foreign opera.

Conversations with old friends gave us insights into the political and economic situation. Zdeněk Rudinger had been fully rehabilitated in 1964 and received financial compensation for the six years spent in prison. He was once more a member of the party, but he complained that it lacked any real democracy and its local cells were lifeless. There was a cult of personality of Novotný, yes — but he was *not* a personal-ity, and his policies were stupid. But Zdeněk believed that the pressure of social forces, produced by the scientific and technological revolution, would eventually bring about social and political changes. His son, Josef, a world-renowned chemist, was a corresponding member of the Academy of Sciences; he did not think that the academy was serving as an effective pressure group. Nor was the Union of Workers in Education, Culture and Science, of which he was a member.

My prewar friend Olga Haningerová and her husband, Bošek, complained of the difficulties and frustrations of life but were happy to report some personal improvements. The children had all been admitted, after many refusals, to higher education. Bošek was a deputy director in an optical firm. He was furious at the inefficiency of management and at the breakdown of working morale. The economic system was in a state of collapse, and economic reforms were ineffective. The party was in disintegration, and most of its members did not believe in the system at all. He was pessimistic about the future and saw the only way out in genuine economic reform and parliamentary control to make sure that it was carried out.

Professor Josef Polišenský was still obliged to conduct research on Latin America and to teach international relations. He was reserved and uncommunicative on matters political but was willing, as others were not, to contribute to the book that Peter Brock and I were preparing in honour of his former colleague Otakar Odložilík, now in exile. Professor Vladimír Soják had been removed from his post as director of the Institute of International Politics and Economics after his return from a semester at Northwestern University in Illinois, presumably because of his favourable attitude toward Western concepts of international relations. He was still associated with the institute and had just received the candidate's degree for his previous scholarly work. He was preparing a book on Marxist and non-Marxist theories of the discipline of international relations and was teaching a course in this field at the University of the Seventeenth of November, which was attended by students from the developing world.

Our car helped us to visit other parts of the country. Gas could be purchased cheaply with tourist coupons, but there were long line-ups at the few gas stations. The roads were not bad, and traffic was usually light. Because of the absence of road signs we sometimes had trouble finding our way. In the south, with the Rudingers, we drove down to Pilsen, Zdeněk's hometown, the site of the Škoda armaments works and four breweries, which was in a state of general decay. We drove through towns originally inhabited by Germans, but they had entirely lost their German character. For 25 kilometres we drove along a restricted frontier zone, with watchtowers every half-kilometre and guards with guns at the ready. The main square of Domažlice, famous for its defence of the frontiers by the Psohlavci (the Dogheads), was marred by a hideous statue of a modern border guard, with dog and rifle. David joined us for a trip to České Budějovice, which, like Pilsen, had a fine arcaded central square, although it seemed more prosperous. But Český Krumlov was a sad sight, with masonry crumbling and renovation just beginning. Once half German, it now had fewer than 500 Germans, and the place of those expelled had been taken by about a thousand gypsies. Nearby we visited Husinec, where Jan Hus was born, and Prachatice, where he went to school; both were originally lovely villages, but now in a bad state of deterioration.

In northeast Bohemia, in the square of Poděbrady, stood a statue to George of Poděbrady, king of Bohemia in the sixteenth century, and the castle offered an exhibit of his plan for a united Europe and of the later development of international institutions, including the United Nations. We searched out the battlefields of Slavkov (Austerlitz), where we found, in the wheatfields, monuments to Prussian soldiers who had died for Kaiser und Vaterland. High up on a tall statue, the Tumulus of Peace, was a famous quotation from Tomáš Masaryk: "Not by violence but peacefully, not by the sword, but by the plough, not by blood but by work, not by death but by life." Liberec, once largely German and a glass-making centre, was very run-down, its seventeenth century timbered houses dilapidated, and there were great piles of construction material everywhere. Near the ski resort of Špindlerův Mlýn we walked on the Czechoslovak-Polish Path of Friendship, which ran along the border in the mountains and was open to access from either side without controls (this was later a meeting place of Polish and Czech dissidents).

Traces of Masaryk were few and far between. We found a plaque on the cottage in Čejc in Moravia where as a boy he had worked as a blacksmith's apprentice. But in Hodonín, his birthplace, all statues of him had been removed. The attendant in a parking lot told us, weeping: "They could not destroy our memories of him or our love for him — tell Americans that we shall never forget him." She pointed to "our own memorial" — an old picture of Masaryk, found in a dump, and framed and decorated with flowers. She showed us down a side street to the site of the cottage where he had been born within the courtyard of a school, but there was no inscription. An elderly lady, leaning from a window opposite the school, whispered: "He lives in our hearts"; a passing cyclist, barely slowing down, pointed to the house and said: "Masaryk was born there."

My work was at first hampered by a bad cold and a severe cough. I had to seek help in a neighbourhood polyclinic, where I enjoyed a foreigner's privilege of free and speedy treatment. I soon got down to my research on Czech politics in the late nineteenth century, I had access to the catalogue of the library of the Institute of Marxism-Leninism, which had absorbed the Masaryk archives and, to my surprise, also included works by Edvard Beneš, by other exiled Czech and foreign authors, and even by Trotsky.

I devoted much of my time to interviews on the current situation with a wide range of intellectuals — writers, economists, lawyers, sociologists, foreign affairs experts, and historians — now, in contrast to earlier visits, easy to arrange. All were agreed that there was much greater freedom than a few years back. Censorship still existed but had been greatly relaxed. In art, socialist realism was a thing of the past, and art exhibits were dominated by abstract paintings reflecting Czech avant-garde traditions and Western influences. Foreign newspapers were available in a few stores, though in limited numbers; people listened widely to foreign radio and television.

Evžen Löbl, a political prisoner for many years, and head of the Slovak State Bank, whom we saw later in Bratislava, expressed the view that the real measure of a nation's wealth was the level of its intellectual activity. The role of leadership in the coming revolution would be assumed, he argued, not by the workers, as Marxism dictated, but by the intellectuals, especially in Czechoslovakia, with its long tradition of an active intelligentsia. This view seemed to be confirmed by my observations of the extraordinary awakening of intellectuals, particularly writers. Everyone praised the Writers Union as an organization exerting great influence on public events. Its congress took place during our stay and demonstrated not only greater boldness of expression but also the regime's heightened fear of this challenge. Although its sessions took place behind closed doors, almost everyone was aware of what was being said each day. I soon learned of the criticism of the government's Middle East policy, the reading of Solzhenitsyn's letter to the Soviet Writers Union on censorship, the dramatic speeches against the regime by Ludvík Vaculík and others, and the anger expressed by the party's cultural commissar, Jiří Hendrych.

The president of the union, Eduard Goldstücker, who had spearheaded the rehabilitation of Kafka, told me how the union, established originally as a means of control over literature and writers, dispensing privileges and advantages to its restricted membership of 700, had become a channel for criticizing the regime and expressing both professional and societal interests. Its weekly newspaper, *Literární noviny*, according to one of its editors, Ivan Klíma, had a circulation of 100,000 and a readership of some 500,000. It published controversial articles by leading scholars and writers, not only on literary and cultural matters, but also on economics, politics, history, and philosophy. One person said that the paper was the equivalent of a political party and the voice of opposition.

A similar part was being played by the economists, especially the Institute of Economics, headed by Ota Šik; it was taking the lead in advocating economic reform. One of its members, Josef Goldman, who had studied at the London School of Economics in 1931-32, had spent the war years at Oxford and then "sat" in prison for eight years during the 1950s. He told me that although there was general agreement on economic reform there was strong opposition from the middle level of management and by many, although not all, of the managers.

The lawyers in the Institute of State and Law were slower to discuss political reforms, said Michal Lakatoš, a Slovak long resident in Prague. He had been dismissed from the institute in 1958 but had been reinstated after two years of factory work. Radical in his views, he frequently contributed to the cultural journals, but because of censorship, he had to resort to Aesopian language. For instance, in a study of "opposition," he could not use this term and could write only of "conflict" and "interests." And in a recent article on "Freedom of Choice," although he wrote of the importance of choice in purchasing food or shoes, and of obstacles in the form of monopoly, he clearly implied that this also applied to political life.

His more conservative colleague, Zdeněk Mlynář, secretary of the party's legal commission, was head of an interdisciplinary team working on reform of the political system. Mlynář admitted to me that he had no illusions about the likelihood that the party would accept its report but hoped that the document would at least contribute to public thinking on the subject. Economic and political reform could come only from above, he believed, from the leadership of the party and through the party apparatus, the main channel for expressing the interests of society. Socialist democracy, he believed, could be attained either through a classic multi-party system, which, however, could not be discussed publicly, or through the development, within a one-party system, of the role of non-governmental organizations and public representative bodies.

The Institute of Sociology was also an arena for the discussion of reform. Miroslav Jodl, a frequent contributor to *Literární noviny*, was completing a book on power, ideology, and elites. The power elite — i.e., the party centre and its officials — possessed the real power. Members of the "influential elite," such as Ota Šik and other experts, however, enjoyed an authority that had to be respected. Then there was the "achievement elite" — creative people, such as film directors and writers, with their influence on public opinion. The latter, he thought, were more important in advocating reform than the economists or sociologists.

Another sociologist, Pavel Machonín, working in the Institute of Marxism-Leninism in Higher Education, headed an interdisciplinary team studying social structure. Through empirical studies, based on questionnaires, it was trying to measure political influence in correlation with functions performed, institutions worked in, positions held, and so on. Having read two of my articles on interest groups, he spoke of the similarity of my approach to his group's in recognizing the self-realization of groups and avoiding labels such as "free" or "totalitarian." He argued that even within the party apparatus and among the managers there was a growing conflict between progressive and conservative forces.

Miroslav Soukup, also a sociologist, told me of his participation in an international, 15-nation study of differing generational attitudes toward society and their images of the year 2000. He was deeply interested in the development of political science as a discipline but admitted that an association of this nature existed so far on paper only. There had been an attempt to form an Institute of Political Science within the academy, but the party had agreed only to such an institute under the Central Committee apparatus.

Even in the field of foreign affairs, scholars were beginning to criticize, at least by implication, Czechoslovakia's dependence on the Soviet Union. The centre of scholarly study was the Institute of International Politics and Economics (UMPE), located in the Lobkovic Palace on the Malá Strana and staffed by some 45 researchers. The director, Antonín Šnejdárek, who had succeeded Soják, was described to me as influential in foreign policy circles, even as a kind of shadow foreign minister. The institute, he told me, was financially supported by the Ministry of Foreign Affairs and in his opinion did exert an influence on foreign policy. As a specialist on Germany, Šnejdárek expounded the official line that there could be no rapprochement with West Germany until Bonn recognized the invalidity of the Munich treaty of 1938. As for the Soviet Union, Czechoslovakia presented its views to Moscow but, as a small country, could not exert much real influence.

His colleague Václav Kotyk expressed a more critical attitude. He showed me a copy of his book, *The World Socialist System,* which had been printed but was not permitted to circulate. In it he had argued that the unity of the socialist bloc must be based on the recognition of the specific conditions of each country and the right of each to develop socialism according to its own conditions. He was openly critical of Khrushchev's policy toward China and Yugoslavia, as well as the policy adopted toward Poland and Hungary in 1956.

History as a discipline appeared to have no direct impact on policy, but historians as individuals could exert an influence on public opinion and affect the legitimacy of the regime. From 1963 there had been a revival of the discipline as scholars sought to search for the truth about Czechoslovak history and to "fill in the blanks." The Historical Institute, which employed 60 scholars, was located in a beautiful palace on the Hradčany, commanding a spectacular view of Prague. One of its members, Jiří Kořálka, told me that it was now easy to get books from abroad (apart from the scarcity of foreign exchange) and that contacts with foreign scholars were frequent. At Charles University, Professor Jan Havránek told me that there was growing recognition that the campaign against T.G. Masaryk had been a mistake and that there was a changing attitude toward him, at least in private and even to some extent in published works. He felt that this would eventually lead to a full recognition of Masaryk's merits.

Václav Král, director of the Institute for the History of the East European Countries, had the reputation of being conformist and conservative. A specialist on Czechoslovak history and Czechoslovak-Soviet relations, he told me that historical writing had moved away from decoration and apologetics toward knowledge and gnosiology. He waxed enthusiastic on the advantages of Czech scholars, citing his own access to the Soviet archives and to those of Masaryk and Beneš. He had no difficulty publishing everything that he wrote, "provided I know what I may write and how." One of his junior colleagues, Jiří Sládek, a specialist on Czechoslovakia and eastern Europe, disagreed and looked on Král as more favoured and official. Sládek had no access to the Soviet archives, and contact with Russian historians was for him dangerous.

I found that a new and more objective spirit pervaded the writing of party history, but progress was slow. For instance, Karel Kreibich, a German co-founder of the Czechoslovak Social Democratic party, had not been able to have his biography published, and his 80th birthday had not been honoured. His books and papers were not readily available at the Institute of Party History, and after he died his bust was not publicly displayed there. Official accounts of his death made no reference to his role in the founding of the party or to his protests against the trials in the 1950s. At his funeral, Pavel Reimann, director of the institute, gave a purely formal address, with no attempt to appreciate Kreibich's contribution. Eduard Goldstücker, in contrast, praised him as a great historical figure; yet the text of his speech was given in full only in *Literární noviny.*

As in Prague, interviews in Bratislava with scholars and journalists were easily arranged. I had several letters of introduction from Prague, each addressed to "Mr. Prof. Dr. Comrade ... ," a curious combination of traditional and Communist honorifics. Although Slovaks were, I found, concerned about the issue of freedom, they placed strong emphasis on the Slovak question and the need for greater home rule or federation.

Bratislava remained little changed since our visit five years earlier. The statue of Stalin was gone from what was once Stalin Square, now renamed the Square of the National Uprising. On the Danube, where the giant statue of Milan Štefánik had once stood, and before 1914, that of Empress Maria Theresa, the square was empty. The only traffic on the "Blue" Danube (it was dirty brown) was the occasional barge, a German or Soviet steamer, and the hydrofoil that ran daily between Budapest and Bratislava. The Old Town was hardly changed, except for the renovation of several fine old buildings. The great Cathedral of St Martin was under repair. The synagogue was slated for demolition. On the steep hill above the city, the Castle was beginning to look as it did before it burned down in 1811, but there was still much work to be done. On the Slavín Hill was the ugly Soviet war memorial, a tall obelisk surmounted by a figure of victory. At its base were hundreds of Soviet war graves, which were tended by volunteers.

At the Historical Institute, Samuel Falt'an, a specialist on the Slovak National Uprising in 1944, gave a positive appraisal of Masaryk's role in developing the idea of Czech-Slovak reciprocity but blamed him for the incorrect concept of Czechoslovakism. The stronger Czechs had imposed their rule on the Slovaks — a form of oppression that contradicted the otherwise liberal nature of the First Republic, contributing to the promotion of the conservative and clerical Populist movement and culminating in the reactionary separate state under Father Tiso. His own book on the uprising stressed its national aspect and was severely censured as bourgeois nationalist by Král, the Czech historian. Falt'an found the present Czech-Slovak relationship thoroughly unsatisfactory. Most people rejected separatism and favoured Czech-Slovak coexistence, but based on the equality of the Slovaks in deeds, not just in words.

The director of the Economic Institute, Pavol Turčan, regarded the economic aspect of the Slovak problem as crucial. He was a strong advocate of economic reform in the republic as a whole but stressed the special problems facing Slovakia as a less-developed region. Could Slovak firms compete in a freer market, without a tariff wall to protect them against more efficient Czech firms? The measures that had been agreed on to meet Slovakia's special problems might, he feared, cause a general paralysis of reform as a whole. Evžen Löbl agreed that the centrally planned system had failed and urgently required economic reform. This would have to be a change not *of* the system but *within* the system and would at least introduce elements of democracy.

Laco Novomeský, noted writer and prominent political figure in the early postwar years had, after release from prison, remained, like Husák, excluded from public life. Writers, he said, were now more or less able to write as they pleased and to express different tendencies of thought, though, of course, always within the framework of socialism. They had no specific political objectives but sought to influence opinion through their writings. As for the Slovak problem, there was general dissatisfaction with the present situation but no thought of separatism; this issue had been settled by the uprising. The basic question was twofold: "Would the Czechs accept the Slovaks as equals?" and "Did the Slovaks accept the idea of living together with the Czechs?"

Alfonz Bednár, distinguished novelist and film writer, took us for a drive to Děvín, the ruined castle on the river, which overlooked the Austrian border, with its barbed-wire fences and watchtowers, and then on to the writers' rest-home in the former mansion of Count Palffy. He told us of the havoc created by censorship in the past and the continuing limits of self-censorship and editorial controls. His own works, dealing with sensitive historical subjects, had to be withdrawn, but his novel on the uprising, *Hodiny a minuty,* had won a state prize. There was indeed much greater freedom, he said, but "we want more!" Czech-Slovak relations were not good, perhaps even worse than before the war, but there was no way of ventilating the problem openly. The crux of the matter was economic, since the economy was run by the Czechs. In the cultural sphere Slovaks had more control of their schools and universities but were still subject to strict rules from Prague.

Conversations at other institutes, usually in large groups, were less productive. At the Institute of State and Law, the director, František Košťa, talked of its study of interest groups and of the emerging discipline of political science. He placed great stress on the need for "lobbying" by the mass organizations and the National Front. At the Institute for the History of East European Countries, Director Josef Hrozenčík spoke warmly of the institute's cooperation with Prague and complained of limited funds. A younger man, František Bystřický, spoke more openly in private. There was greater freedom and objectivity of historical studies than earlier, but one could still not write about the post-1945 years without limitation. At the Institute of Sociology, the director, Jan Mlynárik, told me that the main theme of its research was the evolution of Slovak society and its social structure, including social groups. The class criterion was no longer the decisive one but was supplemented by others such as institutional, regional, and professional.

Miroslav Hysko, a lecturer at the Faculty of Journalism at Komenský University, had been editor-in-chief of the Slovak party organ, *Pravda,* during the uprising and again later, and in 1963 he had been the target of abusive attack by Novotný. He remained a party member, he said, but could not express his ideas with full freedom. He was gloomy about the general situation. What was needed was not only economic reform, but a change in the political system. There had been no fundamental change since 1956, and the Slovak question remained unsettled. The traditional, centralized system introduced by Beneš continued under the Communists. There was no serious movement for separation, but no one was satisfied with the existing situation. František Sýkora, an editor of *Pravda,* agreed with this estimate and thought the real imperative was to achieve greater autonomy for the Slovak National Council and for the Slovak Academy of Sciences. Pavol Berta, an editor of *Kultúrny život,* told me that his paper was a kind of Slovak counterpart of the Czech *Literární noviny* and freely discussed controversial economic and political questions.

We headed north to Nitra, with its walled citadel on a steep hill, a splendid cathedral and bishop's palace, the striking modern building of the Higher Agricultural School, and many new apartment blocks. In sharp contrast, the old walled town of Kremenica was in a state of terrible disrepair. We spent a steaming hot day in Banská Bystrica, headquarters of the Slovak National Uprising, its splendid huge square disfigured by a hideous monument to the Soviet liberators. The museum presented a travesty of the uprising, depicting it as a purely Communist action, with little mention of Husák and Novomeský and none of the non-Communist participants.

In the Low Tatras we made a brief stop on a Sunday morning in the charming village of Vychodná. Since there had been no priest at the Catholic church for years, mass was conducted by the parishioners. They were mainly women, attired in colourful folk costumes. In sharp contrast, the women who streamed out of the Evangelical church after the service were dressed entirely in black. A retired carpenter, Michal Michalka, showed us around the town and, with his wife, gave us raspberry juice in the kitchen of his fine new house. For years afterward we exchanged Christmas greetings with these friendly folks.

We spent a few days in Tatranská Lomnica in the High Tatras, where our visit was spoiled by poor service and constant hassles at the hotel desk. We took long hikes in the mountains and ascended by cable car to the highest peak, Lomnický štít, which we found again, as in 1937, almost totally obscured by fog. We also toured the Spiš towns, settled by Saxons in the twelfth century, and visited castles and wooden churches, all, alas, in an awful state of neglect. The highlight was the church in Levoča, with its magnificent altar sculptures, carved by Pavol of Levoča. Our final stop was the picturesque cattle-raising village of Zd'iar, in the mountains on the Polish border. Its distinctive houses were grey-timbered, with steep roofs. After service on Sunday the peasants, men and women, strolled out in colourful costumes, to the delight of photographers.

We crossed into Poland over a little stream in the Tatra Mountains at the village of Lyšná Połana, where Czech and Polish immigration officials were sitting side by side in the sunshine and detained us for but a few minutes. Lying just beyond was Poronín, a village with low *góral* farmhouses and peasants in folk costume. Here was the house where Lenin had lived in 1913-14, now a museum. The countryside was distinctive for the narrow strip farms, so different from the collective farms in Czechoslovakia. The roads were crowded with many long peasant carts, carrying loads of timber. Zakopané, in the Polish Tatras, was little more than a large, ugly village, with an open-air market and the nearby ski resort. We were surprised to find that Professor Leopold Seidler had come all the way from Lublin by car to welcome us. He entertained us at dinner that evening with a Polish meat dish and Polish vodka. Unfortunately Sally and I were both very sick that night.

Our continuing illness and bad service in the hotel dampened our stay in Cracow, but we were able to see some of its beauties, including the Wawel Cathedral, with the sarcophagi of Polish kings, and the Castle, with its arched Renaissance courtyard and its tapestries, recently returned by Canada from their wartime hideaway. We marvelled at the Church of the Virgin Mary (the Mariacki), with its beautiful altar by Wit Stwosz. From its tower, every hour on the hour, the Cracow trumpeter blew the warning that had sounded against the Turks for centuries — and interrupted still at the point when a Turkish arrow killed him. Once again we were struck by the strong hold that the Church had on many Poles. On Sunday we visited some of the many churches, all filled with worshippers; later we saw hundreds of peasants walking for miles in the country to the nearest village church. In sharp contrast, the regime showed its hostility to religion when it planned the suburb of Nowa Huta, a brand new city of 100,000, constructed for the employees of the huge Lenin Metallurgical Works. In this community, which was of unsurpassed ugliness, there was not a single church.

In Cracow I discussed the role of the Catholic church in a long talk with Jerzy Turowicz, editor-in-chief of the Catholic weekly, *Tygodnik Powszechny*. Founded in 1945, it had been closed down after Stalin's death and resumed publication in 1956, but with a strictly limited circulation of 40,000. Turowicz defended the much-debated practice of pre-censorship as having the advantages of placing the final responsibility on the censors, but he also admitted that self-censorship was necessary. Turowicz strongly denied that the newspaper constituted an opposition either to the church or to the state. The regime appreciated the fact that the Catholic weekly paper was independent of the hierarchy of the church and supported the government's foreign policy, including the alliance with the USSR and the Oder-Neisse line.

At Cracow's famed Jagellonian University I had meetings with two professors. Henryk Wereszycki, a historian who specialized in the nineteenth century, was greatly angered by censorship, which had prevented publication of several of his books. He complained that historical writing had to avoid the delicate subject of the 1863 revolt against Russia or the role of Marshal Pilsudski as interwar leader and to conform to an anti-German interpretation of everything related to Germany. Konstanty Grzybowski, who was writing a five-volume study on the history of political theory, also deplored the pressure on intellectuals, who could express opinions orally but could not publish freely.

We left Cracow on a Sunday and spent some time at the Jasna Gora monastery and church in Częstochowa, the famous place of pilgrimage. With hundreds of others we waited for the unveiling of the famous Black Madonna in the Chapel of the Mother of God. The crowds were huge, including pilgrims who had walked from afar. We also made a stop at the concentration camp of Oświęcim, with its gruesome exhibits of the clothing, suitcases, and even the hair and teeth of the former inmates. The entry into this hellish prison, surrounded by a double line of electrified barbed-wire fences, bore the ironic slogan, "Arbeit macht frei" [work makes one free].

Warsaw was greatly changed since my visit in 1961. All around the Palace of Culture new buildings had gone up, but some empty spaces remained, and occasional gaunt brick buildings stood alone. There were great blocks of flats everywhere, sometimes in quite decent modern style, and many fine palaces had been rebuilt. The new public buildings, including the Opera House, were, however, monolithic and ugly. The ruins of the Ghetto were no more; the great piles of salvaged bricks of 1961 had been used to construct poor-looking apartments. Opposite the Grand Theatre was a striking monument "To the Heroes of Warsaw, 1939-1945" — the figure in stone of a giant woman coursing through the air.

Although it was holiday time I managed to arrange a number of interviews through the good offices of the Foreign Ministry and the Canadian embassy and with the help of Barbara Blake, a Polish student whom I had met in England. The most official meeting was with Gassman, editor-in-chief of the party organ, *Trybuna ludu*, who espoused an orthodox line of support for the Arabs in the Middle East war and evinced complete distrust of the new West German coalition government under K.G. Kiesinger. There could be no diplomatic relations with West Germany until it recognized the Oder-Neisse frontier and the GDR. A similar view on Germany was espoused by Dr Markiewicz, a former journalist, of the Polish Institute of International Affairs, the editor of its journal. He, too, believed that the Kiesinger government still hoped to restore the Germany of 1937; it referred constantly to the GDR as Mitteldeutschland, thus implying that the former German territories in Poland to the east of the GDR also belonged to Germany. In the Foreign Office, Dr Sieradzki followed the same line. How could we have diplomatic relations with a state that did not recognize our frontiers? Moreover, the GDR was a friendly state and was crucial to Poland's security: it should be recognized as a reality.

I was given a rosy picture of the operation of the state institutions by Professor Stefan Rozmaryn, secretary of the Council of Ministers and of its economic committee, and by Dr Gwidź, head of the bureau of the Sejm, or Parliament. Real power rested with the Council of Ministers, which, however, could act only within the framework of law. Gwidź described in favourable terms the role of the Sejm, especially of its all-party committees, which met frequently and submitted proposals and questions. In response to my questions, both men acknowledged the role of interest groups, especially the trade unions, which were consulted and could submit proposals to government and Sejm. According to Rozmaryn, the role of the Academy of Sciences and scientists in general was limited, but advisory committees of experts performed valuable functions.

The role of interest groups was also recognized by Professor Sylvester Zawadzki, of the Legal Institute of the Academy of Sciences. He praised the work of so-called neighbourhood committees, which acted in liaison with the people's councils on schools, housing, health, and so on. However, Stefan Nowak, the sociologist, played down the influence of the trade unions and professional groups, such as the writers and even the economists. A visit to the Union of Writers seemed to confirm his view. Unlike its counterparts in Czechoslovakia and even in the Soviet Union, the Polish union received limited funding and had no publishing house and no organ of its own.

I discussed the role of interest groups with my old friend Jan Strzelecki, the sociologist. Admitting that they did exist, he believed that a real pluralism, with open interest groups, could not exist as long as centralized party control continued. He was making a study of the future of socialist society in Poland. There would have to be more freedom, he believed, since the party could not claim to have the whole truth. The party leaders, most of whom were prewar Communists, feared opposition or even open criticism. The philosopher Leszek Kołakowski had raised the issue of control over power but would lose his job the moment he spoke openly about opposition. The main opposition voice was the newspaper *Polityka,* under the editorship of Mieczysław Rakowski. One of its editors, Zdanowki, admitted that the newspaper did encourage discussion of vital issues (within the limits of censorship) but denied that it was opposed to the party line.

Strzelecki acknowledged that the Catholic church could be considered a kind of interest group or opposition, but only in the negative sense of opposing certain policies of the regime. Some Catholics, however, had a relatively positive attitude toward the regime. People attended mass not just for religious reasons, but because of the social importance of the event in rural society and because of the Polish nationalism of Catholicism. Young people were not blindly devoted to religion and wanted no indoctrination by party or by church.

The most critical voice I heard was that of Karol Lapter, of the Higher Political School, who had been in exile in Prague in the late 1930s and who spoke Czech. He talked openly of an economic and political crisis in the country and a constant struggle for power. Gomułka was combatting both the "Romanians" in the party, who wanted a hard but independent line, and the "liberals," who wanted reform as well as independence. Gomułka was moving step by step toward complete subservience to the Soviet Union. The regime had enjoyed great support for its foreign policy, the alliance with Russia, and the struggle against Germany, but this support was weakened by a growing lack of faith in the Soviet Union, the greater flexibility of Bonn's foreign policy, a lessening of the hatred of Germany among the younger generation. and a warm sympathy for Israel in the war with the Arabs.

After leaving Warsaw we drove north across the great European plain; new brick houses contrasted with old thatched cottages. As we approached the Baltic coast the architecture took on a kind of Hanseatic style — tall, narrow buildings with steep, slanting roofs. At one point we turned off the highway to see a fortress (Ordensburg), of the Teutonic Knights and later to another Teutonic bastion in the town of Malbork. We also visited the battlefield of Grunwald, where in 1410 the Knights had been defeated by Poles, Russians, Lithuanians, and Tartars in one of the great battles of history. As a kind of symbol of former Polish greatness and German aggression there stood a monolithic stone column, with grim faces on opposing sides, and tall metal columns of spears behind.

When we finally arrived on the coast we found that our reservations in the Grand Hotel on the beach in Sopot had been cancelled because of an official conference. We were forced to stay two nights in a run-down hotel in Gdańsk, opposite the main railway station. It overlooked a sad-looking square of poor, newly built flats, garbage pails, and a great pile of debris. Our room with bath did not even have a toilet and was not heated. In the dining-room we experienced our first real taste of what was to become normal — execrable service, with long waits for a table, more long waits for a waiter, for food, and even for the bill, so that we wasted hours on each meal and were driven to take up smoking!

But there were rewards. The city of Gdańsk was a stunning example of restoration. I had seen it in 1950 in total ruins and again in 1961, when it was still largely ruined. Although there were tell-tale open grassy spaces and some badly damaged buildings, the city had been meticulously rebuilt in the original Hanseatic style, including even the exterior sculptures and frescoes. The Long Street and the Long Square formed a unique urban ensemble, with the rebuilt Gothic Town Hall, dozens of patrician houses, and the great Church of Our Lady. We made an excursion by boat to Westerplatte, where the Second World War began and where a handful of Poles had made a brief stand against the German invaders in September 1939. Here, on the open sea, at the gulf leading to the Vistula River, stood a modernistic monument to the heroes of the battle and to the brave feats of Poles in other war sectors. Surprisingly the trip took us straight through the Gdańsk harbour, past factories, shipyards, and ships, including some of Soviet origin.

We moved on at last to Sopot, where we lived in great style in a luxurious hotel of late-nineteenth century style. We had a gigantic room overlooking the beach and the bay. Once again the service was intolerably bad, with long waits in the dining-room and at the desk. We tried to escape this by having breakfast in our room, but this, too, came after long delays and often with items forgotten. Once I ordered boiled eggs cooked for five minutes, and we received five eggs, two of them rotten! When we at last reached the beach, however, it was splendid, covered with hundreds of bathers, mainly Poles, who rented wicker chairs with tops for protection against the blazing sun.

Apart from the beaches, however, Sopot was run-down and depressing. In contrast, nearby Gdynia, with its splendid new port, was a city of wide avenues and a broad seafront. A side-trip to what was once East Prussia took us through empty countryside and the still totally ruined towns of Elbląg, Frombork, and Toruń, the birthplace of Copernicus. The deserted autobahn ended abruptly at the frontier of the Soviet Union to which access was blocked by a great mound of grass-covered earth. Nearby Szczeczin (Stettin) was only partly restored, and broad stretches were still in total ruins. However, its harbour was impressive and filled with ships, both Polish and foreign. Aboard a new Soviet rocket ship, the *Kometa,* we went up the Oder River and through the Gulf of Stettin to the sea. Back home at dinner in the hotel we had a chance meeting with a young man and his wife, who were both employed in the shipyards. We had a pleasant evening of dancing and talking; the next day they kindly took us sightseeing.

Our crossing into East Germany was a minor miracle. Our Polish visa had expired, but the customs officials raised no difficulties and did not check our currency or baggage. One of them even loaned us some small change so that we could buy a bottle of Polish vodka with our remaining *zlotie.* Since we had no German visa and there was no visa office at this crossing point, they doubted that we would be able to enter the GDR and were as surprised as we were when we were admitted at once. This was largely the result of impressive letters of introduction, including one from the GDR's Foreign Office, which assured me help in arranging interviews.

As it turned out, however, these letters proved of no value; I was not able to have a single meeting with German scholars or officials. Moreover the visa, which I eventually received in Berlin, was valid for a single Bezirk (district) — i.e., Berlin. Our guide, after struggling with the bureaucracy, did secure permission for us to travel outside Berlin. We visited Potsdam, with the lovely Rococo palace of Sans Souci, its magnificent gardens, and the mansion of Cecilienhof, where the Potsdam conference was held in 1945. En route we passed through the Western and Eastern controls on the ring highway around the Western zone and stopped at the gigantic Soviet War Memorial in Treptower Park. Our guide also arranged an interesting excursion to the Spreewald, a region of small streams and canals in the Lusatian Sorb country. In a flat-bottomed boat, propelled by a boatman with a long pole, we went through narrow rivers and canals, passing picturesque farms and houses, lush with flowers. In the villages where we stopped we saw little evidence of the Sorb ethnic minority, except in several museums of folk costumes.

With our guide we visited in Berlin the Distel cabaret, with its mild satire of the foibles of East German life. He admitted that it could not go beyond certain limits and was an exercise, he said, in "positive criticism." We also enjoyed an imaginative production of *Schweik in the*

Second World War by Bertold Brecht, with music by Hans Eisler. The play was a bitter critique of the Nazi occupation of Czechoslovakia and of Czech national resistance; this was depicted not in heroic terms but in the passive style of the good soldier Schweik.

Berlin was totally transformed since my earlier visit at the time of the building of the Wall. Unter den Linden was lined with modern buildings and handsome shops. At the Wall there were benches and flowers in front of the Brandenburg Tor. Unter den Linden was lined with solid public buildings, such as the German State Library, the Museum of German History, and the Humboldt University, where Marx had once studied. At a former Nazi monument, now dedicated to the victims of fascism and militarism, every half-hour there was a changing of the guard, with the soldiers using the old Prussian goose-step. And here and there stood statues to famous Prussian army generals. The spacious Marx-Engels Platz was dominated by the cathedral, still in ruins, the restored Art Gallery, which I had visited before the war, and the gigantic, modernistic Ministry of Foreign Affairs, built on the site of the former Hohenzollern Castle. In another part of the city the Karl-Marx Allee (formerly Stalin Allee) was lined with great, monolithic Soviet-style apartment houses and, nearer the centre, more attractive modern structures. The vast empty spaces between these buildings created an inhuman and lifeless atmosphere.

The Wall was painted in bright colours, but this hardly succeeded in making it less forbidding. It had been made much higher, and was patrolled by police with tommy-guns. Every street leading to it was closed off, and at the Wall, a space of 30 to 50 feet, probably mined, was shut off by electrified barbed-wire. At the crossing at Checkpoint Charlie, on the East German side, there was a formidable array of concrete barriers and road blocks and a high watchtower.

Everywhere there were propaganda placards and window displays depicting the Nazi past of West German leaders and American crimes in Vietnam, or proclaiming Communist slogans. The Historical Museum was a giant propaganda display, presenting the Communist interpretation of the whole of German history, from the Prussian military state through the capitalist and militarist Reich to the bourgeois Weimar Republic and Nazi rule and describing the rise and growth of the working-class movement and socialism. In the strikingly modern Congress Hall I attended a meeting in honour of North Vietnam, where, before a highly selected but unenthusiastic audience, Guenther Mittag, a Politburo member, ranted loudly about U.S. aggression, the criminal actions of the Chinese, and worldwide support of the Soviet Union.

Our guide was a bright young postgraduate student and instructor in Marxism-Leninism who was thoroughly indoctrinated but interested in political discussion. His knowledge of Marxism-Leninism was shallow and limited, and he was somewhat surprised by the many interpretations of Marxism that I cited. "Only one can be right," he said. He was critical of certain aspects of East German life but seemed to believe sincerely that power really belonged to the people. He was convinced that communism would triumph throughout the world, even in the United States. He thought that the Wall was unnatural and would eventually have to be eliminated.

When we left the GDR at Checkpoint Charlie we had a long and time-consuming check of our passports and money and an examination of the entire car, inside and out, under the hood and even beneath the car. It was a welcome escape from the East, but the contrast of East and West did not seem quite so black and white as in 1961. We were struck, however, by the handsome hotels and apartment houses, the heavy traffic, the abundant supplies in the stores, and less evidence of war damage than in the East. In our hotel we relished the good service and the absence of endless waiting. West Berlin had inherited fewer of the former public buildings than the East but had the Charlottenburg Palace, the residence of the president of West Germany, and many striking new buildings, such as the Opera and the Congress Hall, and the new TV tower, which gave a panoramic view of both East and West Berlin. The Reichstag was still under reconstruction, but one wing housed an exhibition on the "German East," which seemed to evoke nostalgia for the lost territories.

The purpose of our visit to West Berlin was to attend a conference on eastern Europe. The event was organized by Kurt London and attracted a number of noted German experts, such as Richard Löwenthal, Klaus Mehnert, Boris Meissner, and several old friends: Fred Barghoorn of Yale, Zbigniew Brzezinski of Columbia, Hélène Carrère d'Encausse of Paris, and Bob Tucker of Princeton. There was a wide-ranging and stimulating discussion of the future of Europe and particularly Germany, including even the possibility of a united and neutral Germany. Löwenthal and Mehnert urged the recognition of the Oder-Neisse border but took a very tough attitude toward the GDR; there must be an inner transformation of the Communist state as a condition of good relations with the West. My own contribution was a paper on party, opposition, and interest groups in eastern Europe, which was included in the subsequent volume based on the proceedings.[3] Sally sat in on some of the sessions but enjoyed even more her first opportunity to explore the western part of the divided city.

Our travels in Czechoslovakia, Poland, and East Germany further confirmed for us the change and ever increasing diversity within the Soviet bloc that we had observed five years earlier. This time the change was most noticeable in hitherto-backward Czechoslovakia, which now stood out as much freer in conrast to the GDR and even Poland. There was mounting evidence of crisis in the economy and in politics, and the rift between the leadership and broad social groups, notably the students and the intellectuals, was manifest. The growing influence of intellectuals, especially writers and economists, was also clear. We could not then predict the great reform movement of the following year. In retrospect, however, we realized that we had been witnesses to the last throes of the old system and the burgeoning of a great transformation.

NOTES

1. See my "Ferment among Czechs and Slovaks," in Skilling *Communism: National and International* (Toronto: University of Toronto, 1964), chs. 6, 7; also my chapter in Adam Bromke, ed., *The Communist States at the Crossroads* (New York: Praeger, 1965), ch. 5.
2. For a detailed account of our stay in Czechoslovakia, see "Journey to Czechoslovakia," *Czechoslovak and Central European Journal* (formerly *Kosmas*) 8, nos. 1-2 (1989): 136-67.
3. Kurt London, ed., *The Soviet Union: A Half-Century of Communism* (Baltimore: The Johns Hopkins University Press, 1968).

14

THE INTERRUPTED REVOLUTION

WHEN THE NEWS BROKE of the soviet invasion of Czechoslovakia in August 1968, I was in Palo Alto, attending a conference on the comparative study of change in communist systems. All of the conference participants became immediately preoccupied with the momentous process of reform in Czechoslovakia, the theme of my paper. A straw vote of assembled experts on communism taken in early August revealed that an overwhelming majority shared my view that a Soviet invasion was unlikely. When it came, on August 22, I was both shocked and depressed, and needed little persuasion to embark on a full study of the Prague Spring, its causes and its aftermath. For the next seven years I virtually lived with this theme in my attic study in Toronto. With the help of several research assistants, I combed through the vast quantity of materials I had by then acquired (a collection I later deposited with the Thomas Fisher Rare Book Library at the University of Toronto). I had many opportunities to test out my ideas and explore other views about the Prague Spring in talks with individual participants and specialists in Toronto and elsewhere, and in many seminars in Canada, the United States and Europe.

When the book eventually appeared it was greeted favourably by many reviewers; one Czech émigré scholar called it "a monumental work" which would remain a prime reference for years. In Czechoslovakia Milan Matouš, leading ideologist, condemned my book as a prime example of "systematic and slanderous anti-communist propaganda." In a trial of a dissident the judge ruled that the book should be destroyed as "a thing entirely without value." In unofficial circles, however, it was greeted with enthusiasm; and passed from hand to hand until it was reduced, I was told, to a veritable "salad." Milan Šimečka used to joke with friends that if their name did not appear in the index their role had been minimal. His own copy was confiscated by the police during a house search.[1]

SPRING IN PRAGUE

While the Prague Spring took me by surprise, at Sally's urging I made a quick visit in May 1968 to witness the exciting events at first hand.[2] I was able to absorb a little of the spirit of the reform period, which was to prove so short-lived. Unfortunately time did not permit a visit to Slovakia, which had always been a must during previous trips. The weather in Prague was beautiful, and I enjoyed walks in the Stromovka Park, with its splendid trees and bright flower beds, in the seminary gardens on Petřín, now open to the public, and in the lovely Šárka valley, with its personal memories for me of 1937. In the city many of the old buildings had emerged from scaffoldings and were beautiful in pale pastel colours. Many were still dilapidated, however. It would be many years before Prague would once more become the architectural gem it had once been. At the Hotel International, an ugly monument to Stalinist architecture, where I had to stay for a few days, there was much to remind one of the past — poor service, cold eggs, stale rolls, huge waiting lines, and impolite clerks at the reception desk. It was a relief to move to the Tatran, a modest hotel in the heart of the city on Václavské where I was given a quiet little room at the back with a view of a courtyard.

My old friends, and indeed, intellectuals in all fields had been surprised by the crisis in December and by the fall of Novotný but held widely differing views of the future. Zdeněk Rudinger, still a Communist, said that the outcome was obscure, since Novotný and others in high places still sought to block reform. He saw no need for an opposition party; the Communist party itself must become democratic, with an opposition within itself. His son, Josef, expressed similar opinions and opposed a multi-party system. My old friends the Haningers were sceptical about the future, since the present leadership was not prepared to carry through vigorous reforms. Although people looked on Novotný with contempt, they warned that he still had great influence.

In conversations with intellectuals I questioned them on the causes of the January overthrow and the social forces involved. Pavel Machonín, a sociologist, identified the progressive forces as the intelligentsia, youths generally, and students especially, progressive Communists, victims of past terror, participants in the wartime struggle for liberation, members of banned organizations such as the Scouts and the Sokols, and the Slovaks. Everyone agreed on the paramount role played by the writers and by the Writers' Union. Antonín Liehm, editor of a new daily newspaper that the union planned to publish, described the writers as the "conscience of the nation." Ivan Klíma stressed the importance of *Literární listy*, which had a circulation of 284,000 and a brain trust representing all the main fields of scholarship. The paper stood for a pluralistic and democratic system and was seeking not revolution but evolution, he said. Within the Writers' Union, non-Communists writers had their own independent club, headed by Václav Havel. Jiřina Šiklová, a young sociologist at Charles University, told me that Czech students had no sympathy for socialism and wanted only democracy. Zdeněk Zbořil said that the party was completely discredited among students.

The strongest forces opposed to reform, everyone agreed, were state bureaucrats, managers, and especially the party *apparatchiki*. But even these groups included people of progressive outlook, and there were links between them and the reformers. Some observers reported that the workers were interested primarily in economic improvements and were passive and waiting, but others spoke of growing working class support for reform and for freedom of the press. The peasants, who enjoyed a relatively decent standard of living under the collective farm system, were even more passive. The Slovaks were a significant force for reform, although they often laid greater stress on national aims and autonomy than on democratization.

There was a great disparity of opinion concerning the future of the political system. At the Institute of State and Law, for instance, Michal Lakatoš did not think that the present system, given the party's monopoly of power, could really be reformed. The only hope was a change *in* the system and its replacement by a completely democratic order. This would require creation of a civic society, involving autonomous political parties and interest associations, and a genuinely representative system. Ivan Bystřina, of the same institute, and a member of the official team, headed by Zdeněk Mlynář, for the study of the political system, also advocated a full and complete democracy and a civil society. He hoped that Mlynář would eventually come to accept a pluralism of political parties. The economist Radoslav Selucký, distinguished between a maximum program — a completely pluralist system, with several competing parties — and a minimum program, which would institutionalize some of the gains achieved since January.

Václav Slavík, a Central Committee member, and head of the newly formed Institute of Political Science within the Central

Committee, offered an entirely different alternative. Leadership would continue to be exercised by a single party, but it would have to become an "open system," permitting differing factions and electing its own presidium. Other parties and interest associations would participate in policy-making, but only within the National Front; this would permit differences of opinion and even opposition and would guarantee competing candidates for public office.

I discussed foreign policy issues at length with staff members of the Institute for International Politics and Economics (UMPE), whose director, Antonín Šnejdárek, treated me as a kind of unofficial guest. There was general agreement that the new foreign minister, Jiří Hájek, was open to new ideas but was not likely to introduce dramatic changes in policy. Alexander Dubček, it was said, discouraged public discussion of foreign affairs. Šnejdárek felt that economic and cultural relations with West Germany were improving, but, like his colleagues Alexander Ort and Vladimír Soják, he thought that it was too early to consider formal diplomatic relations. A younger colleague, Jaroslav Šedivý, had been criticized by the Ministry of Foreign Affairs for advocating early resumption of diplomatic relations. Like Václav Kotyk, Šedivý, thought that Prague should follow a more independent line, but both agreed that the alliance with the Soviet Union was essential. According to Colonel Lapáček, of the Military Academy, direct military intervention was ruled out. Prague's military strategy would still have to be based on the alliance with the Soviet Union, but it would display more initiative and independence.

There was uncertainty as to whether the political situation would develop for better or for worse. Dubček was highly regarded by most people, but, it was recognized, he had not been an ardent reformer before January and had accepted the leadership position with reluctance. Much would depend on how he would react to the conflicting pressures on him from outside the country and from conservative and progressive forces within the party. The Central Committee's 15 May plenum was a step forward, but the policy was not as strongly in favour of reform as many would have liked, and there were still strong conservative elements in the leadership. The Party Congress in September would certainly help to resolve these inner conflicts and change the balance in favour of reform.

Public opinion polls indicated an overwhelming majority in support of Dubček and reform. However, there was uncertainty as to the role to be played by the non-party forces in eventual elections. Some feared that the elections would not be really free and that the party would remain the dominant force. There would be little likelihood that the Social Democrats and emerging radical movements would be allowed to participate; in any case, none of them possessed capable leaders who had political experience.

Intellectuals were divided on the likely outcome. Some were hopeful; others were sceptical and did not exclude the possibility of a turn backward. One young historian was cynical about the real chance of democracy. The question, he thought, was not when, but how long it would be before the Prague Spring would turn into the Prague Autumn. The situation was full of ambiguities and absurdities and could be better described, he thought, by a Franz Kafka or a Jaroslav Hašek than by Western sociologists or politologists.

AUTUMN IN PRAGUE

After the Soviet occupation, Sally and I resolved to visit Czechoslovakia as soon as possible. Taking advantage of a sabbatical leave at Toronto, we proceeded to Vienna in the autumn of 1968, not sure whether we would be able to enter Czechoslovakia so soon after the takeover. However, we received our visa in five minutes at the Czechoslovak embassy in Vienna and proceeded by bus to Bratislava. We were uncertain what we could accomplish in an occupied country, but in the event I was able to conduct several dozen interviews in Bratislava and Prague. As usual I worked at a hectic pace, ran myself down, and had to turn to the clinic attached to Charles University for treatment of a bronchial cough.

Our stay in Austria was a useful introduction to the whole undertaking. In Salzburg I attended a seminar organized by the International Political Science Association (IPSA), attended by Soviet and eastern European participants. Czech delegates, especially Alexander Ort of ÚMPE, courageously defended the plans for reform and even mingled with the Soviet delegates socially, in the hope of persuading them of the error of their government's action. The Soviet spokesmen sharply criticized Czechoslovak "democratization" as a threat to socialism but did not openly justify the intervention. The final report by Professor Ghita Ionescu, of Britain, was warmly supportive of Czechoslovak reform and was strongly critical of the Soviet invasion. At the concluding banquet, Karl Friedrich, IPSA's president, was applauded stormily when he remarked that he would have preferred to speak in Czech, rather than in his native German, or in one of the official languages of IPSA.

During our stay in Vienna I served as a volunteer for the Canadian Department of Immigration, screening would-be immigrants to Canada. This gave me useful insights into the mood and motivation of Czech and Slovak refugees. Many had not yet decided to leave permanently; they could still come and go between Prague and Vienna, often returning to Vienna with newly acquired cars laden with their possessions. I also used the opportunity to interview a number of people who had been active in the reform movement.

The trip to Bratislava, only 40 miles from Vienna, took two hours, including half an hour at the frontier. Czech and Slovak officials were smiling and joking and did not even examine our luggage. On the walls of the bank at the border there were pictures of Svoboda and Dubček and the slogan, "Dubček and Svoboda are our freedom." There were no Soviet troops at the border, but just beyond we saw a small Soviet encampment, with several tanks.

Bratislava gave the impression of general decay, except where several historic buildings had been renovated. The Castle, which had been used as Soviet army headquarters, was to remain closed until its ceremonial opening on 29 October, the anniversary of the Slovak declaration in favour of a united Czechoslovak state in 1918. The Old Town was still in a ruinous state. Street names, removed to confuse the invading armies, were still missing, and there were often bullet and shell holes in the façades. Here and there a few Soviet soldiers were to be seen, but most of the troops were stationed in the countryside and were not often permitted to enter the city.

Everywhere there were portraits of Svoboda and Dubček and graffiti on the walls, such as "Russians, go home." The former headquarters of the Soviet-Slovak Friendship Society was empty, and in the windows hung pictures of Gustav Husák and the presidium of the Slovak Communist party, with the slogan: "A nation is not free if it oppresses another." The Hungarian bookstore was closed, its plate-glass windows smashed. On a huge wall by the Castle was scrawled a quotation from a Slovak poet condemning the subjugation of Slovaks by the Romans, now directed implicitly against the Russians. At the Philosophical Faculty of Komenský University, where there had been a huge encampment of Soviet tanks and a massive student demonstration, there was a plaque to "the seventeen-year old girl student who had tragically perished on this spot."

Yet life went on. We spent one evening, in the great underground winecellar At the Franciscans, crowded with people eating, drinking, and singing. This was an expression of their despair, a friend commented. At a political cabaret, in the Theatre on the Corso, where Lasice and Satinský had been lampooning the Novotný regime for years, there were many negative allusions to the Soviet Union and the Russians, which were wildly applauded. At a chamber music concert in the Reduta, Handel and Vivaldi were played to an enthusiastic audience of young people. At the Club for University Students there was a closed "opening" of an exhibition of abstract art; it was a kind of demand for freedom of expression, said a young painter, but "it would be the last of its kind." "We were just beginning to breathe freely after January, and now all that is ended." At the Czechoslovak State Film Office we viewed a documentary on the occupation and the non-violent resistance of the young people, entitled *Black Days*, which had been shown in movie houses during the past few weeks. In the coffeehouse at the Carleton Hotel, where a juke-box played raucously, a young couple, recent graduates of the theatre school, reported that television, and even the newspapers, were still quite daring but were under increasing pressure. Later, at the home of their parents, they told us that everyone was of one mind about the Soviets; friendship had been destroyed forever.

Writers and journalists were most informative. We spent several interesting evenings with Alfonz Bednár, and his wife and two daughters. They were uncertain about the future. Should they stay or go abroad? What could one write? Would there be censorship? They told us that the occupation had been a shock. They were awakened at five a.m. by distant shots. It appeared that the Soviet soldiers did not even know where they were and were often hungry and without water. The invasion created an amazing unity of Czechs and Slovaks, Communists and non-Communists. There were many anti-Russian jokes: "Better a hen were killed by a tank than lay an egg for a Russian"; for Dubček, *slivovice* (Slovak brandy), for Brezhnev, *šibenice* (the gallows).

A favourite spot for conversations was the editorial office of the progressive weekly *Kultúrny život*, published by the Writers' Union, which had been banned after the invasion. It had now become, it was joked, the main discussion club in Bratislava. There I met Pavol Števček, who had been editor-in-chief during the political ferment of 1963-64. The main concern of the Slovaks had been, he regretted, not so much democratization as federation. The Hlinka and Tiso tradition of Slovak statehood had left its mark on the minds of ordinary people, although the Slovak National Uprising had restored the idea of

Czechoslovak unity. Dubček was an honest and decent man, and intelligent, but he was now carrying out the will of Moscow. A co-editor of the newspaper, Rudolf Olšinský, echoed this estimate of Dubček's good and bad qualities and shared Stěvček's fears for the future. Dubček's trip to Moscow had been a catastrophe; he had not been aware of the strong support that he had at home and had not been prepared for a struggle with the Soviets. He should have refused to sign the Moscow communiqué justifying the continued presence of Soviet troops and should have defended the frontiers against all odds. The Moscow agreement had been a tragedy not only for the country but for all of Europe, and it had destroyed the political unity established by the invasion.

Another editor, Agneša Kalinová, who was to become my lifelong friend, agreed with this evaluation of the Moscow agreement. The idea of federation, she thought, was now less important, since the greatest need was for unity with the Czechs. The key question was whether the Czechoslovak party congress would be held in spite of Soviet opposition and would elect a progressive Central Committee. She told the story of the little girl who asked: "Who are these soldiers? Would they shoot?" — "Yes!" "Then why don't the Soviets help us?"

Another journalist, an editor of the party paper, *Pravda*, told me that it had supported the Dubček line after January but now had to exercise strict self-censorship. He wondered about the future of communism in Czechoslovakia after the invasion. In Vienna I had met several other journalists. One who had worked for the trade union paper *Praca* told me that the trade unions had been as useless as "the Pope's penis or a man's nipples." He agreed that Dubček, an honest man, had no clear idea of where he was going but had spoken for the first time in "human terms." Husák, who enjoyed great authority because of his role in the 1944 uprising and his bravery in prison, had not spoken out firmly during the Prague Spring in favour of democratization but had laid stress on federation. He wanted to be first man in Bratislava, not in Prague, and would not, the journalist thought, act against Dubček. Stanislav Budín, editor-in-chief of the progressive *Reportér*, who had decided not to leave the country permanently, praised Dubček but regretted his failure to resist Soviet pressure in Moscow. Husák was conservative but honest and democratic and would not, he thought, betray Dubček.

I interviewed several scholars as well — in history, sociology, economics, and law. A visit to the Historical Institute was not too fruitful, but a conversation that I had at the home of one of its members, Edo Friš, former editor-in-chief of *Pravda*, revealed a very critical attitude toward the Soviet Union. The invasion demonstrated its amazing lack of preparedness and was met with admirable popular resistance. The Soviets were trying to break the party's unity; the leadership, however, was striving to continue the post-January reform course. At the Institute for the History of East European Countries, a young scholar, L.H. Haraksim, regarded the situation as desperate and expected no help from the West. The people recognized that Dubček had had no alternative but to sign the agreement but now regarded him as a puppet of Moscow. Nonetheless, his team still enjoyed general support and could still preserve something of the January program.

At the Sociological Institute, director Jan Mlynárik, now in charge of the ideological department of the Bratislava party organization, expressed less optimism. The leadership was still trying to continue the post-January course as much as possible but was willing, he thought, to make the "necessary concessions." The solidarity of Czechs and Slovaks was greater than ever before in history. The Soviets had not found collaborators as they had expected. There was grave danger of a world war. The only hope was a change in Moscow, but "how long must we wait for that?" His colleague Vladimír Wagner was more hopeful. The Moscow communiqué left some room for manoeuvre. The Soviets would try to play the Slovaks against the Czechs, yes, but Husák would not undercut Dubček.

Andrej Landai, at the Economics Institute, was a strong advocate of economic reform. The Soviets recognized the need for this, he thought, but there should be less talk about a market system and workers' control, which irritated Moscow. As for federation, it was less important than economic reform on an all-Czechoslovak scale. Landai was in favour of a strong federal power, which would preserve a single, unified economic system but would assure more Slovak influence at the centre. Evžen Löbl, head of the Slovak State Bank, said that Slovak politicians wanted more power for Slovakia, but no one advocated a dualist system, with almost complete independence of each part. Some economists wished to have two national economies, linked together in a common economy; a second school wished to have a single economy and economic reform on an all-national scale.

At the Institute of State and Law, I was fortunate to meet Dr Karol Rebro, a member of the all-national expert commission on federalism, who described its discussions at length. Although there were some dif-

ferences between Czech and Slovak members, there was general agreement on the bulk of the final draft. Unfortunately the lack of a system
of free political competition deprived the draft of all meaning, but
there was still room for developing a more liberalized system, he
believed. Democratization and federation should be developed simultaneously and thus strengthen resistance to the Soviet Union. His colleague František Košt'a, former director of the institute, and now
secretary general of the National Front, thought that the present draft
proposal for federation would establish a too powerful central government and blamed this on Soviet pressure as well as on Czech wishes. The
National Front, representing the political parties and important social
organizations, such as those of youths and women and the trade unions,
would, he told me, serve as a medium for the reconciliation of conflicts
of opinions and interests, but the party would retain its leading role.

In Prague discussion of the Slovak question continued. In the
Historical Institute, I met Vilém Prečan for the first time, thus beginning a friendship that was to last for many years. After completing his
historical studies in Prague he had worked for two years as an instructor in Marxism-Leninism in Bratislava. There he had met and married
a Slovak woman, Helen, and had learned to speak her language fluent-
ly. He talked with me at length about the differences in the historical
background of the two peoples; in Slovakia the national question had
not been settled at an earlier stage and still dominated thinking. This
was an important part of democratization, but Czechs were more conscious of the broader political aspects. As for federation, it was a guarantee of the continued unity of the republic, but without democracy it
would collapse and there would be a return to Stalinism. He was critical of Dubček, who had lacked a real political conception of his own
and had yielded to Soviet pressure.

I also had a long talk with Milan Hübl, rector of the Higher Party
School, a Central Committee member, and a specialist on the Slovak
question. He told me that an earlier proposal for federation, advanced
by Professor Miloš Gosiorovský in the 1960s, had been rejected by
Novotný. When it was raised again in 1968, the Czechs had feared that
it would mean Slovak separatism. In August, however, it became clear
that the Slovaks wanted federation, not partition. Moscow, he said, did
not oppose this but had vetoed federalization of the party and urged a
Czech party bureau on the pattern of the CPSU.

In Prague, Professor Rebro reported to me on the last-minute
discussions of the draft law in the commission. The government had

accepted the final version of its report on 17 October, but Czechs and Slovaks were still divided on several issues. The Czechs believed in a unified economy and sought federal control of agriculture and food and of industry; the Slovaks opposed this, fearing a centralized economy. They did not want two separate economies, but they desired greater Slovak influence on joint decisions.

On 27 October, as scheduled, the law on federation was approved unanimously by the National Assembly. At Rebro's invitation, Sally and I attended this gathering in the Spanish Hall of the Castle; we were perhaps the only foreigners present, as the foreign press was excluded. We listened to the proceedings, including major speeches by the prime minister, Václav Černík, and Professor Viktor Knapp, chairman of the Constitutional and Legal Committee, and we watched the unanimous show of hands endorsing the proposal. Rebro later told us privately that discussions at the "eleventh hour" had been hectic, so that what appeared to be a purely formal action by the assembly represented unity based on sincere acceptance by all concerned.

During a break for lunch, delegates and guests mingled together. In a corridor I approached Dubček, who looked younger than I expected and was rather shy, and I requested his autograph, as others had done. He seemed quite surprised at my presence and asked me where I was from and whether I was a journalist or a guest. When I told him that I was writing a book on events in Czechoslovakia from January to August, he smiled wistfully and said: "You should wait until later to write it."

In Prague the people at the reception desk of the familiar Tatran Hotel welcomed us as old friends and gave us the same room that I had occupied so long ago, in the spring. A sign of the times was the behaviour of the chambermaid, who, standing in the hall by our room and shouting at the top of her voice, berated the Soviets, whom everyone now hated, she said.

Václavské náměstí was in complete chaos, not because of the invasion but because of construction of an underpass. At the top of the square the façade of the National Museum was still pockmarked with shell holes. All around it there was complete turmoil caused by the construction of the new National Assembly between the museum and the Municipal Theatre. Outside the Main Station (formerly named after Woodrow Wilson) the square was piled high with construction materials and debris. Further up Vinohradská, the radio station, my old place of work in the 1930s, still bore a slogan from the August days:

"We are with you: be with us!" The buildings around it on both sides of the street were in blackened ruins. At the base of the statue of St Wenceslas — a focal point of demonstrations during the invasion — there lay dozens of little vases of flowers; people constantly crowded around to read the inscriptions. The slogans and posters that had plastered every inch of wall space up and down the avenue during the occupation were all gone. In the shop windows there were pictures of Dubček and Svoboda and decorations for the 50th anniversary of the republic.

There was little tangible evidence of the Soviet occupation, since most of the occupying forces had been withdrawn to outlying areas. Only occasionally did we see officers, or even soldiers; some, off duty, were taking pictures, like tourists, of the famous clock on the Old Town Square. Not far away, on the little square of St Haštal, a hotel had become a Soviet district military headquarters; the church was surrounded by Soviet military vehicles. Just before we left the country, a Canadian diplomat daringly drove us into the countryside where we could see, even photograph, Soviet armed encampments and Soviet tanks being loaded on railway cars ready to leave the country.

The ideological disarray caused by the Soviet intervention was evident, however. In the Gottwald Museum, for instance, the section on the history of the working-class movement was closed, and there was an exhibit on the Munich crisis of 1938, featuring Communist posters calling for resistance to the Germans. There was a large picture of a Czechoslovak soldier, inscribed: "Our soldier was ready to defend!" And at the entrance was an aphorism of T.G. Masaryk, "Better to die in struggle than to live in slavery," and Beneš's slogan of 1938, "We shall remain faithful." Inside the museum one heard the BBC wartime signature tune, the familiar first four notes of Beethoven's Ninth Symphony.

Conversations with friends were full of references to the recent days of occupation. All had been taken completely by surprise. In the early morning hours they had learned of the event through a phone call from a friend, by the rumbling of tanks, or by the roar of planes overhead. They recounted with enthusiasm the events of the next ten days of non-violent resistance to the Soviet forces. Young people marched up and down or rode in trucks or motorcycles waving flags. Prague had been plastered with placards and graffiti. Street signs were taken down or reversed to confuse the invading armies. Everyone listened to illegal radio broadcasts for information and for guidance. Olga Haningerová told me that these were some of the happiest days in her life, as she watched with admiration and pride the young people, including her own children, manifest their will to resist. Zdeněk Zbořil gave me a graphic account of life in the streets and of the fruitless effort of young people to engage the men in the Soviet tanks in discussions of the injustice of the invasion. The soldiers could find no response to Czech arguments and in many cases were not even aware that they were in Czechoslovakia.

Vilém Prečan presented me with one of the earliest copies of the book, *Seven Days in Prague*, which he and his colleague Milan Otáhal had edited and which the Academy of Sciences had published several months after the August invasion. It had been distributed to all libraries throughout the country. Orders were later issued to return all copies, but even the Central Committee did not respond. "The Black Book," as it came to be called, provided an "instant documentation" of the Soviet occupation and Czechoslovak resistance and was an act of courageous defiance of the Soviet authorities.

There was much discussion about why the Soviet Union had decided to intervene. Was it, as some believed, largely a military decision, motivated by fear of the change of the military and political balance of power in Europe and thus determined to a large degree by the Soviet marshals? Or was it a political decision, based on fear of a threat to socialism, at least in its Soviet style, and the danger of the spread of this contagion to other Communist states, including the Soviet Union itself, where it would have struck at the very power of the Soviet leaders? At the Institute of International Politics, Šnejdárek believed that no single explanation was convincing, that both factors were involved.

The former foreign minister, Jiří Hájek, who had been relegated to a newly formed Institute of Political Science, threw further light on this question. He defended the foreign policy pursued under Dubček, which, he said, had not involved any basic change. Czechoslovakia remained loyal to the Warsaw alliance and had no thought of leaving it. Proposals for modifying both Comecon and the Warsaw Pact were designed to improve both systems, not to replace them. Czechoslovakia had no intention of entering into diplomatic relations with West Germany alone and wanted to act together with other Warsaw Pact members. According to Hájek this was anathema to the GDR. At the bloc conferences in Cierna and Bratislava, agreement had been reached only on general principles, and there had been no precise obligations. In his view Moscow did not understand that implementation of these understandings would take a great deal of time and was disappointed that it had not gone as speedily as it expected.

My talks with economists in Vienna and Prague made it clear that the occupation had seriously interrupted economic reform. At the Economic Institute, the acting director, Č. Kožušník, who had taken the place of Ota Šik, admitted that the future of reform was uncertain and would depend on political developments. At the Institute of Sociology, Director M. Kaláb and others talked of the changing balance of social forces, which would affect the course of reform. The chief advocates of reform had been the intellectuals, but during and after the invasion the working class showed a growing pro-reform mood. Even the hitherto-conservative trade unions began to break up into independent organizations, challenging the previously omnipotent central organs and acting as real interest groups. After August the idea of works councils, advocated by certain intellectuals, became more and more attractive to the workers. The invasion brought the managers, many of the *apparatchiki*, and even the security police to Dubček's side. But most of the farmers remained passive or opposed to change.

Michal Lakatoš felt that there was no real escape from what he called a political occupation in which Soviet pressure was the determining factor in policy-making. Few approved Dubček's capitulation in Moscow and his serious concessions after his return. Yet even the most critical realized that had he rejected the Moscow agreement or refused to resume office, the most likely alternative would have been direct Soviet rule, with massive arrests and deportations and the total abandonment of all hope for reform. A few believed that a better course would have been to resist Soviet demands. There was widespread admiration of Kriegel and his three comrades who had voted against the Moscow treaty in the National Assembly. The historian Karel Bartošek was highly critical of Dubček's failure to prepare for resistance long before the invasion and favoured opposition to his increasing collaboration with the Soviets. Other forms of democracy, such as workers' councils and self-rule (*samospráva*). would be more effective than multi-party pluralism or parliamentary democracy.

I met for the first time the non-Communist playwright Václav Havel at lunch at the home of an American diplomat. Havel was also highly critical of Dubček, who had failed to prepare for resistance by mobilizing the people politically and morally, as Tito had done in Yugoslavia. He condemned the party's policy of retreats and concessions and the signing of the Moscow agreement. Havel favoured confrontation, perhaps on 28 October or 7 November, but he gave no indication what form this might take. He saw greater hope in the workers, rather than the intellectuals, as the focus of resistance. As for the Writers' Union, he believed that the foremost task was to democratize this highly bureaucratic organization.

Quite a different alternative was advocated by the Club of the Non-Party Engagés (KAN), a brand-new political movement. My conversations in Vienna with two KAN leaders revealed that this movement did not favour militant opposition or formation of a party of its own. KAN rather sought to assure non-Communists a voice in politics and to encourage them to participate actively. Its ultimate goal was a truly democratic system, based on free elections.

Everyone was greatly concerned about the forthcoming session of the Central Committee in November and the balance of power between the rival tendencies within the leadership. There was some fear of the extreme conservative wing, the so-called Libeň group, which had been discredited by its openly pro-Soviet stance. More dangerous was a broader conservative tendency within the party apparatus and among the party members; this included those who had come to the reluctant conclusion that the only course was to cooperate with the occupying power and to try to preserve something of the gains of 1968. There was little belief that the intransigeants on the other extreme, such as KAN and K231, the organization of former political prisoners, or even the non-Communist parties, such as the former Social Democrats, could affect the ultimate course of events.

The greatest hope lay in the so-called centre, represented by Dubček and the four top leaders. If they maintained their unity — and this was not assured — they might ward off the worst outcome and preserve at least something of the January reforms. Two members of the Central Committee, Milan Hübl and Václav Slavík, with whom I spoke, were both confident that the majority of the Central Committee would approve a resolution defending the post-January reforms and the Action Program. Concessions on these matters would provoke strong resistance from below, especially among the workers.

Michal Lakatoš was much more pessimistic. The Central Committee would meet, probably with Soviet troops outside the building, and the leaders would have to give way on essential matters, removing many people from office and closing down a number of newspapers. The Soviet Union would not be content with compromises or anything short of what it wanted. The only alternative, according to him, would be for Czechoslovakia to build up a system of alliances, including Yugoslavia and Romania, perhaps Hungary and Poland, and even China, as a counterweight to the Soviet Union. The crucial question was democratization of the party itself.

Sally and I were in Prague on 28 October 1968, the 50th anniversary of the birth of the republic in 1918. With hundreds of others we visited the village of Lány and the cemetery where the Masaryks were buried. The graves were heaped high with flowers, including a great bouquet of roses from President Svoboda. As we wandered in the Lány Castle grounds we thought of the unhappy fate of the country that Masaryk had founded. In a little cinema in the village there was a continuous showing of a 30-minute film of the Masaryks in Lány in 1936 and 1937 — a sad and moving reminder of earlier days.

When we returned to Prague in the evening we witnessed a march of some four to five hundred young people on Václavské náměstí; their advance was blocked by heavily armed military units. Later, we were present outside the National Theatre just before a performance of Smetana's opera *Libuše*; the narrow Národní třída was jammed by several hundred young people, waving Czechoslovak flags, chanting anti-Soviet slogans, and booing the arrival of the Soviet ambassador. We were told of other demonstrations at the Castle, in the Old Town Square, and outside the Soviet embassy, where some violence was used by the police.

Student leaders had tried to avoid open confrontations by holding a meeting in the Philosophical Faculty in honour of the 50th anniversary of the republic. There were several long scholarly speeches, one on the role of T.G. Masaryk and of Jan Hus in Czechoslovak history, another on Czechoslovak diplomacy before the Munich crisis in 1938. Under the chairmanship of Zdeněk Zbořil, the meeting adopted a resolution requesting restoration of the statue of Masaryk that had once stood at the head of the main stairway in the faculty. Another expressed appreciation of the few courageous citizens of the USSR and the GDR who had publicly opposed the Soviet intervention. After a heated discussion, a third resolution was adopted deploring the presence of foreign troops, urging their withdrawal, and pressing the leadership not to make concessions that would endanger the nation's sovereignty. Students were urged to refrain from public demonstrations. Several workers from large Prague factories were present and urged solidarity of students and workers.

The television news that night showed once again the ideological confusion of the Communist authorities. The broadcast included the

National Assembly meeting on federation and the placing of flowers on Masaryk's grave in Lány, on the grave of Edward Beneš in Sezimovo Ústí, and on the tomb of one-time President Zápotocký in the Monument of National Liberation. There was not a single mention of Gottwald. This was followed by a documentary film on the events of 28 October 1918, which reported on the foreign liberation struggle and the home resistance but made no mention of the workers' movement, hitherto regarded as crucial in the attainment of independence.

Another occasion that revealed the change of mood was the anniversary of the Bolshevik revolution on 7 November, usually celebrated officially with pomp and circumstance. This year the only official celebrations were a ballet performance of *Swan Lake* the previous evening at the National Theatre, and on the next day the laying of wreaths. Prague was not, as in the past, blanketed with flags; where some did appear, the Soviet flag was rare and was often removed. At one point the workers at the National Assembly construction site showed their spirit by beating their tools on the steel girders; at another nearby building a crowd of over one thousand demanded removal of a Soviet flag. There were other signs of opposition. The students of several faculties conducted a strike and held meetings throughout the day inside the university buildings, with some factory workers present. More militant students demonstrated in the streets and in some cases burned Soviet flags. They were dispersed by trucks that sprayed them with water hoses, and a few people were arrested.

Another indirect protest was the première of Karel Čapek's *Bílá nemoc* (The White Disease), a bitter satire on war, militarism, bureaucracy, and propaganda. The printed program described the play as a hymn to democratic humanism, which placed ideas and truth against tanks, guns, and planes, and it cited Masaryk's definition of democracy as "discussion." At the Realist Theatre, another play, *Jan Hus*, by Josef K. Tyl, was presented for high school students. Although the Czech used was archaic, the references to Czech freedom and independence and Hus's final statement in favour of truth were clear and unmistakable. There were other open or more subtle demonstrations of continuing national spirit and faith in traditions. One was the exhibition of the Bohemian crown jewels, which were put on public display at the Castle for the first time since 1948. There were huge lines of people waiting to be admitted. One morning at eight o'clock we had the privilege of attending with a special group organized by the Historical Institute. Then there was an exhibition in the Strahov Monastery of the pre-1914 cultural and educational program of T.G. Masaryk and his colleague F. Drtina. In a news cinema, a documentary film, *In the Heart of Europe*, recounted the 50 years of the republic, with its great triumphs and its tragedies; many in the audience were moved to tears. The key figure throughout the movie was Masaryk, and Beneš and Dubček played lesser roles. And at an art exhibition in the Belvedere we were struck by a statue depicting a deer attacked by a wolf, representing the Nazi aggression against Czechoslovakia in 1939, but applying equally to the Soviet invasion.

YUGOSLAV AND EXILE PERSPECTIVES

During June and July 1969 a trip to Yugoslavia enabled me to probe Yugoslav attitudes to the events in Prague. Conversations in Belgrade with leading public figures revealed a striking consensus: warm sympathy with the 1968 reforms, criticism of Czechoslovak tactics, and sharp condemnation of Soviet intervention. Najdan Pašić, a professor in the Faculty of Political Science, editor-in-chief of the theoretical journal *Sozializm*, and a member of the Yugoslav Parliament, had taken a strongly pro-Czechoslovak stand and had been the target of attack in the Soviet press. Gavriel Altman, editor-in-chief of the weekly *Kommunist*, thought that Czechs were better suited to be a model of democratic socialism than the Yugoslavs, who were backward and underdeveloped. The Czech error was in not carrying through a more thorough economic and social reform in order to bring the workers into the reform movement; political reform was not sufficient. He felt that the intellectuals had played too great a role and had talked too much. Dubček, he thought, was at fault in not understanding the danger from the Soviet Union and in failing to declare the readiness of Czechs and Slovaks to resist an invasion.

My friend Branko Pribičević, now a professor at the Faculty of Political Science, and chairman of the University Committee of the League of Communists, felt that the Czechs had gone "too far, too fast" and argued that mere words could not overcome the power of the apparatus — police, army, and the militia. He himself was convinced in June that the Soviet Union would intervene or that there would be a coup d'état. Dubček should have talked less about humanism and acted more strongly against the conservatives in the leadership, as Tito had done in 1948, and should have declared his readiness to resist.

These opinions were echoed by Leo Mates, director of the Yugoslav Institute of Politics and Economics, who also felt that the Czechs had gone too far too fast and that their ideas had seemed openly provocative to the Soviet Union. Nonetheless, Mates asserted that the Prague Spring was of immense historical importance in that "socialism with a human face" had been almost established with the support of the people, and prevented only by the forceful intervention of a foreign power. Above all, Dubček had failed militarily. Although armed resistance likely would have been overcome within a matter of hours, a basis for action by the United Nations would have been laid.

Milovan Djilas, the veteran dissident, received me warmly in his home and for an hour and a half spoke frankly about Yugoslav reform and the Czechoslovak events. He had been enthusiastic about the Prague Spring, since it mirrored his own ideas; he favoured radical reform, but without fundamental change in the system — that is, without revolution. His hopes had run high, since Czechoslovakia, unlike Yugoslavia, had a strong tradition of democracy. But Dubček was no leader and had acted in a typically Czech way; he trusted the Russians too much. What the Czechs should have done was to purge the police and army and arrest pro-Soviet elements. Dubček should have taken advantage of the public mood of enthusiasm and threatened resistance; as in the case of Romania and Yugoslavia, this would have deterred the Soviets from intervening.

In July 1971 two conferences in England, in Windsor and Reading, offered me another valuable opportunity to discuss the Prague Spring with specialists and participants. The Windsor meeting, organized by Professor Ionescu, of the LSE, brought together a number of specialists to compare the development of reform in Poland, Yugoslavia and Czechoslovakia. Ota Šik, the architect of Czechoslovak economic reform, spoke of his role in its genesis and the behind-the-scene politics that had brought about Novotný's fall from power. After January, he said, the economists had prepared detailed plans for the introduction of economic reform, but the political situation had prevented anything from being done. He gave a fascinating analysis of the difference of social groups in the battle for change in society, identifying those that were progressive and those that were conservative.

Even more fruitful was the meeting in Reading, organized by the Czech exile Vladimir Kusin, of Glasgow, and attended by a large number of Czech and Slovak exiles as well as foreign experts, including Galia Golan, from Israel, the author of two books on the reform movement. Radoslav Selucký argued that the Prague Spring had represented a culmination not only of political and economic forces, but also moral and cultural ones, and a coalition of reforming groups and tendencies, including scholarship and culture and in Slovakia. There was a heated discussion of freedom of the press and the role of the journalists and the media. A British journalist, William Shawcross, expressed the view that journalists had not been disciplined enough and bore the blame for the Soviet intervention. In reply, Dušan Havlíček, formerly of the Central Committee's information department, argued that the explosion of free discussion had been a crucial element of the Prague Spring and that any attempt to control the press would have negated the entire spirit of democratization.

On the military and diplomatic aspects of reform, Antonín Šnejdárek denied that there had been any real changes in foreign policy after January. The Action Program had been weak on this subject, and no serious foreign policy documents had been issued. He denied that there had been any danger, as alleged by Moscow, of Czechoslovakia leaving the Warsaw pact. Dubček, who did not believe that there was a danger of a Soviet invasion, had rejected the idea of defensive planning against the Soviet Union which had been raised in certain quarters.

AN INTERRUPTED REVOLUTION?

In the title of my book on the Prague Spring I had identified the events of 1968 as an "interrupted revolution," a term not without ambiguity. Were the changes, introduced or planned, fundamental enough to amount to a revolution? Had they been temporarily or permanently interrupted by Soviet intervention? Were reformers seeking an immanent change within the system or transcending it? Was the reform of a one-party system possible at all or was it condemned to failure by its very nature? In my opinion the changes made or envisaged constituted more than surface reform; they were radical transformations and, if they had continued, would have led to fundamental changes in leadership and in the system itself. It was an unusual revolution, one without violence or bloodshed, a movement without chaos. Nor was it certain that the Soviet intervention had put a permanent stop to the process of change. Perhaps the process could resume at some future time. The events of the next two decades and the ultimate overthrow of Communism made it clear, later, that the reforms of 1968, radical as they were, had indeed been incomplete. They had been halted not only from outside, but also by strong domestic conservative forces personified by Gustav Husák. But after a long hiatus, 1968 proved to be the forerunner of a genuine revolution in 1989.

NOTES

1. See my *Czechoslovakia's Interrupted Revolution* (Princeton, NJ: Princeton University Press, 1976), especially the conclusion. See also, Skilling, "Crisis and Change in Czechoslovakia," *International Journal* 23, no. 2 (summer 1968): 456-65; "Czechoslovakia's Interrupted Revolution," *Canadian Slavonic Papers* 10, no. 4 (1968): 409-29; "The Fall of Novotný in Czechoslovakia," *Canadian Slavonic Papers* 12, no. 3 (autumn 1970): 225-42, and my contributions to Robert A. Dahl, *Regimes and Opposition* (New Haven, CT: Yale University Press, 1973), 121-41; and to Adam Bromke and Teresa Rakowska-Harmstone, eds., *The Communist States in Disarray, 1965-1971* (Minneapolis, MI: University of Minnesota Press, 1972), 43-72.
2. See my "Journey to Czechoslovakia, Spring 1968," *Czechoslovak and Central European Journal* 11, no. 1 (summer 1992): 27-42.

15

NEO-STALINISM:
SOCIALISM WITH GOOSE-FLESH

OUR RETURN TO CZECHOSLOVAKIA in the spring of 1969 coincided with a new crisis and the elevation to power of Gustav Husák, the chief architect of the process known as "normalization." This euphemism concealed what was really a counter-revolution: the reversal of the entire course of reform and the restoration of a system that, if not fully Stalinist, was characterized by many features of Antonín Novotný's discredited rule. One immediate cause of crisis was the victory of the Czechoslovak ice hockey team over the Soviet team in Stockholm at the end of March, by a score of four to three. This win was celebrated by massive popular demonstrations, implicitly anti-Soviet in spirit and accompanied by violence not only in central Prague but in towns and cities throughout the country. These events were regarded in official quarters in Moscow as an open challenge to the Soviet occupation and as a threat to the very regime. The Soviet Deputy Prime Minister Semenov and Marshall A.A. Grechko paid a sudden visit to Prague to deliver an ultimatum demanding drastic political changes and threatening military intervention. Outright confrontation was precluded by a Central Committee plenum in mid-April, where Dubček unexpectedly resigned and proposed Husák as his successor.

On our way to Czechoslovakia we stopped for a few days in Vienna and were there during the hockey celebrations. We arrived in Bratislava by bus during the tense days that followed. The symbolic numbers "4 to 3" were scrawled on walls everywhere. At the Theatre on the Corso, famous for its satirical cabaret lampooning the regime, the performance of Becket's *Waiting for Godot* seemed to symbolize the hopelessness that people felt as they awaited the results of the ultimatum.

The Central Committee meeting in Prague mitigated the crisis by replacing Dubček as first secretary with Gustav Husák. Dubček's resignation did come as a surprise, but in spite of misgivings there was overwhelming support for the election of Husák. There had been immense

Soviet pressure, I was told by my journalist friend Miroslav Hysko, who revealed to me the content of major speeches and the results of the voting — 150 voted for Dubček's resignation, 10 abstained, and 22 were against; 156 voted for Husák. This was the only way out, Hysko felt, since Dubček was not ready to take the decisive measures demanded by Moscow. Edo Friš, former Slovak party leader, did not agree; if Dubček had been a stronger leader and had prepared the ground better, he might have "called the Soviet bluff." He doubted that the Soviet Union was ready to intervene militarily again.

There was no open opposition to the change of leadership. There was a general feeling among workers and students that there was no choice but to bow to the realities of the new situation. After August, *Literárny život* (formerly *Kultúrny život*), had been allowed to appear only once before it was stopped. The Writers' Union abandoned its intention of holding a congress. Thus there was no medium for expressing the views of the writers on the crisis and its aftermath. On the whole, it seemed people accepted the change in leadership as a necessary retreat. Some conservatives were enthusiastic about cooperating with the Soviets, while other citizens wanted to resist — "all or nothing." Professor Rebro, the constitutional lawyer, felt it necessary to work with the Soviets for the sake of political expediency: "In this way," he said, "we would at least preserve our ideals and ourselves."

There was great uncertainty about Husák's real purpose. He was an intelligent man and had demonstrated great courage in prison in the 1950s, but as chairman of the Slovak Board of Commissioners, in the late 1940s, he had been utterly ruthless. In 1968 he had devoted his attention mainly to the construction of a federal system. There was a surprising degree of agreement that he was not an open traitor and would not resort to outright terror for political ends. Miroslav Kusý, a professor of philosophy who had been dismissed from his post in the Slovak party secretariat after five months of constant polemics with Husák, believed that Husák simply recognized the utter necessity of working closely with Moscow. The Soviets regarded him as a lesser evil, and wanted, through him, to achieve what they had not been able to achieve after August. Julius Strinka, also a philosopher, thought that the changeover had at least averted the catastrophe of direct Soviet rule. He, too, believed that Husák would eventually resist the worst Russian pressure and achieve some degree of independence. Agneša Kalinová, an editor of *Literárny život*, was more critical but agreed that Husák was a realist, not a collaborator. Like Tito, he wished to get the situation at home under control through a tough policy in order to better resist the USSR.

Relations of Slovaks and Czechs during the crisis had been good, I was told. In general, people felt that the national question had been settled by federalization and were more interested in democratization. Rebro, the chief Slovak negotiator of the federal constitution, was satisfied with the compromise reached. He favoured a flexible federation, where each republic could follow its own course with federal organs dealing with common interrests, but he had received several letters from Czechs complaining of Slovak privileges and Czech financial obligations. The Czech National Council had received hundreds of similar letters. Even in the council there were some members who were, he thought, not willing to accept Slovak equality and wanted a unitary state or a moderately decentralized system, in which the federal organs would be powerful. If this were not possible, some Czechs preferred to let the Slovaks go their own way. In his view Slovaks wanted to work with the Czechs, and there was no support for separation.

The writer Alfonz Bednár, and his wife, Helenka, told us about the difficulties of life in an occupied land. Alfons complained that the atmosphere was not favourable to writing, and there was no certainty as to the fate of what one wrote. One afternoon he took me to view the filming of one of his stories in the village of Dolná Krupa in a castle where Beethoven had once lived and composed. The director, Stefan Uher, joked that they were "all Dubček boys": "We had enjoyed eight months of freedom, but it was a kind of dream and now had ended." We also made an excursion with the Rebros to Bradlo, to see the monument honouring Milan Rastislav Štefánik, the Slovak astronomer, who had worked with Masaryk and Beneš in the struggle for independence during the First World War. En route we stopped at Štefánik's burial place near Ivanka, where, on 4 May 1919, as he was returning from abroad to the republic for the first time, his plane had crashed and he perished. The main memorial, an enormous limestone monolith, stood on a high hill, from where there were splendid views of the Carpathian Mountains. In the Communist years Štefánik had been treated as an enemy agent and had been savagely criticized by the historian Ludovit' Holotík for his Czechoslovak orientation. He was now rehabilitated as a national hero and co-founder of the Czechoslovak state.

Another instance of historical falsification was an exhibition in the Museum of the National Uprising on the Danube quai. Although the museum was closed, an attendant showed us the exhibit — unchanged, he said, since 1967. It was indeed a distortion of history, containing little about the participation of non-Communists and featuring pictures of Husák and other Communist leaders. Another example of politics ignoring historical tradition was the construction of a great new bridge across the Danube, which would enter Bratislava in the very heart of the old town and involve the destruction of many old houses of the former Jewish quarter and the synagogue. Heavy traffic, passing within a few feet of the great church of St Martin, would endanger its very foundations. Academician Alexander Matuška, a specialist in literature, told me that strong protests by historians, artists, and some architects against this desecration of historical sites had had no effect. The huge bridge was an example of the "gigantomania" of the politicians and their lack of understanding of history. "Why do we need a Brooklyn bridge?" he scoffed.

In Bratislava I made the acquaintance of Julius Sedliak, who had worked for 15 years in the Slovak party apparatus; he was head of the newly established Institute of Political Science in the Central Committee and had been elected president of the newly formed Slovak Political Science Association. He felt a strong leader was needed in the present crisis but he did not think Husák would resort to the methods of the 1950s. To my surprise, he invited me to speak on the role of interest groups in Soviet politics at a seminar held in the Higher Party School. My exposition was greeted positively. They, however, accepted the concept of the totalitarian nature of the Soviet system but stressed that the situation in Czechoslovakia, with its quite different national traditions, was quite unlike that in the Soviet Union.

On our way to Prague we also stopped in Brno, to observe the impact of the Prague Spring on the second-largest Czech city and to explore the Moravian movement for a tripartite federal system. The city looked more prosperous than Bratislava; the shop windows were attractive, and the streets were bustling with people and traffic. Temporary street signs replaced the ones removed during the days of the occupation to confuse the invading forces. Preparations were under way for May Day, with big banners praising the liberation by the Soviet army! There were slogans everywhere on the walls declaring support for Dubček and Svoboda, but Husák's name was hardly to be seen. On a bulletin board at the university we saw a quotation from Husák: "Freedom cannot be without limits."

We found the political and cultural atmosphere more relaxed in Brno than in Bratislava or, as we later learned, even in Prague. Life was better here; writers could write more freely, we were told by Milan Uhde, a poet, playwright, and film writer. For 11 years he had edited the monthly *Host do domu (A Guest At Home)*, a paper financially supported by the Writers' Union. The organ was, of course, subject to censorship but had never been banned. He was not surprised by the suppression of the Prague Spring; he felt it was impossible to combine freedom and socialism, at least not when the Soviet Union determined what socialism was to be. Jaroslav Šabata, a university docent in psychology and a member of the South Moravian party's regional committee and of its secretariat, agreed with my use of the term "interrupted revolution." The changeover in 1968 was not really a revolution, but it did involve revolutionary reforms and would continue, in some form, into the future.

I met with two strong advocates of Moravian autonomy or a tripartite federation. Both were lawyers who had been ousted from the Law Faculty in 1950. Professor Vladimír Kubeš had been imprisoned for several years in the fearsome Jáchymov uranium mines, and was rehabilitated judicially only in 1968. He strongly opposed not only Prague centralism but also a binational federation, and favoured a decentralized system, with a strong central government and wide autonomy for Bohemia, Moravia, and Slovakia. The Society for Moravia and Silesia, which had 350,000 members, had elaborated a detailed plan for a tripartite federation. Another advocate of Moravian autonomy, Professor Ctibor Halusa, believed that the powers of the central government under the new federal system should be limited to foreign affairs, international trade, defence, and security. Such autonomism was in keeping with the thousand-year tradition of Moravia and its special status as a *země* (province) under Austria and under the republic.

These autonomist views contrasted with those held by Milan Uhde. While he was opposed to the bureaucratic centralism of Prague he had no interest in the campaign for a separate identity for Moravia. Local officials were of such low quality that Moravia would be "a kingdom of dwarfs," he joked. In any case there were much more important matters to worry about, especially democratization and the Soviet presence. In Šabata's opinion, the idea of Moravian autonomy was progressive in its opposition to centralism, and enjoyed strong popular support, even among the workers. However, it was anachronistic. The North Moravian party organization had condemned it roundly while the South Moravian party endorsed the idea of a special federal position for Moravia.

My interest in Tomáš Masaryk led me to see Lubomír Nový, a university docent in philosophy, who had published a book about him in 1962. Written from a Marxist point of view, he told me, it had sought to establish a link between Masaryk's bourgeois philosophy and the philosophy of Czech socialism. Even during the years when the name of Masaryk was taboo, the former president was revered by ordinary people, he said. After January 1968 there had been a "return" to Masaryk, a rebirth of his ideas, especially his ethical approach to politics. Nový had modified his earlier attitude and written a little book, *Masaryk and Today*, but he was not sure that it would be published.

Professor Jaroslav Sedláček, an architect to whom we had been introduced, was not much interested in politics, he said, but the events of 1968 had restored his faith in the Czech people. One evening, with his wife, he drove us to a 60-year-old wine cellar about an hour from Brno, where we spent several lively hours drinking and singing folk songs. Our friends showed no love for Husák and an intense dislike for the Soviets. Sedláček's father came with us and did not drink, so that he could drive us back to Brno.

PRAGUE

We arrived in Prague on 5 May 1969, just before the opening of the Prague Spring Music Festival, and attended the gala performance of Smetana's *Má Vlast*, conducted by Václav Neumann in the Smetana Hall of the Obecní Dům. Whenever this work was played, under the Habsburgs, during the German occupation, or in the present conditions, its ode to the beauties of the Czech countryside and the greatness of Czech history always awakened strong national feelings. President Svoboda, in the main box, bowed to the audience, and the absence of Gustav Husák was conspicuous. Josef Smrkovský, one of the reform leaders, was given warm applause as he departed.

The anniversary in early May of the liberation of Czechoslovakia, celebrated in the past with great pomp, was now passed over with little formal notice. On 9 May there was a performance of Smetana's opera, *The Bartered Bride*, in the National Theatre. In the centre of the city there were many soldiers and police on duty and the streets were cut off from traffic and pedestrians. There were, however, no demonstrations against the Soviet presence. There had been incidents in Pilsen, at the site where monuments honouring the actions of American soldiers in 1945 had once stood, but these were broken up by the police.

During three weeks in the Czech capital, after a few days in our favourite Tatran Hotel, we stayed again in the home of the Moravčíks, parents of a Czech economist in Canada. I crammed in about 60 interviews with culturally prominent figures and scholars. Later, in England, I talked with other Czechs and Slovaks who had gone into exile or were temporarily abroad. As in Slovakia, I found that people in Prague differed greatly in their estimate of Husák's intentions and prospects. Not surprisingly, people in more official positions tended to favour him. Oldřich Švestka, a high-ranking, conservative functionary whom I met in the Central Committee building, expressed the view that Husák had great support within the party, but he admitted that he would have to try to win over the intelligentsia. Gustav Bareš, the former political leader, now dean of the School of Journalism, strongly criticized Dubček but did not attack Husák. He thought the latter could achieve a certain independence and perhaps even the withdrawal of troops. At a meeting in the editorial office of the party's theoretical journal, *Nová mysl,* several editors admitted that Husák was the "lesser evil" and listed positive measures he had taken. Even independent intellectuals were ready to believe that Husák might resist Moscow and obtain major concessions. Václav Kotyk, a foreign policy specialist at ÚMPE, expressed measured optimism. Husák was a dictator and a dogmatist, but he had fought hard for Slovak national independence in the 1960s and would not want to be dependent on the USSR. Kotyk's colleague, Jiří Štepanovský, thought that Husák might turn out to be a Czech Gomułka and accomplish something for the good of the country. Jaroslav Šedivý, another ÚMPE member, was ready to give Husák six months to show what he could do.

Others were more skeptical and expected increased repression and closer collaboration with Moscow. Legal scholar Michal Lakatoš noted that Husák had no support in society or even within the party apparatus. He feared that the Soviets would exert the same pressure on him as they had on Dubček, and ultimately dismiss him. Even the historian Milan Hübl, who had hoped initially that Husák would do something positive, was already disillusioned.

Later, in England, I heard a severe condemnation of Husák by my friend Vilém Prečan, who was spending a semester at St Antony's College, Oxford. He gave me the details of the memorandum submitted by Husák to Moscow in July 1944, in which he had said that 70 percent of the population wished to be part of the USSR. He described Husák as a neo-Stalinist whose ambition would lead him to give in to the Soviet Union at every turn. Prečan coupled this attack with severe criticism of Dubček's policy before and after August. His signing of the Moscow protocol, he said, had been a betrayal, and his successive retreats prepared the ground for Husák.

As in Slovakia, there were wide differences of opinion in Prague about the future. Some people tried to find reasons for hope and even optimism. The writer Ludvík Vaculík, usually a radical, thought that the present situation was not so catastrophic, although he confessed he could not explain why he felt that way. Many were discouraged, however, by the closing down of newspapers and the ouster of progressive journalists. Milan Jungmann, editor-in-chief of *Listy*, was greatly concerned by the increasing severity of censorship.The most radical analysis of the situation that I heard came from the historian František Šamalík, who spoke bitterly of Dubček's failures after January, and especially after August, when he pursued a policy similar to that of President Hácha in 1939 — i.e., giving up any attempt at an independent course and accepting the necessity of occupation. Šamalík advocated a policy of defiant resistance that he described as more realistic than cooperating with Husák. Michael Lakatoš was equally radical. There were two paths open, he said. The leader, whoever it was, could follow a kind of Titoist strategy by removing reactionary elements from the party and state apparatus (police, army, etc.), and threatening armed resistance if the Soviet Union were to invade again. The second option, which he favoured, was to resist the regime, at first passively, and then actively; if the state took positive actions, these should be supported.

Two Czech law professors who had been closely involved with the establishment of the federal system, Zdeněk Jičínský, now deputy chairman of the Czech National council, and Viktor Knapp, still chairman of the Council's Constitutional Committee, expressed satisfaction with the compromise law that had been adopted in October. It was too early to know how the constitution would work in practice, and much would depend on whether the party remained a single, united, organization, thus promoting a centralized state system, or whether, as Knapp hoped, it was divided into two separate Czech and Slovak parties. According to Jičínský, there was no problem in setting up new Czech ministries, since they could use the same buildings and to some extent the same personnel as the former Czechoslovak agencies. The Slovaks had the more difficult problems of creating new ministries in Bratislava, finding qualified Slovaks for the Czechoslovak ministries in

Prague, and overcoming their unwillingness to move there. Neither Jičínský nor Knapp believed that a tripartite system was practical or realistic. Czechoslovakia was a small country, and federation had to be based on nationality, not on regionalism. The legitimate grievances of Moravians could be met by giving the city of Brno a special status, by locating the Constitutional Court there, and by taking economic measures to aid certain neglected regions.

At a large gathering of economists that I attended, Karel Kouba, of the Economics Institute, chairman of an official advisory committee of experts, gave a frank and realistic appraisal of the economic situation. The principles adopted in 1965-66 remained valid: a change in the role of planning, the establishment of market relations, and increased enterprise authority; these principles had not been implemented during 1968. He admitted that in the existing situation radical and consistent economic reform was out of the question. Concrete measures of state intervention were required to check economic decline and to make recovery possible. Another member of the institute, Jaroslav Habr, an econometrician, was even more pessimistic. He felt that all hope for economic reform on the Šik model was gone. In Cambridge, at the end of May, I spoke with Josef Goldmann and Josef Kon-Flek, two leading economists and former members of the institute. They expressed mixed feelings. Goldmann especially argued that economic reform had had a positive effect in 1968; there had been an increase in productivity and a rise in the standard of living. There was a chance of continuing economic reform, since the Soviet Union itself wanted such changes and objected in the main to the role of Šik and the workers' councils. In London, Hvezdoň Kočtuch, professor at the Higher Economic School in Bratislava, who was a member of a joint advisory committee of Czech and Slovak economists, expressed a more hopeful view. Husák, he believed, understood the need for a system midway between the centrally planned system of old and the new market system.

As for political reform, Petr Pithart, professor of law and former member of the Mlynář team on the political system, told me that the team's report had been almost ready in January and had had a marked influence on the Action Program in April 1968. After the invasion it had ceased to exist. Mlynář had gone through an evolution of thinking and had accepted the idea of pluralism, though not in the form of a multi-party system. Pithart favoured the gradual development of several parties but realized that such a system could develop only over a period of years. The party would have to become more democratic through greater freedom of discussion within its ranks.

Karel Kaplan, a historian, who had been secretary of the Piller Commission on Rehabilitation, met me one day at the Belvedere Palace and gave me some idea of its conclusions. Its 300-page report placed the main blame for the injustices of the 1950s on the Communist party itself and on its leader, Gottwald, and it blamed Novotný for later trials and the delays in rehabilitation. This report was so explosive that it could not be published, but Kaplan had unveiled its essential content in a series of major articles in the party journal, *Nová mysl.*

In this new situation Czechoslovakia clearly had no independent foreign policy, and no public discussion along these lines was possible. My friends at the Institute for International Politics and Economics had all been opposed to Soviet intervention, and their continued employment remained in doubt. Jiří Štepanovský, one of two co-chairmen (Czech and Slovak) of the Czechoslovak Peace Movement, made it clear by implication, in his speeches and in articles, that he did not approve of occupation. Even in Moscow, in talks with members of the Soviet peace movement, he had spoken openly of the disaster of the invasion. Václav Kotyk had some hopes that the realities of the international situation would force the Soviet Union to adopt a better policy, but feared that this might take five or ten years. Wide differences of opinion among the Communist parties would prevent any decision on, or even discussion of, the Czechoslovak question at the upcoming international Communist conference in June.

The heavy hand of censorship and repression was evident in the scholarly, educational, and cultural fields, but it had not extinguished the flame of freedom. In the Academy of Sciences the process of purging research scholars was already beginning, but resistance was strong. In the Chemical Institute, a letter from four conservative scientists had stirred a storm of controversy and was unanimously rejected. A real danger existed that the whole Academy, or individual institutes, might be dissolved. A widely-read magazine for the popularization of history, *Dějiny a současnost,* was still appearing, though a ban on it was expected at any moment. In a current issue censors had actually approved the reprint of an article of mine on opposition in communist societies.

In the educational field an extremely conservative minister of education had been appointed. According to Zdeněk Zbořil, student leader, the official student organization had no appeal for most students. Jan Palach, who had burned himself to death in protest against the Soviet occupation, personified the unsuccessful search of many students for meaning in life. His suicide had led students to turn away from direct politics and return to serious study. At the Czech Technical College, Jan Bárta, a lifelong Communist who had suffered eight years of imprisonment in the 1950s, was a severe critic of the present system. He said the current regime had nothing in common with socialism and was lagging years behind the capitalist world. In England, Jan Kavan, an active member of the Czechoslovak Youth League, whose diplomat father had also spent long years in prison in the 1950s, expressed the view that while most students were members of the League, they had virtually no sympathy for it. At present no more than 6 percent of members were Communists. The prospect, he thought, was for a very slow and long process of resistance and preparation for a distant future.

In the cultural field there were contradictory tendencies at work. For instance, an opera by Bohuslav Martinů, *Plays About Mary*, was based on folk plays but had a decidedly religious character, and it was performed with magnificent music and staging. Bishop Tomášek, the apostolic administrator, attended in his church robes and red skull cap, and was greeted with enthusiastic applause. In the Theatre on the Balustrade Václav Havel's play, *The Increased Difficulty of Concentration*, well acted and beautifully staged, was an excellent example of the theatre of the absurd, depicting, through a police investigation of a man and his wife, the conflict of science and humanity, of brain and heart. At the Viola, a small, central wine-café, we enjoyed an evening of baroque poetry and music, strongly religious, but also national and "popular" in character. The director, Vladimír Justl, spoke of his fear that censorship would be restored. Justl was also an editor of the Odeon publishing house. He declared that he could not imagine leaving Prague; intellectuals should stay with the poeple. We went back to the Viola to hear Jiří Suchý read poems and dialogues from a new show to open soon at the satirical theatre, Semafor. His sallies stirred the audience to laughter. Later, in a tiny private bar below the stage of the Semafor, Suchý and his partner, Jiří Šlitr, told us that they could now do things that they would not have dared to in the 1960s. The censors were often too stupid to understand the hidden meaning of the skits, which the audience grasped very well. A few days later we attended a one-man performance by Šlitr, with strong political overtones and a receptive audience. Such people, we realized, were helping to keep up the morale and resistance of the young people, but they walked a tightrope, and their ultimate fate was uncertain.

One night at the *Zlatá studně* we had dinner with Zdeněk Mahler, a playwright and television writer, and member of the Writers' Union, who had been elected to the presidium of the film and television workers' union. The Writers' Union was planning to protest the banning of its newspaper, *Listy*, but he feared that this and other creative unions would soon have to dissolve themselves. He was highly critical of television, especially the news service, and of censorship.

We made an excursion to the *chata* (cottage) of the Moravčíks, on the Berounka, a quiet little river with great limestone cliffs. Their son-in-law was a stage designer for a puppet show in Banská Bystrica, in Slovakia, and a member of the Czech theatrical workers' union and the artists' union. He reported that most members, Czech and Slovak, were opposed to Husák. So far, censorship had not been reintroduced, and self-censorship prevailed. However, he was highly critical of what he called the "old-fashioned" Soviet puppetry, which had adulterated the traditional style of puppeteering. Like so many others he, and his wife, who was a textile designer, were bitterly hostile to the Soviet Union and feared Husák.

The artists suffered similar woes. Ota Janeček, the painter and sculptor, had been expelled from the Union of Artists and could no longer exhibit in Czechoslovakia; nor was he permitted to attend openings of exhibitions of his work abroad. He had done a series of paintings of Jan Palach — the reason for his expulsion — and presented me with one of them, a tragic portrayal of Palach's face in torment. A younger painter, Jan Špála, son of the well-known painter Václav Špála, had a studio in his father's house right on the staircase leading to the Castle — a veritable gallery of his father's and his own paintings. Although the younger Špála had begun as a socialist realist painter, he later turned to abstract art, some of it based on a cosmic theme.

On the Hradčany, there was a service in progress in St Vitus Cathedral. Afterward the bishops and priests left the altar and walked, singing, to the chapel of St Václav, followed by members of the congregation. On the other side of the square, the Archbishop's Palace looked beautiful after its recent restoration. We sneaked inside the main door to look at a large picture, banked with flowers, of Cardinal Beran, who had died in exile in Rome the previous day. At what used to be the Royal Riding Academy, there was a splendid exhibit of seventeenth century religious paintings by Petr Brandl, and, in the former

Castle stables, a gallery of paintings by old masters from the collections of Emperor Rudolf II.

My old friends the Haningers took us by car to Mělník, home of the famous Czech wine. The cathedral was crowded for evening mass. At dinner on a terrace overlooking the vineyards and the juncture of the Elbe and Vltava rivers, we watched the sun go down behind the Central Bohemian Mountains; the sky was black and cloudy, and the red glow made it look like an inferno. The view seemed somehow symbolic of the country's situation. In the distance we could see the legendary hill of Říp, which had been a favourite place for patriotic demonstrations in the nineteenth century. In bad times, according to legend, St Wenceslas would come out from beneath the hill on a white horse and rescue the Czech nation. How bad did things have to be?, we wondered.

PRAGUE, 1969

In the autumn of 1969 I returned to Poland and Czechoslovakia as a member of the Canadian delegation to colloquia in Warsaw and Prague, organized by the Canadian Institute of International Affairs in association with the Polish Institute of International Relations and the Czechoslovak Institute of International Politics and Economics. The delegation included John Holmes, director of the CIIA, Professor Robert Spencer, of the University of Toronto, Professor Adam Bromke of Carleton University, and David Lewis, the New Democratic Party M.P. Both conferences had a common theme: European security, with particular emphasis on the Soviet-bloc proposals for holding a conference on European security and cooperation. In Poland we met in a beautiful small palace not far from Warsaw, and conducted our discussions with several high-ranking officials, including Richard Frelek, head of the Polish Institute, who was soon to be appointed deputy minister of foreign affairs. Whenever the Czechoslovak question was raised — and I made a point of doing this several times — the Poles refrained from comment and made no attempt to justify the invasion.

Conversations with Polish intellectuals after the conference revealed that the reform movement in Czechoslovakia had awakened great sympathy. Jan Szczepanski, a leading Polish sociologist, had had high hopes of its success and blamed Czech and Slovak journalists for acting irresponsibly and forgetting the Czech tradition of caution. Jan Strzelecki felt that the Czechs had been naive in expecting radical reform under existing circumstances. Stanisław Ehrlich, professor of law, observed that, although Poles did not like Czechs much, they had felt great sympathy with them after the invasion. Dubček had made mistakes, he thought, and should have resigned after the Moscow conference. Two Catholic intellectuals, Tadeusz Mazowiecki, editor of *Więź*, and the scholar Jacek Woźniakowski, regretted that the Czechs had abolished censorship but considered the invasion a great tragedy. A former member of the Politburo, J. Morawski, who was now deputy director of the Polish Institute of International Affairs, also referred to Polish support for the Czechs but felt that they had gone too fast and too far. He believed that Soviet intervention, nasty as it was, was necessary under the circumstances.

The conference in Prague was much less formal and official than the one in Poland. The delegation was headed by the institute's director, Antonín Šnejdárek, and consisted of institute members Vladimír Soják, Alexander Ort, and Julius Sedliak from Slovakia. Several others whom I knew well, including Kotyk, Šedivý, and Štepanovský, were not present, no doubt because of their more radical views. Once again the meeting avoided discussion of the Prague Spring and the Czechoslovak situation. The atmosphere was even more unreal because the very futures of the institute and its members were highly uncertain, as Šnejdárek intimated in private. In fact, right after the conclusion of our meeting, he used his diplomatic passport to leave Czechoslovakia permanently and settled as an exile in France.

After the close of the meeting I learned from talks with other Czechs and Slovaks that the situation had deteriorated since April and that there was complete uncertainty about the future. Some thought that Husák, in response to Soviet pressure, had taken unnecessarily harsh measures. He had some support in the army and in certain party circles, but none at all among the intellectuals, or even among the workers. The economy had deteriorated, and there were widespread meat shortages. There was little hope of economic reform, and none at all of political. The universities were threatened by purges under the new minister of education, Jaromír Hrbek. In the Philosophy Faculty of Charles University the Students' Academic Council had been dissolved; the newly formed Union of Students had little or no support. Most students were apathetic and passive, and the links that they had established with workers had been broken. In the Academy of Science the relatively progressive František Šorm had resigned as its president. The Institute of the History of East European Countries had been renamed the Czechoslovak-Soviet Institute and had been placed under the arch-conservative, Václav Král. The future of many other institutes, whose leaders were often displaced, was uncertain. The Institute of International Politics and Economics was under attack in the party press and was in danger of being incorporated into the Ministry of Foreign Affairs. The Gottwald Military Political Academy, which had studied changes in defence strategy in 1968, had been dissolved. Within the Central Committee, the Institute of Political Science, under the progressive CC member Václav Slavík, had been shut down, as had its Slovak opposite number, under Sedliak. A similar fate awaited the Institute of the History of Socialism (formerly the Institute of Party History). The Higher Party School had been placed under the conservative ideologist, Jan Fojtík. Many individual scholars had been dismissed or lived in fear for their personal future.

In spite of everything my friend Vilém Prečan remained hopeful, saying jovially that he still held his job and could continue his research; he had his wife, Helenka, and he had not yet been arrested. It soon became clear that he was wrong on most counts; he was to be charged with criminal activity for his part in the publication of "The Black Book." He and Helenka had been busily engaged for three years in building a new home — a desperate effort to defy the regime by showing that they could still act independently. Vilém said that he would not go abroad under any circumstances, but some years later, having given up all hope of resuming historical work at home, he did, reluctantly, go into exile.

The elevation of Husák to power marked the end of the Prague Spring and the beginning of the era of counter-reform or, as it was euphemistically called, "normalization." By 1970 all traces of Dubček's reforms had been erased. The "temporary" Soviet occupation was to continue for many years; Husák made no attempt to resist Soviet pressure, and dispelled all illusions to the contrary. Indeed, he showed himself ready and willing to accept Moscow's leadership in world affairs and to follow its example in matters domestic. Although he had been the architect of federation, Husák had no compunctions about centralizing power in Prague and nullifying the autonomy of Slovakia. In any case the forms of the federal system were rendered meaningless by the continuance of a single, centralized party and the absence of democratic procedures. Although Husák had personally suffered from the terror of the 1950s, he did not hesitate to pursue a policy of severe repression, both judicial and existential, against all forms of opposition.

In the words of a student slogan, which played on the meaning of the word *husa* (goose), Husák had replaced "socialism with a human face" by "socialism with goose flesh." This system of neo-Stalinism was to last almost two decades and ended only with the "velvet revolution" of 1989.[1]

NOTE

1. See my chapter on Czechoslovakia, in Adam Bromke and Teresa Rakowska-Harmstone, eds., *The Communist States in Disarray, 1965-1971* (Minneapolis: University of Minnesota Press, 1972), 43-72.

IV

SOWING THE SEEDS OF FREEDOM

16

CHARTER 77

THROUGHOUT THE 1970s we led busy and active lives in Toronto. I travelled a great deal in North America, attending scholarly conferences and giving lectures and seminars on interest groups and on the Prague Spring. In view of the ever-intensifying repression under the Husák régime, I felt little incentive to return to Prague or to write about the Czechoslovak situation. I had already acquired most of the materials needed for my book on the "interrupted revolution" and was able to devote most of the first half of the 1970s to its completion.

After working for almost a decade on the exciting ideas and activities of the Prague Spring, I could not bear to return to research in the old way on the Communist systems. I found an escape in the study of the fascinating materials produced by the human rights and dissident movements of eastern Europe. The conclusion of the Helsinki Final Act in 1975 opened up new possibilities for the defence of human rights in the Communist world and led, in Czechoslovakia, to the Charter 77 Declaration of January 1977. For the next four years I devoted much of my time to writing a book on Charter 77 and I prepared articles and gave speeches on this theme. I travelled to Czechoslovakia in 1975 and again in 1977, and twice in 1978, to conferences in Yugoslavia and Italy in the summer of 1977, the Soviet Union in 1979, and to Poland in 1978 and 1979. During those years my life became intimately linked with the human rights movement in Czechoslovakia and with its leaders.

I was much encouraged by the Conference on Security and Cooperation in Europe (CSCE), in Helsinki in 1975, whose Final Act included the "Basket III" on human rights. As early as 1965, and again in 1967 and 1972, at conferences at Carleton University in Ottawa, I had advocated a Canadian initiative for the formation of such a permanent body in the interests of European security, although I had not included human rights within its purview. In the autumn of

1976 I published an article on Czechoslovakia and Helsinki in which I welcomed the Final Act and its guarantees of human rights and freedoms. Although the document recognized the territorial and the political status quo in eastern Europe and proclaimed the obligation of states not to intervene in others' internal affairs, it implicitly condemned the Soviet intervention in Czechoslovakia in 1968 and the repressive policy of the Husák régime. It also provided, through periodic follow-up conferences, a platform for the expression of international concern about denials of human rights and a means to put pressure on delinquent Communist governments.[1]

In March 1977 I organized in Toronto an informal group, including John Holmes of the Canadian Institute of International Affairs and Professor Robert Spencer of the university's History Department. We met several times to discuss the implications of the Helsinki Final Act and sent a letter to the Department of External Affairs in Ottawa, urging that Canada give strong support to its human rights provisions. We finally received an encouraging reply, but only after waiting for seven months. In April I attended a briefing session in Ottawa, at which Tom Delworth, head of the Canadian delegation to the forthcoming CSCE follow-up conference in Belgrade, outlined the Canadian position.

After leaving Prague in July 1977 I paid a brief visit to the conference in Belgrade. Ambassador Delworth took me to lunch in a Serbian restaurant in the countryside and told me what had been happening in the opening two weeks. The handsome conference centre had been completed just in time for the opening and was guarded by strict security measures. Sessions were not open to journalists and the general public. Delworth, however, made it possible for me to sit in as a temporary member of the Canadian delegation and to observe the meeting of the 35 delegates seated around a long oval table. This introduced me to CSCE procedures, thus preparing me for later meetings that I was to attend. The principal task of this preparatory meeting was to determine the agenda and the procedures for the main conference that was to open in August. No momentous issues were discussed at the meeting that I attended. The purpose of the main conference, in Delworth's view, would be to discuss all aspects of the Helsinki Final Act and its implementation, including human rights. Canadian policy was to insist on discussion of this theme and to put the Soviet Union and other Communist states on the defensive concerning their record in human rights.

CZECHOSLOVAKIA, 1975

In the summer of 1975 Sally and I had spent two weeks in Bratislava and Prague. Conversations disclosed, as I wrote later, the shocking results of the intellectual, spiritual, and moral earthquake that had devastated the land since 1969. The fear, apathy, and despair that prevailed were documented in an eloquent letter to President Husák sent by Václav Havel in the summer. But there was evidence of a new spirit of opposition, a rebirth of history, as Havel put it.

By this time President Gustav Husák had concentrated all power in his own hands and seemed to be free of serious challenge from even more extreme conservative leaders, such as Vasil Bil'ak. There was very little support for the regime, and there had been a massive flight from active politics to private work and life. Punishment for those ousted after the Prague Spring did not usually take the form of trials and imprisonment, although a small number who had voiced opposition were put in jail. The penalties were more refined and took many forms. People were expelled from their professions and forced to do manual or menial work. Many were subjected to frequent interrogations and house searches. Listening devices were installed in their homes, and their children were debarred from higher study. There was widespread moral degradation; lying and deceit, bribery, corruption, stealing, and moonlighting were rampant.

Culturally, Czechoslovakia had become, said one of our friends, a Soviet province. If this were to continue for seven or eight years, said another, Czech and Slovak culture would eventually be destroyed. Many writers and scholars had been silenced and were forced to work as stokers or window cleaners; many had fled into exile. Official cultural and scholarly work usually lacked any value. The best work was published in samizdat — i.e., in underground scholarly and literary publications. Exile literature, such as the novels of Josef Škvorecký, was circulated and read. He and his wife set up Sixty-Eight Publishers in Toronto, which published most of the Czechoslovakia manuscripts smuggled out of the homeland.

People who had taken an active part in the reform movement suffered a range of subjugations. In Slovakia Milan Šimečka, who had taught political theory at the Faculty of Music in Bratislava, had been dismissed and worked for five years as an excavator on construction sites. He said that most of his fellow-workers worked only a few hours a day and were often drunk on the job; they openly expressed their

Sixty-Eight Publishers, with Zdena Skvorecká and Sally, 1977

deep hatred of Husák. Agneša Kalinová spent weeks in prison and was often interrogated at home. Her husband, Laco, had been sentenced to a year in prison after publishing a book entitled *One Thousand and One Jokes*. Karol Rebro, a constitutional lawyer, had been expelled from the party, but was readmitted after a personal appeal to Husák. One of the lucky ones, he was able to continue as a professor and a member of the Academy of Sciences.

In Prague I heard many similar stories. Zdeněk Mlynář, a former member of the party presidium, who had resigned in the autumn of 1968, was struck from the staff of the Institute of State and Law. He prepared a memorandum of appeal to the Italian, Spanish, Yugoslav, and perhaps the Romanian parties as a possible platform for discussion at the international Communist conference in June. Some people were highly critical of the memorandum and regarded it as an appeal to Brezhnev by "a loyal Communist." Mlynář's colleague, Michal Lakatoš, had also been removed from the Institute but had been lucky enough to secure employment as a lawyer in a communal enterprise. Václav Kotyk was working eight hours a day as a stock-keeper in a factory with 6,000 workers. Josef Polišenský managed to keep his university professorship but was confined to research on Latin American history. Jan Havránek still worked in the archives but was no longer director. Jiří Kořalka, who had been instrumental in ousting many members of the Institute of History in 1968, had himself been dismissed — he was later relegated to the Hus Museum in Tábor.

Other close personal friends suffered similar experiences. Jiřina Šiklová was luckier than many others. Having lost her job in sociology at Charles University, she was working in gerontology at the Krč nursing home and hospital. She published articles under the name of her boss in *Rudé právo* and the popular press and had written a book, *Socialism for the Housewife*, under a pseudonym. She was busily engaged as a "postman," as she called it, sending samizdat documents abroad and receiving and distributing Western books and journals at home. The Haninger family had survived many blows. In 1973 my dear friend Olga, about to enjoy a well-earned retirement, had been struck by a streetcar on her way home from work and died at once. Her husband, Bošek, had attained the rank of deputy director of an optical firm, the only non-Communist in a high position in the enterprise. Their son, Milan, was finally admitted to study at the Higher Technical School and was now teaching there. Because of her great interest in riding, the oldest daughter, Gina, got a job managing the riding clubs of the Youth League, though she was not a party member. Later she became editor-in-chief of *Chovatel,* a magazine about pets and small animals. Her younger sister, Jelka, trained in library school; though she, too, refused to join the party, she became editor-in-chief of a magazine in information science.

Soon after my visit to Czechoslovakia in 1969, Vilém Prečan had been dismissed from the Institute of History and then interrogated for months on a charge of sedition, later changed to subversion, for his part in the editing of "The Black Book" on the Soviet occupation. He was not imprisoned, and no trial was held. Forced to work as a stoker in a hospital, and later as a cloak-room attendant in a luxury restaurant, he was dismissed from the latter because it gave him contact with foreigners. His wife, Helenka, was working at the box office of a cinema. Her duty was to show as many Soviet films as possible, but these were poorly attended in comparison with American or Czech movies.

In March 1975, Vilém had written a letter to President Husák, complaining that he had lost all hope of finding work appropriate to his training and requesting permission to leave the country. The only reply was a search of their house, which lasted seven hours; at the end a protocol was signed, listing 45 books and papers confiscated. Up to then Vilém had confined his oppositional activity to writing private letters to Husák and several anonymous articles. He told me that he had finally decided to make a public appeal for support to the World Congress of Historians in San Francisco in August 1975 and was sending there a brochure, *Acta persecutionis*, listing 145 historians dismissed from their positions.

My first venture into human rights activity was connected with Prečan's appeal. Although I did not attend the historians' conference in San Francisco, I did what I could from afar by lobbying certain well-known historians and shipping copies of the brochure. The congress passed a resolution deploring the treatment of the Czech and Slovak historians and appealing to the authorities for correction of the injustice. In the following month, I pressed in person for similar action at the conference of the American Political Science Association in San Francisco. When the American Association for the Advancement of Slavic Studies (AAASS) met in Atlanta in the autumn I again lobbied, from a distance, for an airing of the plight of the Czechoslovak historians.

As a result of the unfavourable publicity that Prečan had caused abroad, the Czechoslovak regime decided to get rid of him by granting him permission to emigrate. This he did, with Helenka and his three teenaged children, in July 1976; they settled down in the small town of Edemissen, near Hannover, in West Germany, for what was to be 14 years in emigration. For the time being he did not want to make an open break with the Prague regime but was determined to give what assistance he could to his fellow Czechs at home; he eventually set up a documentation and information centre on Czechoslovak scholarship, using his kitchen as his workplace. He began to write to me regularly, in Czech, and I replied, in English; we thus began a correspondence and a partnership that were to last for more than 20 years.

In January 1977 a group in Prague issued what it called Charter 77 — a declaration based on the international covenants on human rights and on the provisions of the Helsinki Final Act, which described the violations of these rights in Czechoslovakia. Charter 77 was established as "a free, informal, open community of people of different convictions, different faiths and different professions," which would strive for respect for these rights. Several hundred people signed, and the number grew to more than one thousand by the mid-1980s. I was enthused by this rebirth of a spirit of resistance in what had been a largely quiescent country and began to do what I could in support.

I began to receive Charter publications from Prečan, Ivan Medek, an exile in Vienna, and Jan Kavan, who had also gone into exile and established the Palach Press in London as an information and documentation centre. Sally and I photocopied some of the more important materials and sent out packets by mail to about 30 people in Canada and the United States. I supplemented the money thus raised by holding a sale of books from my personal library and by donating honoraria received for articles and radio talks on Charter 77. By the end of the year we were able to send money to Prečan to help defray the costs of copying and mailing Charter materials, and we later took money with us on our journeys to Czechoslovakia.

I received other Charter documents through the regular postal service. These were addressed to Sally Bright (Sally's maiden name) or to fictitious names — for instance, Sybil Heatherington and Larry McAteer, at our address at 90 Cheritan Avenue (thereafter Prečan used the code name AC90 when he wrote people in Prague about me) — or to several of our friends and neighbours. Over a period of years, with the financial assistance of Rudolf Fraštacký, a wealthy Slovak émigré in Toronto, and with grants received from other sources, we built up a rich collection of Czechoslovak samizdat publications in the Thomas Fisher Rare Books Library in at the University of Toronto, ably assisted by librarian Luba Hussel (who was Fraštacký's daughter).

In 1978 I wrote an article on the first year of the Charter in which I welcomed it as making the issue of human rights a focal point of world politics and urged Western governments to act decisively in support of the Helsinki Final Act.[2] I had decided to write a small book on Charter 77 and had naively expected to complete it by the time of the CSCE conference in Belgrade in the autumn of 1977. In fact, there were many delays and interruptions, and I did not finish it until 1980. During trips to Czechoslovakia in 1977 and 1978 I was able to talk with many of the leading Chartists and established enduring friendships with them. Vilém Prečan jokingly referred to me as Charter 77's "ambassador abroad" and as his emissary in the homeland.

CZECHOSLOVAKIA, 1977

In the summer of 1977 I travelled to Czechoslovakia, this time without Sally. Vilém Prečan gave me detailed instructions and hints concerning the trip, as well as messages for friends. He sent Jiřina Šiklová my itinerary; she in turn informed people in Bratislava that "Byron" was coming and arranged many interviews for me in Prague. I went to Czechoslovakia by what was to become a favourite route — the "back door," via Vienna, and then by bus to Bratislava and on to Prague by air; I returned to Vienna via Bratislava. In Vienna I had several long talks with a prominent Chartist Zdeněk Mlynář, who was now in exile. The official campaign against the Charter had dissipated his hopes that there might be a change of official policy and that he could conduct any meaningful political activity. Finding it impossible to secure employment at home, he had taken advantage of the asylum offered all Chartists by the Austrian president and had left Czechoslovakia in June 1977. He described the Charter declaration as but the tip of an iceberg of discontent.

I had several meetings with my old friend Leopold (Poldi) Grünwald, whom I had known in Prague in 1938 and 1939, and his new German wife. We walked in the mountains above Vienna and had a *heuriger* dinner in a garden restaurant in Nussdorf. Poldi had spent the war years in Moscow and afterward had gone not to Czechoslovakia but, at his own request, to Austria. As correspondent of the Austrian Communist party newspaper, *Volkstimme*, he had covered Czechoslovakia from the 1950s on. Fully sympathetic with the goals of the Czechoslovak reform movement, he had been expelled from the Austrian party.

In Czechoslovakia I tried to avoid the attention of the police. I made no reservations beforehand and usually arrived in a town early in the morning so that I could contact friends before the police were aware of my presence. I prepared a special coded address book and sent my cards to Sally under a pseudonym. In Bratislava and Prague I stayed a night or two in a hotel, which registered me, as required, with the police, and then I moved to private quarters. During the two weeks I did not have the impression that I was being followed by the police. For safety, I scribbled my notes, with many abbreviations, and with no names, so that it was later difficult even for me to decipher them.

In Bratislava I was asked to leave my room at the Hotel Carleton because all rooms were reserved for a conference, but was lucky to find a place in a private apartment. The landlady was permitted by the Čedok Travel Agency to rent only to persons from socialist countries, but she was happy to let me have her son's room in exchange for my American dollars. I spent much time with the Kalinas, both at home and at their *chata*. They told me of wire-tapping of their apartment, bugging of telephone conversations, and police interrogations. Laco had finished a large book on the theory and practice of comedy and humour but could not publish it. Agneša had a job as a translator. Julka was about to try, for the seventh time, to be admitted to university. Acceptance depended on "pull" and on "a good moral profile." If rejected again, she was resolved to study abroad. She had made one failed attempt to arrange a marriage of convenience with a foreigner in order to get permission to emigrate.

Charter 77, they told me, had, for the first time since 1968, reawakened interest in public affairs. Most people knew of the Charter and sympathized with it; the official campaign against it had only increased their sympathy. Most, however, were dissuaded from signing it by the fate of those few who did. Agneša herself had not signed it. In spite of impediments to travel, Charter 77 documents were reaching Bratislava, but the circle of readers was narrow. The Slovak authorities were afraid of the Charter and made every effort to prevent communications with the Czechs, or even travel to Prague. People felt isolated and were afraid to act. Even her former colleagues at *Kultúrny život* shunned political activity; few of them were writing anything. Many were even willing to sign the anti-Charter declaration, hoping to improve their position or protect their children. One prominent reformer from 1968, Pavol Stěvček, disavowed his previous activity but was nonetheless expelled from the Academy of Science and forced to take a minor post at a publishing house.

I met with Milan Šimečka at a parking lot near the Hotel Děvín, and we walked along the Danube, with a beautiful quarter-moon reflected on the river. We had dinner at a lovely little baroque fish restaurant below the Castle, which was illuminated at night. I met him again at the Kalinas' cottage where, at a wooden table outside, he proposed a toast and jokingly awarded me the highest Czechoslovak order, the White Lion (which I would actually receive from President Havel 15 years later). Milan had a somewhat better job now, as a dispatcher. With Miro Kusý, Šimečka was almost alone as an oppositionist and was busily engaged in writing what became a steady stream of provocative samizdat essays. He had almost completed his book, *The Restoration of Order*, a brilliant analysis of the "normalized" system, which was later translated into several languages.

The Charter was well-known in Slovakia through Vienna radio and television, but it was regarded as a Czech product. Milan had received a big bundle of copies of the original declaration but had been on holiday skiing in the Tatras and had been unable to distribute it. Most people were, however, afraid to sign it. As a Czech in Slovakia, he decided that he would not sign. The workers in a big factory refused to sign the anti-Charter declaration without knowing the contents of the Charter, but the party committee issued it anyway. The Charter had been important, Milan believed, because it re-established a degree of morality, at least among a small group. Most people were, however, not concerned with political issues or human rights and feared the loss of their jobs.

Rebro and his wife twice took me to dinner in hotel restaurants, but he was unable to invite me to the Institute of State and Law without permission. People felt that it was too dangerous even to read Charter documents. His wife confessed that she had not read the declaration. Rebro admitted that he had not signed the Charter, but he had refused to speak against it on television, as requested.

I was delighted to meet Miro Kusý at a friend's farmhouse, where we sat under the trees and talked as we ate. He had signed Charter 77, not expecting the persecution that would follow. He had not been arrested but was viciously attacked in the press and had been turned down for thirty jobs. During police interrogation he was offered another chance to live normally if he withdrew his signature, but he refused. He was repeatedly urged to emigrate. Although he did not want to do so, there seemed no alternative. Unlike the Czechs, not many Slovak intellectuals had been dismissed after 1968, and even these had decent jobs and were not badly paid. As a result, those in opposition in Slovakia were far fewer than in Prague and had less moral and financial support; they were closely watched by the police. Kusý was critical of Dubček's behaviour before and during 1968 and of his silence and passivity after the Charter. Husák, he said, had no real support in Slovakia and was very tough towards any sign of opposition. As for federation, Slovaks considered it meaningless in view of the lack of democracy.

In Prague that summer of 1977, I stayed a few days in my favourite hotel, the Tatran, but lived much of the time at Gina's, in a new house built right beside the old one, the building of which had taken years and exacted a heavy toll in terms of effort and energy on the whole of Olga and Bošek's family. I met several times with their other children, Milan and Jelka, who still lived in the old house, where I had first met their mother, in 1937. All the family worked at decent jobs and refused, in spite of pressure, to join the Communist party. Jelka had abstained from voting on an anti-Chartist resolution at her workplace. She had been interrogated once or twice because of visits by French friends and her travels in France. Although Charter 77 reflected the truth as they observed it, they had not dared sign it. Most people were afraid to do so out of fear for their children, their jobs, their cars, and their cottages. My friends were surprised to hear from me how much Charter material had appeared and read with fascination some of the documents that I showed them. Other old friends told me of their lives since January 1977. Lisa Rudinger lived alone in the far-off suburb of Spořilov. Zdeněk had died, due, she was certain, to the failure to get urgent medical attention. Despite her advanced age she remained active behind the scenes, supporting Charter activities. She said that everyone was afraid. The motto was, she said, "Don't think, don't speak, don't write, and don't sign — and don't be surprised!"

My friends at the Institute of International Politics and Economics were unable to continue their scholarly careers. Jaroslav Šedivý, after a short spell in prison, had been working for six years as a window-cleaner. Václav Kotyk had been employed for the same period as a store-keeper in a large factory. Alexander Ort was luckier than others; he was able to write articles on international affairs in various daily newspapers under a pseudonym and on a freelance basis. The historian, Jan Havránek, was still at work in the university archives and was able to conduct historical research and to publish. All of them approved of Charter 77, but none had signed it. Milan Otáhal, historian and co-editor with Prečan of "The Black Book" in 1968, had signed the Charter and was editing a historical journal that appeared regularly in samizdat.

My friend Ota Janeček, the painter, had a large new studio in Široká Street and was even able to travel abroad to attend the openings of exhibits. I bought a picture of his, this time through the official art centre, at a high price. It was entitled "A Little Bird Creeps out of His Hole and Sings" — a reference to Charter 77, I joked; he laughed and said that was a good idea. Ivan Klíma, the writer, had not signed Charter 77 but strongly supported it and was writing novels for publication in samizdat.

I had a long talk with Michal Lakatoš at his beautiful villa in the village of Černošice. He had signed Charter 77, which, he thought, had a moral purpose — namely, to show the reality of the system of uncontrollable power, of lies, and of bribery and the denial of human rights. The West, he urged, should make the Belgrade follow-up conference a tribunal of human rights, even though this was not likely to produce concrete results. Petr Pithart, a former law professor, had at first worked as a water-measurer but was now employed as a mason. The work left him tired at the end of the day, but he was doing some

clandestine writing. Charter 77, he said, was a realistic movement, dealing with real problems and making real proposals, but it had a moral
side, too — people had to decide whether to sign or not to sign and
whether to sign the anti-Charter declaration.

After the death on 13 March 1977 of the philosopher Jan Patočka,
one of the three initial spokespersons of Charter 77, and the detention
of a second, Václav Havel, former leading Communist Jiří Hájek held
the fort alone as the one remaining Charter spokesman. I was not able
to see him, but at Lisa's apartment I had a long talk with Milan Hübl,
former member of the Central Committee, who was close to Hájek in
his political views. The purpose of Charter 77, in his opinion, was to
make people aware that the present leaders were ignoring their own
laws and were not solving the country' s problems. It was time to
"make a noise" about human rights at Belgrade, even though a compromise on this subject was not likely. As a specialist on Slovak history, Hübl talked at length on the situation in Slovakia. He had visited
Dubček three times in Bratislava and had met Kusý in Brno. Dubček,
he said, agreed with the Charter and would have signed, but he had
first heard about it on the radio from Vienna. By achieving federation,
Husák had achieved some financial gains for Slovakia and more job
opportunities in central offices and had, he thought, gained prestige as
the first Slovak president in Czechoslovakia's history.

I came away from Czechoslovakia with the impression that Charter
77 was likely to continue. Unlike the 1968 reform movement, it was
not a Communist initiative but represented a real consensus of former
Communists and non-Communists. Its objective was not the revival of
the Prague Spring but the defence of human rights in general. Despite
the vicious official campaign against it, it had helped to break down a
little the *anomie* that had prevailed for ten years, and it enjoyed substantial support. In Slovakia it had less influence, partly because of the
weaker tradition of democracy there and the stronger appeal of nationalism as compared with human rights, and partly because of the formal
achievement of federation.

CONFERENCES, 1977

My stay in Belgrade for the CSCE conference in July 1977 gave me an
opportunity to meet some prominent Yugoslavs. I had two long meetings with Milan Djilas, the celebrated dissident, in his apartment in
central Belgrade. He did not seem to be under surveillance and spoke

freely and openly. I gave him a copy of my book on Czechoslovakia's interrupted revolution; when he saw its dedication to a number of Czechs and Slovaks, he asked me to inscribe his name there, "where he belonged." As in our earlier meeting, Djilas was critical of Dubček's naiveté about the Soviet Union and his unwillingness to fight the Soviets. "A state which is not ready to fight is not worth preserving," he said. Djilas considered Charter 77 "perhaps the best document that we have had in Eastern Europe since the beginning of Communist rule"; he had supported it from the start. He admitted that there was no human rights movement in Yugoslavia, although there were many violations of human rights.

I also met with Svetozar Stojanović, one of the eight Belgrade professors (the Praxis group) who had been removed from their posts in 1975 but were permitted to teach and to publish abroad. There was no real opposition, he told me; an informal group met regularly to discuss ideas and occasionally published statements. He was well informed about Czechoslovakia and sympathetic with Charter 77, and he regretted that there was nothing comparable in Yugoslavia and that there was no samizdat there. I also had meetings with other Yugoslav friends who held important positions, such as Najdan Pašić, a member of the presidium of the Republic of Serbia, and Professor Jovan Djordjević, chairman of the Serbian Constitutional Court. They were all warmly sympathetic with Charter 77 but were not aware that it was continuing its activity. In Zagreb I had dinner with the sociologist Rudi Supek, a former member of the Praxis group, who, unlike his Serbian colleagues, had not been ousted from his university post, and Eugene Pusić, a specialist on public administration. They, too, were surprised to hear that Charter 77 was still alive and active.

I proceeded directly from Belgrade to Italy to a conference on stability and change in eastern Europe; it was held in an idyllic setting, at the Hotel Il Ciocco, in the mountains near Lucca. Czech and Slovak exiles and some Western scholars (Leszek Kołakowski, Wolfgang Leonhard, Richard Löwenthal, Hugh Seton-Watson, and others) came together for three days of discussion. The highlight of the proceedings for me was an address by Zdeněk Mlynář, who spoke on Charter 77. According to him, the document reflected the end of all hope of reform from above. It was not so much a political movement as a moral necessity. It was designed to reveal, prior to the Belgrade conference, the failure of the regime in Prague to respect the human rights guaranteed by the international covenants and at Helsinki. Its supporters did not expect, he said, that the regime would fully recognize human rights, but they hoped for some relaxation of political pressure and a decrease in subservience to Moscow.

In December I was back again in Italy, this time in Venice, to attend the so-called Biennale on "Dissent in Eastern Europe and the Soviet Union." This was a gathering of exiled dissidents from all over eastern Europe, including several Soviet Russians who had staged a sit-down strike in Red Square to protest the Czech occupation of 1968. There were exhibits of writings from the entire Soviet bloc. I was disappointed that I was not given the opportunity, which had been promised me, to speak on Charter 77, but I listened with interest to the reports on other dissident movements.

CZECHOSLOVAKIA, SUMMER AND FALL 1978

In the summer of 1978 I returned to Czechoslovakia — to Bratislava, Brno, and Prague — this time with Sally, to explore at first hand the situation of Charter 77 after what some considered a crisis of its existence. Some Chartists were impatient with its failure to produce results; others felt that it had served its purpose and had no future role. It had been racked by heated inner controversies concerning tactics, particularly over whether it should develop a more political approach, as advocated by Jaroslav Šabata. Even more militant was the position taken by the historian Jan Tesař, who had sharply criticized what he considered Jiří Hájek's conservative and legalistic leadership. The discussions were linked with a change in Charter spokespersons. In late 1977 Hájek had been joined by two others — Ladislav Hejdánek, a Protestant philosopher, representing non-Communist intellectuals, and Marta Kubišová, the popular singer, speaking for the cultural community. In January 1978 Hájek was replaced as spokesman by Šabata.

In Paris, while we were en route to Prague, Pavel Tigrid told me of the recent conference of Communist and non-Communist exiles in Franken in Bavaria. There the "victors" and the "vanquished" of 1948 had had an open and honest discussion of their differences and had finally reached a consensus. At home, he said, there was a similar unity of action within Charter 77, despite the controversy about future tactics. Tigrid had published selections in his journal, *Svědectví*, about another controversy at home — over the morality and wisdom of the transfer of the Sudeten Germans in 1945.

In Vienna, my friend Poldi Grünwald also talked of this controversy and condemned the transfer as a decision based on the idea of collective guilt and imposed on Czech and Slovak leaders by Stalin personally. He had published a three-volume book that documented widespread Sudeten German resistance to Nazism. He was busy writing his memoirs, which recounted his gradual awakening to the realities of Communism and his complete break after 1968.

I also met with Mlynář, who was working in etymology, an old hobby of his, but also devoting much time to politics. He told me of his conversations with Communist and Socialist parties in Italy, Spain, France, and England. He seemed to have little confidence in the future of "Euro-Communism" and to have identified himself with European social democracy. He introduced me to a recent émigré from Prague, Josef Hodic, a former Communist and a Chartist, who had worked as a historian in the Military Academy. Little did I suspect that he would soon return to Prague and be revealed as an agent of the Czechoslovak security police.

In Bratislava my arrival was a surprise, since my friends had not yet heard from Prague of my coming. The Kalinas told me that conditions had deteriorated since my previous visit. Efforts to conduct a few seminars in private apartments on the Prague model had been suppressed by the police, who were frightened by even the slightest activity and of any contacts with Czechs. There had been frequent interrogations and house searches. Julka told me that she had had to become accustomed to lying in these ordeals in order to avoid saying anything about her parents or friends. After her eighth application to university was rejected, the Kalinas had applied for permission to emigrate.

Milan Šimečka told me that he had no intention of emigrating; he would do so only if the alternative was prison. The police had questioned him about me and had confiscated his copy of my book. He was torn with doubt as to whether to publish his own book, and his wife, Eva, urged him not to do so. He felt that it was his duty not to give in and to adapt; this would destroy the solidarity that he felt with his friends here and in Prague. As for the Charter, Milan did not sympathize with the idea of making it more political. He did not expect a complete change of the system but favoured a step-by-step approach, via small changes. He confirmed that people were on the whole satisfied with their lives and were afraid to do anything that would endanger their livelihoods.

Miroslav Kusý said to me that he felt less desperate than a year earlier and had adapted to his new life. He had no employment and was earning a meagre living by catching fish bait in streams. He had been glad to take part in the seminars organized by the students and had been falsely accused of organizing them. His house had been searched recently, and much of his library, including a copy of my book, had been seized. He was in close touch with the Czechs and had been in Prague recently for discussions on the purposes and methods of Charter 77.

While I was in Bratislava, the press announced the death of Edo Friš, historian and former Slovak leader, but since he had been expelled from the party in 1969, no obituary appeared. Although I was told that the police would be taking photographs of all those present with a hidden camera, I decided to attend the funeral; Šimečka and Kusý agreed that we would pretend not to know one another. It was a sad and moving ceremony, but its dignity was marred by the political character that the regime had given it. The main speaker paid tribute to Friš the man, but said nothing of his work as historian and party leader. Eight Czechs, including Rudolf Slánský and Karel Bartošek, had journeyed from Prague by car to attend. After the ceremony I walked alone among the grave stones, and the Czechs at first mistook me for a security policeman but were told my real identity by Kusý!

In Moravia, Brno was the main centre of Charter activity, with 70 signatories; in the industrial city of Ostrava there were none, I was told. I was unable to meet Jaroslav Šabata, who had been detained by the police because of Leonid Brezhnev's state visit to Czechoslovakia. Jan Tesař met me at the station and spent the entire day with me, talking excitedly of the Charter and criticizing its work. Hájek and other former Communists, he said, hoped that a "dialogue" might bring real changes and were hoping for an eventual change of policy in Moscow. Šabata and others wanted to press for immediate reforms, even though they expected few concrete results. "We want to prepare society for any eventual chance" by taking "civic initiatives," such as the forming of the Committee for the Defence of the Unjustly Persecuted (VONS). Later in Prague I had two more long meetings with Tesař, who was obsessed with the need to follow the more political tactics of the Polish dissidents and to cooperate with them.

In great contrast to this highly political talk was a historical discussion that I had with Professor Božena Komárková, an elderly philosopher who had spent six years in Nazi concentration camps and had been unable to teach or to publish for almost 30 years. In her study, lined with books, a small bust of T.G. Masaryk looked down on us. She was Evangelical in her orientation and was close to Jan Patočka and

Ladislav Hejdánek. She compared the Charter to the rebirth of freedom of conscience after the Catholic Counter-reformation, which had
forced Catholicism on the Czech people; this had actually revived the
ideas of Jan Hus, which to that point had seemed to be disappearing.
Similarly, under Communism, democratic ideas could not be expressed
publicly, but they remained latent and had expressed themselves in
1968 and in 1977. Although many did not know much about
Masaryk, he remained a kind of mythical figure in whom people
believed. The Charter's moral approach was comparable to Masaryk's
"non-political politics."

The centre of Prague was still in shambles that summer because of
the construction of the metro to be opened in August. Banners were
going up to welcome Brezhnev and to celebrate the voyage in space of
the Czech cosmonaut, Vladimír Remek. Police were everywhere, and
many Chartists were detained. No one understood the purpose of
Brezhnev's visit, but it was presumed that it was intended to show
Soviet support for the present regime. There were rumours of conflict
among the top leaders and of the resignation of Husák, but these
turned out to be false.

Since the Tatran Hotel was full, we stayed at Gina's house on
Petřín. In gatherings of the whole family we found that they knew little about Charter 77 and were divided in their opinions of it. Milan
wondered whether it could achieve anything, since it had influence
only on a narrow circle. Jelka admired the courage of the Chartists but
thought of them as a closed society; she was willing to help but did not
know how to reach them. Her husband, Jirka, was the most sceptical
and kept stressing the workers' lack of interest and the general absence
of information for most people.

This time I was able to see Jiří Hájek, a former spokesperson. A specialist on the human rights aspects of Charter 77, he agreed with me
that the discussion of the issue at Belgrade had refuted the argument
that this amounted to interference in domestic affairs. Charter 77
would continue, he said; "it was part of our life and could not be erad-
icated." Its purpose was to seek a restoration of values and a renascence
of citizenship. He confessed that he did not understand Tesař's criticism of the Charter's non-political approach but said that he believed
that discussions on tactics were natural and valuable.

Jiřina Šiklová was still performing a crucial role as a link between
the people at home and those abroad and tried to be neutral as between
the conflicting groups. As an old Communist herself, she had a guilty

conscience and was highly critical of the sectarian attitude of the "old Communists." She regarded Šabata highly and thought that Hejdánek, as a non-Communist, was now the moving spirit of the Charter.

Michal Lakatoš, the lawyer, saw the greatest significance of Charter 77 as lying outside the country, in showing the world the Communist system as it really was. Inside the country it touched people's consciences and offered an alternative system of values. It stimulated a sense of responsibility and of courage on the part of a few involved persons. Petr Pithart did not think that the Charter was in decline but felt that "we must wait for years to see results." Rudolf Battěk, a former sociologist, had served three years in prison and was now earning a living by washing windows. No great changes could be expected as a result of Belgrade, he said. The totalitarian system could not go beyond certain limits in making concessions. Charter 77 represented a general agreement on law and human rights, but this did not exclude the forming of narrower, more political groups, such as the Catholics, Protestants, Trotskyites, former Communists, and his own independent socialist group.

I spent an evening in the apartment of Rudolf Slánský, son of the party's former general secretary, executed in the 1950s, who was engaged in technical work in housing construction. He thought that Charter 77 would continue, although the regime was showing signs of greater harshness and had used violence. The Charter grouped together persons of different political tendencies and therefore could not itself be political. Outside the Charter framework, however, informal political groupings, such as the ex-Communists, to which he belonged, could seek more political goals.

I had meetings with several historians and other scholars. Milan Otáhal, a former colleague of Prečan's, told me of a revival of historical writings, mainly in samizdat, including a symposium of articles to be presented to the world congress of historians in Bucharest in 1980. In general he thought that Czechs were not willing to look critically at themselves and their past, and he welcomed the criticism of the transfer of the Sudeten Germans and of the capitulations of 1938 and 1968. He felt that Charter 77 would continue as a permanent movement to defend humane values and to stir up people's consciences. Jan Havránek was no longer permitted to teach history students but had been allowed to go to a conference in Cracow — his first trip abroad in five years. Jaroslav Opat had been working as a construction worker for four years and was now on disability pension. He spoke of the beginning of a more objective historical approach in the 1960s and of a more positive attitude to Masaryk and Beneš. Jaroslav Šedivý was still washing windows for a living; he had published some articles abroad under his own name and several books at home under a friend's name. Charter 77 had been a great achievement, he felt, but it had no broad popular basis and was too narrow in scope. Instead of concentrating on human rights it should deal with economic and other problems. Václav Kotyk told me that in the big factory where he was employed most workers were very dissatisfied with their standard of living and were working as little as possible, but they were not interested in politics. He had secured a new job as a documentation worker for the subway and hoped to be able to do more writing and, for the first time in his life, to do so out of real conviction and not within the framework of the party line.

It was a relief to leave Czechoslovakia at last after the strain and excitement of two weeks of conspiratorial meetings and to proceed to the different worlds of West Germany and later, England. In Edemissen, near Hannover, I stayed a few days with Vilém Prečan, whom I had seen twice since he went into exile, first at the Lucca conference in 1977, then in Toronto. Later that year I gave him a detailed report of my conversations in Czechoslovakia and my impressions. When I left him I carried with me a massive bundle of the latest Charter documents, including those that I gathered in Prague and those I had received from Prečan. It was fascinating to see his embryonic archive, which already contained a fantastic collection of documents. He was in constant touch by letter and telephone with people at home, and was working closely with Pavel Tigrid and Jiří Pelikán abroad. With Jiřina Šiklová he had worked out an elaborate coding system based on citing pages and lines of a certain book that they possessed. In Prečan's opinion, the main purpose of Charter 77 was domestic: to arouse citizens from their resignation and demoralization and to cultivate citizenship and knowledge, thus preparing for an eventual crisis.

In London I had talks with several Czechs — George Steiner, at Amnesty International; George Theiner, editor of *Index on Censorship*; and Eduard Goldstücker, now professor at Sussex University. All were full of questions about my impressions and interpretations and glad to see the samizdat materials that I had brought with me. I spent some time with Jan Kavan at the Palach Press, which distributed materials from Czechoslovakia to the British media and had been shipping Western books and journals to Prague in trucks with secret compartments. The latest shipment had been seized by the police and as a result, Kavan had lost the confidence of other exiles, such as Prečan and Tigrid. I enjoyed seeing a new play by Czech-born Tom Stoppard, *Every Good Boy Deserves Favour*, a brilliant depiction of a Soviet dissenter in prison, with music by André Previn. I gave a long interview on Charter 77 on the BBC Czech service and wrote an article on the 10th anniversary of the Soviet invasion (*The Times*, 18 August 1978). Back home in Toronto I wrote an article on the invasion and its aftermath for the *Sunday Star* (20 August 1978). I made the pieces anonymous in the hope that my chance of returning to Czechoslovakia in October would not be jeopardized.

In Edemissen I learned of a conference to be held that autumn in Kreuz, in the Bavarian Alps, on the theme "Czechoslovakia in Europe, 1918-68," and I resolved to attend. I also decided to make a quick detour to Czechoslovakia on my way. Prečan told me that my task was "to take the pulse of a sick country" and to report on the status and future of Charter 77. I felt like I was bearding the proverbial lion in his den.

In Prague I stayed only two nights, from Saturday to Monday (14-16 October), checking in at the Hotel Yalta but sleeping at Gina's. Although her telephone had been taken, Jiřina Šiklová was still active and as reckless as ever; she gave me my program of meetings, in writing, replete with names and places. On the first evening, at Lisa's apartment, I met Hejdánek, and later I went with him by bus and metro to Rudolf Slánský's apartment, where we were joined by Václav Havel. Hejdánek told me of the independent activities of Protestant and Catholic dissidents and of their role in Charter 77. The Charter, he believed, would continue. The regime could put a stop to it if it wished — but this would be too much a challenge to world opinion. I learned more about the several attempted meetings of the Czechs with Polish dissidents in the mountains on the Czech-Polish border. At one of these they had agreed on a joint declaration, which was issued on 21 August, the anniversary of the invasion.

Havel told me that the rock group Plastic People of the Universe was still playing and taping new compositions, including *The Easter Passion*. This was played at Havel's farm, with over one hundred people present. There had been private performances of one of his plays and of *Macbeth*, with Vlasta Chramostová, celebrated actress, banned from the stage, taking the role of Lady Macbeth. His book series Expedice was continuing; 40 titles had been released, and 20 more were under consideration. When we left late at night it was amusing to see Havel standing on the broad Leninova Avenue, trying to flag down passing cars, including a police car, for a lift into town!

The next day, in the Kinský Garden, I met Dana Němcová, a Catholic laywoman, who had made her home a gathering place for young people. She had seven children of her own but was extremely active in Charter work, especially attending and reporting on all the trials. She told me of several Catholic priests and laymen who had signed Charter 77, even though this was opposed by the Catholic hierarchy. That evening Šiklová and I went together to Petr Pithart's. He was quite critical of the Charter 77 spokesmen for their lack of contact with people, including signatories. The next day I met him at a café in town with Milan Otáhal. The latter had been to the Canadian embassy, as I had suggested, to pick up copies of an article I had prepared for the conference in Bavaria. Both gave me their comments as well as a written critique by Jaroslav Opat. All of these, alas, were later taken from me by the police in Bratislava. On my last day in Prague, early in the morning, I went out by tram to Jiří's Hájek's little house in a distant suburb. He talked of the difficulties of preparing Charter documents, since each had to be approved by the spokespersons. He told me of the work of VONS, which was designed to relieve the spokespersons of the burden of dealing with questions relating to prisoners.

In Bratislava my trip was short but packed with excitement. On 16 October I went directly to the private flat where I had stayed on previous visits, and I was based there for two nights. I went by taxi to the Šimečkas, who were taken completely by surprise. Milan proudly showed me a painting by Jiří Kolář, a collage of the crucifixion, which he had received from the Czech writers as an unofficial award for writing what they called "the best book of the year." He had gone by train to Prague but had been escorted back to the station at once and thus missed the award ceremony. When I told him of the likely publication of his book abroad in Czech, German, and French, he put his hands to his head and gazed out the window; he was proud of his book but worried about the probable consequences.

The next day I went to see Miroslav Kusý, who was a casual labourer at a construction site and arrived home late, tired and dirty, in his work clothes. Police had confiscated his driving licence so that he had to go to work on a bicycle. He had, however, been able to go to Prague recently with his wife and had attended a conference of Czech writers in Havel's house and watched the performance of *Macbeth*. Charter 77 was still limited in Slovakia, he told me, although several active Catholic priests had been defrocked. He gave me a one-page *feuilleton* that he had written on an accident which he had suffered in the work-place. Before I left I hid some money for him under the tablecloth in the dining-room.

As I learned later, the police had been watching his house and fol-lowed me for the rest of the day; they even knew that early in the morn-ing I had gone to the Kalina flat again, although they never learned that I had left a letter and some money for Šimečka in the mail box. Worse still, as it turned out, at lunch at the Hotel Děvín I met David Taylor, a Canadian commercial attaché, who was heading for Vienna by car the next day and offered me a ride. I declined, but he agreed to take my notes with him. This led me to spend an afternoon writing these up more carefully than usual, since I assumed that there was no risk of police seizure. But alas, overnight, Taylor changed his mind, pleading that he was new to the diplomatic job and was afraid to take the risk, so I had to take the notes with me.

In the evening the Kalinas were having a farewell party before their emigration in ten days. I dropped in unexpectedly and was warmly wel-comed, although Laco seemed somewhat alarmed because my visit might cause them trouble with the police. They told me of the heavy costs of emigration, which they covered by selling their *chata* and many books, and of his fear for the safety of his manuscripts. They were allowed only a total of ten dollars for emigration. I gave them some additional money. Julka was to enter the university in Cologne on a scholarship arranged by Prečan. It was a sad occasion, since these close friends were prepared to separate, perhaps forever. They opened a bot-tle of Scotch, a gift from someone, and discussed the questions of polit-ical commitment and emigration.

The next morning (Wednesday 18 October), when I went to the bus station at an early hour, to catch the bus to Vienna, I was followed by the police, although I did not know it at the time. At the border all passengers were forced to leave the bus and their bags were thoroughly searched. The officials took me to a small room for a body search. In the bus they found the Kusý *feuilleton*, which I had hidden inside a newspaper in my coat, and also my notes, which I had concealed beneath the seat under some *koláče* (Czech cakes), which Gina had given me in Prague. By the time they concluded the search, my bus had left for Vienna.

I was taken back, in a police car, to Bratislava, to the office of the Slovak Ministry of the Interior. There I was held the rest of the day for a "conversation," as they called it. This was in Slovak, with an interpreter doing a poor job in English. They told me that I was not under arrest; I had only to answer a few questions and I would soon be on my way. They rejected my repeated requests for permission to telephone the Canadian embassy in Prague. There were several persons present, including a man with red hair and gold teeth, who said not a word and whom I took to be a Russian. A young man who acted as chairman was very polite; a tall elderly man, "the colonel," as I nicknamed him, remained standing and from time to time pointed at me with his arm raised and asked me threatening questions.

During the whole morning they questioned me closely about my meetings in Prague and Bratislava, asking me where I stayed, whom I met, what I had talked about, and whether I had given or received any written materials. I managed to evade answering most of their questions and invented stories about where I had stayed. I refused to say anything about my conversations; having received a visa, I claimed that I had the right to meet and talk freely with Czech citizens. As for the *feuilleton*, I told them that someone I did not know had slipped it into my hands in the hotel lobby.

After lunch they told me they knew that I had been lying all along and that they were aware of everything that I had done after my visit to Kusý's. They had translated my notes into Slovak and questioned me about them. Unfortunately these included notes on my conversations in Prague and some coded messages from Jiřina Šiklová for Prečan. At one point they produced a copy of my book on the interrupted revolution and asked me if I had written it and whether I had given it to Šimečka. Later I thought that I ought to have asked them if they had read it and would like me to autograph it! At about seven o'clock I was requested to sign the final written protocol. Knowing that they were anxious to get home to supper, I deliberately took my time about it, reading it carefully and making several corrections. I added a note that my requests to talk to the embassy had been refused.

I was taken to the border in a police car, and the colonel handed my passport to the official for stamping. Finally, at dusk, I walked across the space between the Czechoslovak and Austrian frontier barriers and was warmly greeted by the Austrian official. Since there were no bus or rail connections at that time of night, he called a taxi to take me to Vienna. I was free at last. It was a great relief to reach my hotel an hour later. I called Sally at once to explain the delay and report my safe arrival. I spent the next morning at the Canadian embassy, where

I recounted my adventure to David Taylor and to a resident Canadian diplomat. The interrogation, though somewhat unnerving, had given me a personal taste of what the Chartists were constantly suffering and added a new dimension to my academic study. The experience, Šimečka wrote later, was all that I needed to complete my understanding of human rights in eastern Europe; all Western specialists, he joked, should request an opportunity for such field work!

At the conference on Czechoslovakia in Kreuz (19 October) I gave my paper on 1968 in the context of Czech history. Ironically, in view of his later role, I had a long talk with Josef Hodic and told him in detail what had happened in Bratislava. No doubt this was transmitted back to the Czechoslovak security police. Later in Munich, I spent an evening with Vilém Prečan, who was of course fascinated and disturbed by my report of the border incident. The next morning he telephoned Šimečka and Kalina and learned that both had been interrogated about our meetings. Fortunately this had no effect on the Kalinas' emigration; they arrived in Munich two weeks later, as planned. I was also concerned that my confiscated notes might have had some ill effects on people in Prague, but Jiřina later assured me that there were no untoward results.

When I returned to Canada I launched a diplomatic campaign through the Department of External Affairs; I sent it a full memorandum of what had happened and urged them to demand the return of my notes and an assurance of future entry for me into Czechoslovakia. The Canadian ambassador in Prague made several official protests concerning my detention but did not receive an apology or the return of my notes. The Czechoslovak Foreign Ministry later admitted that an error had been made but accused me of talking with anti-state elements. I decided to "go public" on the case and sent off a press release to friends in Austria, Britain, France, and West Germany and to the Canadian newspapers and opposition leaders. All of this took place at the time of an official visit to Canada by the Czechoslovak foreign minister, Bohnslav Chňoupek! I later wrote signed articles on the situation in Czechoslovakia for Toronto's *Sunday Star* (19 November 1978) and for the *Globe and Mail* (14 December 1978). I had burned my bridges and perhaps made unlikely an early return to Czechoslovakia.

MOSCOW, 1979

In August 1979, in spite of my encounter with the police in Czechoslovakia, I decided to take advantage of a world conference of the

International Political Science Association (IPSA) in Moscow to visit the Soviet Union for the first time in over ten years. There had been some opposition in the West — for example, within the Canadian Political Science Association — to holding the IPSA meeting in Moscow for fear of potential limitations on free discussion and on granting of visas. However, it was finally decided that it provided a unique opportunity for open debate on controversial issues in a country where such debate was otherwise strictly limited. In spite of some misgivings, I registered as a delegate and was granted a visa without problem. According to conference rules, I was entitled to take with me copies of my paper as well as other supporting materials. I interpreted this broadly and took some Charter 77 documents and several copies of *Czechoslovakia's Interrupted Revolution.* We passed through customs control at the Moscow airport without a hitch.

Sally joined me for her first trip to the country about which she had heard so much from me. In Moscow between sessions I was able to show her places of historical interest and beauty, sometimes in the company of our good friend from Paris, Hélène Carrère d'Encausse, a specialist on Soviet Asia. On one occasion, to avoid being overheard, Sally and she walked and talked in Red Square. In Leningrad our time was completely free to explore that city and to make excursions to Pushkin and Petrodvorets.

The program of the conference covered every possible theme of political science, including such highly controversial ones as human rights and pluralism, arms control and the Middle East. The scholarly character of the proceedings was often marred by ideological confrontations. For instance, at the panel on Helsinki and human rights, Professor Harold Berman, a Harvard specialist on Soviet law, gave what seemed to me a balanced analysis of the achievements and the failures of both the United States and the USSR in the observance of human rights. He was, however, sharply attacked by Samuel Zivs, of the Soviet Institute of State and Law, who stoutly defended the Soviet human rights record and cast grave doubt on some of Berman's sources, such as Amnesty International. At a panel on the transformation of systems, my paper on pluralism in Czechoslovak history was severely condemned by the chairman and by other Czech and Soviet scholars.

Other events cast shadows on the congress as a free forum for intellectual discourse. A controversy erupted when a distinguished Soviet cyberneticist, Alexandr Lerner, was not permitted to attend and to read his paper in person. A compromise proposed by the IPSA committee, which would have allowed someone else to read Lerner's paper, was bitterly attacked by some delegates as a capitulation to Soviet pressure and was rejected outright by Lerner. In the end he had to give his paper in a private apartment to an audience of 50 or so. Then at the very end of the congress a Canadian delegate, Irwin Cotler, was summarily expelled from the USSR because of his meetings with relatives of the imprisoned dissident Anatol Shcharansky.

Sally and I had the rare opportunity to visit the home of Jurij Kalensky, a scholar at the Institute of State and Law who had attended my panel. I knew him as the author of an excellent study of American political science; he told me that he had read some of my work. His young wife was studying at the Institute of Foreign Languages, specializing in English. Jurij spoke openly of the lack of serious scholarly work at the institute and of his hope to leave the country (this he did within a year).

In Leningrad we had another revealing encounter with a cousin of my Toronto colleague Gleb Žekulín, Irina Kern, who was employed at the Institute for the Study of Social Problems. She was an indefatigable guide but spoke only Russian. Her daughter, Katya, spoke some English. Irina was a bitter critic of all aspects of Soviet society and spoke of the disintegration of the family, widespread alcoholism, and all-pervasive corruption. She painted a devastating picture of the lack of real scholarship at her institute. Katya was extremely religious and completely alienated from Soviet society. Irina was determined to emigrate at the earliest opportunity, to join another daughter in California. Although she was not Jewish, she was confident that she would get permission to leave the country — and in fact she did emigrate within a year or two.

An unexpected by-product of the congress was an opportunity for me to have conspiratorial meetings with Soviet dissidents, including Andrei Sakharov. Professor Peter Reddaway, of the London School of Economics, a specialist on Soviet dissent, gave me the names of people to contact and a little map showing me how I should go to a designated meeting place. With some trepidation I made my way by a circuitous route to a tiny private apartment. There I met a young man, Slava, and a young woman, Irina, both computer mathematicians, and a half-dozen other dissidents who were actively involved in the Moscow Helsinki committee and the committee on the abuse of psychiatry. On another evening I went back to the same place for an even larger gathering, which included Jurij Kovalev, who had just visited his father, who was serving seven years in a remote prison, and a spokesman of the Pentacostalists, who had come from Siberia to inform the Helsinki committee and foreign journalists of their plight. It was exciting to spend time with these brave souls — one of them was imprisoned soon afterwards; another went into exile abroad.

My friends later sent me a cryptic message at the hotel that they were willing to escort me to Sakharov's apartment. We were to meet at a certain subway station, and I was to get off the final car. We met as planned, walked to his address, and climbed the stairs to his sixth-floor apartment. There I found to my surprise that Sakharov was not alone but was in fact conducting a kind of seminar with some 15 or 20 delegates to the IPSA conference. There he sat, with the hot setting sun streaming in the window on his bald head, patiently answering questions, in Russian, about prison conditions, religious persecution, the human rights movement, and problems of emigration for Jews, Germans, and Pentacostalists. He argued strongly that in the absence of human rights détente would be fragile; without détente, human rights were in constant danger. He thought that the congress was valuable if we were able to present views other than the official Soviet ones, but argued that all Soviet scholars should have been permitted to attend and that the proceedings should have been reported in the Soviet media and eventually published in full in the conference protocols.

Sakharov's wife, Elena Bonner, invited us to their tiny kitchen for tea and cakes. Before leaving I had a short talk alone with Sakharov in the hallway and presented him with a copy of my book on Czechoslovakia's interrupted revolution. He expressed his admiration for the Czechs and Slovaks and had me inscribe his name after the dedication to Czech and Slovak dissidents in the frontispiece. He confessed that he knew little of the Charter 77 movement and suggested that I meet with one of his colleagues to give them information.

Again I met Slava at a subway station, this time near the Kremlin, and we spent several hours together sitting on a bench within the Kremlin walls — an oddly incongruous place to talk about human rights! He was amazed to hear of the manifold activities of the Chartists and was glad to receive copies of Charter documents. I offered to take a message to the Czechoslovak and Polish dissidents and later did receive a greeting of solidarity signed by Sakharov and a half-dozen fellow dissidents. On my return to London I transmitted this message to Warsaw and Prague and in due course sent their reply to Moscow. In a small way I had bridged the gap between the dissident movements, which had almost no direct contact with each other.[3] On my last day in Moscow I met Slava and a friend at a subway station not far from the U.S. embassy. He gave me a shopping bag full of samizdat materials, including the latest reports of the Helsinki committee and the committee on psychiatry, which I hurriedly took to the embassy. Mark Garrison had promised to ship this material back to North America. Alas, in Washington, DC, the U.S. State Department appropriated these documents and sent only copies to me in Toronto. Fortunately, with the help of Peter Reddaway, I eventually recovered the originals.

Within six months of my meeting with Sakharov he was illegally exiled to Gorky, one day after signing a protest of Moscow's Helsinki monitoring committee against the invasion of Afghanistan.[4]

POLAND, 1978 AND 1979

On the way home from the Soviet Union, Sally and I stopped for a few days in Warsaw, which I had visited in 1978. During these two stays I was able to observe the extraordinary world of active dissent that paved the way for the rise of Solidarity. I had no problem in meeting leading figures in all the human rights movements, secular and Catholic, and outstanding scholars who were actively engaged in independent intellectual activities. In Paris and London, on my way to and from Poland, in 1978, and in London on our return in 1979, I was able to supplement what I learned in Poland by talks with prominent Polish exiles, especially the Polish economist Włodek Brus, an old friend from St Antony's College, Oxford. I also met with the two Smolar brothers, Alexander in Paris and Eugenius in London, who were in close touch with the dissent movement at home.

In 1978 I had stayed at the once splendid, but now shabby and dilapidated, Hotel Bristol. In 1979 Sally and I stayed with Tadeusz Kowalik, an economist and former student and close friend of Włodek Brus's, and his wife, Irena, also an economist. Tadeusz had worked for years in the Institute for the History of Science, Education and Technology, where he was editing the collected works of the great Polish economists Oskar Lange and Viktor Kalecki. His position was tenuous, however, and he had recently been deprived of the right to travel. He listened with interest to my report on Charter 77 and on the Moscow congress. He told me that my book on the interrupted revolution had been circulating widely and agreed to pick up another copy at the Canadian embassy and deposit it in the "free library."

Tadeusz was close to the Committee for the Defence of the Workers (KOR), as it was called when it was founded in 1976; in 1977 it was renamed the Committee for Social Defence (KOS). I gained further insight into its activities by talks with two of its prominent leaders, Jacek Kuron and Adam Michnik. Kuron was a big, vigorous, dynamic man, and his "office" seemed like a kind of general staff, with aides coming in and out and phones ringing constantly. He spoke to me in Polish, through an interpreter. The movement had no political or economic program, he said, but sought to defend the interests and the rights of society through what he called the "self-organization of society" (*samo-organizocje*). Through an independent press and publishing and an unofficial educational system, it aimed to develop a mass movement of intellectuals, students, workers, and farmers; this would exert constant pressure on the authorities and thus effect changes in the totalitarian system. It was trying to organize independent trade unions but had so far not achieved a great deal. He admitted that it had to adjust its demands to the reality of Soviet power; he hoped that the Soviet Union would not intervene as it had done in Hungary and in Czechoslovakia.

The historian Adam Michnik was a slight, thin man, who talked to me in halting French and in Polish, with the aid of an interpreter. Like Kuron, he believed that the only way to dismantle totalitarianism was through the self-organization of society. Like Kuron, too, he thought that much depended on political change in the Soviet Union. No one knew what would happen — this meant that anything could happen, he said. But they were not simply waiting for this — they were trying to do something now so that they would be prepared for whatever might come. They were not seeking power; they were striving to be ready to affect the power relations if and when conditions changed. In 1978 I had heard him give a lecture in a private apartment in which he expounded a favourite idea of his — namely, that the Polish situation was similar to Spain's in the 1960s. The urgent need was to attain unity of action of all groups, whatever their past political positions. In 1979 Michnik felt that the situation in Poland was very different from that in Czechoslovakia. In Poland repression was tolerable; there were no political prisoners, and there was no general fear. He regarded the trial of Chartists in Prague as a serious matter and told me of various Polish protests. This time he was quite prophetic about the future. "We were standing before great changes in society and in the establishment," he said. "These were the last days of the present establishment." The dissidents, who were engaged in a great discussion of tactics, did not exclude the idea of collaborating with the establishment — a foretaste of what actually happened in 1980.

In 1978 I had meetings with two other KOR activists. One was Barbara Toruńczyk, a young woman student, who was secretary of the samizdat literary journal, *Zapis*. This came out in 3,000 photocopies but was also published in printed form in London and smuggled back into Poland. Jan Lytiński, a mathematician, told me about the many publications of Now-a, a samizdat publishing house, the great variety of newspapers and journals, and new copying techniques which, in contrast to Czech methods, allowed production of large numbers of copies. He was the editor of *Robotnik*, a small newspaper for workers that had a circulation of some 25,000.

I also had several meetings with two leading figures of another quite different organization, the Movement for the Defence of Human and Civil Rights (ROBCHiO), which had started in March 1977 but was at this very time in the process of splitting up into two separate organizations. Leszek Moczulski, a historian of an older generation, had been editor of the movement's monthly newspaper, *Opinia*. Andrzej Czuma, a young lawyer, had led the breakaway and was assuming the editorship. Czuma described ROBCHiO as a human rights movement that published several newspapers, issued leaflets and documents, and organized protest demonstrations. He spoke of the right of self-determination of the nation as a whole as one of the basic rights. Moczulski expressed this view even more forcefully. ROBCHiO was a continuation of the movement for national independence that had been initiated in the 1920s by Josef Piłsudski (whose picture hung on his wall). Without independence Poles could have no human rights; without human rights, no independence. The task, he admitted, was a romantic one, but the movement sought to replace Communism with a new system in a pragmatic way, step by step, by building up a free press, discussion clubs and, later, parties and free elections, free trade unions, free universities, and so on.

In many ways these goals did not seem to differ fundamentally from those of KOR. The differences were subtle and seemed to reflect the different personalities of the leaders and the different traditions and groups to which they appealed. KOR was more socialist or leftist and was more attractive to intellectuals. ROBCHiO was more nationalist and conservative, and perhaps more plebeian, with fewer prominent intellectuals. Moczulski professed a desire to cooperate with KOR but admitted that their relations were not good. KOR, I found, had no desire to cooperate with ROBCHiO.

The Polish situation was markedly different from that of Czechoslovakia in terms of the role of the Catholic church and of the manifold trends of Catholic activity. The church, under Cardinal Wyszyński, had always presented a strong challenge to the Communist regime. The cardinal, however, was a traditionalist, who followed narrow church interests; only gradually had he come to show an understanding of the broader interests of society and of the struggle for human rights. The church did not identify itself directly with any dissident groups, Catholic or non-Catholic, but often showed its sympathy with movements working for human rights and cultural independence. Karol Cardinal Wojtyła, in Cracow, was more open and liberal, and his elevation to the papacy in late 1978, and his visit to Poland in 1979, had had a great impact.

I tried to assess the situation in conversations with leading lay Catholics, among them Tadeusz Mazowiecki, editor of the monthly journal, *Więź*, S. Stomma, former leading member of the Znak parliamentary group, Bohdan Cywiński, former editor-in-chief of the monthly, *Znak,* and Andrzej Wielowieyski, secretary of the Club of Catholic Intelligentsia (KIK). These groups varied greatly, both in their attitude to the church hierarchy and to the state, and they did not directly cooperate with each other, but there was a general consensus on human rights. An example of the spirit of cooperation was Cywiński, a young freelance writer, who was writing a book on the Catholic church in Communist eastern Europe. He was not a member of KOR or ROBCHiO but was associated closely with the Flying University. He was a close friend of the new Pope and believed that his visit had been influential even among non-Catholics.

A distinctive feature of the dissident landscape in Poland was the Flying University, which was sponsored by a group of distinguished scholars who formed the Society for Scientific Courses (TKN). They organized an extensive program of courses by outstanding scholars in literature, history, politics, psychology, sociology, and so on. Lectures took place in private apartments and had to be moved from place to place. Occasionally police broke up seminars, and apartment owners sometimes had to pay heavy fines. I met with several independent intellectuals who participated actively in the Flying University — for instance, the sociologists Stefan Nowak, of the Academy of Sciences, and his wife, Irene, who taught at the University of Warsaw. His theoretical work could be published abroad, but his empirical writings, especially studies of public opinion, were circulated only in mimeographed form. Other instructors were Tadeusz Kowalik and my longtime friend Jan Strzelecki, who was still employed by the Institute of Sociology.

I visited Jan and his wife several times in their small, dingy apartment. He seemed discouraged and dispirited and confessed that he had done little writing or research. When I presented him with a copy of my volume on the interrupted revolution, he thanked me, almost in tears, and asked me to add to the dedication — "to a Polish Jan." Although he was a non-believer, he showed his excitement at the Pope's visit and admitted that it had had a great impact on Catholic and non-Catholic, Communist and non-Communist. He spoke positively but critically of KOR; he thought that it was too political and mistakenly sought a general reform of the system. In his view there could only be small reforms within the system, although he was not hopeful even about this. I was at a gathering in his house in 1979, at which his son, Turek, and a young woman economist, Jadwiga Staniszki, were present, there was a heated discussion of the possibility of the reform of Communism; all were agreed that it was not possible.

CHARTER 77 AND HUMAN RIGHTS IN CZECHOSLOVAKIA

The completion of my book on Charter 77 was delayed by my frequent travel and many other activities. In any case it was like shooting at a moving target. There were constant changes in the Charter's spokespersons and its tactics, and continuing controversy as to its purpose. Vilém was tireless in sending me the ever-increasing amount of samizdat material from Prague and in trying to answer my many questions about Charter developments. He admitted that even he, and those at home, sometimes found it difficult to understand what was actually going on within the movement.

I had seriously considered making a brief stopover in Czechoslovakia on my way to Moscow in 1979. This would have been risky in view of my encounter with the police in 1978 and my public activity in protest against the arrest of leading Chartists in May 1979. Friends in Prague warned me against coming, and Prečan expressed doubts. Nevertheless, at my request, the Canadian Department of External Affairs talked with the Czechoslovak ambassador in Ottawa about a visa and transmitted my request for conversations with Czech specialists on the CSCE; he postponed making a decision by saying that he would have to consult Prague, and in the end I left without obtaining a visa.

In the summer of 1979 I sent a first draft of my book to Princeton University Press and was devastated to hear that it had doubts about publishing it because of its great length and a negative report from a reader. However, George Allen & Unwin, a British publisher, had already expressed a willingness to publish it, sight unseen, and in June 1980 it gave me a firm commitment. I continued to work on the revision of the manuscript in the light of current developments and criticisms received from Vilém Prečan and other readers. Because of a postal strike in Canada, I took the revised manuscript to England with me on my way to Madrid in September and mailed it at Heathrow Airport. Even during the Madrid conference I kept making changes so as to bring it up to date and mailed these revisions at Heathrow on my way back to Canada. It was set in type in Toronto by Sixty-Eight Publishers, so I was able to make last-minute changes. As always, Sally did a prodigious job of editing the manuscript and preparing the index. It was a relief to send it off in final form by courier in April 1981.

When *Charter 77 and the Human Rights in Czechoslovakia* finally appeared, it covered the first four years of Charter activity to the end of 1980. I was able to send several copies to delegates at the Madrid conference. Through the good offices of the International Literary Center in New York, 35 copies were sent to Czechoslovakia and elsewhere in eastern Europe. In 1983 the samizdat bulletin *Informace* hailed it as a worthy continuation of my book on the interrupted revolution and a valuable record of Charter 77 activities; the volume was written, it said, with rigorous scholarship and a real commitment to the cause of human rights.

NOTES

1. See my "Czechoslovakia and Helsinki," *Canadian Slavonic Papers* 18, no. 3 (Sept. 1976): 245-65, also given in Adam Bromke and Derry Novak, eds., *The Communist States in the Era of Détente, 1971-1977* (Oakville, ON: Mosaic Press, 1978).
2. Skilling, "Socialism and Human Rights, Charter 77 and the Prague Spring," in a festschrift for Richard Löwenthal, H. Horn et al., eds., *Sozialismus in Theorie und Praxis* (Berlin: De Gruyter, 1978); in revised form in *Canadian Slavonic Papers* 20, no. 2 (June 1978): 157-75.
3. For texts of these letters see my *Charter 77 and Human Rights in Czechoslovakia* (London: George Allen & Unwin, 1981), 278-80.
4. See H.G. Skilling, "Why Sakharov was Muzzled," *Sunday Star*, 3 Feb. 1980.

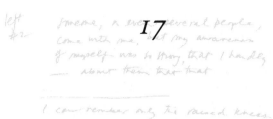

IN DEFENCE OF HUMAN RIGHTS

DURING THE 1980S HUMAN RIGHTS and independent activities in Czechoslovakia and eastern Europe were the principal objects of my concern and activity. I became an activist in human rights and lent my support to the dissidents in eastern Europe. I attended the meetings of the Conference on Security and Cooperation in Europe (CSCE) in Madrid and Ottawa and published several studies of these stages of the Helsinki process. Despite this concentration on contemporary affairs I also found myself turning back to the study of Czechoslovak history and of the Czech political leader Tomáš G. Masaryk. In 1982 Sally and I spent three months in Japan, and in 1984 and 1987 we made two exciting return visits to Czechoslovakia.

SOLIDARITY AND THE STATE OF WAR

We followed with hope and enthusiasm the birth of Solidarity in Poland in 1980 and the subsequent struggle for reform, so reminiscent of the Prague Spring, and were depressed by its similarly violent termination with the establishment of the state of war (*stan wojenny*) on 13 December 1981. At a conference in May 1982, at Carleton University, I sought to compare and contrast the two movements for reform and the two "interrupted revolutions."[1] I noted the striking similarity of the general objectives of economic and political reform. In Poland, this was a massive popular movement from below, by the working class and the trade union movement Solidarity. Like the Czechoslovak case, this was a virtual revolution, non-violent and self-limiting. It did not, in my opinion, threaten Poland with anarchy or civil war. The Communist party — its legitimacy eroded by events in 1970 and 1976 — dragged its feet during the 18 months that followed. In the end General Jaruzelski, who had become head of the party as well as military commander, used force to ward off radical reform and the disintegration of the party's rule. The establishment of the state of war in December

1981 unquestionably had the support of Moscow and relieved the latter of the need to intervene.

The initial reaction of the Canadian government to the state of war seemed, in my view, to condone the use of military measures and to absolve Moscow of responsibility. I was highly critical of the West's slowness in recognizing that these measures and the ensuing liquidation of civil rights and freedoms were flagrant violations of international law and of the Helsinki Final Act. It was necessary, I believed, to impose sanctions against the Polish regime and to offer large-scale Western aid if a reform policy were resumed.[2]

After the declaration of the state of war I was swamped with requests to give interviews and commentaries on radio and television on the Polish situation. I gave lectures on Solidarity and martial law in Toronto and elsewhere and took part in conferences on Poland in Windsor, at Harvard, and in California and Honolulu, as well as in Japan. As chairman of the Royal Society of Canada's recently formed Committee on Freedom of Science and Scholarship, I took advantage of the society's centennial meeting in Ottawa in May 1982 to arrange a meeting between the president, Professor Michael Tremblay, and the distinguished Polish historian Alexander Gieysztor, president of the Polish Academy of Science, who was present as a guest. Acting on the recommendation of our committee, Tremblay issued a statement protesting the round-up of Polish intellectuals in the wake of the proclamation of martial law. When Lech Wałesa was awarded the Nobel Peace Prize, I wrote a letter to the *Globe and Mail* (17 December 1983) calling attention to the significance of the award in emphasizing the close link between human rights and peace.

CSCE: MADRID, 1980

During the first half of the 1980s I immersed myself in the study of the Conference on Security and Cooperation in Europe (CSCE). In 1978-79 I worked with a team of Canadian scholars organized by Professor Robert Spencer, director of the Centre for International Studies at the University of Toronto, to prepare a full-length book on this theme. We met regularly in Toronto to discuss our project and in July 1980 had a week-long sojourn at the Rockefeller Study Center in Bellaggio on Lake Como. There we were joined by scholars from Britain, France, Italy, the Netherlands, Poland, Sweden, the United States, and West Germany, for a discussion of our draft chapters. My own contributions were two chapters on Belgrade and Madrid.[3]

In September 1980 I flew to Madrid to attend a week of the preparatory meeting and to find lodgings for Sally and me for when we returned in November for the full conference. From Madrid I joined Sally in West Germany for a few days with Vilém and Helena Prečan in their new home in Hanover. We proceeded to Munich for a visit with our Slovak friends the Kalinas and then to Garmisch-Partenkirchen in the Bavarian Alps for the International Congress of Soviet and East European Studies. I gave a paper there on pluralism and Czechoslovak political culture in a panel arranged by Archie Brown, of Oxford; it eventually appeared in a book that he edited.[4] During the conference Julia Kalinová and I went from room to room to distribute to delegates copies of Vilém Prečan's book *Acta Creationis*, on the plight of Czech historians, prepared for the world congress of historians in Bucharest.

After the congress we drove along the spectacular Alpenstrasse, stopping a night or two in lovely inns. In Konstanz we visited the memorial to Jan Hus. Then we took the train through the mountains to the Rockefeller Center in Bellaggio on Lake Como, where I was to spend a month as a visiting scholar. We lived in the Villa Serbelloni, perched on a small hill and commanding views on all sides of the lake and the Alps. It was a life of extreme comfort, with servants and superb Italian cuisine, but its formality and luxury soon palled. I devoted my time to my chapter on the Belgrade conference. Sally worked hard on an index for my book on Charter 77. In this idyllic environment it was hard to believe that the outside world existed, but our short-wave radio brought us news of the events in Poland.

We went from Milan by air to Madrid, where we spent six weeks in November and December. It was our first visit to Spain, and, blessed with glorious sunshine, we took advantage of the weekend breaks to explore Madrid and the lovely towns nearby, such as Avila, Segovia, and Toledo. Since the only way to observe the conference proceedings at close hand was to be a journalist, I had secured accreditation from the *Toronto Star*. This did not entitle me to attend the actual sessions, which were held *in camera*, but gave me access to the conference building and its facilities. It was somewhat frustrating trying indirectly to get a clear picture of what was going on behind closed doors by buttonholing delegates in the lounge, attending press conferences, and conducting lengthy interviews. I arrived at the conference in early November, when the preliminary conference was deadlocked and the opening of the permanent conference was still in question. For the next five weeks, until the conference recessed for Christmas, I covered the sessions as a working journalist, doing a number of broadcasts for the CBC domestic service and Radio Canada International. Back in Toronto I did several more broadcasts and published several articles in Toronto newspapers.[5]

The Madrid conference placed human rights in the centre of international diplomacy and made Madrid a kind of "city of dissidence." Hundreds of delegates of human rights organizations and former dissidents and exiles from eastern Europe staged demonstrations, gave press conferences and interviews, and held public discussions on human rights and détente. There was an exhibition of samizdat documents from eastern Europe. I did my best to inform delegates and the press of the latest Charter 77 documents. I attended the inaugural meeting of the newly formed International Helsinki Federation on Human Rights.

The official conference offered a renewed opportunity for a detailed and often highly polemical review of human rights performances, in which the Soviet Union and several other Communist states bore the brunt of criticism. Western delegates denounced the major trial of Chartists in Czechoslovakia, the Soviet invasion of Afghanistan, and the establishment of a state of war in Poland. The Soviet Union was thus placed on the defensive and found itself isolated, except for its bloc partners. After I left the conference continued, with long interruptions, for nearly three years of almost constant controversy and came to an end only in September 1983. After months of wrangling, it finally reached agreement on a concluding document representing a substantial development beyond the Helsinki Final Act. Concrete results included the decision to hold a further follow-up conference in Vienna in 1986, a conference on military security in Stockholm, and a number of meetings of experts, including one in Ottawa on human rights, sponsored by Canada.

Some observers concluded that Madrid had been a failure: it had no serious effect in promoting the observance of the human rights provisions of the Helsinki Final Act or in preventing severe reprisals against human rights advocates in the Soviet Union and Czechoslovakia. Others judged, however, that the widespread discussion of the violations of human rights in the Soviet bloc states had vindicated the principle that these matters were a matter of legitimate concern to all signatories. In view of its decisions concerning future meetings, the CSCE had emerged, it seemed to me, as a more or less permanent forum for discussion of the Helsinki obligations and had confirmed the legitimacy and importance of citizens' initiatives and monitors in the Soviet Union and in other Communist states.

CSCE: OTTAWA, 1985

During 1984-85 I was associated with a symposium on human rights and Canadian foreign policy initiated by Professors Robert O. Matthews and Cranford Pratt of the University of Toronto. A team of Canadian specialists on human rights held a series of meetings in Toronto.[6] During April, May, and June 1985, I went down to Ottawa from time to time to attend sessions of the conference, once again in the capacity of a journalist, attending briefings and press conferences and conducting interviews with the heads of the Soviet, American, British, and other delegations.[7] When in Toronto I kept in close touch with current developments by long telephone conversations with the Department of External Affairs. Harry Jay, the chief Canadian delegate, made himself available for several extensive interviews and gave me critical comments on my chapter.

Unlike the meetings in Belgrade and Madrid, the gathering in Ottawa devoted itself exclusively to human rights — something that the Western negotiators of the Final Act could not have foreseen in their most pleasant dreams or Soviet diplomats in their worst nightmares. The time in Ottawa was spent mainly in a polemical and somewhat one-sided discussion of the non-observance of human rights by the Soviet Union and by other Communist states. Despite strenuous effort on the part of neutral and non-aligned states to reconcile conflicting viewpoints between the two main camps, it was impossible to reach agreement on a concluding document. The conference ended without even the briefest communiqué to show after three months of work.

In Ottawa, as at Madrid, non-governmental and human rights organizations were active, holding press conferences, mounting demonstrations, and organizing "hearings" on human rights. The case of Andrei Sakharov, who had been interned in Gorky, was the subject of a widely attended press conference by two of his stepchildren, who also lobbied many delegations. Anatol Shcharansky's wife demonstrated outside the Soviet embassy on behalf of her husband and other imprisoned human rights monitors. As at Madrid, I made it a point to inform delegates of the views of dissidents, especially members of Charter 77. I also spoke on the Czechoslovak situation at meetings of the International Helsinki Federation and of the Czechoslovak Association of Canada.

Despite its failure to agree on anything, the conference put a spotlight on human rights as a proper subject of international diplomacy. The proposals of the two blocs for the final document showed clearly the unbridgeable chasm between democratic beliefs and Communist doctrine and the wide gap between the theory and the practice of the Soviet-bloc countries. In the end each bloc amalgamated its own proposals into a separate document. The Western text served as a kind of blueprint for follow-up conferences. Repeated discussion of human rights, though not widely publicized in the East or the West, certainly contributed to the ultimate collapse of Communism in eastern Europe several years later.

LOBBYING, BRIEFING, ADVOCACY

During the late 1970s and the 1980s I was active in human rights activities, lobbying the Canadian and U.S. governments in support of Charter 77 and human rights in eastern Europe and presenting the case of the dissidents in various public forums. I sought to influence Canadian policy directly by writing several long letters to successive ministers of external affairs — Mitchell Sharp and Don Jamieson. I also kept in close touch with the departmental officials who were responsible for the CSCE and eastern Europe. On several occasions (July 1980, April 1985, and October 1987) I gave testimony on human rights in Czechoslovakia before the Subcommittee on Human Rights of the parliamentary Committee on External Affairs and Defence. In February 1985 I took part, with other specialists, in an all-day briefing for Joe Clark, then minister of external affairs, prior to his official visit to the Soviet Union. Several times newly appointed Canadian ambassadors to Prague, such as David Peel, in 1981, Terry Bacon, in 1984, and Barry Mawhinney, in 1987, visited me in Toronto before proceeding to their posts.

In April 1979 the U.S. State Department invited me, along with four or five other specialists on Czechoslovakia, to take part in an all-day briefing of the newly appointed U.S. ambassador to Prague, Francis Meehan. There was a repeat performance in November 1983 for his successor, Bill Luers and his wife, Wendy. Both of them were keen to establish contact with the dissidents. During their tenure in Prague they were in fact of great help to independent Czech and Slovak intellectuals. In April 1981, at the State Department's Foreign Service Institute, I gave a talk to foreign service officers who had been posted to Prague and other eastern European capitals. During these visits to Washington I visited the State Department's Bureau of Human Rights and its Soviet and East European divisions, where former students of mine at Dartmouth held several of the highest posts. I also often visited the joint (administration-Congress) Commission on Security and Cooperation in Europe (CSCE) in Washington, DC. In 1980 I had long interviews with Max Kampelman, head of the U.S. delegation to Madrid, and Spencer Oliver, director of the U.S. CSCE. Several times I gave testimony on the situation in Czechoslovakia and eastern Europe before the public hearings of the CSCE in Washington. In New York City, I kept in touch with people involved in human rights support, especially at the Helsinki Watch Committee, the International League for Human Rights, and Freedom House. In February 1982 the Ford Foundation, which had been funding the Helsinki Watch Committee, asked me to make recommendations for its financial support of human rights in eastern Europe. In a detailed report I proposed an alternative strategy, one that emphasized direct assistance to human rights activists in those countries and to the Czechoslovak, Polish, and other organizations outside those countries that were supporting the people at home. In August 1984 I was the guest of Random House, whose director, Robert Bernstein, was chairman of the Helsinki Watch Committee, to brief him prior to a visit to Czechoslovakia.

I used every opportunity to publicize the plight of Chartists and other dissidents in newspaper articles and occasional broadcasts to Czechoslovakia on Radio Canada International, Radio Free Europe, the BBC, and Voice of America. When leading Chartists, including Benda, Dienstbier, and Havel, were tried and received long prison sentences in October 1979, I wrote an article about the matter in *Queen's Quarterly* and was able to distribute it to delegates to the Madrid conference in November and December 1980.[8] A year later, a number of leading Chartists, including my close friends Jiřina Šiklová and Milan Šimečka, were arrested and charged with treason. The *Toronto Star*, using materials that I provided, published a full page about the victims, with their pictures. I also published a letter on this event in the *New York Times* in August 1981. Then came the sensational news that Josef Hodic had returned to Prague and revealed himself to be an agent of the Czechoslovak security police. I had had several meetings with him in Vienna and also, alas, acknowledged his help in the preface of my book on Charter 77. In an article in the *Toronto Star* published with the lurid title, "Communist Master Spy Comes in from Cold," I described the serious effect that this defection would have on dissidents at home and their supporters abroad, with whom Hodic had been in close touch.[9] The continued detention and interrogation of "Šiklová and company" seemed to point toward a major trial, in which the accused would receive long sentences. It was a great relief when, for reasons that remained obscure, they were released from prison, without trial, in the first half of 1982.

GALVANIZING THE ROYAL SOCIETY

Soon after becoming a fellow of the Royal Society of Canada (FRSC), I urged formation of a Committee on Freedom of Science and Scholarship to advise the society on infringements of scientific freedom throughout the world. It took several years of steady pressure on the society's elected organs to overcome a general lack of interest in human rights and the open opposition to my idea from some members. Finally, in December 1981, the committee was approved, and I became its first chair. There followed a long struggle to define our terms of reference. In the end we were not authorized to issue our own statements. However, successive presidents of the society were more than willing to issue statements in their own names, protesting the persecution of people such as Sakharov and Shcharansky in the Soviet Union, the mathematician Professor Masserra in Uruguay, and, as noted above, Polish scholars imprisoned after 1981. Later we prepared special reports on human rights abuses in Chile, Iran, and South Africa, and circulated them to fellows. In May 1984 I organized a special panel on freedom of science and scholarship on a global scale at the society's annual meeting in Guelph, Ontario.

In 1985, at my request, CSCE Ambassador Jay received the president of the Royal Society of Canada, Alexander MacKay, who presented him with our committee's proposal of a CSCE conference on freedom of science and scholarship. Jay did not think that this proposal was suitable for the Ottawa meeting but urged that we present it to the next follow-up conference in Vienna. Ambassador William Bauer, head of the Canadian delegation in Vienna, warmly welcomed our idea and incorporated some features of it in an official Canadian resolution, which was in turn accepted by the entire NATO group. Although this NATO document did not include our idea of a scientific forum, it did emphasize the need to respect scientific freedom and for direct contacts between scientists. The Vienna conference document, accepted by all countries, recognized the need for unimpeded communications and personal contacts among scientists throughout the world.

In 1987, when my tenure as chairman of the committee ended, my place was taken by the human rights expert Justice Walter Tarnopolsky, of the Supreme Court of Ontario, who had given me great support in the struggle to get the committee established and in its subsequent activity. I continued to serve on the committee for some years, and helped to plan an international conference on Freedom of Science and Scholarship, which took place in 1991.

SPREADING THE WORD

I kept in close touch with Vilém Prečan, regularly exchanging long letters and meeting him at every available opportunity. One of his greatest concerns was to secure the publication abroad of Charter 77 documents and other materials produced by independent writers in the homeland. I supported his efforts to find publishers for major samizdat books but had little success. For a time I hoped that the Centre for Russian and East European Studies in Toronto might publish the Charter 77 news bulletin, *Informace* (*Infoch*), and I sounded out the Ford Foundation regarding financial assistance. In the end we had to give up the idea for lack of funds and of translators. We had to be satisfied with the publication of selected documents by the CSCE in Washington and Freedom House in New York City, and provided them with translations of important materials. Prečan and I edited a special issue of the *International Journal of Politics* (1981), a collection of essays on politics by Rudolf Battěk, Miroslav Kusý, Jan Patočka, Petr Pithart, Milan Šimečka, and others.[10] We were happy to be able to send honoraria to all the authors.

We were particularly anxious to publish the work of independent historians, whose samizdat writings were challenging Communist distortions of Czech and Slovak history and searching for historical truth. Prečan had documented the rise of this independent historiography in his *Acta Creationis*. In a long review of this work in the *Canadian Slavonic Papers*, which I dedicated to Prečan on his 50th birthday, I analysed this remarkable revival of history. I wrote another study on this theme, "The Muse of History — 1984," which appeared in the cultural journal *Cross Currents*; it was reprinted in a Polish samizdat journal, *Czas*. Together Prečan and I edited a special issue of *Kosmas*, containing samizdat essays in history by Havel, Kusý, Pithart, Šimečka, and others. I brought this up to date in a brief article in *Kosmas* in 1987. I had become fascinated by samizdat as a general phenomenon throughout central and eastern Europe and gave a paper on this theme in 1981 in Halifax, at the annual meeting of the Royal Society of Canada.[11]

I became involved in several enterprises that sought to give financial support to Czechoslovak scholarship at home and abroad. One was modelled on the Jan Hus Fund, in Britain, which had been very successful at raising money for individuals and groups engaged in research or writing in Czechoslovakia, and in sending philosophers to speak at living-room seminars. In 1982, Charles Taylor, the McGill University philosopher, Paul Wilson, the translator of Czech materials, and I joined forces with several Americans to found a counterpart organization in the United States. The following year, with Josef and Zdena Škvorecký, Gleb and Lilit Žekulin, and others, we formed a Canadian Hus Fund. For the next four years we raised money and gave stipends to Czechs and Slovaks. We cooperated closely with the British Hus Fund and I attended several of its meetings during visits to that country.[12]

Another kind of aid was offered by the Sixty-Eight Publishers, organized in Toronto in 1977 by Josef and Zdena Škvorecký. Over the next 15 years Sixty-Eight published several hundred works by writers at home or in exile. This helped Czech and Slovak culture to survive at a time when it was under siege at home. I served as president but my duties were largely honorary and I presided over our annual meetings.

For some years the Masaryk Trust had been giving grants to support publications by and about T.G. Masaryk. It was headed by my old Czech friend René Wellek, of Yale University, now a distinguished scholar in comparative literature; its secretary was Professor George Gibian, of Cornell University, a specialist in Czech and Russian literature. I joined this group in 1983 and attended its annual meetings in New Haven, New York, Washington, and Toronto.

TRAVEL IN JAPAN, ENGLAND AND GERMANY

In 1982 Sally and I spent three months in Japan as the guests of the Japanese Society for the Promotion of Science. It was a complete change of scene for us and a fascinating introduction to the complex and confusing politics and culture of Japan, with its fusion of the deeply traditional with the strikingly modern. Our hosts were Professor Hiroshi Kimura, a specialist on Soviet politics at the Slavic Centre of the University of Sapporo, and Professor Osamu Nakanishi, of Soka University, near Tokyo, who hoped to publish our book on interest groups in Japanese. Gen Kikkawa, my former student, now a professor at Shudo University near Hiroshima, was very helpful behind the scenes in planning our stay.

We spent the first six weeks at the University of Sapporo, on the northern island of Hokkaido. The only Slavic centre in the country, it had the strongest Slavic library, with 30,000 volumes. There were six professors — specialists on Russian history and literature, Soviet politics and economics, and Poland. We enjoyed the company of a young graduate student in law, Yutaka Akino; passionately interested in Czechoslovakia, he had learned Czech and studied at SSEES under Hugh Seton-Watson. I spent most of my time working on a concluding chapter for the Japanese translation of our book, but I also gave a seminar on the Polish and Czech interrupted revolutions and did six broadcasts on Japan and Slavic studies for Radio Canada International. At the end of our stay in Hokkaido, a meeting of the Japanese Association of Soviet and East European Studies brought Slavic specialists from all over Japan. The sessions were almost exclusively in Japanese, except for a lecture by Norman Davies of SSEES on Poland, and one by me on samizdat in eastern Europe. Among the participants was another Czechophile, Tadayuki Hayashi, a specialist in history and politics, who had spent two years in Prague.

During our stay in Tokyo we enjoyed comfortable quarters in the beautifully designed International House, set in a secluded garden. We drank in the beauty and antiquity of Japan and visited the ancient capitals of Kyoto and Nara. We enjoyed five weeks there with our son, Peter, our first reunion for three years. Professor Nakanishi welcomed me warmly to Soka University, where I gave a seminar and lecture. Although he knew some English, he insisted on talking with me in Russian — "our professional language," as he called it. He talked endlessly of his plans for the publication of our book — it eventually appeared in truncated form, with an introduction by him, and comprised only three chapters of the original and the new conclusion I had written in Sapporo.

We found, to our surprise, that in Japan we were still close to the Communist world, not only geographically but also through constant discussion of events with Japanese and with Western visitors. There was much talk of the Polish crisis with Norman Davies and with Yoshia Umeda, a young Japanese who had lived in Poland for some years and was then acting as a representative of Solidarity. Zdeněk Mlynář and his wife, Irina, were also in Japan and we heard our old friend give a lecture on the Prague Spring and the Polish events. Like other listeners there, we came away with the impression that he had not shaken free of his belief in the possible reform of Communism. At one meeting of the East European Association, where I gave a seminar on Czechoslovak political culture, I was astonished to learn that all of the 20 or more students present were specializing in particular countries of eastern Europe and had learned the appropriate languages. At least eight or ten of them were working on Czechoslovakia. At the invitation of Professor Osamu Hirai of Osaka University I later gave a seminar on Soviet and eastern European studies in the West at the nearby Ryukoku University and lectures at his university on the "two interrupted revolutions" and on interest groups.

We then proceeded by the world-famous "bullet train" to Hiroshima, to visit Gen and his wife, Yumiko. I spoke to one of his classes on human rights in the Soviet Union and eastern Europe, translated at intervals by Gen. In Hiroshima we experienced vicariously the horrors of the atomic bomb attack in the Memorial Peace Park, with its museum, and through conversations with survivors. Some Japanese, especially those in the peace movement, gave the highest priority to the struggle for peace and nuclear disarmament. At a small seminar on "Human Rights and Peace" at the Institute of Peace Studies I made an effort to place the "right to life" in the context of human rights in general, emphasizing the need to strive equally for all these principles. Back home in Toronto I pursued this theme of the indivisibility of peace and human rights, most notably in my address upon receiving an honorary degree at the University. (The text was published in a Czech samizdat journal.) Years later, in 1988, Gen invited me to return to Japan to speak at a meeting of the Japanese Peace Association on "Socialism, Human Rights, and Peace." I argued that there were certain features of real socialism — notably the absence of democratic procedures and human rights — that made the Soviet Union prone to aggression and the conduct of war. I cited a number of Charter 77 and CSCE documents to elaborate the view that human rights were a condition of peace.

In the summer of 1983 we made a nostalgic visit to England, this time to attend a reunion of Rhodes Scholars in Oxford and a conference at SSEES, my old "School" in London, on central and east European history, in honour of the retirement of Hugh Seton-Watson, the son of my own thesis supervisor. In Oxford we stayed in my old college, Christ Church, and attended a garden party for the Queen and the Duke of Edinburgh at Rhodes House. We paid a visit to my cousin Jack, and his wife, Marjorie, in a small town in Norfolk, and met friends such as Dorothy Galton, the former secretary of SSEES, who lived nearby. In London we were bombarded by memories of SSEES days and of our time as students in Bloomsbury. We made a sort of pilgrimage to Brighton, where my parents had once lived, and I visited Lord Longford, my former tutor at Christ Church, who pumped me with questions about Czechoslovakia.

At the SSEES conference I gave a paper on historical writings in samizdat in Czechoslovakia. It was well received by British and American scholars there, and some of the eastern European historians, especially the Hungarians. However, the one Czech scholar present, Miroslav Hroch, of Charles University, protested against what he called my "political manifesto"; in criticizing official historiography I had insulted his colleagues, who, like him, were still working in the universities and institutes. As a result of Hroch's intervention and later conversations in Prague, I added a reference to the fact that some good work was being done by "official" historians.

After Sally's return to Canada I travelled to Germany for a week with Prečan in Hannover, West Germany. We had the usual strenuous days of talk interspersed with occasional outings into the beautiful countryside of Lower Saxony. Prečan had prepared an extensive documentation of human rights violations and dissident activities, which was circulated to the delegates at the Madrid conference. The Prečans' small apartment was crammed with samizdat material and with books and magazines in English, French, and German, to be shipped home to dissidents in Czechoslovakia. He had developed an effective system of smuggling materials in and out of Czechoslovakia, mainly through German diplomatic channels. Vilém was constantly on the phone with people in Czechoslovakia, including Václav Havel, who had been released from prison in April. When Prečan mentioned to him my praise for something that Havel had written, the author was moved almost to tears — a reaction that he explained was part of the post-prison syndrome he was still labouring under. Havel expressed warm appreciation of what Prečan was doing to support the people at home, and he congratulated me on my books on 1968 and on Charter 77.

CONFERENCES AND MORE CONFERENCES

Our lives seemed to consist of a constant succession of scholarly conferences. In 1982 Sally and I had flown out to Honolulu for a Pacific conference of the AAASS, where I gave a paper on Poland. On the return journey we stopped in Vancouver for a major address that I gave on Poland at the Vancouver Institute. In 1983 I took part in a conference in Bloomington, Indiana, on media and communications in eastern Europe, where I gave a paper on "independent communications" in Communist countries. In 1984 we both went to Cambridge, Massachusetts, for a conference on Poland at Harvard University. I gave the opening address on the crisis in eastern Europe. Shortly afterward, on our way to Prague, we stopped over in Bonn for a meeting on Soviet foreign policy, where I gave a report on the role of dissidents in foreign policy questions. In November I presented a paper on independent activities in eastern Europe at a meeting of the AAASS in New York. In July 1985 Sally and I went together to the meeting of the International Political Science Association (IPSA) in Paris, where I spoke on the Helsinki process. Our son Peter joined us in Paris and returned home with us to Toronto. In November of the same year we attended the International Congress of Soviet and East European Studies in Washington, DC.

In March 1985 I went alone to an IPSA conference on "Interests and Politics" in Zagreb. I restated my theory of conflict among interest groups in Communist systems, modified in light of the experience of Czechoslovakia and Poland in 1968 and 1980, respectively, and the development of the dissent movement in the 1970s. The flowering of dissent and independent activity went far beyond "primitive" interest group articulation and represented a limited pluralization of the authoritarian systems. My analysis was welcomed by Jerzy Wiatr, a political scientist whom I had met in Poland, and by William Smirnov, a young, open-minded Russian political scientist, from the University of Moscow. Both, however, thought that I had neglected the growing amount of legitimate articulation of interests by organized groupings in their countries. I made a special trip to the beautiful city of Dubrovnik on the Adriatic to see the radical dissident Mihailo Markovic.

In early 1986 I took part in a conference at the University of Michigan on "Politics and the Intellectuals in Central Europe"; it was attended by a number of eastern European intellectuals, among them Danilo Kiš, György Konrád, Czesław Miłosz, and Tomas Venclova. Miłosz generated a lively debate by expounding his view that central Europe constituted a distinctive cultural and historical entity; its common features were exhibited in its literature and its architecture. In the discussion I expressed some doubt as to whether his thesis did not exaggerate the degree of unity, and I noted the deep conflicts within and between these states. I also felt that it was difficult to draw a sharp line between central and eastern Europe and wrong to exclude such states as Romania and Bulgaria, or even western Soviet Russia from the former category.

Later that year I suddenly required a heart bypass operation and was compelled to forego a conference on Masaryk in England, attended by leading Masaryk specialists from Europe and North America. Prior to the meeting, Prečan and I had urged the organizer, Robert Pynsent, a Czech specialist at my old "School" in London, to extend invitations to some of the dissident historians. He strongly opposed this suggestion and insisted on inviting only official historians. In the end none even of the latter got permission to come. Prečan helped to set the record straight by preparing and distributing at the conclave a booklet that contained a summary of articles from a samizdat symposium on Masaryk. The only guests from Prague were the sisters, Anna and Herberta Masaryk, granddaughters of Tomáš.

At the meeting Pynsent denigrated the quality of samizdat writing and of the work of the dissidents. Two years earlier he and Professor K. Brušak, a Czech literary specialist at Cambridge University, had written a joint letter to *The Times* ridiculing the award of the Nobel prize in literature to Jaroslav Seifert as "a reward for mediocrity." Outraged, I had written to the *Globe and Mail* (10 November 1984) justifying the award to a great Czech poet.

Two important conferences in 1987 and 1989 were the National Association of Soviet and East European Studies (NASEES), which met in Cambridge, England, and the Freedom Society conference in New York City; for both I spoke on the independent or parallel society in eastern Europe. In the winter of 1987-88 I went to New York for several meetings of the East-West Project, sponsored by the Seagram Corporation under the chairmanship of Edgar Bronfman, head of the World Jewish Congress.[13] After some initial hesitation because of the sponsor — the U.S. Central Intelligence Agency (CIA) — I accepted an invitation to attend a conference in Washington on eastern Europe. I gave a report on dissent in Czechoslovakia before an audience of U.S. intelligence officers and diplomats, including the newly appointed ambassador to Prague, Shirley Temple Black.

MASARYK AND CZECH HISTORY

For many years my work concentrated on contemporary questions in central Europe, but I had longed to escape from Communist studies and to return to my first love, history. During the 1970s and early 1980s I planned to prepare, with my colleague Andrew Rossos, a volume on Czech politics from 1848 to the present, and I did a good deal of preparatory reading. But both of us became involved in other pressing lines of research — in my case, on 1968 and Charter 77, and in his case, on the Macedonian question — so that we were not able to pursue our plan.

My predilection for Czech history was stimulated anew by the revival of interest, at home and abroad, in T.G. Masaryk. There had been, for instance, two-large scale symposia on him, one published abroad, and the other in samizdat. My first step in this direction was a long article in which I reviewed the two symposia and other books on Masaryk.[14] Meanwhile, in anticipation of further research, I sought out his writings and material about him whenever I visited libraries in North America or Europe, and built up a large collection of "Masarykiana." Between 1989 and 1992 I published a number of articles and most of these came to be included in a later book on Masaryk.

In the spring of 1988 Sally and I spent six weeks at Indiana University in Bloomington, where, at the initiative of my friend Bob Byrnes of the History Department, I was appointed a visiting scholar at the Institute of Advanced Studies. Bob had also nominated me to give the Patton Lecture Series, and I put in a good deal of work preparing six lectures on Czech history from 1848 to the present. His proposal was not, however, accepted by the lecture committee. Hence, apart from several classroom and public lectures, my time was free for research on Masaryk and Czech history. At a luncheon meeting of the Midwest Slavic Conference, I gave a talk entitled "Lions and Foxes" (borrowing Masaryk's own terms in his Česká *ofzka* [The Czech Question]), on Czech and Slovak leadership from Masaryk to the present. I gave another university address on "An Independent Society in Central and Eastern Europe," which I repeated at the University of Illinois in Urbana and at the Hudson Institute in Indianapolis. We made a nostalgic return to Wisconsin, where we visited several old friends, including Merle Curti, and I gave a lecture in the Department of Political Science, where I had been a professor over 40 years earlier.

I took another dip into history in the autumn of 1988 by initiating a conference in Toronto to honour the 70th anniversary of the founding of the Czechoslovak republic. I bore the main burden of organizing the meeting and editing the resulting volume.[15] The conference brought together outstanding specialists from Canada, the United

States, Britain and continental Europe and attracted capacity audiences. Each chapter sought to analyse a single theme — for example, the German question, or the Slovak question — throughout the entire 70 years. Without embellishing the record under the republic or denigrating it under Communist rule, we tried to present an objective account of the achievements and failures of the period. In my introductory chapter, a new version of my "Lions and Foxes," I argued that most of the Czech and Slovak leaders, non-Communist as well as Communist, had shown themselves to be foxes, rather than lions — lackeys rather than heroes, in Masaryk's terms. Only Masaryk had shown the qualities of leadership necessary to establish and preserve independence. In my conclusion, added in 1990, I described Havel as a leader of intellect and courage in the mould of Masaryk. The 1988 conference received a letter of greeting from Charter 77 and replied with a message of solidarity to a similar anniversary symposium planned in Prague. When that assembly was broken up by the police I addressed a letter of protest to Ladislav Adamec, the Czechoslovak Prime Minister and included it in an appendix of our book.

I also made a return to my own past, when Sixty-Eight Publishers published a Czech translation of my *Letters from Prague, 1937-1940*, which had appeared in abridged form in English in *Kosmas*. It came to the attention of Václav Havel, who published it in his samizdat series Expedice in 1986. A copy of this book, with a personal dedication by Havel, became one of my most treasured possessions.[16]

HONOURS AND ANNIVERSARIES

In 1981 I had ceased teaching entirely, and a year later I was appointed to the rank of "professor emeritus." Honours followed in rapid succession: in 1981 the Innis-Gérin Medal from the Royal Society of Canada and life membership of the Canadian Association of Slavists (CAS), and in the Czechoslovak Society of Science and Art (SVU). In 1982, in Ottawa, the CAS held a joint session with the Canadian Political Science Association (CPSA) in my honour, with a panel on the theme of "Human Rights — International and Eastern Europe," chaired by my former student Bohdan Harasymiw, and including Frank Griffiths, Stefania Miller (another former student), Josef Škvorecký, and Walter Tarnopolsky. There followed in 1985 the Masaryk Award from the Czechoslovak Association of Canada. In 1981 I was elected a member of the board of the American Association for the Advancement of Slavic Studies (AAASS) for a three-year term, and six years later I received the association's "award for distinguished contributions to Slavic studies." In 1989, as luck would have it, I was nominated for the presidency, together with my close friend, Bob Tucker, of Princeton University. Neither of us was happy about running against one another. When Tucker was elected I thought that he fully deserved the honour, and was glad to be spared the immense and time-consuming burden.

In November 1982 the University of Toronto awarded me an honorary degree — the LL.D. — on the nomination of Gleb Žekulín, then director of CREES, who read the citation at the ceremony. The following year my colleague Susan Solomon organized a Festschrift in my honour, published under the title *Pluralism in the Soviet Union*, with contributions from Susan and other Soviet specialists, such as Fred Barghoorn, Archie Brown, Włodek Brus, John Hazard, and Jerry Hough.[17] Susan presented a copy of the volume at a meeting of the centre held on the 20th anniversary of its founding. It was, of course, a great honour, but I was disappointed when contributions by some good Czech friends and others, Vladimir Kusin, Zdeněk Mlynář, Vilém Prečan, and Richard Löwenthal, were not included.

1987 was a year of anniversaries. On my 75th birthday Charter 77 sent a warm message of greeting, and the Czech paper *Listy* (February 1987) published articles on my life by Vilém Prečan and Milan Šimečka. The next year, when Sally caught up with me, there was a flood of telegrams and cards from abroad, and some wonderful parties in Toronto. Then there was our 50th wedding anniversary, which we celebrated not only in Prague with our Charter friends, but also with friends and relatives in England, with the Prečans in Scheinfeld, with friends in Toronto, and with Sally's sister Tacy and the families of her two sons in Pennsylvania.

Our own sons continued to live at a distance, but we were able to join them from time to time — once in British Columbia, and once in Thailand. In 1980-81 Dave's "girlfriend in Montana," Joan, moved with her four children to East Sooke, where Dave was living, and they married soon afterward. We acquired four "instant grandchildren," Jean, Joe, Amelia and Ben. In 1985 Dave gave up planting trees in favour of a more settled job in real estate and moved to Victoria. Peter, after working for several years in what was called the "orderly departure program," which processed Vietnamese refugees entitled under American law to go to the U.S., decided in 1985 to devote himself

Honorary Degree, University of Toronto, November 1982, with
President James Ham and Chancellor George Ignatieff

entirely to research. Sally and I supplemented his small grant from the
Pali Text Society in England by regular payments from what we jokingly called the Fund for Assistance to Indigenous Scholars of the
Name of Skilling (for short, *Faisons* — "let's do it"). In August 1988
he witnessed the violent suppression of massive demonstrations in
Burma and wrote several articles for the *Bangkok Post*, illustrated with
his own photographs; he became a vigorous advocate of Burmese freedom.

Sally led a busy life at home, looking after the household and the
budget (including the income tax). It must have tried her patience to
endure my constant preoccupation with research and other scholarly
activities, but it was a pleasure for us both when we travelled together.
We were on the whole blessed with good health and did not feel as old
as the calendar said, although aches and pains, fatigue, and the deaths
of people we knew, kept reminding us of the passing years. In 1986 I
survived a by-pass operation, but more serious was Sally's stroke in the
autumn of 1988, which left her somewhat handicapped. In February
1988 we had moved from our old house on Cheritan Avenue into a
condominium on Sylvan Valleyway, which we were able to enjoy for all
too brief a time before Sally's death.

NOTES

1. Skilling, "Two Interrupted Revolutions," in J.L. Black and J.W. Strong, *Sisyphus and Poland: Reflections on Martial Law* (Winnipeg: Ronald P. Frye, 1986), 65-82.
2. "The Silent Canadian," *Graduate* 9, no. 4 (March-April 1982): 4-5.
3. We were unable to interest a Canadian publisher in the book, so it was eventually published independently by the Centre for International Studies in Toronto. See Robert Spencer, ed., *Canada and the Conference on Security and Co-operation in Europe* (CIS, University of Toronto, 1984), 283-307, 308-48. See also my "Belgrade and Human Rights: Success or Failure?" *International Perspectives* (July-Aug. 1978): 19-22; "CSCE in Madrid," *Problems of Communism* 30, no. 4 (July-Aug. 1981): l-16. For the chapter on Belgrade, the Department of External Affairs gave me highly unusual access to the departmental archives, normally not available for at least 20 years. The chapter on Madrid I based largely on my attendance at the opening stage of the Madrid conference. These sources were supplemented by departmental briefings in Ottawa for non-governmental and human rights organizations before and after each conference. I also had several long interviews with Louis Rogers, head of the Canadian delegation in Madrid, who later gave me detailed comments on the draft of my chapter.
4. "Czechoslovak Political Culture: Pluralism in an International Context," in A.H. Brown, ed., *Political Culture and Communist Studies* (London: Macmillan, 1984), 115-33.
5. *Toronto Star,* 7 Sept. 1980 and 21 Jan. 1981; *Sunday Star,* 23 Nov. 1980 and 7 Dec. 1980; *Globe and Mail,* 17 Aug. and 14 Feb. 1981.
6. A final two-day conference took place in 1986. These papers were published in book form: Robert O. Matthews and Cranford Pratt, eds., *Human Rights in Canadian Foreign Policy* (Montreal: McGill-Queen's University Press, 1988). My contributions were chapters dealing with the Ottawa Conference in 1985 (283-307), and evaluating the Helsinki process as a whole (308-48).
7. See *Sunday Star,* 23 June 1985.
8. "Czechoslovakia on Trial," *Queen's Quarterly* 87, no. 3

(autumn 1980): 387-96. This was also published in 1980 in garbled form in a journal called *Phoenix*, published in Texas.

9. *Toronto Star*, 16 Aug. 1981; *New York Times*, 17 Aug. 1981.

10. "Parallel Politics: Essays from Czech and Slovak Samizdat," *International Journal of Politics* 2, no. 1 (spring 1981).

11. "Independent Historiography in Czechoslovakia," *Canadian Slavonic Papers* 25, no. 3 (Dec. 1983): 518-39, later republished in the Czech samizdat journal *Kritický sborník* (1985). "The Muse of History — 1984, History, Historians and Politics in Communist Czechoslovakia," *Cross Currents: A Yearbook of Central European Culture* 3 (1984): 29-47; *Czas* (winter 1987-88): 213-18; "Real Socialism in Czechoslovakia and the Search for Historical Truth," *Kosmas*, nos. 3/4 (winter 1984); nos. 1/2 (summer 1985): 1-7. "Czech and Slovak Independent Historical Writing, 1985-1987," *Kosmas* 7, nos. 1/2 (summer 1987/winter 1988): 213-18; *Transactions of the Royal Society of Canada, 1981* (Ottawa, 1982): 51-66.

12. Barbara Day. *The Velvet Philosophers* (London, Claridge Press, 1999). Also in Czech.

13. My paper on Czechoslovak politics was published in William Griffith, ed., *Central and Eastern Europe: The Opening Curtain?* (Boulder, CO, Westview Press: 1988).

14. "The Rediscovery of Masaryk," *Cross Currents* (Ann Arbor, MI, 1983): 87-114.

15. Skilling, ed., *Czechoslovakia, 1918-1988: Seventy Years from Independence* (London: Macmillan, 1991).

16. See Skilling, *Listy z Prahy* (Toronto: Sixty-Eight Publishers, 1988), published under the same title in samizdat in 1986. It was translated by Eva Šimečková in Bratislava and edited by Jiřína Šiklová and Petr Pithart. See also, "Letters from Prague, 1937," *Kosmas* 1, no. 2 (winter 1982): 63-73; "Letters from Prague, 1938," *ibid.* 2, no. 1 (summer 1983): 85-97; "Letters from Prague, 1939," *ibid.* 2, no. 2 (winter 1983): 87-89. I began a new series, "Journeys to Prague (Czechoslovakia)," which were detailed reports of my trips to Czechoslovakia from 1948 to 1968. *Kosmas* 5, no. 1 (1986): 139-56; *ibid.* 6, no. 1 (summer 1987): 127-43; *ibid.* 7, nos. 1 and 2 (summer-winter 1988): 219-38; and *Kosmas: Czechoslovak and Central European Journal* (new title of *Kosmas*), 8, nos. 1 and 2 (1989): 136-67.

17. Susan Solomon, ed., *Pluralism in the Soviet Union, Essays in Honour of H. Gordon Skilling* (London: Macmillan, 1983).

18

AN EMERGING CIVIL SOCIETY:
VÁCLAV HAVEL

ONCE I HAD COMPLETED MY BOOK on Charter 77 in 1981, I felt a little fearful that I had written a kind of obituary for a movement that was not likely to survive. In spite of repeated crises, however, it did not die, and in fact it became a catalyst for ever more independent writing and activity. I began to think that I should write something — perhaps a long article — which would bring things up to date and, above all, that I should return to Czechoslovakia to see with my own eyes what was happening in the human rights movement. This I did, with Sally, in 1984 and 1987.

PRAGUE, 1984

Six years had passed since my encounter with the police in Bratislava in 1978, and in the intervening years I had been actively and publicly engaged against the Czechoslovak regime. We were not at all sure that we would receive visas and be able to carry out our plans without harassment. It was encouraging to receive from Canadian Ambassador David Peel, whom I had met before his going to Prague, an official invitation to go to Czechoslovakia as his guests and to stay with him in the official residence. This did not guarantee us visas, he warned, but in fact we secured them from Montreal in just six days. As guests we had a kind of official status, which afforded us some protection against harassment by police. Of course, we could not exclude the possibility of some kind of provocation or scandal designed to discredit the Chartists or endanger our non-Communist friends.

As in the past, Vilém Prečan informed a few people in Prague of my forthcoming visit and forwarded messages to me from Jiřina Šiklová, telling me of meetings arranged with coded instructions as to times and places. He also sent us an invitation from Václav Havel to visit him in Hrádeček, his home in the country. Prečan took a three-

and-a-half-hour trip by train so as to spend three hours with us during a stopover in Frankfurt on our way to Prague. Through his secret channels and through Canada's Department of External Affairs we were able to send books and papers to Prague, some reaching us within days of our arrival. We could not be sure that these arrangements might not be interrupted forcefully by the police or that we might not be expelled from the country. In fact, however, apart from some missed appointments, usually resulting from misunderstandings, everything went smoothly. I was able to meet with close friends just released from prison for Charter activities, writers and independent historians, religious Chartists, leaders of the famous Jazz Section — and the highlight — Václav Havel at Hrádeček.

We lived a kind of triple life in Prague. First, on the diplomatic level, we lived in Hadovka, the residence, a lovely building in a strange English gothic style, with a very large garden. We lived in a self-contained apartment with its own entrance, which gave us a sense of security; we were insured against night visits by the police and could keep our documents and notes safely. The Peels often invited us upstairs for drinks or a meal but did not interfere with our lives. They took us on several excursions through the countryside to Bílá hora, Lány, and Lidice and to the Castle of Křivoklát. On one occasion we drove to the mill and studio of the artist Ota Janeček, in southern Bohemia, where we had the chance to look at his paintings and buy several of them.

On 1 July some 500 Czech guests came to the embassy to the Canada Day reception, among them Ivan Havel, Václav's brother, a computer scientist and mathematician, Petr Pithart, and many other old dissident friends. Peel asked me to speak on the dissident scene to his fellow diplomats — once, to some of the ambassadors of the NATO countries, and another time, to political affairs officers of Western embassies. It seemed strange to talk on this subject to diplomats who had been in the country for several years, but they often knew little about what was going on below the official level.

We were warmly welcomed by the American ambassador Bill Luers, and his wife, Wendy, whom we had helped to brief in Washington. He had already established contacts with writers and scholars and often invited them to meet visiting American intellectuals. When the historian Arthur Schlesinger, Jr, visited Prague, Luers included me in a luncheon with a small group of leading Czech historians. Schlesinger presented a cyclical interpretation of American politics, which must have surprised people accustomed to a strictly Marxist view, but few were bold enough to make comments. Luers himself could not easily meet dissidents, but several of his officers were assigned to keep in touch with them. On one occasion we went to the residence of a young American diplomat to listen to a jazz group — the Blues Berries, who played in the garden before an audience of about a hundred Czechs. Several other diplomats, including two Canadian officers, knew the dissidents well and gave them much moral support.

There was also the second, scholarly level of my life in Prague. At first, in order to avoid stirring suspicions among the authorities, I devoted most of my time to research in the National Library in the Klementinum, where I was permitted to use the professors' reading room. I had a good deal of material copied on the one Xerox machine available, but in the end they ran out of paper and could do no more for me. I found that the main card catalogue had no entries under the name of T.G. Masaryk, the greatest figure in modern Czechoslovak history! All his works had been removed to special closed collections, and I was unable to secure access to them. On my last day in Prague I discovered that many of his works were listed in the catalogue in the library of the Institute of Marxism-Leninism (which also listed my books on the interrupted revolution and on Charter 77).

The most important level of life for me was the dissident one, the life of the Charter 77 activists and others who were trying to lead independent lives after expulsion from their professional work. I tried to keep my activities *sub rosa,* using public telephone booths outside the embassy to make appointments. I had some 30 to 40 meetings, occasionally in private homes, but more usually in a number of favourite spots, such as the Vltava *quai* near the library. Another handy place was the snack bar of the library, where Markéta Němcová, a young dissident, worked behind the counter and willingly passed on messages and arranged rendezvous. As far as I knew I was not kept under surveillance by the police.

Sally and I were depressed by the decay of the old city we loved so much. Some buildings looked beautiful after renovation, but there were scaffoldings everywhere. We found some places disgustingly dirty — for example, the toilets at Charles University — and, in Soviet style, there were piles of debris in streets and courtyards. The new metro was very efficient and made communication much easier, but it was still under construction. We had the impression of almost total stagnation in all fields of life. There had been no political changes since 1969. The economy was in bad shape, although it assured people at least enough

With Jiřina Šiklová and Milan Šimečka in Prague, 1984

to live on. Culture had been badly harmed by censorship and propaganda. The truth about history was concealed or distorted. For instance, most traces of Masaryk had been removed. However, his monument still stood in the Pantheon in the National Museum, and we were surprised to see a new plaque in his honour in the foyer of the National Theatre.

We had a reunion in Prague, in the apartment of Lisa Rudinger, with our close friends Jiřina Šiklová and Milan Šimečka, not long out of jail. Both had expected to spend many years in prison and did not know why they had been released, without trial. Who knows? they asked. Perhaps it was because of pressure from abroad and the regime's desire to make a good impression on the Madrid conference. In prison they had been confined in cells with common criminals, who regarded them as heroes. When they returned to work after their release, they received a warm welcome from their fellow workers. Since then Milan had not been under surveillance and had rarely been interrogated. He had no work, however, and lived from small honoraria from his articles and books published abroad. Unfortunately he suffered serious eye trouble and was to have an operation soon. Jiřina had been able to get her old job back and had at once resumed her clandestine activities.

Milan strongly denied that the Charter was a ghetto, as some claimed. Perhaps in the first two or three years it had been isolated, but now ordinary people knew about its activities and its documents from Voice of America (VOA) broadcasts. The number of signatories was not important. The main thing was for people to act independently. The inner circle of Charter 77 was a kind of family, with deep and close friendships; there had been few betrayals. Milan's slogan was "Live your own life and ignore the system." We now know that we cannot change the system in a few years, he said. It was more important to change people and their values, and this was slowly happening, little by little. Even among those who worked within the system, there were many decent, honest, and intelligent people seeking to improve it. Oppositional tendencies were widespread, but they took the form not of opposition to the system as such but of bitter criticism of the way in which the system operated and its undemocratic procedures.

Sally and I took Jiřina to dinner on her 50th birthday. We went to the Palace of Culture, a huge and hideous building, constructed by the party at vast expense. Its best feature was the beautiful panorama of Prague from the dining-room. Jiřina was as dynamic and energetic as ever and looked hardly more than 40! She recounted the story of a French van that had been detained and searched at the border. This had led to the discovery by the police, in a garage near Prague, of a cache of materials prepared for the return trip, and to the arrest of many people. She confided that she now had good arrangements for shipping materials through German diplomatic channels. In view of the impending recall of the helpful German representative, the dissidents would soon need someone else; she wondered whether there was a new Canadian diplomat who would be willing to carry on the job. There had been a great deterioration in standards and in morale, she thought; it would take more than a generation for people to change. She feared that even if there were major political reforms, people would be unable to change their habits and behave differently, and this might lead to a catastrophe

On a visit to Brno we met Milan Šimečka again, this time with his wife, Eva, at the *chata* owned by her parents in Bystrc, near Brno. Miro Kusý and his wife, Jolka, and one of their children came up from Bratislava. Also present was Eva's brother-in-law, Homolek, who had given evidence to the police that had led to Jiřina's arrest, but this had been forgiven, and he was accepted by the others. It was a wonderful evening of friendship and talk; it seemed almost a miracle for us to be together again.

Milan asked me to tell Vilém that they were happy and looking forward to the time when they would be together with him, as we were here. They admired his work abroad and were grateful to him. We were not really dissidents, he said, or even political people. We enjoyed life as much as we could. Independent writing would continue, he thought, and perhaps even increase. Writers must not only criticize the existing system, however, but begin to think of something new. It was useless to look toward any kind of utopia, and certainly not toward revolution. Kusý was no longer doing manual work but had a part-time job as a documentarist in an urban planning institute. He devoted much of his free time to writing. He had been offered a chance to return to scholarly work if he gave up writing in samizdat and publishing abroad, but he had refused. He was still writing as a Marxist, he said, in order to show the true Marxist interpretation, in contrast to official dogma.

We were able to glean from our friends some information about the situation in Slovakia. Federation had no real value, they said, except that it provided some Slovaks with jobs in Bratislava and Prague. The Slovak ministries and even the Slovak party had no real power. Charter 77, they admitted, did not enjoy wide support in Slovakia. According to Milan, Dubček gave no support to the Charter; he still hoped that things would change and that he would be able to resume his political career.

In Brno it was an added bonus to meet Jiří Müller, student leader in the 1960s and now an active Chartist. On the way home by street-car he was afraid that we were being followed. Even at lunch at home, he urged us to speak cautiously for fear of being overheard. Brno, as a small city, was worse than Prague, he said; the very small group of oppositionists could not easily escape police supervision. I returned to his place for lunch to meet Dr Milan Jelínek, a literary scholar in the Academy of Sciences, who had to take special care not to be seen by the police in Müller's company. Both Müller and Jelínek praised independent thought and action as a means of preserving traditional values. There were not only literary and cultural activities, but more prosaic actions, such as caring for the family and raising children; building a chata and growing vegetables, even selling some private produce; meeting in small reading groups; and taking outings into the countryside. Since the system was based on control by the party of everything and everybody, the regime feared all such activities and tried to limit and control them. Charter 77 could claim three achievements: it linked together people of different political and ideological orientation, it circulated information and documents and it established links with western Europe and North America. Its negative feature was its separation from society; its goal was to escape from this ghetto.

Müller was one of the few people involved in a tiny independent socialist group whose leading personality, Rudolf Battěk, was still in prison. Negotiations by the French government for his release had been in vain. Unlike the ex-Communists, the independent socialists had no support abroad. Their appeals for solidarity to the Socialist International had had no success. Jaroslav Šabata, once a Communist, and now also a former Charter spokesman, was not a member of any political group, he said, and was open to influences and ideas from every side.

Shortly thereafter Šabata came to Prague, and we had a long talk together. As we sat on a bench on the *quai* and strolled over the Charles Bridge, he was sure that we were being watched and photographed by a police agent. There were diverse political tendencies among Chartists, he told me, but their level of activity was low, and they could hardly be called real political groups. A declaration on one hundred years of socialism, issued by the democratic socialists on the anniversary of the founding of Czech Social Democracy, had been signed by people of many outlooks, including Havel. The ex-Communists were themselves divided between those who defended the 1968 reform course and those, such as Šabata, who were more critical of it. He was trying to bring all the various groups together on the basis of a document on the peace movement.

A meeting with all three Charter spokesmen was arranged at the home of Jiří Ruml, but I had the wrong address and arrived very late. On the way, in seeking the right address, I stopped in at the home of Petr Uhl, editor of the Charter bulletin, *Informace o Chartě* (*Infoch*). Although I had never met him and he was not expecting me, he immediately introduced me to his wife, Anička, as "Pan Skilling." In spite of five years in prison, he said, he was well, physically and mentally. The trial in which he had been sentenced was really directed against Charter 77 and led to the imprisonment of two of its spokesmen, Václav Benda and Jiří Dienstbier. Uhl said that he was "a revolutionary socialist" and joked that there had been only two Trotskyites in Prague, and one had just emigrated. Despite his political views he found common ground with the other Chartists. His wife, who had edited *Informace* during his imprisonment, was surprised and delighted to hear that I had a complete collection of it in Toronto.

When I finally arrived at Ruml's, I found that two of the spokesmen, Václav Benda and Jana Šternová, had already left, but I had a long talk with Ruml and his son, Jan, and with Rudolf Slánský. As they all worked in factories they were in close touch with the workers; they reported that there was great dissatisfaction with economic conditions and that complaints were openly expressed. But the "social contract" was still valid — people had enough food to eat and could buy clothing and shoes. Although the economy was functioning, there was stagnation and danger of a crisis. The party leaders talked endlessly of reform but did nothing about it. Politically this was the most stable regime in eastern Europe — it had survived 15 years, and there was no prospect of change, they thought. Charter 77 had never had a great impact on the population as a whole and had much the same status as eight years ago. The important fact was that it had survived; the regime had not been able to liquidate it. It was regarded by many people at home as their mouthpiece and had acquired great authority abroad.

Their views on the economy were confirmed by Vladimír Kadlec, an economist and former minister under Dubček, whom I met in the buffet at the library. The economy was functioning, even without economic reform, but not effectively. He did not think, however, that it was in a state of crisis or was likely to collapse, as it had in 1961. Bad management and poor morale prevented high productivity, however, as did lack of innovation and out-of-date equipment. Certain independent economic activities were beneficial. For example, independent artisans did jobs for citizens after hours, or even during working hours; the Tuzex stores made goods available to those who had dollar coupons sent from abroad; and the black market in currency brought in much-needed dollars to the economy.

I was able to probe the attitude of Chartists to foreign policy and the peace movement in conversations with Jiří Hájek, who had been minister of foreign affairs under Dubček; with Jiří Dienstbier, former foreign corespondent (who was to head the same ministry in 1990); and with other specialists in international relations. I made two long treks out to Hájek's home in Zahradné město. There I sat beside a huge teddy bear, which he jokingly called "Big Brother," and drank tea. Hájek had drafted the Charter's document on Madrid and was interested to hear my report on the conference. He had prepared some of the other peace documents and had reviewed my book on Charter 77 for *Infoch*. The Charter was not, he thought, merely a ghetto; it was broader than that and was supplemented by other forms of independent activity. It met the demands of our consciences, he said, and had some influence, however slight, on public opinion and even on official policy. But it had not been able to establish a mass movement as in Poland.

Hájek took me to the home of Alexander Ort, to one of the regular gatherings of a few international relations specialists, formerly members of ÚMPE. There I met old friends Jiří Stěpanovský, who worked as a lawyer in a construction agency, and Jaroslav Šedivý, who was still washing windows. No one there had any contact with UMPE, which had been renamed the Institute of International Relations and was completely changed in staff and in spirit. Another former colleague, Václav Kotyk, was not present, but I met him by chance the next day in the courtyard of the Klementinum. He said that it was a red letter day, since he had got a new apartment on Hradčanské Square and had secured permission to work as a freelance writer; now, as a climax, he had met me!

I had two long meetings with Jiří Dienstbier, each time at the Smetana monument on the *quai*. He told me at length of his prison experience. When he had been confined in Heřmanice with Havel and Benda, they were able to see one another at meals or at work and even to talk a little. They were not permitted to write anything, but managed to smuggle out their ideas on the Madrid conference. He was pleased when I told him that I had passed these proposals on to delegates and had used them in my own broadcasts. He admitted that adapting to ordinary life after release from prison was long and difficult. He found it hard to write anything, since his books had been confiscated.

A group of Chartists were planning a series of essays on the topic of economic, political, and cultural tendencies leading to 1988. He did not know why 1988 — it could equally be 1990! The basic premise of the regime was "no change"; in fact, no changes had taken place in 15 years. He did not entirely rule out the party as an instrument of change, as had happened in the 1960s, but he did not expect such action from its present members. Charter 77 remained mixed in its composition and would break up if it did not keep to its original non-political stance. Dienstbier criticized a recent Charter document as being too critical of the Western peace movements; they were, it was true, often one-sided, but they had valuable ideas. On the occasion of the recent officially sponsored Peace Assembly in Prague, the Czech dissidents had had no real chance to talk to the delegates of foreign peace movements, but they had been able to present their views through interviews with representatives of foreign press and radio.

I was particularly anxious to meet with some of the independent historians to discuss both their work and my own plans for historical research. Petr Pithart was no longer working as a gardener but was employed in an office; he was devoting all his spare time to historical writing. With two others he had edited a three-volume collection of articles on Masaryk and had seen and liked my long review article of this work. With another team of three, including Milan Otáhal and a third person who remained anonymous (Petr Příhoda), he had been working for some years on a wide-ranging reappraisal of the whole of Czech history. Pithart was sharply critical of a recent Charter 77 document on Czechoslovak historical writing, especially for its failure to recognize that some good work was being done by "official" historians. Pithart was equally critical of Charter 77's work as a whole. The Charter should try to reach beyond its signatories to broader circles and to break down old labels, such as Communist and socialist, left and right.

I had several meetings with Milan Otáhal, who invited me to his home for dinner. When I arrived he was quite nervous and cautioned me that our conversation might be overheard by a hidden listening apparatus. He and his wife, also a historian, were without employment and were subsisting on their pensions. He was still a member of the Historical Club, which had recently rejected an official attempt to exclude him. He agreed with the view that some good historical work was being done by people in the established institutions, including Miroslav Hroch, my critic in London.

When I met Otáhal later at the Klementinum he admitted that there were personal conflicts among dissident historians, so that two separate issues of the samizdat historical journal had appeared. Pithart explained this conflict in terms of differences of opinion on questions such as the 1945 transfer of the Germans, with one group — Jiří Hájek, Miloš Hájek, Milan Hübl, and Jaroslav Opat, defending it — and others, including Otáhal and Pithart, condemning it. Otáhal charged that some of the ex-Communists remained Communists at heart and had become extremely nationalist, whereas they, who had broken completely with Communism, were more ready to criticize national traditions. Although he recognized that his former colleague Prečan was doing more to help historians at home than any other exile, they had had misunderstandings about the symposia prepared for the world congresses of historians in Bucharest and Stuttgart.

I heard from the other side of the controversy among historians from Miloš Hájek and his wife, Hana Medrová, both ex-Communist historians. Miloš was engaged in a major study of the Communist

International. He explained the appearance of two separate historical journals as reflecting differences over proposed content but noted that the two groups still had many links. There were also strong differences among historians over Charter 77's document on history, which it had issued, he said, without consulting historians and which was one-sided and simplistic. Like Pithart and Otáhal, he argued strongly that there was good historical work being done by younger established scholars.

I later talked with another ex-Communist, Milan Hübl, whom I met in, of all places, the Army Club restaurant. He was highly dogmatic and criticized almost everyone. He, too, was very critical of the Charter's document on history and called it the "tip of the iceberg" of growing conservative Catholic influence, as represented by the spokesman Václav Benda.

Jim Connell, an American diplomat who was leaving Prague, invited me to a farewell party in the home of the writer Ivan Klíma in Bráník. When I arrived, Klíma and Ludvík Vaculík were talking together in a little square outside the house and exclaimed loudly: "What a surprise to see you in Prague!" Both agreed that conditions were easier than before; they were not being interrogated as often. According to Vaculík, the quality of official Czech literature was poor, but published Slovak writing was on a higher level. Klíma was writing a play and two novels and had an invitation to go the University of Michigan again; he had a passport and could go, but he feared that he would lose his Czech citizenship. On the shelves in the living-room were complete collections of some of the samizdat journals. I witnessed the unpacking of one of Vilém's huge parcels of books; each item was greeted with cries of delight. After a huge buffet supper, Vaculík started up a sing-song and conducted it with great gusto. We all joined in, singing from Xerox copies of songs arranged by Jan Masaryk. Vaculík liked my translation of one song so much that he wrote it down and had me dedicate it to him and sign it.

On our first Sunday we went to the Cathedral of St Vitus, where Cardinal Tomášek was conducting mass. The church was filled with people of all ages, including many long-haired youngsters. Slow lines waited for communion. At the end of the service the cardinal, who was over 80 years old, walked through the congregation, smiling, touching people, and blessing them. He continued on foot through the courtyards of the Castle to the Archbishop's Palace, followed by a large crowd, and joined with them in singing hymns. From the gateway of the palace and from the balcony he greeted the faithful as they chanted: "Long Live John Paul II." This event was a testimony of people's affection for him and also a kind of confrontation of church and state, as the head of the church passed under the president's windows.

Later I had a meeting on the *quai* with a young Catholic priest, Václav Malý, who had lost his official permission to act as priest because of his signing of Charter 77 and had been working as a stoker. Malý saw no hope of a change in the system, but only the possibility of a slow evolution in people's values over many years. In the past few years the cardinal, largely under the personal influence of the Pope, had changed his attitude to Charter 77. At the official Peace Assembly, the cardinal had delivered a message that was similar in spirit to the viewpoint of Charter 77. In fact, I was told, it had been drafted with the aid of Catholic Chartists. There had been a strong development of independent Catholic journals and samizdat books. The church was not, however, closely linked with the nation, as it was in Poland, and did not have the same commanding influence.

In the same place I met with another prominent Catholic Chartist, Václav Benda, a layman, trained in mathematics, who had just emerged from four years in prison and had resumed the role of Charter spokesperson. Charter 77, he said, had been hit hard by repressive measures and had been more or less destroyed in smaller communities. It was, he felt, isolated from the people because of official repression and what he called the information blockade. Its ideas and proposals had some influence, even on members of the *nomenklatura*, who heard about its activities on foreign radio; issues raised in some of the documents were discussed openly in the press. The Charter's international authority had grown greatly, he thought, and its relations with the Western peace movements had improved.

Benda also felt that the Charter's relations with the church and with Catholic laypeople were better. The cardinal was quite friendly to him as Charter spokesperson. When a local parish priest had refused to baptize Benda's sixth child, the cardinal performed the service himself in his private chapel in the palace. The campaign for an invitation to the Pope to visit Czechoslovakia, he told me confidentially, had been organized by church people and Chartists. In Slovakia there was a strong development of religious protest.

I became well acquainted with a young Catholic Chartist, Markéta Němcová, the eldest of seven children of two prominent dissidents, Jiří Němec and Dana Němcová. She had not been able to continue with higher education because of her parents' activities. Only 28 years old,

Jazz Section, with Karel Srp and Josef Skalník, 1984

she had been active in the movement for six years and went regularly to the Hejdánek seminars. She often travelled to smaller towns where trials of dissidents were taking place and also attended rock concerts held in the countryside. She told me of many interrogations over the past six years; memories of them used to keep her awake at night, but she now accepted them as routine.

Among Protestant Chartists I visited the home of Ladislav Hejdánek, a lay philosopher, who had studied privately under Jan Patočka and was a former Charter spokesperson. I knew him as the author of regular samizdat *Letters to a Friend*, in which he frankly expressed his personal views on politics and life, and as the organizer of a philosophy seminar conducted in his home. There were some 20 other seminars, but his was frequently targetted by police.

I had known and written about the Jazz Section, a semi-official agency under the Union of Musicians, and made a pilgrimage by metro out to Kačerov to visit the big old mansion that was its headquarters. Over coffee and a bottle of Becherovka, Karel Srp, the president, and Josef Skalník, vice-president, told me of their work over 12 years. They had 4,000 members but had influence, they said, over 80,000 to 100,000 young people. Their Jazz Festivals were hugely successful but had been banned since 1981. Now they could only arrange private concerts and make tapes. They put out a regular bulletin for members and several book series that were not subject to censorship. They were responsible for the graffiti I had seen on the walls on Na kampě ("Although John Lennon is dead, he is still with us"; "Peace, not war"). Whenever the police painted over the space, they filled it again. The following year they sent me the entire Jazz Section archive for safe-keeping in our library in the University of Toronto. Later, when the Jazz Section was closed down by the authorities and Karel Srp arrested, I wrote a letter of protest to the *Globe and Mail* (13 September 1986).

We had a number of pleasant social evenings with our old friends, members of Olga's family, Gina and Alex, Milan and Jiřina, and Jelka and her new husband, Jožko. Their views provided us, as Sally joked, with a kind of "control group" of non-Chartist people. Gina had a new job, as assistant editor of an agricultural newspaper published by Comecon — very surprising, since she still refused to join the party. She felt that most people, though not satisfied, had, like Švejk, adapt-ed to the system and did not rebel, for the sake of their children. She did not expect basic changes and hoped only for small improvements. I made the long trip by metro out to Zlíčín, a remote and drab suburb, to see Jelka, her husband, Jožko, a Slovak, who worked in a nearby con-struction engineering firm, and their little daughter, Olga. As editor of an information science magazine, Jelka lamented that she had little access to Western data and doubted whether she would have it in her lifetime — "perhaps in Olinka's time," she sighed!

The highlight of our trip was the 24 hours that we spent with Havel at his farm in Hrádeček. His brother, Ivan, met us at a Prague metro station and drove us there at high speed in about two hours. Although other visitors had been stopped by police as they approached Hrádeček, we drove right through without incident. Olga had been called away by the illness of her mother, so the two brothers prepared dinner and breakfast. We ate lunch in a plebeian tavern nearby, where people paid little attention to our presence.

Hrádeček — the name meant "little castle" in Czech — included the castle ruins, two or three other cottages, and Havel's large, hand-somely renovated farmhouse. A few hundred metres away stood a tiny chata, on stilts, presumably a police observation point, but there seemed to be no one in residence. Outside the farmhouse there was a spacious courtyard, dominated by a geometric iron sculpture painted yellow. Upstairs was a huge open space, used by groups that stayed overnight. Havel's study had many bright pop paintings and posters, including one inscribed "Make Love Not War." On his desk were the letters that he had written to Olga from prison, some 160 of them, in their envelopes stamped by the police censor. Samizdat books and journals were everywhere. On the windowsill was the entire collection of his book series, Expedice. Above his bed hung a crucifix and a large photograph of the Pope.

Although his place was no doubt bugged, we talked openly on many subjects that evening and the next day. I did not find it easy to follow Havel's Czech because of his guttural voice and his rapid diction. I often had to turn to Ivan for interpretation; he confessed that it was sometimes difficult for him to translate because of Havel's unique style. Havel told us of his life in prison, from which he had been released about a year earlier. Fellow prisoners, he said, often turned to the dissidents for advice and treated them with respect. No writing was allowed except in letters to closest relatives, and these were heavily censored and sometimes confiscated. It was difficult to concentrate on writing in a crowded cell; since he was not allowed to have writing paper, he had to use toilet paper or other scraps.

Charter 77 had become, in his opinion, a kind of conscience of the nation, although this was not what they had intended it to be. People regarded it as a kind of example, even if they themselves did not follow it. The active minority of a nation made history, Havel thought, but the non-active majority gave the minority authority. The Charter community embodied a wide spectrum of political viewpoints, but there was a consensus on its basic purposes. Most of the sharp differences in the past had centred on tactics and had been ironed out over the years. The main point of disagreement now was the content of each of the documents issued by the spokespersons. In order to reach a consensus, they often had to water down the texts, which became colourless, he thought.

It was not the task of Charter 77 to help ordinary people to solve their problems, Havel felt. Each individual had the responsibility to decide how to act. He himself wanted to live like a human being; in fact he found he could do many things that made it possible to live in this way. His actions were not based on the hope of early change and reflected a realistic optimism, or perhaps an honest pessimism. "Do you have faith in what you are doing?" I asked. "Yes, it was satisfying to hear from others that the Charter had a meaning not just for ourselves, but also for them, too." He likened Charter 77 to a kind of path in the jungle; it had become a mere trail and might be obliterated, but it might also broaden into a path again. When we died, he said, we could at least feel that we had done all we could to achieve its goal. Havel did not believe in a personal God, but he felt that there was some kind of limit and measure to people's actions — something absolute, above men and women. Havel did not think that independent alternative activity could be suppressed, although there were bound to be ups and downs in its development. There was little point in making prognoses. Chartists' interest was in the here and now, in confronting the totalitarian society with a more natural one. He felt that the forces at work below the surface of events were unknown and unforeseeable. A random event might suddenly trigger an avalanche.

Among the young people, he told us, there was no enthusiasm for real socialism and no support for the party, even among the children of top party people. There was great interest in rock music, although it was officially forbidden. There were about two hundred bands — some good, some bad. The Plastic People of the Universe still existed and had changed its name to Hovězi porážka (Beef Slaughter-House). It could not play in public and usually did its recording at Hrádeček. Havel played us its latest recording, "Midnight Mouse," made in an unusual collaboration with Marta Kubišová, pop star of 1968 fame.

The Chartists were in favour of a dialogue with the peace movements in the West, with which they shared common points and a concern for the fate of the world. True, Western movements often had simplified ideas and illusions, which the Chartists did not share, about Soviet policy. We have had personal experience with appeasement, Havel said, and were critical of the view that it was better to give in and not to fight. People were tired of peace slogans, he acknowledged; they did not believe official pronouncements and sometimes rejected Charter statements, too.

On our departure from Prague we were taken to the airport by David Peel and passed through immigration and customs without any problems. He said that he would not leave the airport until he had seen us safely on board the plane. Jiřina also came to Ruzyně to say goodbye. At the airport in Hanover it seemed right to find Vilém Prečan waiting for us and to spend the rest of the day with him and Helenka, regaling them with stories of Prague. Vilém had already heard from Jiřina of some of our activities and thought that these had been nothing short of a miracle. Šimečka, he said, had called our visit the greatest event in his life since his release from prison. Kusý and he both now felt that the other world still existed and had not forgotten them. The Czechoslovak authorities had been very inefficient, he joked. He had received a card signed by Havel and by us from Hrádeček, and another from Bystrc, signed by all our friends.

There followed busy days, as usual, as I reported in detail on my meetings and examined the latest materials that Vilém had received from Czechoslovakia. We had long discussions on historical questions and on Charter 77. He told me of the excellent communications he now had with Prague. Every week he sent and received materials through the German Foreign Office diplomatic bag. He also met regularly with a West German diplomat from Prague in the little town of Vohenstrauss, close to the Czechoslovak frontier, where they exchanged larger shipments of materials. Sally and I made some excursions with the Prečans into the countryside, including a trip to Hamelin, a beautiful old town, where a special performance of *The Pied Piper* was taking place.

Shortly after my trip I prepared a long article, "Independent Currents in Czechoslovakia," which appeared in January 1985 in *Problems of Communism*, published by the U.S. Information Agency. In this I brought the development of Charter 77 up to date and analysed other forms of independent activity. I began to plan a book that would discuss parallel politics and the concept of an independent society. Macmillan, which had developed a remarkable interest in things Czechoslovak, gave me a contract for this.

In 1986 Prečan enlisted my aid in preparing a study of the first ten years of Charter 77, which he was planning with Václav Havel. *Nározeniny* (Birthday), as he referred to it, would include an introductory essay on the meaning of Charter 77 by Havel, a chapter by me describing the international impact of Charter 77, biographical sketches of all the spokesmen, a full annotated listing of Charter documents, and translations of some of the major texts. Prečan did not succeed in getting everything done in time to publish it for major anniversary celebrations planned in Oslo, Copenhagen, and elsewhere, but he did put out abridged versions in Czech, English, Swedish, German, Polish, and Dutch.[1]

PRAGUE, 1987

During my visit with him in 1983, Prečan, in a telephone conversation with Havel, told him of my plan to come to Prague to celebrate our 50th wedding anniversary and of my idea of a party at the Hrad, "where," I joked, "Havel would be president!" Havel laughed heartily and said that it would be too soon for that. He added, however: "If not the Hrad (the Castle), then come to Hrádeček (the little Castle): here I *am* president," he said.

Three years later Havel was not yet in the Castle, but Sally and I did go back to Prague. We had no difficulty in receiving our visas, perhaps because Canada's Department of External Affairs and the ambassador in Prague had urged favourable action on the Czechoslovak authorities. The Canadian ambassador, whom I had met in Toronto, was not especially interested in the dissident movement and somewhat to our relief did not invite us to stay at the residence. One of his junior colleagues, Peter Bakewell, however, had become a close friend of Jiřina Šiklová and of other Chartists. He had taken over the risky task of acting as an intermediary between the Chartists and their friends abroad and making the regular trips to the German border town. Because of the recent defection of a Czech employee at the Canadian embassy he had to be extremely cautious and discreet. Peter met us at the airport in the early evening and drove us through the grey, drab streets of Prague to the city centre. The newly created malls were almost totally deserted at nine p.m. After a search we found a Čedok office open and purchased our hotel coupons and changed the required amount of money. Peter then saw us safely ensconced in a comfortable suite in the Hotel Ambassador in the heart of the city on Václavské náměstí. Outside the hotel we were greeted by Jiřina, who, without regard for watching police, embraced us both, much to Peter's embarrassment.

The next two weeks we devoted to a hectic schedule of meetings arranged, as usual, by Jiřina, with historians, former Communists and Socialists, religious Chartists, diplomats, old friends — and Václav Havel. Our visit was in some ways a kind of repeat of 1984, but I had the impression that tension had relaxed somewhat; there were fewer interrogations and fewer trials, and we did not have the sense of being followed. Some people were still extremely cautious and nervous about meeting us, but others met us openly and without hesitation. We had all too little time with Jiřina herself. On one occasion she gave us an old Austrian coin dated 1768 as a gift — and as a kind of reminder of another '68, two centuries later. She told us of the death of our dear friend Lisa Rudinger in the spring; we both regretted that she had not lived to take part in our wedding anniversary celebration.

As in 1964, I tried in 1987 to cram into our busy days a little historical work on Masaryk. In the Klementinum, Otáhal and Pithart met me openly outside the entrance or in the buffet. I talked with them about their study of Czech history and my own book on an independent society and about Masaryk. Pithart was hoping to have his book on 1968 translated into English; this time he would publish it under his own name. His attitude to the Charter had changed somewhat. He cooperated on specific Charter activities or documents but did not go regularly to Charter meetings because of the endless controversies. He was dissatisfied with the concept of an independent society, which ran the danger of becoming an island and drifting away from the mainland. There were good people within the "official structures" who often acted independently. What was needed, he thought, was to expand to other sectors of society and not to confine ourselves in a special community. Otáhal expressed his view that Charter 77 was of great moral significance and was irreplaceable. He reported that, after six years of being divided into two separate publications, a single issue of the historical journal was being prepared by a joint editorial board and would include a symposium on the 65th anniversary of the republic. They were also preparing for the 70th anniversary in 1988 and invited contributions from abroad, including one from me.

It was a special privilege to visit Karel Kučera, a dismissed historian, who lived in the apartment that Masaryk had occupied prior to going into exile in 1914 and where his wife, Charlotte, had lived during the war years. Since the house was right opposite the Canadian embassy I had often noticed the bust of Charlotte by the ground-floor window; it had surprisingly not been removed by the Communists at any time. Kučera showed me a picture of the study as it was when Masaryk had used it and the mark on the door jamb when the room had been padlocked in 1915. The furniture was new, and the library had been taken away to the Institute of Party History. For me it was exciting to imagine Masaryk at work there and to look out of the window at the garden below.

I visited Vladimír Kadlec, the former minister of education, in his home, which was a kind of meeting place, with people dropping in and out all morning. Václav Slavík, former Central Committee member, arrived unexpectedly, and so did Jiří Hájek. There was much talk of Gorbachev and his visit, of the Czechoslovak leaders and their attitude to reform, and of the role of Dubček. There was scepticism about the likelihood of reform in Czechoslovakia. I made a long trip by streetcar out to the suburb to see Jiří Hájek again. He had no great confidence in the likelihood of reform but had some hope that there might be steps in this direction, citing speeches by Husák and Lubomír Štrougal as evidence. He was confident that the Charter would continue. Indeed it would be necessary to have such an organization, even if things opened up a little, since there was always a need to criticize evils in any country.

We spent an afternoon at tea at Jiří Dienstbier's. The Soviet Union, Jiří felt, was 40 years behind the West and would cease to be a world power if it did not make changes in its system. Gorbachev did not understand this, however, and in any case would not be able to carry the population with him. Although people liked his visit, they were upset by the tight security around him, with 50 or 60 security police accompanying him everywhere. Dienstbier himself was followed for hours by five or six men. Jiří did not agree with those who said that Charter 77 was a ghetto. People were much more sympathetic to the Charter than previously and were expressing their views more openly. Charter documents were being reproduced by xerox, but the number of copies was still limited because of the paper shortage. Every word of the Prague Appeal, addressed to the Western peace movements in 1983, had been subject to discussion, but a consensus was finally reached. Many Western peace groups, he thought, now understood that peace was not just a matter of control of armaments but involved human rights.

I had a good conversation with Rudolf Battěk, the leading spirit of the Independent Socialist group. We met in the little park behind the Tatran Hotel, and he was quite nervous about being watched. In spite of his five years in prison he seemed to be in good health; he and his wife were living on a meagre pension. Life in prison had been difficult at first, as he was confined in a cell with drug addicts. Later he had two rooms and could use one for reading and writing. He presented me with an inscibed samizdat copy of his letters from prison — a philosophical work entitled *Strast z nekonečna* (Anxiety over the Infinite), handsomely bound, with a colourful scene of high mountains on the cover.

The socialist group had been weakened by Battěk's imprisonment and was not very active. Battěk wanted to engage the former Communists in dialogue: he had good relations with Rudolf Slánský, who, he felt, did not consider himself a Communist any more. Battěk thought that Charter 77 was putting out too many documents, and some were not of high quality. Yet he was sure the organization would continue, despite conflicting views, since it did represent a general meeting of minds. He had organized a seminar, the Prague Club, and hoped that some leading Canadian socialist might attend. I later wrote to Ed Broadbent, leader of the Canadian New Democrats, about this possibility.

The Protestant philosopher Ladislav Hejdánek and his wife received us at their home for tea. He was continuing his seminars this year on the theme of ethics; they had not been interrupted by the police at all. As before, he waxed bitter about the failure of the Protestant synod and its senior to support independent activities or to give assistance to endangered Protestant Chartists. With Mrs Hejdánek and the wife of the pastor, Sally and I later attended a service at the largest Evangelical Brethren church in Prague. Alfréd Kocáb, a Charter signatory, had surprisingly just been appointed as substitute pastor. In his sermon he said that it was the duty of the church to care for the sick, the poor, the old, the unjustly treated, the "powerless," and the persecuted, and he condemned "the arbitrariness of power."

On Good Friday we attended the more formal Catholic service at the Church of St Salvator. Václav Benda and Radim Palouš had agreed to meet us there, but the congregation was so large that we missed each other. On Sunday we went to the Easter Mass in Strahov, a church of extraordinary beauty, with lovely painted ceilings and golden rococo statues and pillars. Mass was served by the cardinal, who was 88 years old. As in 1984, he was greeted with affection by many believers before and following the service. Afterward Peter Bakewell took us to Benda's to surprise him. Happily, Benda invited Sally and me to have lunch with his wife and six children and prepared the meal himself. We waited in his library, which was piled high with samizdat materials. He told us that he had had four police searches; in one case ten policemen had taken ten hours to examine every book and every scrap of paper.

Benda lamented the position of the church, with only two of thirteen bishoprics occupied in the Czech lands. In Slovakia there was no archbishop, but a former archbishop, who had lost his licence as a priest and had served eight years in prison, had great influence, he said. The Czech cardinal was also influential among Slovaks. There had been a revival of religion in the past ten to fifteen years, especially among youths, who found Marxism empty and were seeking for truth and for a sense of community. The Catholic church had a greater appeal than the Protestant, he thought, because young people were seeking order and authority, not democracy.

As for the parallel or independent society, it continued to exist, and it was much more advanced than when he had first written about it in 1978. Like several others, he did not believe that this concept was a barrier within society as a whole; there was a reciprocal influence of the official and unofficial societies. He showed me confidentially a manifesto on central Europe that was to be circulated for signing in Hungary and Poland as well as in Czechoslovakia. It called for an international struggle against totalitarianism and for independence, democracy, and friendship among nations.

Early one morning Sally and I went out to the distant suburb of Hlubočepy to visit the youthful Father Malý in his modest apartment. He had been in prison for 11 months in 1981, along with Šiklová and others, but, like the others, he had been released without trial. Although he had lost his licence to be a priest, he secretly (and illegally) continued his priestly duties, even hearing confessions and conducting services in small groups. Malý did not think that Charter 77 was as isolated as some said. People knew about it from foreign radio and asked him questions about it. The Charter tried to reach out to the population and to create "space" and justice for all citizens, not just for Chartists. Malý confirmed the turn to religion among youths, but it was a matter not of thousands, but of individuals and small groups. He did not fully understand the reasons but speculated that the young people had no belief in Communism and were searching for certainty. They turned to the Catholic church because of its colour, its music, its symbolism, and its mystery, and they found in it a kind of community that they could find nowhere else. The cardinal was a symbol of protest and resistance, and the Polish example was greatly admired. Others turned, however, to the Protestants, including the Jehovah's Witnesses and the Baptists, and even to Buddhism.

In contrast to the young Father Malý was the venerable Father Josef Zvěřina, 73 years old, who had been a priest for 50 years. He had spent 14 years in prison but looked well and vigorous. He did not feel at all isolated, he said, waving to the books in German, French, and Polish that lined his walls. We joined him for lunch, prepared by Sister Agneša. Charter 77 was still a constant challenge to the people, he said, a kind of moral imperative. Signature was a matter of conscience; Chartists were not satisfied with their own exclusive circle and tried to break out of it to reach society as a whole. The Charter was open to people of all age groups and all tendencies of thought; its documents dealt with questions that concerned the whole of society. He was ready to work with everyone; this required spiritual openness and the abandoning of all prejudice.

Father Zvěřina denied that the church was in crisis or that it could ever be driven underground. "We act in the light of day and are not in the Catacombs. We must fight fear, hatred, and the lie." The situation was not as bad as in the West, he said, since the church faced here not an inner crisis but a crisis caused by outside pressures. The seminary in Litoměřice took in 95 students each year, and there would be more if a theological faculty existed in Prague. He had three hundred young students of theology, who were taking regular underground courses, with examinations. He was critical of the bishops, many of whom sought peace with the state and were ready to make compromises with it. Most of the people, and 90 percent of the priests, were pro-cardinal; only 10 percent of the priests favoured the pro-state clerical movement, Pacem in Terris.

Diplomatic events were fewer for us than in 1984. The Canadian chargé d'affaires gave a lunch for us at Hadovka with half a dozen ambassadors, including the American, Dutch, French, Swedish, and West German, some of whom seemed well informed about the dissident scene. We spent a good deal of time with Peter Bakewell, who was a great help in taxiing us back and forth to meetings and took us to several new restaurants and pubs.

We had an evening at the residence of the American diplomat Bob Norman, who was in close contact with dissidents. Among the guests were Jožka Skalník and several other members of the Jazz Section who had been released from prison, as well as the wives of those still detained. The trial of Karel Srp and the others had been a farce, they said, like an "absurd play." Srp was still in prison and was showing great courage under the ordeal, they reported. The headquarters of the Jazz Section had been thoroughly searched; most of its publications and papers were confiscated, and the place was padlocked. The members who were not in prison assured me that they would continue the work of the Jazz Section in some form — legally if possible, illegally if necessary.

We did not see much of Olga's children. I met Jelka for lunch one day. She told me more of the difficulties of her work as editor of the information journal. The editorial council was supposed to decide on everything, but the members, including Jelka, were afraid to voice their real opinions. Worst of all was the self-censorship; everyone knew the limits and taboos that had to be observed. Foreign articles were often cut so much that they could not be published at all. The visit by Gorbachev had brought a glimmer of hope that things would change and that at least her children would have a better life. She soon became aware — her eyes filled with tears — that this was not likely to happen. The words that Gorbachev used were a little different than those of the past, but there were no signs of glasnost in Prague; no one could believe Husák or have any trust in Štrougal. I met her briefly at the Klementinum on my last day to say good-bye. As we stood on the Charles Bridge, Jelka warned me that we were being observed by several police agents, including two "lovers," who watched us as they embraced.

I saw Havel three times — once by pure chance. Sally and I were searching for a table for lunch at the Bílá Labuť on the Hradčanské náměstí, and he invited us to join him. A few days later I met him for lunch at the Klášterní winecellar in town. Havel joked about his role in society. His name was well-known, but people could hardly believe that he really existed. Once he was in a pub alone; the young people, and a policeman who came in, would not believe that he was really Havel. When he said that the popular singer Jaroslav Hutka had written a song about him, they all began singing it, with its refrain "Havlíček-Havel." He talked a lot about the reconstruction of his apartment on the *quai*. It was a slow and difficult process, involving many permits. He also had to provide the workers with food and drink and to carry up cases of beer to them on the fifth floor.

Expedice, his book series, had now published over 250 volumes. With the help of his brother, Ivan, he was turning to the computer for his writing. Charter 77 was also beginning to use xerox machines, which were smuggled in from abroad. He told me of the slow progress of the collected works of Jan Patočka, which were nearing completion. Like most people Havel did not expect anything to come out of Mikhail Gorbachev's visit to Prague and did not anticipate that it would encourage Husák to introduce economic reforms. He told me that he liked my chapter in *Ten Years of Charter 77* and had given the book to journalists during Gorbachev's visit. I told him about my book on the independent society, and we talked at length about this concept. He rejected the criticism by Pithart that this idea established a barrier within society and created a ghetto. There were many mutual contacts of the first and second societies, and each influenced the other.

The highlight of the visit was, of course, the celebration of our marriage 50 years before. Jiřina had organized two events — one, a buffet dinner in the historic Obecní dům (Community House), and the other, the next day, an official ceremony in the Old Town Hall. The dinner took place in a private dining-room, ironically called the Red Salon, and was ordered under the name of Sara Breitová (a German-Czech version of Sally's maiden name, Bright). Jiřina had invited Václav Havel and his wife, Olga; the Šimečkas, from Bratislava; the

Our 50th wedding anniversary, with Václav and Olga Havel

Dienstbiers; the Battĕks; and the Palouš's; Jaroslav Opat and his wife, Dana Nĕmcová, and her daughter, Markéta; and a dozen other leading Chartists, most of whom I knew personally. At the beginning Ludvík Vaculík came to excuse himself because of another engagement and presented Sally with a single red rose. The only foreigner present was my fellow Canadian, Peter Bakewell. We learned much later that there were five police agents among the waiters, but the affair passed off

Rudolf Battěk, Petr Pithart, and Father Václav Malý

without any police intervention. One of the Němec sons, Oldřich, took many black and white photographs of the evening and of the ceremony the following day. These were "lost" for some time at the photographic studio (were they being examined by the police?) but were later discovered.

At Sally's suggestion, Father Malý said grace, thus exemplifying the solidarity of believers and non-believers in the Chartist movement. Charter spokeswoman Libuše Šilhanová presented us, on behalf of Charter 77, with a coloured engraving of early eighteenth century Prague. There was much speech-making, as Havel and others informally expressed their appreciation of the work that we had done for the common cause. Jiří Dientsbier praised my *Letters from Prague* and jokingly suggested that a railway station should be named after me, in the same way that the French scholar, Ernest Denis, had been honoured after the First World War. Sally and I responded with words of praise for the work of the Chartists. I spoke of the great contrast of present-day Prague with the Prague that I had first visited in 1937. It was an evening of warm friendship, during which our guests had the rare opportunity to get together for a purely social evening, and we experienced the thrill of meeting good Chartist friends in a convivial atmosphere. After the event we repaired with the Šimečkas to Jiřina's apartment for whiskey and tea and a friendly chat. Milan said that the occasion had been the most wonderful event in many years and had brought tears to his eyes.

The next day came the ceremony in the Old Town Hall in the very same Marriage Room where we had said our vows in 1937. Jiřina had arranged it this time for Professor Harold Skilling. As we walked in an organist was playing. To the surprise of the lady in charge we were followed in by many friends, almost all dissidents, including Havel, Pithart, Dienstbier, Radim Palouš, the Šimečkas, some 35 people in all, including several children. The only foreigner present was the wife of Karl Schmitt, chargé d'affaires at the U.S. embassy; he had been my student at Dartmouth College.

Presiding was the chair of the National Committee of Prague I, a portly, Brunhilde-like figure with blonde hair, wearing a long black robe and her chain of office. In a warm and dignified manner she read a speech in which she praised our long marriage and my historical work. She did not mention and no doubt was unaware of my books on 1968 and Charter 77. There was a delicious irony, in which our friends took great delight, in this tribute to an "enemy of the state" by a Communist functionary in the presence of so many dissidents, whom she no doubt did not recognize. At the end she gave Sally a bouquet of flowers and presented both of us with a scroll of "renewal of vows" and a bronze medal of Prague. We also received, to our amusement, a large parcel of "refreshments," which contained egg cognac, assorted cheeses, and even some American chewing gum. At the close the guests filed past to embrace and congratulate us. Havel gave us a lovely black and white etching of the ascension of Wenceslas to Heaven. As we left the Town Hall we were greeted by Jelka and Olinka, who had been unable to reach the city hall in time because of the construction in the square. They gave me some flowers and a beautiful engraving, *Ecce homo*. The next day there was an amusing report of the event in the *Večerní Praha* (Evening Prague), headed "marriage over the ocean." In language quite unusual for a Communist newspaper, the writer praised this couple who had returned over the ocean from a great distance because of their love of Prague. The event was also reported in Charter 77's *Informace*.

After the ceremony, with Jiřina and the Šimečkas, we drank some wine in the Old Synagogue Restaurant. Milan joked that the wedding had been a historic moment — the "reconciliation of us and the state!" Things were changing in the Soviet Union and in Czechoslovakia, too. Social development, not power struggle, would eventually bring about change in leadership and policy. He could not have imagined three years ago that the situation would be so much better; he thought that in another three years things would be better still, and Vilém Prečan would be sitting with us. (This in fact did happen!) Things were moving in Slovakia, too. Milan was meeting regularly with about a dozen people, something that would have been quite impossible just two to three years ago.

Early on the morning of our departure from Czechoslovakia Šiklová joined us for breakfast and farewell. An American diplomat drove us to the airport, stopping for a brief moment at the burial place of Jan Patočka, one of the first Charter spokespersons, who had died under interrogation, in an ancient monastery outside Prague. We placed flowers on the grave and took some photographs. At the airport there were no problems at customs or immigration! I bought a bottle of Becherovka for Prečan, and a few hours later he met us in Nürnberg. Peter Bakewell had just arrived by car from Prague, bringing with him our notes, films, and gifts and a trunk full of the latest batch of Charter materials. In the parking lot at the airport, in contrast to their customary secrecy, he and Vilém openly transferred the loads from one car to the other.

We spent a week with the Prečans, this time in the fairytale Schwarzenberg Castle, high above the lovely old town of Scheinfeld, with its timbered houses, old inns, and a tower in the main street. Prince Karel Schwarzenberg, descendant of one of the great Bohemian aristocratic families, was a patriotic Czech who had lived in Vienna for many years and had been active in the international human rights movement. In 1986 he had offered space in his Bavarian castle, at a nominal rent, for the newly formed Documentation Centre for the Promotion of Independent Czechoslovak Literature, which had been established that year with a generous grant from the National Endowment for Democracy in Washington, DC. Prečan proudly showed us his well-equipped offices and facilities. The centre had already become a focal point for communications with the homeland and with other exiles abroad. Shipments to the homeland sometimes included xerox machines and tape recorders.

We had decided to hold the first meeting of the Academic Advisory Council, of which I was chairman, during our stay in Scheinfeld. Its members gradually arrived: Jan Vladislav, exiled writer, who chaired the centre's executive committee, from Paris; Jacques Rupnik, political scientist, also from Paris; and two historians, Eva Hartmannová, from Munich, and Anton Staudinger, from Vienna. A Czech exile, Milan

Horáček, who had formerly been a member of the West German Bundestag for the Green party, sat in on some of our meetings. So did the prince. Our agenda included reports by me on our trip to Prague and by Prečan on the centre's activities, including the plans for a quarterly journal, *Acta*, and the progress of the publication of the works of Jan Patočka. We discussed at length ways and means to extend the influence of the Documentation Centre in scholarly circles and among the foundations, especially in West Germany. During the conference we ate together at the great oval table in the dining-room. On one occasion the prince, to our amusement, personally carried over a huge tray of food and drink left over from the recent visit of French guests from Nancy, Scheinfeld's sister city. Sally had great fun opening up the parcel of food and drink given us by the city of Prague at the wedding ceremony.

AN INDEPENDENT SOCIETY

By this time, I had been studying and writing on samizdat and independent societies in central and eastern Europe for several years. During my trip to Czechoslovakia in 1987 I gathered new ideas for a book on the subject. Borrowing Benda's concept of the parallel *polis* and the similar concept of a "second society" from Elmer Hankiss, the Hungarian sociologist, I developed their ideas in theoretical terms and examined the contrasting patterns of this phenomenon in the Soviet Union and in the Communist countries of central and eastern Europe. The second, or independent society included the second culture, the second public (opinion), unofficial education and scholarship, social deviance, the second economy, and what I called para-politics, or a second polity. The last expressed itself in movements for the defence of human rights, for peace and European unity, and for opposition to nuclear weapons, as well as in ecological protests and various informal political groupings. There was even what some Czechs called an embryonic international *polis*, involving cooperation with dissidents in other countries, especially the Poles, and with Western peace movements.

In late 1988, extraordinary things were happening in central and eastern Europe. There was an outburst of new forms of unofficial activity and a blurring of the lines between the two cultures and the two societies. Barring new repression, I wrote, the independent society might fuse more and more with the official society, and society as a whole might increasingly escape the thrall of the state. This would still be a far cry from the genuine civil society envisaged by some authors in eastern and western Europe. The crucial question, as yet unanswered, was whether existing autonomous spheres would be greatly broadened and recognized and legally guaranteed by the state and whether the state itself would be subject to democratic control.

I finally completed the book late in 1988. After some delay, Ohio State University Press reached an agreement with Macmillan to co-publish it in the United States. St Antony's College, Oxford, decided to include it in its book series. Macmillan agreed to use my design for the cover — an old Underwood typewriter, with padlock and chain.[2]

In preparing the book I had distributed to leading Czechoslovak, Hungarian, and Polish dissidents an *anketa* (questionnaire), which asked them to give their opinions on the meaning of the term "independent society" and on its purposes and potential. The Czech responses were miniature essays, which contained prescient remarks about what had happened since they were written in 1986 and 1987 and seemed to be still relevant to the present and the future. Paul Wilson, who had lived for many years in Czechoslovakia and translated materials for me in the past, helped me in preparing some of the Czech essays for publication in English. We published several of these essays, together with Benda's article on the parallel *polis*, in a special issue of the journal *Social Research*.[3] Later we published a small book, under the title *Civic Freedom in Central Europe: Voices from Czechoslovakia*, which contained all 18 of the Czech responses and several more recent essays, together with a historical introduction. The book did not appear until 1991, so I had to write and rewrite the introductory essay to keep up with the rapid flow of events. It was too early, I wrote, to predict whether this struggle of competing political forces would lead to the gradual erosion of state power or would be forcefully terminated by the regimes. The final outcome was still uncertain but the seeds of democracy and pluralism were planted, and the way had been opened for the building of genuine civil societies in central and eastern Europe, especially in Czechoslovakia.[4]

NOTES

1. English version: V. Prečan, ed., *Ten Years of Charter 77* (Scheinfeld: Dokumentationszentrum zur Forderung der unabhängigen tschechoslowakischen Literatur, 1986).
2. Skilling, *Samizdat and an Independent Society in Central and Eastern Europe* (London: Macmillan, 1989).
3. *Social Research* 55, nos. 1/2 (spring-summer, 1988).
4. Skilling and Paul Wilson, eds., *Civic Freedom in Central Europe: Voices from Czechoslovakia* (London: Macmillan, 1991).

19

THE VELVET REVOLUTION:
INDEPENDENCE AND PARTITION

THE ACTUAL COURSE OF EVENTS in Prague in late 1989 and early 1990 overtook what I was writing. During our visit in 1987 Sally and I had observed a greater spirit of freedom and sensed greater hopefulness, but we did not seriously expect dramatic change. In fact, in a long article published in the *Globe and Mail* (4 November 1989), I described Czechoslovakia as "a rock of stability and calm in the turbulent seas of communism" in eastern Europe. It was "out of step" with its allies, East Germany, Hungary, and Poland, and even Bulgaria, which were undergoing revolutionary changes. I referred to the growth of civic courage during the past several years and the huge, spontaneous demonstrations on 28 October in Prague and Brno, but I did not think that popular resistance on the scale of East Germany was likely. Czechoslovakia stood in a period of transition, I concluded, in which the future could not be predicted. It would be determined by the outcome of the conflict between the rising tide of civic freedom and a panic-stricken but still powerful regime.

Within days, events had contradicted my cautious prediction, as a series of massive demonstrations shook the regime to its foundations and led to negotiations between the Communists and the Civic Forum, headed by Havel, and the formation of a government with a non-Communist majority. I was sorely tempted to go to Prague to witness this turning point in Czechoslovak and European history. One of the American television networks asked me whether I would be able to rush off to Prague, to cover these happenings. I reluctantly declined, fearing that it would have been risky at my age to travel in midwinter and engage in the hectic job of international broadcasting.

The democratic revolution of the late 1980s in central and eastern Europe was a dramatic turning-point in Czechoslovak and European history. We shared the euphoria of most Czechs and Slovaks, along with their hope that the revolution would completely replace the system of despotic rule with a democratic one, where civil and human rights, and free elections, were restored. The new order would differ greatly from the First Republic, whose traditions had been severely damaged, if not destroyed, during the 50 years since Munich. However, I believed that the democratic ideas and principles of Masaryk would be revived and the goals of Charter 77 at last attained. I was well aware that it was impossible to predict with any certainty what would happen in the next few weeks, let alone in the years to come. Yet the way had been opened for a new beginning within a democratic framework and for a rational approach to the solution of the myriad problems left behind by Communism and those presented by the construction of a new order.

Vilém Prečan, in frequent telephone calls, kept me in touch with exciting events — most particularly, the election of Václav Havel as president of the republic and his inauguration in The Hrad! Dubček became chairman of the National Assembly; Jiří Dientsbier, minister of foreign affairs; and Petr Pithart, premier of the Czech Republic. In the academic world a full-scale revolution was underway. Radim Palouš was elected rector of Charles University, and Miroslav Kusý, rector of Komenský University in Bratislava. Prečan, in one of his letters, wrote that the great changes had given him a sense of "historical satisfaction" and had seemed to vindicate his work in exile.

In Canada there was widespread public interest in the Velvet Revolution and its consequences. I received many invitations to speak on the situation and to give interviews in the press and on radio and television. In December 1989, the Czechoslovak community organized a gala celebration at Toronto's St Lawrence Centre for the Arts, with dance, music, plays, and speeches. I spoke a few words in Czech, observing that my joking prediction to Václav Havel in 1987 of his return to the Castle had been confirmed. In March 1990, I spoke to a gathering of Canadian Czechs and Slovaks in support of the newly formed Civic Forum Fund. I paid tribute to Charter 77 and the other independent movements that had been catalysts for the formation of the Civic Forum and had provided leadership in the democratic revolution.

For me an unusual by-product of the events in eastern Europe was a 25th anniversary reunion of the students who had taken part in my Toronto seminar on eastern Europe in 1965-66. One of them, Colleen Taylor, who had taken a doctorate in Slavic literature, called me from

Convocation Hall during Havel's state visit, 1990, with (left to right)
the author, President Havel, the Chancellor of the University of Toronto,
John Aird, and Josef Čermák at the microphone

Chicago and suggested that we meet to discuss these momentous happenings. She was no longer in the academic world but was working
with the Institute of Gas Technology. Five of the others were professors at Canadian universities, specializing in the literature, politics or
history of eastern Europe; one was a deputy minister in the Ontario
government. All of them joined Sally and me for dinner at Solo Maria,
our favourite restaurant across the street; afterward, at home, we talked
until midnight about the extraordinary changes unfolding half a world
away.

In February 1990 Václav Havel, newly elected president of
Czechoslovakia, paid a state visit to Canada. Sally and I were invited by
the governor general, Ray Hnatyshyn, to a dinner given in Havel's honour in Rideau Hall. We flew down to Ottawa for this occasion and
joined the crowd of Czechs and Slovaks who were eagerly awaiting the
arrival of Havel's plane at the Uplands Airport. We attended a luncheon at the University of Ottawa in honour of university rectors,
including Radim Palouš and Miroslav Kusý, who had accompanied
Havel, and we heard their fervent plea for Canadian assistance to
Czechoslovak higher education. In the afternoon there was a huge
meeting of the Czechoslovak community in Nepean, a suburb of

Ottawa. Although I had special tickets, we were unable to get into the overcrowded hall and had to wait to see Havel at the reception. In the receiving line, Havel embraced me with a great bear hug and called me "our Canadian father." At the state dinner, attended by some four hundred guests, Havel and his wife, Olga, astonished everyone by greeting us with warm embraces and kisses. Havel gave a formal address in Czech, and the governor general responded in part in Ukrainian, his mother tongue. There seemed to be a personal rapport between them, not only because of their use of two Slavic languages, but also in a common understanding of the importance of human rights.

In Toronto I had several opportunities to meet Havel during his ten-hour visit. In Convocation Hall at the University of Toronto a crowd of 1,500 awaited him with impatience and gave him a standing ovation. He arrived late from an official lunch with the Ontario premier; he had insisted on walking from the legislative buildings at Queen's Park and through the neighbouring university campus without a coat in cold Canadian weather! On the way he hammed it up with the press by posing on one of the motorcycles of the police escort. The program at Convocation Hall was long, with many greetings and gifts from local Czech and Slovak organizations, including the World Slovak League. Based in Toronto, the League represented extreme Slovak nationalism and advocated separation of Slovaks from Czechs. To the discomfiture of the chairman, and the annoyance of the audience, the spokesman of the League, Rev. Dušan Toth, spoke at great length and stressed the need for Slovak equality and sovereignty. I had the honour of introducing Havel. I compared his faith and courage to that of Andrei Sakharov, Lech Wałesa, and Nelson Mandela. In his speech Havel expressed deep thanks for what Czechs and Slovaks in emigration had contributed to the Czechoslovak cause. He called for the two nations to live together in a democratic federation. He irritated some Czechs in the audience by urging that Czechs should acquire a Czech national consciousness, separate from their Czechoslovak consciousness, to parallel Slovak national feelings.

After the meeting Havel rushed to the Sixty-Eight Publishers to meet his good friends Josef and Zdena Škvorecký. Again he greeted me with a hug and laughingly said: "You are everywhere — like God!" He embraced Sally warmly and then at my request repeated it for a photograph. After no more than half an hour he was off with his motorcade to the airport for the flight to Washington. It had been a memorable visit, and Havel endeared himself to everyone, including those who were not Czech or Slovak, by his openness and simplicity and by his eloquence. One relished the irony of the metamorphosis of a dissident and former political prisoner to a president hailed by the world.

Sally and I soon received an official invitation from Charter 77 to be present at a gathering of all signatories and friends of the Charter in Prague in March 1990. Prečan urged us to come and talked of my giving lectures in the Academy of Sciences and at Charles University and of receiving other honours, including a reception by President Havel. During Havel's state visit in Ottawa, Joe Clark, Canadian external affairs minister, told me that Jiří Dienstbier had asked him if there were any objections to the granting of some kind of award to the Canadian diplomat Peter Bakewell and to me, for our services to the Czechoslovak cause. Barry Mawhinney, the Canadian ambassador to Prague, invited us to stay as his guests in the embassy residence. It was to be Sally's last trip to Prague before her death in May.

Sally and I were cordially received by Ambassador Mawhinney and his wife, Islay, with whom we stayed in Hadovka. Mawhinney organized a large reception in honour of Charter 77, of us, and of two representatives of the Czechoslovak Association of Canada who were visiting Prague. President Havel was travelling abroad and was unable to join us. There were about 160 guests, including ambassadors and high officials, and many old friends whom we had met conspiratorially in the past. Jaroslav Kořan, mayor of Prague, who had taken photographs at our anniversary wedding ceremony in 1987, showed me a picture that he had taken of the Denisovo (Denis) railway station, under demolition, with a placard in the ruins bearing the name Skilling Station.

At a luncheon given by the ambassador and his wife, the only guest, Rector Radim Palouš, broke the news in confidence that I was to be awarded an honorary degree at Charles University. The approval of the Committee on Degrees had not yet been given, so that the ceremony could not take place during this visit. He invited me, however, to give a lecture at the university. On that occasion, a few days later, Palouš presented me with a bronze medal and gave Sally a huge bouquet of flowers and two exquisite china cups. He presided over my seminar in the small Aula of the ancient Carolinum. Vilém Prečan read a *laudatio* (citation) of my life and work. I gave a lecture on Masaryk, in Czech, which I had carefully prepared and rehearsed in Toronto. I summarized the main theme of my book, which was in preparation, depicting Masaryk as a "permanent non-conformist," a courageous critic of conventional thinking and of official institutions. I documented this by describing his activity as an academic iconoclast, a radical feminist, a religious heretic, and a foe of anti-semitism.

Vilém Prečan, by a miracle of hard work, was successful in completing the Czech version of the book on Charter 77's tenth "anniversary," extended to cover thirteen years, in time for the celebration on 17 March. When Sally and I arrived, Smetana Hall in the Obecní dům was filled to overflowing for the gathering of Charter 77 signatories — the first time they had met together publicly. There were many speeches by leading Chartists about whether Charter 77 should continue to function under the new conditions and what its role should be. Jiří Ruml argued that no society was so healthy that it did not need a Charter 77 to correct its mistakes. Jiřina Šiklová, in her remarks, made mention of the aid that Wolfgang Scheur, the German diplomat, Peter Bakewell and I had given to the Charter movement. She insisted on escorting me to the platform, but I was not called on to speak.

In the evening Sally and I attended a festive celebration in the Lucerna Concert hall. On the stairs Havel gave us a hurried greeting as he rushed by, a few minutes late. We sat with Peter Bakewell in reserved seats next to the presidential box, where Zbigniew Brzezinski was one of a large entourage of other guests and advisers. Havel spoke very briefly, rejoicing in the fact that the Plastic People of the Universe, after being banned for so many years, had realized an old dream of performing publicly in the Lucerna. Surrounded by his bodyguard, he left before the intermission, so there was no chance to talk with him. We shared in the rejoicing but felt a little deflated by the fact that the honour that we had expected did not materialize. Peter Bakewell was especially upset, since the Canadian Department of External Affairs had given him leave of absence to come to Prague for this purpose. Sally was so upset that she even said that there was no point in staying longer in Prague.

The fiasco of the mysterious "honour" that was not granted was never explained. Prečan was furious that Havel had not received us and next day telephoned the Presidential Chancellery as well as the offices of the Foreign Ministry and the premier. Perhaps as a result of his intervention, Peter Bakewell and I were invited at short notice to come, early one morning, to the Černín Palace, to meet Jiří Dienstbier, the foreign minister. He sought to atone somewhat for the diplomatic blunder concerning the promised award by issuing a communiqué expressing warm appreciation of what we and several other diplomats, British and American, had done for the Czechoslovak cause. Although he was leaving for Spain that morning Dienstbier talked with us about foreign policy for more than an hour. In view of the uncertainty of the situation in the Soviet Union and the possibility that it would soon break up, he believed that Germany, now united, should remain a member of NATO. In time a new security framework, stretching from San Francisco to Vladivostok, must be created, perhaps within the Helsinki Final Act. Seemingly unhurried, he escorted us to the offices that Edvard Beneš had occupied as foreign minister in the 1920s and the 1930s, to which Dienstbier was planning to move. He also took us to see the little room in which Jan Masaryk had lived — and from the windows of which he had fallen to his death in March 1948. Dienstbier was still not sure whether this had been suicide or assassination.

On the day after Sally and I arrived a state visit by the German president, Richard von Weiszäcker, dramatically illustrated the complete reversal of history. The visit was scheduled for 15 March, the day Nazi troops had occupied the country over 50 years earlier. The Vladislav Hall in the Castle was a splendid setting for a ceremonial meeting, which I attended in the company of the Canadian ambassador. The two presidents expressed their friendship and mutual respect; the German president openly condemned the German invasion in 1939, and the Czechoslovak president condemned the brutal expulsion of the Sudeten Germans in 1945. It was a moving experience to watch the two heads of state stroll across the courtyard of the castle where I had stood, with Sally, in 1939 and caught a glimpse of Hitler at the window above.

Sally and I saw pictures of Havel posted everywhere. At the top of Václavské náměstí the statue of St Wenceslas, the site of many demonstrations in the past, was plastered with posters and pictures. Nearby was a high mound of wax produced by candles that had burned there for hours, now covered with flowers and pictures of Tomáš and Jan Masaryk, Edvard Beneš, Jan Palach, and other great figures of Czech history. At the foot of the wide avenue was a reproduction of an octopus, lampooning Communism. Nearby a rock-and-roll group played. The Old Town Square, so long marred by scaffoldings, had been restored to its former beauty. Down on the Vltava the ghastly white statue of Klement Gottwald, the Communist leader, had been removed. Up at the Castle, there was an operetta-like changing of the guard in its newly designed uniforms. In the Černín Palace opposite Sally and I visited an exhibit on the life and work of T.G. Masaryk. Spring was coming and Czechoslovakia was free.

The political situation had changed almost beyond recognition. Václav Havel was in the Castle, and it seemed likely that he would run again for the presidency; there was really no alternative to him, we were told. The Civic Forum (OF), although it was not a party or the government, exercised decisive influence on policy at the centre, in the localities, and in individual enterprises and institutions. Although it had not been elected, it was an indispensable agent of democratic change. I paid several visits to the OF headquarters, which was lodged in the cramped five-storey building formerly occupied by the League for Czechoslovak-Soviet Friendship, at the foot of Václavská náměstí. I found it a hive of activity, humming with young political volunteers. In conversation with one of its leading figures, Martin Palouš, I learned that the OF was expected to be a kind of umbrella for a number of parties in the forthcoming election and, if victorious, the basis of a coalition government. I attended a joint session of the Federal Assembly, held in the same building where the Communist rubber-stamp parliament had met. Although these people had not been elected, they were clearly acting as a genuine parliament, debating and deciding issues of public policy in a democratic fashion. My old friend Michal Lakatoš, now back in his old room at the Institute of State and Law, was optimistic about the future in the Czech Republic and did not did not think there was an imminent danger of Slovak separation. The Slovaks were fearful of Russia and wanted the relationship with the West that the Czechs already had achieved. We both agreed that the democratic revolution was in its first phase and that there was a long road ahead before a civil society — with a free press and organized opposition parties — was attained.

Prečan was director of a newly formed Institute for Contemporary History, where he had assembled a staff of 13 scholars, many of whom had been ousted by the Communists. At the Academy of Sciences we met with Viktor Knapp, former Communist legal scholar and now head of the Social Sciences Division, to discuss the possibility of publishing an abridged Czech version of my book on the interrupted revolution, but in the end nothing came of it. I also attended the opening of an exhibition of books published in samizdat and abroad during the Communist years. Vilem Prečan and Karel Srp, now a high official of the Ministry of Culture, spoke on the significance of this documentation of independent activity in defiance of the Communist regime.

There was also evidence of the extraordinary, and often ironic, changes in the personal lives of former dissidents. Jiřina Šiklová had been reappointed to the Department of Sociology at Charles

University. Milan Otáhal, dismissed in 1968, was back in the Historical Institute. Jaroslav Opat, after many years of manual work, had been named director of a revived Masaryk Institute. Václav Kotyk, excluded from scholarly work for 20 years, had been appointed director of a new Institute of International Relations. Father Malý, who had become a kind of hero during the November events, had spurned high office and was now priest at the sadly run-down St Wenceslas church on Malá Strana. With Mawhinney and Bakewell, both of whom were Catholic, I attended high mass in his church. Father Malý praised the work of Charter 77 and prayed for its future. Spotting me far back in the congregation, he spoke warmly to the congregation of the work I had done for Charter 77.

My old friends in the Haninger family suffered less drastic changes in their fortunes. Gina had been elected editor-in-chief of all the magazines published by the agricultural department of a former Communist publishing house, and was also back as the editor of a magazine on small animals and pets. She talked of the exciting days of November and December, when, with her two sons, she had taken part in demonstrations every day. Her sister, Jelka, still editor-in-chief of the information journal, told me of interrogations and house searches that had followed our last meeting in 1987. She told me that the most emotional experience of her life had been in hospital, listening on the radio to Havel's speech before the U.S. Congress. She had felt proud to be a Czech, she said! When I suggested that Communism had perhaps brought some advantages, she challenged me to name one — and was not able to offer an example herself. Her brother, Milan, told me of the great changes in the technical college where he worked, and the growing role of students in the new Academic Council.

Courtesy of Petr Pithart, the Czech premier, we were given the use of a car and a chauffeur for a trip to Brno and Bratislava. We were accompanied by Derek Paton, a former Toronto student, who had been living in Czechoslovakia for several years on a fellowship. We stayed in the home of Iva Kotrlá, a Catholic dissident writer. She spoke nostalgically of "the golden days of dissidence" and was highly critical of the present situation, particularly in education. We spent the first evening at a performance of *Animal Farm* in English by students of Don Sparling, a Canadian who had taught at the Masaryk University for many years. His students had been reading Orwell for a long time, he said, although this could not be publicly revealed at the time. The next day we chatted with the university rector, Milan Jelínek, who had never lost his post as professor of Slavic literature despite close contact with the dissident movement. It was a slow and difficult process, he said, to ease out of the university former Communists who had no qualifications and to reintegrate into the faculty dissidents who had been barred from scholarly life for many years.

On the way to Bratislava we made a stop in Hodonín, the birthplace of Masaryk. We were happy to see that the huge statue of the former president had been restored to its place and a square had been named after him. In Bratislava we stayed in the spacious but dilapidated apartment of Mrs Anna Abrahám, the mother of Samuel Abrahám, who had been a student in Toronto. She spoke strongly in favour of Masaryk and Havel and was emphatically Czechoslovak in her orientation. A walking tour of the Old Town revealed that it was still sadly in need of repair. We stopped in to look at an exhibit of Masaryk's writings.

At the Komenský University, Miro Kusý, now its rector, presented me with a medal and gave Sally a bouquet and some pieces of china. At a seminar that he chaired I repeated the lecture on Masaryk I had given in Prague, but introduced it with a few words in Slovak, carefully prepared beforehand. Later, the Dean of the Faculty of Law, who had been a party member but, I was told, behaved well in 1968 and November 1989, told me that only a small sector of public opinion favoured Slovak independence and that there was no danger of separation. Professor Karol Rebro agreed with him and was critical of the idea of confederation; he preferred a federation with strong central powers. At a celebratory luncheon we had a happy reunion with Milan and Eva Šimečka and Dana Němcová, now a parliamentary deputy, who was visiting Bratislava. Due to Sally's sudden illness I had to go alone to tea at the Šimečkas and then to dinner with them in a Hungarian restaurant. Milan felt sure that separatism was not strong in Slovakia and that it was being promoted mainly by North American Slovak emigrants. He talked with nostalgia of the dissident days when life was exciting and of the initial period of euphoria after November.

A month after our return from Czechoslovakia Sally suffered a stroke, and she passed away peacefully in her sleep on 3 May. Sally had been a devoted partner in my life and work for more than 50 years and had given me unstinting support in good times as well as in bad. She had been a meticulous and creative editor of everything that I wrote so she was, in an important sense, their co-author. The Centre for Russian and East European Studies arranged a memorial service in the Univer-

Sally at the International Slavic Conference, Garmisch, 1980

sity College Union. There was no funeral service, as she had donated her body to the university's medical school. Letters poured in from all over the world from people whom she had known at every stage of her life — from Norristown and Barnard, London and Oxford, Dartmouth and Wisconsin, and Czechoslovakia. They wrote of a wonderful woman — intelligent, warm and friendly to others, with high moral standards. From Czechoslovakia came many letters of appreciation for her life, including a message from the spokespersons of Charter 77 and a telegram from President Havel. He referred to "that rare and good Sally who did so much for our nation, long ago in 1939, but also later in the difficult years between the Soviet occupation and the velvet revolution." During the last ten days of Sally's illness and after her death I was buoyed up by the support that I received from friends and neighbours and from our two sons. On the day before she died David, who had spent a year travelling in Australia, Thailand, and Japan with his friend Jan, arrived in time to have a final visit with her. During the next difficult three weeks David was with me, and soon after he left Peter arrived for a long stay. With the help of good friends in Toronto I was able to work out a new pattern of life in the next years.

WITH PETER TO CZECHOSLOVAKIA

I made a second trip to Czechoslovakia, in August 1990, this time with Peter. On the way we stopped off in England for the International Congress of Soviet and East European Studies, in Harrogate, fine former bath town in the Midlands. I presented a paper on T.G. Masaryk, in which I summarized the theme of my book — Masaryk as a dissident who had worked against the current in the years before 1914. Peter, who had spent some days in London, rejoined me for the Channel crossing by overnight ferry to the Netherlands. There we stayed in a *pension* in Leiden and explored this ancient town and its canals on foot and by boat. We visited The Hague, Haarlem, Amsterdam, and Utrecht by bus or express train, and made a special excursion to the walled city of Naarden, where the Czech educational philosopher, Jan Amos Komenský, had lived and died in exile.

We travelled through Germany by train to spend a few days with the Prečans, and then went on to Prague by car with Vilém by his usual route — a four and a half hour drive. We spent nine days in Prague, the first time Peter had been there since his childhood. Like so many others he fell in love with the city and came to know my old friends. It was good to explore Prague with him and see its beauties through his eyes. We stayed in a little *garsonka* (*garçonnière*) which was to become our favourite "*byt*" in Prague. Located in the heart of the city, it was a bizarre place — a single large room, with one wall entirely covered by an enlarged photograph of a mountain spot in the Krkonoše and crammed with artificial flowers, knickknacks and souvenirs. Prague was crowded with Germans, Italians, and tourists from other parts of the world. Restaurants were too few and usually overcrowded. At every turn we heard the music of buskers; the Charles Bridge was alive with young people and handicraft sellers. Before a concert given by the Rolling Stones in the stadium, pandemonium reigned in the streets below. President Havel received them in the Castle; by chance Peter saw them waving from the window in the third courtyard.

This was not a customary working trip, but we did visit the headquarters of the Civic Forum, It was no longer a place of hustle and bustle. The elections were over, and its major personalities occupied posts in the government and in Parliament. The Civic Forum had its own nationwide organization, which met regularly and sought to achieve a consensus on policy. It also sought to influence government and Parliament directly and to influence public opinion. Although I had little time for academic work I put in a few hours at the Klementinum and had some talks with historian friends. Jan Havránek took us on a walking tour of the Old Town, of which he knew every stone.

We were in Prague on 21 August and witnessed great demonstrations in memory of that day of infamy. From the office of Gina Makariusová at the top of Václavské náměstí we observed President Havel laying a wreath at the statue of St Wenceslas. Then on television we watched the scene at the foot of the avenue, where Havel and Dubček spoke from the balcony of the Civic Forum building. Havel called for a second or "continuing revolution" to press forward to a completely reformed system. Dubček made a forceful defence of the unity of Czechs and Slovaks.

While in Prague we visited Milan Šimečka, who had been pressed into service as an adviser to the president on relations with Czechs and Slovaks abroad. He took us for a walk through the "corridors of power" and showed us the office of the president. Outside the room leaned the famous scooter that Havel used to dash around the huge Castle. Šimečka seemed not to feel at home in high office and openly admitted that he would have preferred to stay in Bratislava as an independent critic. Foremost in his mind was the problem of Slovakia. He was convinced that 80 percent of Slovaks wanted to remain in a union with the Czechs. Havel had decided to establish a presidential office in Bratislava Castle to give the Slovaks the feeling that he was also *their* president. We were joined by the Prečans and Jiřina Šiklová for dinner in the nearby Lion's Court, and we had an old-time chat about politics. Like many others to whom we talked, they were obsessed with the fact that after the fall of Communism, many people lacked a spirit of independence and a readiness to work. Little did we realize that this was to be our last meeting with Milan. It was shocking to learn only one month later of his sudden death from heart failure — wrongly diagnosed as something less serious. He was about to come to Canada for a lecture in Vancouver and was planning to stop over with me in Toronto.

Prečan proudly told me that "The Black Book" on the Soviet occupation of 1968 had been published and 100,000 copies had sold out — another 50,000 would be printed. Jiřina was back at her academic work, but frustrated by lack of funds and space for the Gender Studies Department which she had set up. She gave me the tiny figure of a sleeping cat (representing the "inactive" KAT, her underground pseudonym). She gave Peter a little owl — for wisdom, she said.

HIGH HONOURS IN PRAGUE

In 1990 I returned to Prague for two thrilling occasions — the granting to me of an honorary degree by Charles University and a reception by President Havel at the Castle. Both my sons went with me, and it was the first time they had been together for some years. We three drank in the beauties of Prague. David and I shared a guest room in the oldest university building, the Carolinum, where we had a spacious room, with high beamed ceilings decorated with ornate floral patterns. Peter lived not far away in Jiřina's flat. We spent much of our time as tourists, armed with cameras, exploring favourite corners of Prague that Sally and I had known so well. Sometimes I was an amateur guide, pointing out spots where historic events or incidents in my life had taken place. On two occasions we had the expert guidance of Professor Jan Havránek — once in Malá Strana, another time in the New Town. Vilém Prečan was away in Moscow during most of our visit but before he left he took me to see the new chairman of the Academy of Sciences, the distinguished chemist Otto Wichterle, and told him of his plan to establish a Skilling Fellowship to enable a Czech student of history to study for a year in Canada. At Jiřina's apartment we had a wonderful farewell dinner, at which she regaled us with tales of conspiracy in the Charter days and told us of three hidden "bugs" in her apartment, which she had learned about only recently.

The big event was the convocation at Charles University. The Karolinum was crowded with guests, including many old friends from the dissident days. The ceremony, dignified but warm, took place against the backdrop of the great tapestry that represented (rather unhistorically!) the granting of the university seal to Charles IV in 1348 by the long-deceased King Wenceslas. The deans wore red robes, the professors their Hussite black gowns and hats, and the beadles carried maces. Fanfare, organ music, and the playing of the Canadian and Czechoslovak national anthems sent shivers down my spine. I was "promoted" by my old friend Josef Polišenský, who, in Latin, presented me with the diploma and placed a gold chain around my neck. I then spoke, in Czech, paying tribute to the greatness of Charles

Honorary Degree, Charles University, October 1990, with Professor Josef Polišenský

With Jiří Dienstbier, Minister of Foreign Affairs, and Jiřina Šiklová, at a reception following the ceremony

University and to its early rector, Jan Hus, and to distinguished past professors, such as Tomáš Masaryk, Otakar Odložilík, and Jan Patočka.

It was a moving occasion, a high point in my life, when I received the highest honour from the university that I had first known as a student in the 1930s. How I longed to share it with Sally! Then we rushed off by taxi to a luncheon given by the Canadian chargé d'affaires, Rob McRae, trained in philosophy, who had been close to the dissidents. It was a small group, including Jiřina, Dana Němcová, Zdeněk Urbánek, and the foreign minister, Jiří Dienstbier, who, he told us, had to tear himself away from a cabinet meeting to attend.

Equally exciting was our visit to the Castle to be received by President Havel. In the reception room, beautifully decorated with his own modern paintings, Havel greeted us warmly, with a small battery of media representatives recording the event. David took many pictures, including one of Havel and Peter in front of the gorgeous wall hanging given to Havel by the Dalai Lama. For half an hour we chatted informally at a great conference table. We reminisced about previous meetings in dissident days: he recalled my joking remark about him moving from Hrádeček, the little castle, to the Hrad, the big castle. Citing his famous essay on "the power of the powerless," I asked him whether he felt powerless now that he was in power! He laughed and said that he had discovered that even under the constitution his powers, except as commander in chief of the armed forces, were limited. Often when he proposed measures he was told by his ministers or advisers that it was politically impossible to do what he wanted. People, he said, wanted action and complained that he was only making promises or giving speeches. I also touched on a theme that ran through his dissident writings — the importance of ethics in politics. Had he found it possible, in his new position, to act morally? Havel replied that he did not consciously lie, but he could not always tell the people all the facts or reveal his own personal feelings. Would he someday write a play about the absurdity of power? Yes, perhaps he would in the distant future, but now he had no time to write anything but his speeches.

In the twilight, the boys and I walked down to Malá Strana and encountered, by chance, Markéta Fiálková (Němcová), now ambassador to Poland. She took us to her sister, Pavla's, who lived just below the Charles Bridge on Na Kampě. There followed a good evening of drink and talk. Martin Palouš, Pavla's husband, came in later; he had just been appointed one of four deputy ministers of foreign affairs, to replace another former dissident, Luboš Dobrovský, who had been named minister of national defence. Palouš told us that in his new job a central question was the relationship of Czechs and Slovaks. Although this was not intrinsically a foreign policy question, its solution was vital for the stability of the country and for foreign investment. He insisted that there must be unity of foreign policy in a newly federated state.

We encountered Havel on two other occasions. One was the opening of *Libri prohibiti*, a samizdat library based on the collection of a young dissident, Jiří Gruntorád, and located in the local National Committee in Prague VII. Jim Čert, a member of the Plastic People of the Universe, was playing the accordion in the crowded hallway. When Havel finally arrived he opened a bottle of champagne to celebrate the event. Informally attired in windbreaker and slacks, he seemed very much at home among his fellow dissidents, away from the cares of office.

The second occasion was 28 October, Czechoslovak National Independence Day, celebrated for the first time since the democratic revolution. I had an invitation from the president's office to attend the gala concert in the Castle; it was held in the newly restored Spanish Hall, a magnificent room of white and gold, with glittering chandeliers. In a brief speech Havel frankly acknowledged that many people were dissatisfied and full of doubt and fear and that some Slovaks were seeking separation. Everything must be done, he said, to maintain the unity of Czechs and Slovaks as equal nations within a federation that had enough competence at the centre to deal with common problems. The concert was moving, with music by Dvořák, Martinů, and Smetana, played by the Czech Philharmonic Orchestra under Jiří Bělohrádek. At intermission drinks were served, and we met our friends, Prince Schwarzenberg, Milo Kusý, and Radim Palouš, and some of the guests, including the U.S. ambassador Shirley Temple Black, who remembered my lecture in Washington just before her coming to Prague. Havel, who was for a moment standing alone, came toward us and asked how we liked the renovation of the hall: he apologized for the old carpet, which for budgetary reasons could not be replaced. Olga Havlová came over to speak to us about her work with a humanitarian fund to aid the disadvantaged that she had founded and headed.

I had little time — and, I must say, little inclination — to pursue my customary interviews about political life. However, when Dana

Němcová invited me to lunch at the parliamentary cafeteria, she said that as member of parliament she worked 14 hours a day, and found herself a frequent target of criticism. Conversation with other deputies, who joined us at our table, revealed that the Civic Forum, while it agreed on matters of principle, represented a wide spectrum of views on specific issues; its members were taking different directions politically, some to the left, others to the right. The more conservative Václav Klaus, minister of finance, had been elected chairman of the Civic Forum, defeating the more liberal Martin Palouš. Václav Benda, of the main Catholic party, represented another conservative tendency. His party had left the Civic Forum, against his own wishes. Rudolf Battěk, a member of the presidium of Parliament, had recently been expelled from the Social Democratic party because he had wanted it to join the Forum. He thought that the totalitarian system was deeply rooted and was difficult to change quickly. People continued to think and behave in the old way and were not used to the free exchange of opinions. Another deputy, Zdeněk Jičínský , a constitutional expert and a member of the commission of legal experts on the federal question, was hopeful that the new constitution would preserve strong federal competence; he rejected the idea of a loose federation or confederation. All who were at the table, including a Slovak deputy, Rostislav Rašín, of the Public Against Violence, agreed on the undesirability of Slovak separation and were highly critical of the nationalism that some Slovaks were promoting at home and abroad. Most Slovaks did not want separation, they assured me.

Later I pursued these themes at lunch with Zdeněk Kotrlý, a Brno deputy of the Czech National Council, now housed in the historic building of the Bohemian Diet. He, too, did not anticipate a break-up. A tripartite federation was not, he believed, a realistic possibility; only a minority in Moravia really wanted it. As in the past, Michal Lakatoš was a mine of information and interesting ideas. He was now head of the Department of the Theory of Law, in the Institute of State and Law. He regretted that the country had not yet been able, as the dissidents had hoped, to establish a civic society, replete with many parties and movements. The government was divided and found it difficult to agree on policies. The bureaucracy was made up mainly of members of the old *nomenklatura*, who often blocked reforms. President Havel was good, he thought, but his advisers, drawn from his dissident friends, were not well qualified. The Czech-Slovak relationship was uncertain; what was needed was a strong federal government, with power over foreign affairs, defence, foreign trade, finance, and economics.

I attended briefly the local Helsinki Citizens' Assembly, a newly formed body set up as an independent citizens' movement on an international basis. In his opening address Havel urged that the Helsinki process, based on the common ideas of a civic society, be consolidated as an all-European institution. One of my Chartist friends, Libuše Šilhanová, co-chair of the assembly, was privately very critical of the conference — there had been nothing but generalities and no really concrete decisions.

After my return from Prague in late October I resumed life without Sally; I stayed busy socially and became absorbed in research and writing on Masaryk. I now found that a word processor was indispensable to my work, and took a further step into the modern world by purchasing a fax machine. The even tenor of my life was rudely interrupted in May 1991 by an aneurysm of the aorta, detected in the nick of time. Ten days after the operation I was home again, having survived another crisis and entered on what I jokingly called my "fifth life." Shortly after I came home a memorial service for Sally and others was held by the medical school at St James in the Necropolis, the oldest cemetery in Toronto. Sally's ashes were deposited in a burial place marked by a small plaque honouring those who had given their bodies for science and teaching.

There was a happy by-product of my hospitalization. David came to be with me before and after the operation. While he was in Toronto he met several times with Jane Francis, the daughter of Cheritan Avenue neighbours, whom he had known since her childhood. They fell in love, and after visits back and forth between Toronto and Victoria, Jane moved to Victoria in 1992. A couple of years later they were happily married. Peter came home for his annual visit in August and stayed with me for six weeks. He was deeply immersed in his comparative literary analysis of the texts of a dozen of Buddha's discourses, using principally Tibetan sources, but also Sanskrit and Pali. During a visit to Cambridge Peter met, for the first time, Michael Ares, a Tibetan scholar from Oxford and husband of Suu Kyi, the imprisoned Burmese leader and winner of the Nobel Peace Prize. Michael and Peter were good friends until the former's untimely death in 1999.

After Peter's departure I flew to Ottawa for the Royal Society of Canada's International Symposium on Constraints to Scholarship and Science. There was a wide-ranging discussion by delegates from five continents and 17 countries on the economic, cultural, ethnic, and disciplinary limitations on freedom of scientific research. The conference closed with a statement, which I drafted, proclaiming the need for freedom of scholarship and science and the duty of scholars and scholarly bodies to take steps to resist threats to this freedom. I was glad that the conference had put the Royal Society on the map of international human rights activity. Alas, publishing the proceedings was quite another matter, in spite of great efforts by Justice Tarnopolsky, our committee chairman. At the time of his sudden death in 1994 the book had not come out, but it did appear later, dedicated to his memory.

THE ORDER OF THE WHITE LION

A milestone in my life occurred on 28 February 1992, my 80th birthday. I was awakened early in the morning by a fax message from Karel Schwarzenberg, Havel's chancellor, congratulating me on my birthday and informing me that President Havel had awarded me the highest honour for non-citizens, the Order of the White Lion, Third Class. A few moments later I was awakened again by a letter of congratulation from Miroslav Kusý, head of the President's Chancellery in Bratislava. Vilém Prečan had forewarned me by telephone about the coming award and jokingly explained that First Class was given to heads of state only, Second Class to government heads or foreign ministers, and Third Class to those "who had really done something!" I also was informed that I had been awarded the Palacký medal by the Academy of Sciences. There followed a deluge of letters of congratulations from old friends who now occupied high positions in the Czechoslovak Republic, from the spokesmen of Charter 77, and from other Czech and Slovak friends.

In going to Prague to receive these honours I was returning to a country that had, after the Velvet Revolution, established, without violence, a relatively stable democratic system independent of Soviet control. However, the future was uncertain. The Civic Forum, the basis of government, had won the general election in June 1990 but was in danger of disintegration because of internal differences; the outcome of a new election was unpredictable. Most serious of all was the future of the relationship of Czechs and Slovaks and the threat to the very existence of a united Czechoslovakia. When Kusý had written me about the Order of the White Lion he had expressed his confidence that I "would be coming to one country, not two." In fact he was right, but only in the short run, and by the end of the year the republic that Sally and I had first visited in 1937 would break in two.

Receiving the Order of the White Lion, Prague Castle, 1992

I wanted both David and Peter to be with me in Prague for these great occasions. The high point of our visit was the reception at the Castle by President Havel. This was not without its amusing aspects. When we arrived on foot at the great gates to the Castle the guards barred our entrance because we had no invitation. The guards used a walkie-talkie to communicate with the president's office but were still hesitating when we spied our friend Dana Němcová, whom I had invited to the ceremony. She vouched for our security, and we reached the president's offices just in time. And when Havel presented me with a certificate of the award, he apologized that the medal itself was being redesigned from its Communist version and was not yet ready.

Then, as in 1990, we had a drink at the big reception table, and chatted with the president for half an hour. He reminded me of my joke in 1987 of his eventual move to the Hrad from Hrádeček and asked me how soon I thought it would be before he could leave the

Hrad and return to Hrádeček. "Not soon, unfortunately," I replied. Little did we know that within months he would resign from the presidency and, like Cincinnatus, return to his farm.

It was to be ten months before I received the medal through the Canadian embassy and the Department of External Affairs. While waiting for it I borrowed from Zdena and Josef Škvorecký one of the medals that each of them had received earlier, so that I could show it to friends. Theirs' were ironically, the old Communist model, with the logo of the mountains and bonfire on the lion's chest; the only change had been to remove the Red Star from the lion's head. Just ten days before the breakup of the Republic I received the newly designed medal, with the crown restored to the lion's head and the partisan logo removed. It was thus a unique exemplar, the first and only medal awarded in both a post-Communist and united Czechoslovak (pre-separation) form.

The other great occasion in Prague was the awarding of the Palacký medal at a ceremony sponsored jointly by the Institute of History and the Institute of Contemporary History, as well as by the Czechoslovak National Committee of Historians, of which Prečan was president. This took place in the old Emaus monastery, where the Institute of History was located, and was attended by about 50 persons. Prečan had prepared a little book, in Czech, which contained a biographical sketch, an essay published in samizdat by Milan Šimečka on my 60th birthday, and a bibliography of my work. I was given the medal — named after the great nineteenth century Czech historian František Palacký — by Viktor Knapp, on behalf of the Academy of Sciences. I then gave a lecture in Czech on Masaryk as a champion of democracy and defender of Czech-Slovak unity.

Happily, there were occasions when I could reciprocate Vilém's kindness to me. When he decided that he must move the Documentation Centre back to Bohemia, I wrote letters to President Havel, Pavel Tigrid, minister of culture, and Milan Uhde, urging them to help in finding a suitable location and in assuring financial support. Support came from the Czech foundation Patriae, which had also helped to finance publication of my book. It was planned to return the valuable collection to its rightful home in Bohemia at a location near Prague. In an article, "The Archive of Freedom," which was included in the volume published on the anniversary of Charter 77 in 1997, I recorded the great work of Prečan in documenting and supporting the dissident movement and preparing the ground for the Velvet Revolution.

Vilém Prečan presenting the Palacký Medal on behalf of the Historical Institute and the Institute of Contemporary History, Prague, 1992

I had been informed I was also the recipient of another Academy of Sciences medal, named after Josef Hlávka, the Czech Maecenas of arts and scholarship in the nineteenth century. Strangely, I did not receive the medal during this visit, nor did my fellow-recipient, Marketa Goetz-Stankiewicz, of the University of British Columbia. To our great surprise, however, we both received our medals a year later through Canadian diplomatic channels.

Peter, David, and I found Prague vibrant with activity and new private shops and restaurants. We attended a play by Havel, *The Garden Party*, performed in the beautifully restored Stavorskí Theatre. We made a pilgrimage to the grave of Franz Kafka in the modern Jewish cemetery and to the museum of Dvořák in a beautiful small palace called Amerika. We also visited a splendid exhibition of samizdat that Prečan had organized in the Institute of Literature at Strahov, where I was delighted to see three books of mine on display! I also enjoyed a visit to Alma and Herberta, the grandchildren of President Masaryk, in Anna's simple upstairs flat in Malá Strana, and we talked with them about their grandfather.

With David as driver, we made two long trips by rented car. Once we drove to a conference at the Documentation Centre in Schein-

With sons David and Peter after Palacký award ceremony, 1992

feld in Germany. Organized by Prečan, this was the first meeting of Czech and Slovak writers who had been prominent in the dissident days, including Ivan Klíma, Milan Uhde, and Ludvík Vaculík. Prečan proudly showed them the archive of samizdat, which included many works of the writers present. The future of the Documentation Centre was discussed, and I helped to draft an appeal for financial support so that it could continue its work in Germany.

We made a second trip eastward, to Slovakia, driving through Moravia and stopping en route in beautiful Telč. In Bratislava we were depressed by the run-down look of the old city and the smog hanging heavily over the ugly suburb of Petržalka, across the Danube. I had an opportunity to see my friend Miro Kusý, who had resigned from the President's Chancellery and was the head of the Institute of Politology at Komenský University. The newly elected president of the Slovak Academy of Sciences, Bronislav Lichardus, whom I had met several times in Toronto, took me to dinner at the academy's castle in Smolenice. Later David, Peter, and I drove north to the High Tatras. Once again we took the chairlift up to the highest peak to view the nearby mountains. As in the past, they were shrouded in cloud and mist.

CRISIS AND PARTITION

Within six weeks of returning to Canada I was off to Prague again, this time alone, to attend the conference of the Czechoslovak Society of Science and Art (SVÚ). I stayed in the same beautiful room in the Karolinum. Radim Palouš, who had arranged my accommodation, received me in the rectorate with great warmth and, at parting, sang Auld Lang Syne. He had been surprised by the complete defeat of the Civic Forum in the election and the victory of nationalism in Slovakia, but he still hoped that the two premiers, Klaus and Mečiar, would reach an agreement to preserve the country as a union. I had dinner with the Prečans in their small apartment in Prague 6. Vilém felt no resentment toward the Slovaks, and felt that the Czechs shared much of the blame for the conflict. He agreed with Havel in his call for *vzájemnost* (reciprocity) of Czechs and Slovaks, whatever happened. During the SVÚ conference he held a reception in the Slovak House of Culture, to which he invited a small group of Slovak and foreign scholars. As usual I spent some time with my "Prague family" (Olga's children), all of whom were saddened by the prospect of Slovak separation and had no liking for the Slovak premier, Mečiar. They continued to have great faith in Havel, and spoke favourably of his weekly radio speeches from Lány.

The conference was a historic occasion for the exile SVÚ, which was meeting for the first time on Czechoslovak soil. Hundreds of Czechs and Slovaks came from abroad, sometimes for the first time in many years. My fellow political scientist Jan Triska, of Stanford University, president of SVÚ, spoke at the opening ceremonies in the Great Hall of the Karolinum and at the closing gala reception in the Spanish Hall of the Castle. Strangely, President Havel, who was present at the former, did not speak, although he came prepared to do so. His chief adviser, Pavel Tigrid, spoke in his place and gave a speech that Vilém Prečan sharply criticized as "a funeral oration for the republic." My main reason for going to Prague had been to attend two sessions devoted to T.G. Masaryk. At one I gave a paper on Masaryk as a champion of democracy. It was wonderful to listen to papers given by Jaroslav Opat, director of the Masaryk Institute, and other members of the institute, and by exiled scholars, such as Jiří Kovtun of Washington, DC, on a subject so long taboo. There was a reception at the institute at which Opat told us of the difficulties that he was experiencing in finding assured funding for the institute and permanent locations for it and for the invaluable Masaryk archive. I had a chance to chat once more with the Masaryk sisters; they spoke of their grandfather's warm relationship with the Slovaks and his knowledge of the Slovak language.

I was in Prague at a time of political crisis. I arrived shortly after the elections in which the Civic Forum, as well as its Slovak counterpart, had suffered resounding defeat, and Václav Klaus and Václav Mečiar gained majorities in the two republics. The policies of the new governments in Czechoslovakia and in the republics were not yet known, nor was it certain that Havel would run again for the presidency — and if he did run, whether he would be elected. Some felt that Havel had done all that he could to preserve the republic and was not to be blamed for its break-up. It was widely believed that the majority of both Czechs and Slovaks would reject separation in a referendum, but it was not yet certain that a vote would be held. All these events cast into doubt the entire future of the republic as a union of Czechs and Slovaks.

The SVÚ conference held its concluding sessions in Bratislava, so that I had some opportunity to study the problem of separation on the spot. Upon arrival I was whisked away, without prior warning, to the Philosophical Institute, where the director Julius Strinka, my friend from the 1960s, chaired a seminar highlighted by a long and lively discussion in Slovak and English on Masaryk and Czech-Slovak relations, past and present. I expressed the view that Masaryk's idea of a common Czechoslovak nation, based not on language but on common values, had failed to recognize the full nature of Slovak national consciousness. Strinka argued that Slovak national consciousness had developed later than Czech, so that Slovaks at first understood the necessity of Czech-Slovak cooperation. When Slovak consciousness did develop, Czechs did not fully acknowledge it, and Slovaks saw much less need for cooperation. Similarly civic society was less developed in Slovakia between the wars and during the Prague Spring, and civic values were subordinated to ethnic nationalism after liberation. Most members of the institute, I was told, opposed separation and favoured a federation. They still hoped that a compromise could be reached between the Czech and Slovak points of view.

Another meeting for delegates at the Institute of History, chaired by the director, Dušan Kováč, was devoted largely to questions of Slovak history and avoided the issue of the Slovak future. Later, however, at lunch with Kováč in a huge wine garden restaurant, we had a fascinating discussion of this question. He said that he would be sad if Czechoslovakia broke up and hoped it could still be kept together. Most Slovaks, he felt, still supported the republic; most scholars, though supporting a single state, favoured a strong Slovakia *à la* Mečiar. Kováč preferred a loose confederation, with certain areas, such as foreign policy, defence, and finance run in common. He feared, however, that Klaus now wanted full Czech independence and that most Czechs would vote for independence in a referendum. Mečiar seemed to want to postpone a referendum and maneuvre the Czechs into taking the first step toward separation. Kováč recognized that Slovakia was isolated in the world and would face a certain danger from Hungary, but he did not fear military intervention.

At dinner with the Kusýs' when one of Milan's sons, Martin Simečka, was present, we talked about the crisis at length. It was a sad evening as the television news reported Havel's defeat in the presidential election in Parliament as a result of Slovak votes against him. For Kusý and Šimečka this was a personal defeat. As dissidents they had laboured for the restoration of democracy, but when it came it had led to the break-up of the state. Kusý thought that Havel had done his best to avert separation; he had tried to apply the universal values in which he believed to all nations, including the Slovaks.

I was lucky to have a ride to Brno with Samuel Abrahám and his wife, Debby, and in spite of extreme heat we had a good tour of the city with Don Sparling. Then I had dinner at the Hotel Slavic with rector Milan Jelínek, who had arranged for me to use a guest room in the university residence. He was a strong supporter of Czechoslovakia: in his office there were busts of Masaryk and Beneš. He spoke about the deep historical roots of the Czech-Slovak conflict from 1918 onward and the failure to reach a consensus in the past two years. He favoured a federation, and had not thought that the loose confederation sought by Mečiar would afford political stability. Jelínek was now convinced that the republic was at an end and favoured separation as soon as possible. As for Moravia, Jelínek denied that it had a distinctive language or nationhood. No one wanted Moravian independence, and few sought a tripartite federal system; all anyone wanted was autonomy for Moravia-Silesia.

It was a hot and tiring evening. On my return to my room I felt a dull pain in one shoulder and called for emergency medical assistance. I spent four or five days in the hospital under examination. In the end the doctor dismissed me, with no ailment discovered. and recommended "armchair therapy" in Prague. Rector Jelínek kindly provided me with a car to take me back to Prague.

It was a relief to arrive home in Toronto safe and sound. I continued to push ahead with the final chapters of my book on Masaryk, but I had some difficulty finding a publisher. In early 1993 Penn State Press and Macmillan (London) reached an agreement on joint publication, and it finally appeared in the summer of 1994. A year later, thanks to Prečan's efforts, it came out in a Czech translation sponsored by his institute.[1] I also prepared a brief essay comparing the work of Masaryk and Havel as dissidents and as architects of democratic revolution.[2]

Meanwhile, in Czechoslovakia, things went from bad to worse. On 18 July Havel chose to resign rather than preside over the dissolution of the republic. Long negotiations between the three governments to preserve the republic were unsuccessful. The people, both Czechs and Slovaks, opposed separation but were given no opportunity to express their opinions in a referendum. The decision to separate was made by the Czech and Slovak premiers, Klaus and Mečiar, who had both come to the conclusion that there was no alternative. This put an end to Masaryk's dream of Czech-Slovak unity, and to Havel's hope that the republic could be preserved. It was a sad day, on 31 December 1992, when, at midnight, the republic that Sally and I had known since 1937 and visited so often came to an end. I was in Victoria at the time. David had strung Christmas lights in the shape of the old Czechoslovakia on the trees in his back garden. At four p.m. Pacific time, he took out the two lights that linked the republics together. Fortunately, the separation was a peaceful one, unlike other cases in Europe, but it was bound to produce all the bitter feelings of a divorce and a host of economic problems. Czechs and Slovaks had lived separately prior to 1914 and between 1939 and 1945, but they had still much in common. I hoped that the two nations would continue to cooperate and preserve the mutuality of relations of which Masaryk had often written before their union in 1918.

THE LAST LAP

In the years that followed, life in Toronto flowed in its usual channels. I continued to live in my Valleyway eyrie on the top floor of a low condominium, with gorgeous flowers and trees, even a waterfall down below, and a garden on my balcony. I was in good health although I continued to suffer from some side effects of my operation more than 40 years ago, largely unalleviated by various forms of therapy. In 1998 I began a rehabilitation program of regular walking for a mile or two daily. This was rudely interrupted when I was knocked down by a car and suffered a fractured shoulder. I entered on my "seventh life," and engaged in regular therapy to repair my damaged limb.

After completing my book on T.G. Masaryk I turned to the writing of my autobiography and finally completed it. After many years of searching for a publisher I was delighted when Carleton University Press decided to take it on. At about this time I had my portrait painted by a Czech-Canadian artist, Maria Gabánková. I was already at work on research on other members of the Masaryk family, notably his American-born wife, Charlie, and his daughter Alice. I prepared two long articles on these great Czech women, to be published in *Kosmas*. During a trip to Ljubljana in 1998 I secured copies of Alice Masaryk's correspondence with Josip Plečník, a Slovenian, who was the architect of the Prague Castle and for many years had close relations with Alice, who served as "First Lady" during her father's presidency. I launched into the translation of these 450 letters with a view to publishing them in English and Czech.

My two sons, while living at a distance, provide me with companionship from time to time, and sometimes accompany me to Prague. Each year I spend Christmas and New Year's with David and Jane in Victoria. In September 1994 they were married in a simple ceremony in a small wooden chapel on the shore of the Lake of Bays, in Ontario. Peter was present, and Sally's sister, Tacy, a lifelong Quaker, came for what was to be our last time together before she died in 1995. In her honour, and in memory of Sally, the service included the reading by me of the Society of Friends marriage declaration. In 1996 David gave up his work as a realtor and embarked on a new career as partner with Jane in her design business, which flourished.

It was a pleasure to have Peter at home for a month or six weeks every year. In 1994 the first volume of his monumental study of Buddhist sutras was published by the Pali Text Society. A second volume appeared a year or so later, and the final volume is underway. In April 1995 he was appointed by the same society as curator of Burmese manuscripts smuggled out of Burma and sold promiscuously in Bangkok markets. He was able to secure grants for the purchase of a house where the manuscripts could be stored and made accessible to scholars. Peter was appointed visiting professor of Buddhist studies at Harvard University for the first term of the year 2000.

The most exciting and stimulating new development in my life was my "living-room seminar" which, like the Prague or Warsaw seminars, met in my home. Unlike the Flying Seminar in Poland, we did not have to change our meeting place to escape police supervision. At the outset in 1996 the participants were six young women, graduate students at the University of Toronto and York University, all of whom were working on Czech(oslovak) history or politics. Later others joined, both men and women, and we met every month or so, and usually had a guest-speaker on a Czech subject. Once, in Prague, I organized a seminar at the Karolinum, with Jan Havránek as speaker. It was attended by three students from my Toronto group, and four graduate students from Germany and the U.S. I continued to communicate with these external associates via e-mail. It was a great satisfaction, after years of retirement, to work with young people who were deeply interested in "my country," and to gain new insight from them while advising them on their work.

I took advantage of my freedom from responsibilities at home to travel, including an exciting trip to Israel in January 1993 to attend a conference on leadership in Soviet Russia at the Hebrew University in Jerusalem. My usual destination, however, continued to be the Czech Republic, which I visited almost every year at least once and, less frequently, Slovakia. There was often a conference to attend — for example, one in Opočno in 1993 on the transition to Communism of 1945-48, and another in Prague in 1994 on the Prague Spring. There were also two conferences on Masaryk, one in 1993 in the château of Liblice, north of Prague, and another in Brno in 1994. In June 1998 there was still another conference to mark the 30th anniversary of 1968, this time in Paris. At home I headed east and west to scholarly conferences in Newfoundland and Seattle, and once to Washington, DC, to celebrate the 80th anniversary of the Czechoslovak Republic.

Unlike earlier trips to Prague, I had no hectic program of interviews, and I did not try to follow the complicated politics of the two new countries. Happily, there were always interesting conversations with former dissidents, such as Jiří Dienstbier and Petr Pithart, who were no longer in high office after the elections, with scholars in Prague and Bratislava, and with my old friends. There were even reunions in Prague with my Japanese friends Gen Kikkawa and Tadayuki Hayashi. In my search for Masaryk's roots I took a tour, with Dáša Švihlová, head of the Masaryk Archives, of his various dwelling places in Prague. On another occasion Jan Havránek took me to Osvěta in Vinohrady, where Masaryk had lived when he first came to Prague in 1882. In Brno I took a fascinating all-day bus tour to places in Moravia where Masaryk had lived, including Hodonín. In Čejchovice, breaking with Masaryk's rules of abstinence, we spent two merry hours in a wine-cellar, drinking and singing.

New honours came my way. In early 1994 I was elected a member of the Sněm (Assembly) of the Czech Academy of Sciences, although I was not able to attend its sessions. The same year I was presented with a medal in honour of Edvard Beneš, given in the name of the George of Poděbrady Foundation for European Cooperation. And in 1999, a Masaryk medal was awarded to me by the Masaryk Democratic Movement, which Jiřina Šiklová accepted on my behalf.

Most exciting of all, after the appearance in Czech of my book on Masaryk, was a book-signing in the Fišer bookstore in the Old Town, near the University, in October 1995. I was also received by Milan Uhde, chair of the Czech Chamber of Deputies, in the old Bohemian Diet building, and interviewed on the main evening television news. All of this, and a number of excellent reviews of the book in Czech newspapers, gave me the feeling that my work was appreciated in my second homeland. During an audience that Prečan had with President Havel that year, Vilém presented him with a copy of the book, which I had autographed and dedicated to him as "a worthy successor of Masaryk." He was greatly moved, I was told, but expressed doubts as to whether he deserved such a compliment. Later, my good friend Markéta Fialková (Němcová), who was acting as an assistant to Havel, reported on a vigorous discussion that he had with advisers as to whether or not he should veto the renewal of the screening legislation designed to debar former Communists from public office. In justifying his veto, she told me, Havel cited my dedication and argued that this was what Masaryk would have done.

*

As I look back over these more than 80 years I realize how lucky I have been to live during a period when extraordinary changes were reshaping the world, to witness some of these forces at first hand, and to have played some part in these happenings. My life has spanned two world wars and the rise and fall of fascism in Germany and Communism in the Soviet Union and eastern Europe. I had known Germany as a single country under the Nazis, witnessed the building of the Berlin Wall in 1961, and visited both parts of the divided country. I welcomed its unexpected reunification in 1990 as terminating an unnatural partition. The Soviet Union, whose existence had more or less coincided with the whole of my life, went through a series of dramatic changes and came to a sudden end in the 1990s. I rejoiced at this sudden and surprising transformation as a victory for democracy and national freedom. I had personally experienced the successive stages of the history of Czechoslovakia — democratic republic, Nazi protectorate, liberation after the war, subjugation to Communism, the end of Communist rule, and subsequent break-up into two republics in 1993. On a broader international front I had watched with dismay the decline of the League of Nations in the 1930s and with great expectations the forming of the United Nations in the 1940s and the Conference on Security and Cooperation in Europe (CSCE).

For both Sally and me this series of astounding events provoked a continuing process of learning, deepening our understanding of the world and dissipating some of our illusions. Certain of these dramatic events were tragic and depressing; others awakened our enthusiastic approval. In particular, the fall of Communism and the liberation of Czechoslovakia in the 1990s aroused great hopes. Some of these were soon dispelled by the subsequent instability and violence in the states of the former Soviet Union, the frightful wars in Yugoslavia, and the peaceful break-up of Czechoslovakia. There were great difficulties, too, in the process of reunifying Germany. Conflicts throughout the world revealed the weaknesses of the United Nations, NATO, and the CSCE. It was evident that continuing vestiges of the old order and the strength of nationalism were great obstacles to the maintaining of peace and the establishing of stable democracies.

In retrospect I realize, too, that the course of my life was decisively affected by pure chance. It was a lucky accident, for instance, that I met Sally in Tom Quad in Christ Church in 1935 and thus found a life partner of such rare character. It was also largely fortuitous that we were in Czechoslovakia at a time of world crisis. Had we gone a year or two earlier we might have missed events that had a crucial influence on our lives. Had my visit been prevented by the start of war, I might have been unable to complete the research for my doctorate, and my career might have been quite different. I was also fortunate to be exempt from military service during the war and to escape arrest and perhaps long imprisonment while visiting Czechoslovakia during the terror of the 1950s.[3] It was equally good luck that I survived serious medical crises that might have cut short my life.

Whether because of planning or chance, my life had been a happy and satisfying one. Apart from the death of my parents and of my brothers Don and Andy, I did not experience major personal tragedies until Sally's death in 1990. Our two sons have been blessed with good health. Ours was a life of financial security, without unemployment or economic suffering, and with adequate social benefits after retirement. In spite of humble origins, I was fortunate enough to acquire a higher education, the only member of my family to do so, and to study at major institutions of higher learning, such as Toronto, Oxford, and London, and later to teach at distinguished universities and colleges — Wisconsin, Dartmouth, the Russian Institute at Columbia, and the University of Toronto. Such seats of learning and my associations with St Antony's College, Oxford, and the Russian Research Centre at Harvard, brought me into contact with a galaxy of academic stars. Some of them — for instance, Frank Pakenham, R.W. Seton-Watson, Merle Curti, John Hazard, and Archie Brown — inspired me in my scholarly work. As a teacher, though often discouraged by my own performance, I derived great satisfaction from helping along several generations of students. I learned much from outstanding ones, and kept in touch with them long afterward. During these years Sally and I had the opportunity to live in fascinating places in Europe, the United States, and Canada, and to travel widely in other more exotic parts of the world such as Thailand, Japan and Israel.

My life was enriched by a curious medley of scholarship and political activism. At Toronto I was active in student affairs and an ardent advocate of Canadian socialism. At Oxford and London, Sally and I were involved in politics, taking part in demonstrations, meetings, and strikes, this time in favour of the more radical left. In the United States during the war and postwar years I supported left-wing causes and the Soviet Union, and felt increasingly out of step with prevailing political opinion during the years of Cold War and McCarthyism. This climate had serious consequences for my academic career. The atmosphere was freer in Toronto than in the United States, but I refrained from domestic political activity at the university and in Canada and devoted myself largely to professional and scholarly work. My research and publications were, however, directly concerned with the politics of the Communist countries. After 1975 these were designed to contribute to the reform of Communism in that part of the world, and were combined with intense activity on behalf of human rights and greater freedom in those countries.

My life has not been without shortfalls and disappointments — my failure to get first-class standing at Oxford and to get tenure at

Wisconsin, my victimization at Dartmouth in the McCarthy era, my slowness in understanding the real nature of Communism, and time spent on books that were never published. But there were also substantial successes — the founding of the centre at Toronto, the exchange program with the Soviet Union and the impact of my writing on the scholarly study of Communist countries. It was satisfying to win praise in the Western scholarly world and in the eastern countries, too, for my publications and to be awarded high honours in Canada, and in Czechoslovakia.

As a Canadian I was proud to have contributed something to the renaissance of democratic life in Czechoslovakia and to be recognized and honoured for these efforts. I was immensely proud when a leading dissident, who became minister of foreign affairs in the liberated republic, dedicated a book to me. Originally published in samizdat, it was inscribed to one who, he said, "had, since the time of [French historian] Ernest Denis, contributed most to the understanding of the fate of Czechoslovakia in the world."[4]

Sally was a true partner in everything that I did and shared with me both successes and failures. Without her love and support I would not have been able to overcome the difficulties and attain certain successes. Our life together was a happy one and lasted for more than 50 years. We were sustained by the affection and support of our two sons, who were blessed with good health and were able to live happy and successful lives. After Sally's death I was able to work out a new and satisfying new life on my own, and I have had the companionship and friendship of a number of people in Toronto and in Prague.

NOTES

1. *T.G.Masaryk: Against the Current, 1882-1914* (London: Macmillan with St. Anthony's, 1994) and, in Czech, *T.G. Masaryk Proti Proudu 1882-1914* (Prague: Prah 1995).

2. This was first published in Czech in a special Canadian issue of *Lidové noviny* (25 June 1991). It was included in a festschrift in honour of Marketa Goetz-Stankiewicz on her retirement from UBC, and also in *Critical Essays on Václav Havel*, ed. Marketa Goetz-Stankiewicz and Phyllis Carey (New York: G.K. Hall, 1999).

3. During my many visits to communist Czechoslovakia I was normally unaware of whether or not I was being watched by the

police. The one exception was in 1978 when I was apprehended and held for a day of questioning. However documents from the archives of the Ministry of the Interior, released to me in 1998, revealed that during at least two of my trips to Czechoslovakia — our family visit in 1962 and my visit with Sally in 1975 — I was subjected to strict surveillance by the State Security Police (STB), in each case under the heading "Action Professor." In 1962 the purpose of this surveillance was said to be "to check on his activity, his interests and relationships and whether he is carrying out espionage activity or other activity hostile to the CSSR or our allies." In 1975 it was assumed that my visit was designed for intelligence or espionage, with two purposes: to learn about the political and economic situation in the CSSR through conversations with "rightist elements" and to assess which "rightist elements" might be "counted on in the future." It was noted that I had been in touch with Western sovietologists and émigrés (Zbigniew Brzezinski, William Griffith, Josef Svorecky, et al.) and that these individuals sought to activate "right-wing opportunist elements for further hostile activity and ideological diversion." It was reported that I had secured specific materials and would pay for reports on the political and economic situation, which would then be sent abroad through the Canadian Embassy.

The files described the extensive preparations made by the Ministry for each of these two visits, including gathering information about previous visits and about my publishing activity, preparing my hotel rooms for the visit, including installation of listening devices, selecting persons who would conduct "investigation and study (*rozpracovani a obsazeni*) of Skilling'" and others who would follow my movements and conversations, including those in Bratislava and elsewhere. Although the names of their agents and the people with whom I met (or planned to meet) were blotted out, a prominent role was played in the 1975 surveillance by a former member of the Institute for International Politics and Economics, known under the code name T.S. (Secret Collaborator) 'Václav'.

The dossier indicated that the Ministry had a complete list of all my previous visits — during the period of worst repression in 1948, 1950, and 1958, and in the more relaxed year of

1961. It was explicitly stated that there were no reports by agents about these visits and no program of observation had been undertaken. No files were released concerning my later visits in the period of greater relaxation in the 1970s and 1980s when I was in close contact with those active in Charter 77. More recently, however, I have received a file containing surveillance of my meetings with Charter 77 activists in 1987. Materials about this may have been removed from the files, destroyed, or not made available.

4.   Jiři Dienstbier, *Snění o Europě*, (samizdat, 1986), (Prague: Knihovna Lidovyéh novin, 1990).

INDEX

250, 255-6, 267, 291, 296, 328; freedom
of 320, 388-9; Poland 316; Soviet Union
166, 194, 195-7, 219, 223-4, 311;
Western 223
scholarships (Skilling) 26, 29, 68; Mackenzie
30; Rhodes 40, [43], *42-57*, 66, 72;
Southam 30
Schönerer, Georg von 85
Schwarzenberg, Prince Karel 367, 368, 386,
389
Schwarzenberg Castle (West Germany) 367
science: Japan 328; Poland 313, 316; Soviet
interpretation of 194. *See also* freedom of
science and scholarship
scientists: attitude on the atomic bomb 101;
repression of (Czechoslovakia) 278
Scínteia (newspaper) 210
Scotland 54, 55, 62
Scott, Frank 34
Scotus Viator (pseudonym) *see* Seton-Watson,
R.W.
Second International 5, 55, 63-4, 98
second society phenomenon 363, 368
Second World War *see* World War II
security *see* Conference on Security and
Cooperation in Europe
Security and Cooperation in Europe,
Commission on (CSCE) (Washington,
D.C.) 325, 327, 330
Šedivý, Jaroslav 251, 275, 282, 296, 304,
348
Sedláček, Jaroslav 274
Sedliak, Julius 272, 282
Seidler, Leopold 184, 239
Seifert, Jaroslav 118, 333
Sekulić, Nikola 216-17
Selucký, Radoslav 250, 266-7
Semenov (Deputy Prime Minister, U.S.S.R.)
269
Semenov, V. 190
seminars: Flying University (Poland) 316,
399; Hejdánek 352, 360, 398-9;
Karolinum 399; "living-room" 328
(Czechoslovakia), 398-9 (Toronto)
separation (Czech and Slovak) 271, 276-7,
373, 377, 379, 386, 387, *394-7*
separatism (Slovakia) 10, 236-7, 257, 379
Serbo-Croatian language 156, 213, 215, 219
Seton-Watson, Christopher 61
Seton-Watson, Hugh 61, 298, 329, 330
Seton-Watson, R.W. 7, 56-7, 58, 59, 60-1,
64, 66, 69, 74, 75, 79, 80, 81, 113, 116,
402; tribute to T.G. Masaryk 71

Seven Days in Prague (Prečan, Otáhal, eds.) 260
Sezimovo Ústí (Czechoslovakia) 118, 264
Shapiro, Henry 135, 189
Sharp, Mitchell 324
Sharp, Walter 86
Shcharansky, Anatol 311, 323, 326
shoe-repair shops (W. Skilling's): Brooklyn
(New York) 18; College Street (Toronto)
[17], 18, 20, 22
Sholokhov, Mikhail 219
show trials *see* political trials
Shudo University (Japan) 329
Shulman, Marshall 135
Shvernik, Nikolai 55
Siberia (U.S.S.R.) 312
Sieradzki, Dr. 241
Šík, Ota 232, 261, 266, 277
Šiklová, Jiřina 250, 290, 292, 302-3, 304,
305, 306, 308, 309, 339n16, 340, [343],
344, 355, 357, 361, 363, 365, 366, 367;
arrest and imprisonment 325, 326, 343;
post-1989 375, 377-8, 382- 3, [384],
385, 400
Silesia: autonomy for, in Moravia 396;
Czechoslovakia 69, 273, 396; Poland 183
Šilhanová, Libuše 365, 388
Šimečka, Martin 396
Šimečka, Milan 248, 288, 294-5, 300, 301,
306, 307, 309, 327, 336, [343]-344, 345,
355, 363, 365, 366-7; arrest and impris-
onment 325, 343; post-1989 379, 382,
391
Šimečková, Eva 339n16, 344, 363, 365, 366,
379
Simmons, E.J. 122, 131, 155
Simon, Frau Pfarrer 47
Simons, Jennifer Allen xi
Sirluck, Ernest 155
Široký, Viliam 128
Sixty-Eight Publishers (Toronto) 288, 289,
318, 328, 335, 339n16, 373
Skalník, Josef [352]-3, 362
Skilling, Alice (mother) née Stevenson 16,
17, 18-19, 20, 21, 24, 26, 55-6, 65,
75n1, 82, 83, 108, 124, 132, 134, 138,
331, 401
Skilling, Andrew Douglas (brother) 12, 16,
17, 20, 23, 25, 124, 138, 402
Skilling, David Bright (son) v, xi, 107-8,
109, 112, 123, 124, 132, 133-4, 149,
152, 164-5, 180, 198, 201-2, 218, 227,
336, 380-1, 383, 385, 388, 390, 392-3,
[393], 398, 403